The World of Villa-Lobos
in Pictures and Documents

The World
of Villa-Lobos
in Pictures and Documents

Lisa M. Peppercorn

Scolar Press

Published by
Scolar Press
Gower House
Croft Road
Aldershot
Hants GU11 3HR
England

Ashgate Publishing Company
Old Post Road
Brookfield, VT 05036-9704
USA

British Library Cataloguing in Publication Data
Peppercorn, Lisa
The world of Villa-Lobos in pictures and documents
1. Villa-Lobos, Heitor, 1887-1959
2. Composers – Brazil
3. Music – Brazil
I. Title
780.9'2

ISBN 1 85928 261 X

Library of Congress Cataloging-in-Publication Data
Peppercorn, L.M. (Lisa Margot)
The world of Villa-Lobos in pictures and documents / Lisa M. Peppercorn
336p. 208cm
Includes bibliographical references and index.
ISBN 1-85928-261-X
1. Villa-Lobos, Heitor. 2. Villa-Lobos, Heitor—Pictorial works.
3. Music—Brazil—20th century—History and criticism. 4. Brazil—Intellectual life—20th century. I. Title.
ML410.V78P465 1996
780.9'2—dc20
[B]
95-44199
CIP
MN

This publication received financial support from the Paul Sacher Foundation, Basel, Switzerland

Edited for the publishers by John Taylor Book Ventures, Hatfield, Herts

Designed by Harold Bartram

Keyboarded by Museum Rietberg Zurich, Switzerland

Films produced by Banbury Pre-Press Centre, Banbury, Oxon

Printed in Great Britain by Biddles Limited, Guildford

Contents

Foreword

More and more do we learn that we all must live with our past in order to ease the future. Not only is it necessary to understand objectively but in a very human way subjectively, so that we may assume the right proportions in matters of value of our own contribution, its scope and importance, and so that loose and frayed ends may be smoothed.

No human gift is able to resurrect the past in all its vibrant immediacy like music, and a book about a unique personality, who embodied his culture and his time, leaving us its very voice in his music, such a book reinforced with pictorial corroboration and providing an image and 'feel' of the world which produced the man, gives the reader a profound insight into the whole living fabric of a passionate people and an era unbounded in energy and talent.

Although I have played several works of Villa-Lobos and have already admired the intensity of his orchestral compositions as a boy in San Francisco, I deeply regret that I did not come to know him personally as I would have longed to. Certainly this book fills a gap in my life as a contemporary musician, and it will likewise enrich my colleagues and audiences forever.

We are fortunate that so distinguished, well-versed, and so mature a musicologist, whom I had the great pleasure of meeting in Rio some fifty-three years ago on my first trip, brings *her* experience and impressions of a lifetime to us. Often an outsider is better able to fathom and to explain his or her adopted country than one born to it.

Would that all 'outsiders' would bring the sympathy, the judgement and the commitment to their host countries that our author has shown in her attachment to Villa-Lobos and *his* Brazil.

Yehudi Menuhin

Preface

This book is not a pictorial biography but offers source
material towards a biography. It includes autograph
letters, in facsimile, many of which are published here
for the first time, reprints from newspaper and
periodical articles and interviews, as well as original
programmes to attest dates, places and artists of
premières – often conflicting with statements printed in
reference works –, facsimile reproductions of illustrations, documents, instruments, tunes and legends that
Villa-Lobos studied to prepare himself for the creation
of a Brazilian style, and comprehensive records relating
to the historical background and contemporary cultural
trends during various phases of the composer's life.

Old theatres, long since demolished, where Villa-
Lobos's music was once played, are recorded in photographs and with an account of their history. Institutions
such as the Chamber of Deputies, the Senate, the
Music School, the National Museum, the National
Library and others, which all played a part in Villa-
Lobos's life or that of his family, are depicted in this
book with both the original and new buildings where
they have been housed over the years and with an
outline of their history.

Rio de Janeiro and São Paulo, where Villa-Lobos and
his forebears had lived for most of their life, are recorded at various periods. These illustrations mirror the
fundamental modifications which the two cities have
undergone over a period of more than one hundred
years, and, in an impressive way, demonstrate how the
cities' transformation over an entire century reflects the
change in living conditions in Brazil. They provide a
cross-section through the world of yesterday and in
some may evoke nostalgia.

Some documents reproduced depict the historical
background of Villa-Lobos's own time. Other
illustrations provide evidence of life during the colonial
period which the composer studied as part of his
musical preparation. History is captured here by means
of reproductions of watercolour paintings, engravings,
lithographs, drawings and old photographs. Some of
this material will be relatively unknown to the average
reader.

The book also tells of the musical and cultural trends in Rio de Janeiro and São Paulo during the composer's lifetime and that of his forebears. Craving success and recognition, Villa-Lobos was, at the same time, subject to the influence of the contemporary cultural directions of his era. Thus, his life is, in a sense, a mirror of his age.

The book portrays Villa-Lobos's contemporaries in music, literature and the world of affairs and thus enlarges the subject-matter to describe the whole epoch in which the composer lived. Also presented are those who participated directly in Villa-Lobos's life, such as artists, performers, those who commissioned works, poets, friends, his principal publisher and, of course, his family. This is done by means of illustrations, and captions which provide brief biographical notes about the personalities involved.

The book is designed to appeal to music lovers as well as professional musicians and musicologists. Experience has shown me that laymen and scholars alike, and particularly young people, are curious about the composer's world and wish to know more about it. So I have attempted to describe the 'world of Villa-Lobos' and hope that this book may, at least partly, satisfy such legitimate curiosity.

Research for the book posed a number of difficulties and obstacles. Some valuable documents, programmes and letters, reviews and illustrations, proved to be unavailable from archives, universities, theatres, concert organisations and individuals. Much material had been destroyed for lack of space. Some of the ancient buildings in Brazil and elsewhere which would have offered important pictorial and documentary evidence had been demolished and no photographs had been taken before their destruction. Some newspapers in various countries no longer possessed negatives for photographs of contemporaries of Villa-Lobos which prevented me from getting prints. This obliged me either to omit them or to use rather inadequate photocopies from newspapers.

Many requests for information or illustrations remained unanswered, in spite of repeated reminders. There are also instances in which various published reference sources give conflicting information. The reader will, therefore, find in a number of cases discrepancies between dates in this book and those given elsewhere.

The documents which are reproduced in facsimile are not translated. Readers today tend to be so fluent in foreign languages that I have assumed that those interested in Villa-Lobos and his world are sufficiently well acquainted with the foreign languages reproduced here.

The book's general outline is chronological, but I have also on occasion deviated from strict sequence in order to group texts and illustrations around certain themes, for a better understanding of the subject.

I am indebted to many persons and institutions both in Brazil and other countries who have lent their most valuable assistance in the preparation of this book. Arminda Villa-Lobos generously offered information and illustrations from the vast collection of the Museu Villa-Lobos and graciously consented to the facsimile publication of an autograph letter reproduced here for the first time, for which I am most thankful. I am equally grateful to Mercedes Reis Pequeno, chief, Music Division, Biblioteca Nacional, Rio de Janeiro, and her assistants for their indefatigable help in looking up dates and details and providing me with microfilms and photocopies. Dulce Martins Lamas, holder of the chair of folklore at the Music School in the Federal University of Rio de Janeiro, is remembered with deep affection for her extraordinary assistance in furnishing me with addresses and details of various kinds that were hard to come by. I am most thankful to Villa-Lobos's brother-in-law, Oldemar Guimarães and his brother, Luiz Guimarães, who spared no effort in providing me with innumerable details concerning the letters in their possession and kindly consented to one of the letter's reproduction in facsimile. They were also kind enough to supply me with pictures of Villa-Lobos's sisters and brother, published here, thus adding important documents of the composer's family, otherwise unavailable to me. Ary Vasconcellos has been of inestimable assistance. He has provided me with photographs that had proved extremely difficult to secure. I am most grateful for his offerings and all the details made available whenever I consulted him. Gilberto Ferrez, holder of the invaluable photo archive of his grandfather, Marc Ferrez, granted me permission to reproduce from his comprehensive collection. His consent was given during a most delightful afternoon over tea in Zurich when in a nostalgic mood we reminisced about old times in Rio de Janeiro. Grasping quickly what I still needed, as soon as he had returned to Brazil he sent me some more documents he thought I might like to have.

In Paris, Luiz Heitor Corrêa de Azevedo, the great Brazilian scholar and an old friend of mine to whom I am much indebted, allowed me to publish from his private collection some photographs he had taken himself. He also sent me photocopies of many programmes from his own archives. Always helpful and interested in the endeavours of others, he graciously presented me, on his own initiative, to Raquel Braune, Assistant to the Cultural Attaché at the Brazilian Embassy, London, who revealed herself to be prodigiously supportive in helping to assemble material for the book and to whom I am most grateful. She had a microfilm made of a Villa-Lobos exhibition, held at the Embassy in London in 1964, and spared no effort in letting me have quite a number of prints from this film. Philippe Marietti, Director of Éditions Max Eschig, in Paris, also gave me valuable information and some photocopies of reviews and programmes for which I am thankful.

To Minister Sérgio Paulo Rouanet, the Consul General, and Celia Flores Gangl, Attaché, both at the Brazilian Consulate General in Zurich at the time, I express my deep appreciation for their great kindness in offering generous assistance and in providing me through the Ministry of External Relations, the Ministry of Education and Culture and other bodies with illustrations for which I had previously searched without success.

The indefatigable Hugh Ross entered into a most delightful correspondence with me over many years, recounting incidents and details concerning his old friend Villa-Lobos which was both a pleasure and a great honour for me. Stella Pacheco Werneck, Coordinator of the Museu dos Teatros in Rio de Janeiro, combed her archives on my behalf and to her I am most grateful for photographs that I would not have had another opportunity of securing. Bruce Bohle of New York City obtained for me a number of addresses and precious dates for which I am most grateful. Wayne D. Shirley, Music Division, Library of Congress, Washington DC generously offered many autograph letters in the Library's possession and graciously responded to further inquiries about details. The letter reproduced in this book for the first time in facsimile appears by kind permission of the Library of Congress with the consent of Arminda Villa-Lobos.

I am most obliged to the Zentralbibliothek, Zurich, and its generosity in kindly reproducing free of charge a considerable number of photographs in a most cordial spirit of cooperation.

I am much indebted to John Taylor who has edited my text with diligence and good humour. I would also like to express my profound gratitude to the Paul Sacher Foundation, Basel, for its extremely generous financial support without which this publication would not have been possible. Finally, I wish to express my deep appreciation to Lord Yehudi Menuhin who very kindly honoured me by offering to write an introduction to this book.

The book is the result of about twelve years of preparation, involving no less than sixteen files of correspondence. In the course of preparation I have made many new friends and, hopefully, not too many enemies. Further research I undertook in libraries and archives. The volume is thus the outcome of investigation and study of and selection from a wide range of material.

When I decided to do the book, I was guided by the thought that I had had the good fortune to live in Brazil during the last twenty years of Villa-Lobos's life and be a contemporary of his and to have experienced the age in which he lived. I can recall it all with an immediacy that goes beyond what can be grasped from his works alone. May future generations be blessed with wisdom to love and respect the past.

Preamble: Time chronicle

It is natural to start our story around 1859, the year Noêmia Umbelina Villa-Lobos was born in Rio de Janeiro on 25 February, the daughter of Antônio Santos and Domitildes Costa Santos Monteiro. She was the mother of Heitor Villa-Lobos, the Brazilian composer, who died one hundred years later.

When Noêmia was born, barely seven million people lived in Brazil, and about one third were slaves (by the time her son died, in 1959, the population had risen tenfold to seventy million). It was a leisurely, slow-paced period devoid of hustle and bustle. Streets were gas-lit, the electric bulb had yet to be invented by Thomas Edison (1847-1931). There were no cars, no aeroplanes, no satellites and no computers. There was no telephone, no radio and no television. The main form of communication was by mail.

The first regular shipping line from Brazil to Europe had been opened only eight years before Noêmia was born, and the first railroad was inaugurated in Brazil

1 In 1854, five years before Noêmia Villa-Lobos was born, Iluchar Desmons engraved a beautiful view of Rio de Janeiro, taken from the Hill of Santo Antônio. It was printed by an anonymous firm. Seen here are: Sacco do Alferes, Cidade Nova, Campo de Santana, Rua Espírito Santo, Rua dos Ciganos, Campo da Acclamação, Academia Imperial das Bellas Artes, Teatro de São Pedro and Rua do Teatro.

1

2 Street scene from *Voyage pittoresque et historique au Brésil, ou séjour d'un artiste français au Brésil depuis 1816 jusqu'en 1831 inclusivement,* by Jean Baptiste Debret (1768-1848), Paris 1834-1839.

3 A mulato family leaves to spend Christmas in the country (Debret op. cit.)

4 Marriage of Negroes in the house of rich people (Debret op. cit.)

barely five years prior to Noêmia's birth. As a result of the Queiróz (1812-1868) Law that abolished the slave trade in 1850, capital previously invested in it was, in the 1850s, applied to public utilities.

Rio de Janeiro was a beautiful city with lush vegetation ablaze with thousands of varieties of flowers. Crystal-clear water sparkled in the bay, and the Atlantic Ocean, whose murmuring waves reflected the deep blue sky over the tropical city, was rimmed by endless lily-white and unpopulated sand beaches. Public transport was by means of horse-buses which people of any colour could only board when wearing a coat and tie, a custom still adhered to long after World War II.

5 Negroes arriving at church for baptism (Debret op.cit.)

6 View of Rio de Janeiro from *Malerische Reise in Brasilien* by Johann Moritz Rugendas (1802-1858), Paris 1835.

5

6

7

8

7   Street scene in the Rua Direita in Rio de Janeiro (Rugendas op. cit.)

8   Aqueduct in Rio de Janeiro, built in 1740 (from *Reise in Brasilien* by Johann Baptist von Spix (1781-1826) and Carl Friedrich Philipp von Martius (1794-1868), Munich 1823-1831.

9   Church of São Francisco de Paula, the new façade of the Hospital dos Terceiros and the first horse-drawn buses.

9

10

10 The new building of the Municipal Chamber, opened on 12 July 1825, between the Rua do Sabão (General Câmera) and Rua S. Pedro (Lithograph by Pedro Godofredo Bertichen *c.* 1855).

11 Praça do Poço (after 1870: Dom Pedro II) as seen in 1880 (Photo: Marc Ferrez, Rio de Janeiro 1843 – Rio de Janeiro 1923).

12 A bird vendor in 1890 on the Praça Dom Pedro II near the Municipal Market (Photo: Marc Ferrez).

11

12

Raúl Villa-Lobos and his time

Raúl, the father of the composer Heitor Villa-Lobos, was born in 1862, the son of Spanish parents, Francisco da Silveira and Maria Carolina Serzedelo Villa-Lobos. An intellectual, amateur musician, writer and translator of scholarly books with a versatile interest in a vast range of subjects, Raúl had wanted to be a medical doctor. But for lack of funds, he had to give up his studies. He found work, at the age of twenty-eight, at the Biblioteca Nacional (National Library) in Rio de Janeiro. This, in fact, was much more suited to his talents.

13   Facsimile of records concerning Raúl Villa-Lobos's appointment and promotions at the National Library in Rio de Janeiro.

14   The National Library Building in the Rua do Passeio where it was housed from 1858 to 1910.

15   The National Library Building in the Avenida Rio Branco 219-239 where it was installed in 1910.

SERVIÇO PÚBLICO FEDERAL
FUNDAÇÃO NACIONAL-PRÓ-MEMORIA
BIBLIOTECA NACIONAL-S. DE REFERÊNCIA

RAUL VILLALOBOS

NOMEADO PARA TRABALHAR NA BIBLIOTECA NACIONAL, POR PORTARIA DE 13.10.1890. TOMOU POSSE NO DIA 16 E COMPAREOEU O RESTO DO MES, COMO OFICIAL AMANUENSE, GANHANDO O ORDENADO DE 86$021 E GRATIFICAÇÃO DE 43$011.
TRANSFERIDO POR PORTARIA DE 2/8/1892 PARA A SECRETARIA DOS MINISTERIOS DA INSTRUÇÃO PUBLICA.ATÉ O DIA 13/11/1892
NOMEADO POR DECRETO DE 6/10/1892, PARA A BN, COMO 1º OFICIAL. TOMOU POSSE NO DIA 14/11/1892.
SUSPENSO POR PORTARIA DE 26/11/1892 ARTIGO 70 PARAGRAFO 4º E ARTIGO 71, SEGUNDO O DECRETO 5659 DE 6/6/1874.
SUSPENSO DE 26/11/1892 ATÉ 17/9/1893, POR NÃO TER ASSUMIDO AS SUAS FUNÇÕES NA BIBLIOTECA NACIONAL
REASUMIU NO DIA 18/9/1893 ATÉ O DIA 12/7/1899, FICANDO DOENTE, ONDE VEIA A FALECER NO DIA 18/7/1899, GANHANDO 120$430 E DE GRATIFICAÇÃO 25$806.

13

14

15

16 Facsimile of the Inauguration Document of the National Library in the Avenida Rio Branco.

On 29 October 1810 the National Library was officially installed in the Catacumbas das Religiosas do Carmo. This is considered the Library's official date of inauguration. When it opened to the public in 1814 it housed 60,000 items. Dom João VI returned to Europe in 1821 and left his library behind; it then became the property of the state by a treaty of 29 August 1825. A new building was acquired in 1855 to which the Library was transferred on 4 August 1858. Here in the Largo da Lapa (Rua do Passeio) was installed at a later date the Instituto Nacional de Música. Since 1878, the library has been designated as the National Library. By the end of the Empire it contained 170,000 items. With the Proclamation of the Republic (1889) and Emperor Dom Pedro II's exile in Paris, he donated 50,000 volumes to the National Library. The donation was called Coleção Teresa Cristina Maria (1822-1889) after Dom Pedro II's wife. The present building in the Avenida Rio Branco was opened on 29 October 1910. It now holds more than 2.5 million items.

1) Dulce Martins Lamas, 'O Samba de Escola (Carnaval)', *Revista Brasileira de Música* (Rio de Janeiro), Vol. XI, 1981, p. 31.

16

In the period from Raúl's birth until he took up his post at the National Library, Rio de Janeiro was a fascinating city with its beautiful landscape, lovely buildings and picturesque street vendors.

In 1892 Raúl was promoted to first library assistant, the Tunel Alaor Prata, later commonly known as Tunel Velho (Old Tunnel), in Rio de Janeiro was opened on 6 July, and on 8 October the first electric tramcar line to the Flamengo district was inaugurated. A year later, in 1893, the first *bloco carnevalesco* (carnival group), called 'Rei de Ouro' (Gold King), was organised in Rio de Janeiro.[1]

Ever since 1850 visiting soloists have performed in Brazil and splendid performances by the great European singers have taken place in the Teatro Fluminense. When Raúl and Noêmia Villa-Lobos were young during the second half of the nineteenth century, they witnessed the emergence of several concert organisations in Rio de Janeiro and São Paulo, and Raúl, being interested in music, probably attended

17

18

17 Street vendors in Rio de Janeiro in 1865 (Photo: Marc Ferrez)

18 Museu Nacional (now: Arquivo Nacional) at the Campo de Santana (now: Praça da República) about 1855. Design and lithograph by Pedro Godofredo Bertichen (*b.* 1796).

19

21

19   Largo de São Francisco de Paula. In the streets can be seen the horse-drawn buses and on the right the Hotel e Hospedaria, the origins of the famous Park Royal department store, *c.* 1875 (Photo: Marc Ferrez).

20   The Botafogo district in Rio de Janeiro with Sugar Loaf mountain in the background.

21   Rio de Janeiro harbour.

some of the performances. In Rio de Janeiro, the first to appear was the Sociedade Filarmônica (founded in 1834), followed by the Clube Mozart (1867), the Clube Beethoven (1882) and the Sociedade de Concertos Clássicos (1883). In 1883 the first performance in Brazil of Wagner's *Lohengrin* took place and in 1892 that of *Tannhäuser*. São Paulo was no less active. There the Clube Haydn (1883) and the Clube Mendelssohn came into being. The concert life in both cities was extremely lively, great international artists gave performances and regular series of symphony concerts were presented.

22 The Glória area of Rio de Janeiro with the Glória do Outeiro Church in the background.

23 The Flamengo district and a panoramic view of Rio de Janeiro in 1874 (Photo: Marc Ferrez).

24 Teatro Real de São João, opened on 12 October 1813 and three times destroyed by fire (1824, 1851 and 1856). It was modelled after the São Carlos Theatre on the Praça da Lampadosa (today: Praça Tiradentes) in Lisbon. The Teatro Real de São João was called successively Teatro Imperial de São Pedro de Alcântara, Teatro Constitucional Fluminense, Teatro São Pedro and eventually Teatro João Caetano which is its present name. The Teatro Real São João had 1020 orchestra seats and 112 boxes. In the illustration can be seen, on the left, at the corner of Rua do Sacramento, the house in which lived José Bonifácio de Andrade e Silva (1763-1838), advocate of Brazil's independence and, on the right, Rua do Ouvidor. Watercolour painting by Thomas Ender (1793-1875).

22

23

24

In 1896, three years before his premature death of malaria, at the age of thirty-seven, Raúl was entrusted with the reorganisation of the Senate's library.

25 The Senate was installed in the old Palácio do Conde dos Arcos, built on the Chácara de Antônio Elias in the old Praça da Acclamação (later Campo de Santana, and today: Praça da República). It was opened on 6 May 1826 in the presence of Emperor Dom Pedro I, Empress Dona Leopoldina and Princess Dona Maria da Glória and continued to meet in the same building until 31 December 1924. The street scene (in the illustration) depicts daily life in Rio de Janeiro and Brazilian customs and habits.

25

26 The Senate moved to the Palácio Monroe in 1925. It had its first meeting there on 3 May and remained in that building, constructed in 1906 on the occasion of the Third Pan American Conference, until 20 April 1960. The Palácio Monroe was demolished in 1976.

27 The Senate held its first session in Brasília on 21 April 1960. The Senate meets in the tower on the left and the Chamber of Deputies in the one on the right.

26

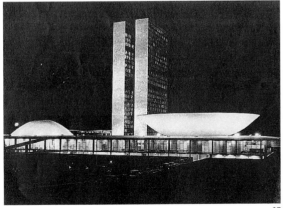

27

The Villa-Lobos family

28

29

28   Heitor's mother,
Noêmia Umbelina Santos
Monteiro (25 February
1859-13 March 1946).

29   Heitor's father, Raúl
Villa-Lobos (7 January 1862-
18 July 1899).

In 1884, at the age of twenty-two and six years before
he was employed at the National Library, Raúl, a
teacher, married Noêmia, who was twenty-five. Legend
has it that the couple had seven or eight children; only
four survived. Their firstborn arrived a year after their
wedding, on 3 November 1885. Called Bertha and
nicknamed Lulucha, she later married Romeu Augusto
Borman de Borges. They had three children: Clélia (*b.*
11 September 1908), Haygara (*b.* 10 May 1917) and
Paulo Emygidio (*b.* 10 October 1922). Bertha died in
1976 aged ninety-one in Belo Horizonte in the state of
Minas Gerais. Two years after her birth, her brother
Heitor Villa-Lobos was born on 5 March 1887. His
father died when Heitor was twelve years old. But his
mother, who lived to be eighty-seven, witnessed the
development and recognition of her son's great musical
talent. The next child Carmen was nicknamed Bilita.
She was born eighteen months after Heitor on 10
October 1888 and died on 20 April 1970 at the age of
eighty-two in Cruzeiro in the state of São Paulo. She
married Danton Condorcet da Silva Jardim; they were
survived by a daughter, Ahygara Iacyra (26 August
1933 - 1996). Othon, the youngest offspring of the
Villa-Lobos family, was a premature child. He was born
on 23 June 1897, shortly before his father, Raúl, died
on 18 July 1899. Othon's life, too, was short. He died
at the age of twenty-one on 27 July 1918. An
electrician, he had married Octavia.

Heitor's date of birth has long been in doubt and a
matter of speculation according to various documents
that are available. No birth certificate is available
because between 1881 and 1891 Brazil had no general
registers of births; hence many Brazilians were not
registered. The only document that refers to Heitor's
date of birth is his certificate of baptism. It is given as 5
March 1887. He was baptised, together with his
younger sister Carmen, on 17 January 1889 in Rio de
Janeiro's São José Church. Maria Carolina Serzedelo
Villa-Lobos, the composer's paternal grandmother, was
godmother.

30

31

32

30 Heitor's older sister, Bertha Borman de Borges (3 November 1885-1976).

31 Heitor's younger sister, Carmen Condorcet da Silva Jardim (10 October 1888-20 April 1970).

32 Heitor's brother Othon (23 June 1897-27 July 1918).

33 Facsimile of the certificate of baptism.

Conego Dr. Benedicto Marinho de Oliveira
Vigario da Freguezia de S. José
do Arcebispado de Rio de Janeiro

Certifico que no livro 18 de termos de baptismos desta
freguesia, á folhas 55, consta o seguinte:

- H e i t o r -

"A dezessete de janeiro de mil oitocentos e oitenta e
nove, batizei solenemente HEITOR, nascido a cinco de março de
mil oitocentos e oitenta e sete, filho legitimo de Raul Villa
Lobos e Noemia Villa Lobos, foram padrinhos José Jorge Rangel
e Maria Carolina Villa Lobos. Conego R. P. dos Santos Lemos,
Parocho Encomendado. - À MARGEM LE-SE: Casou-se com Lucilia
Guimarães em 12 de novembro de 1913. O Vigario Conego Dr. B.
Marinho. - NADA MAIS CONSTA. ITA IN FIDE PAROCHI.

33

34

34   The São José Church
(exterior and interior). The
church was built on ground
donated in 1608 by the
governor of Rio de Janeiro,
D. Luís de Almeida. In 1711
Rio de Janeiro was invaded
by the troops of Duguay-
Trouin (1673-1736). This
also affected the church: its
archives went missing.
Hence, the date of the
church's construction is
unknown. The first priest
gave his opening sermon on
31 January 1751.

Villa-Lobos's childhood

In 1887, the year in which Heitor Villa-Lobos was born, the city of São Paulo, which would be the first to recognise his talent in years to come, was still a small, quiet place and not much different from what it was in the middle of the nineteenth century, a small town with 25,000 inhabitants.

Villa-Lobos's birth and early childhood took place during the last two years of the Second Empire under Emperor Dom Pedro II, the son of Emperor Dom

35 São Paulo's Rua da Glória in 1860. When Villa-Lobos died almost a century later in 1959, it had become one of the principal avenues in the industrial centre which by then had five million inhabitants.

36 Quitanda Street in São Paulo in the year Villa-Lobos was born (1887).

35

36

37 The Imperial Palace in São Cristóvão in Rio de Janeiro in 1885.

38 Dom Pedro I (Pedro de Alcântara de Bragança e Bourbon 1798-1834), first Emperor of Brazil, son of Dom João VI.

39 Leopoldina (1797-1826) (Maria Leopoldina Josefa Carolina of Habsburg, Archduchess of Austria, first Empress of Brazil and wife of Emperor Dom Pedro I).

40 Dom Pedro II (Pedro de Alcântara de Bragança e Bourbon 1825-1891), second and last Emperor of Brazil. Son of Dom Pedro I of Brazil and Leopoldina. He reigned from 7 April 1831 until the Proclamation of the Republic (15 November 1889). The war against Paraguay took place during his reign. He furthered European immigration, stimulated the economy and sponsored the arts and sciences. During his reign the first railroad and telegraph lines were constructed.

Pedro I and Empress Leopoldina. Slavery still existed then. Although in 1885 the Saraiva- (1823-1895) Cotegipe (1815-1889) Law had freed all slaves when they reached the age of sixty, it was only on 13 May 1888 that Dom Pedro's daughter, Princess Isabel, signed – during her father's absence – the Golden Law *(Lei Áurea)* which abolished slavery without compensation for slaveholders.

The political consequence of this was the dethronement of the Emperor by the army, led by Marshal Manuel Deodoro da Fonseca, head of the provisional government, and the Proclamation of the Republic on 15 November 1889. This in turn introduced an American-style Federation, replacing the British-style monarchy. The Emperor and the Imperial family went into exile in France.

Two years after the Proclamation of the Republic, in 1891, the year Dom Pedro II died in exile, Brazil was governed by Marshal Floriano Vieira Peixoto (1891-

37

38

39

40

41 Isabel of the House of
Orléans and Bragança,
Imperial Princess and Regent
of Brazil (1846-1921).
Daughter of Emperor Dom
Pedro II and Empress Teresa
Cristina Maria de Bourbon,
she married Prince Luís
Felipe Maria Fernando
Gastão de Orléans, Count
d'Eu, on 15 October 1864.
They had three children.
During her father's absence
in Europe, she represented
the Emperor as Regent. In
her first regency, she signed
the 'Free Womb' Law (28
September 1871) which
freed the slaves' future
children. During her third
and last regency she signed
the 'Golden Law' (13 May
1888) which abolished slavery. After the Proclamation
of the Republic she and her
family went into exile in
Europe. (From 1865 from
the Collection of Dom Pedro
de Orléans and Bragança).

41

42 Newly-arrived Negro
slaves and the slave market
(Rugendas op.cit.).

42

43 Facsimile of the 'Golden Law'.

44 The Imperial Family in Petrópolis. *Left to right:* Empress Teresa Cristina Maria, Prince Dom Antônio, Princess Isabel, Emperor Dom Pedro II, Dom Pedro Augusto, Dom Luís, Count d'Eu, and Dom Pedro, Prince of Grão Pará, in 1889, shortly before they went into exile in France (Collection: Prince Dom Pedro Orléans e Bragança).

43

44

45   Marshal Manuel
Deodoro da Fonseca (1827-
1892).

46   Marshal Floriano Vieira
Peixoto (1839-1895).

47   Prudente José de
Morais Barros (1841-1902).

48   Manuel Ferraz de
Campos Salles (1841-1913).

49   Portuguese tiles which
embellish Brazilian houses
(four examples).

1894). Law and order was re-established by President
Prudente José de Morais Barros (1894-1898) and
finances stabilised under President Manuel Ferraz de
Campos Salles (1898-1902), a former Senator (1891-
1896) and Governor of São Paulo (1896-1897).

By the turn of the century, the nostalgia for the
Empire was a matter of the past. The Republic was
already well established when one of Brazil's great
Presidents, Francisco de Paula Rodrigues Alves, took
the reins from 1902 to 1906. During his administration
the fight against yellow fever was successful and Rio de
Janeiro became urbanised under engineer Francisco

50   Francisco de Paula
Rodrigues Alves (1848-
1919).

50

Pereira Passos (1836-1913), the city's mayor from
1902 to 1906. Elected for a second Presidential term,
Rodrigues Alves (as he was generally called) declined to
serve on grounds of health.

Background of Villa-Lobos's early years

51   Euclides Rodrigues Pimenta da Cunha (1866-1909), Brazilian essayist, historian and engineer. The publication of *Os Sertões* (Rebellion in the hinterland) established his literary reputation and earned him election to the Brazilian Academy of Letters and the Brazilian Historical and Geographical Institute.

52   José Pereira da Graça Aranha (1868-1931), Brazilian writer and diplomat. Descendant of a patriarchal family from the north of Brazil, he studied law at Recife, state of Pernambuco. He was a founding member of the Brazilian Academy of Letters. At the beginning of the 1920s, he supported the modern movement which led to 'The Week of Modern Art' in São Paulo, 1922. His book *Canaan* (1902) was epoch-making. His play *Malazarte* (1911) is written in Portuguese and French and was produced in Paris.

The year 1902 in which Francisco de Paula Rodrigues Alves took over Brazil's Presidency also witnessed two important literary events: the publication of *Os Sertões* by Euclides Rodrigues Pimenta da Cunha and *Canaan* by José Pereira da Graça Aranha.

The appearance of these two works was an event that marked the end of the great Brazilian literary era of the nineteenth century, an epoch into which the Villa-Lobos family was born. Undoubtedly, the intellectual Raúl was attracted by the works of these poets who also left their mark on his composer son, Heitor, during his adolescent years. The famous classics created by these and other important cultural figures were enormously influential. However, within the first two decades or so of the twentieth century, most of these writers had died. The most illustrious of them all, Joaquim Maria Machado de Assis, died in 1908, followed in 1909 by Euclides Rodrigues Pimenta da Cunha. In 1910 Joaquim Aurélio Barreto Nabuco de Araújo died, followed in 1912 by Barão do Rio Branco, in 1918 by Olavo Brás Martins dos Guimarães Bilac, and five years later, in 1923, by Ruy Barbosa de Oliveira.

51

52

53

54

53   Joaquim Aurélio
Barreto Nabuco de Araújo
(1849-1910), Brazilian
abolitionist, statesman,
author and diplomat.

54   Joaquim Maria
Machado de Assis (1839-
1908), Brazilian writer of
fiction, drama and poetry,
criticism and essays. He was
the son of a Portuguese
mother and a mulato father.
Suffering from epilepsy and a
speech defect, he was largely
self-taught. At the age of
fifty, he was acknowledged as
Brazil's greatest writer.
Founder and President of the
Brazilian Academy of Letters.

55   Barão do Rio Branco
(José Maria da Silva
Paranhos) (1845-1912).
Well-known historian,
geographer and diplomat.
Emperor Dom Pedro II
made him a baron in 1888.
Foreign Minister, fought for
Brazil's recognition as a
leading nation in South
America and the
establishment of her
frontiers, and strengthened
relations with the USA.

55

56

56   Ruy Barbosa de Oliveira (1849-1923), Brazilian statesman and lawyer. He was the chief architect of the 1891 constitution modelled upon that of the United States. He was known for his eloquent pleas for the rights of the younger nations at the Second Hague Conference (1907). He was a prolific writer, co-founder of the Brazilian Academy of Letters and its one-time President.

57   Olavo Brás Martins dos Guimarães Bilac (1865-1918), Brazilian poet. Defender of the abolition of slavery. He spent some time in Europe (1890) and was co-founder of the Brazilian Academy of Letters.

57

Villa-Lobos's youth

58

58 Ernesto Júlio de Nazaré (1863-1934), self-taught Brazilian composer and pianist. Played the piano in cinemas, music stores and in public in the state of São Paulo and the south of Brazil. He was famous for his Brazilian tangos (he wrote about 120), and also composed waltzes and polkas. An ear ailment from childhood onwards led to deafness in old age. In his last years he was mentally disturbed and ended his life tragically. *Chôros No. 1* is dedicated to him.

59 Colégio Pedro II in Rio de Janeiro at the time when Villa-Lobos attended in 1901. Founded in 1789, it acquired its name in 1837.

Little is known of Heitor Villa-Lobos's childhood. His father introduced the boy to music which was played at home, taught him the rudiments of the cello and exercised considerable influence over his son. Not one single likeness of the composer as a child has been unearthed. It is likely that much that has come down to us may be based on legend.

There is proof, however, that Heitor entered Colégio Pedro II on 3 April 1901. Regrettably, we have been unable to establish with the college how long Villa-Lobos was a student there.

It must have been during his final years at college or shortly thereafter when the musically-minded Villa-Lobos began to mix with composers and poets from the world of Brazilian popular music. He also participated as a guitar player in such groups and occasionally wrote small pieces for their get-togethers. Some of these musicians, though half-forgotten today, were prominent in their time. They include: Ernesto Júlio de Nazaré, Catulo da Paixão Cearense, Eduardo das Neves, Joaquim Francisco dos Santos (Quincas Laranjeiras), Anacleto Augusto de Medeiros, Irineu de Almeida, Francisca (Chiquinha) Hedwiges Gonzaga and others.

Two years after the first automobile licence was granted in Rio de Janeiro (29 August 1903) and four

59

60   Catulo da Paixão Cearense (1863-1946), Brazilian poet who moved to Rio de Janeiro in 1880 from his hometown São Luís in the state of Maranhão. His poems were set to music by many contemporary composers of popular music. Villa-Lobos used the poem *Rasga o Coração* (Rend the heart) in his *Chôros No. 10* but the melody is from Anacleto Augusto de Medeiros.

60

62

61   **Not illustrated** Irineu de Almeida (1873-1916), Brazilian composer of popular music and ophicleide player. Around the turn of the century he was known under the name of Irineu Batina (*Batina* means 'soutane') because he always wore an overcoat. Together with Anacleto Augusto de Medeiros he was a founding member of the Fire Fighting Band in which he played the ophicleide and trombone (1896-1916). Between 1904 and 1905 he frequented the Cavaquinho de Ouro (Golden Fiddle), a saloon and meeting place for Villa-Lobos, Quincas Laranjeiras and others. From 1907 he was a regular guest of Alfredo da Rocha Vianna's father in the Rua Vista Alegre in the Catumbi district where, from 1911 onwards, he instructed his son, Alfredo da Rocha Vianna Júnior, who later became a well-known composer of popular music under the pseudonym of Pixinguinha (1898-1973).

62   Eduardo das Neves (1874-1919), Brazilian singer and composer of popular music who was a favourite artist at the beginning of the twentieth century. Appeared in circuses, in cafés and other places of entertainment in Rio de Janeiro and other parts of Brazil. Played the guitar and was author of satirical poems.

63   Francisca (Chiquinha) Hedwiges Gonzaga (1847-1935), Brazilian composer of popular music and pianist. Descendant of a well-to-do family, she obtained a good education. Pupil of Arthur Napoleão (1843-1925) with whom she gave concerts. She visited Europe (1902, 1904, 1906) and was an emancipated lady, piano-teacher and member of a dance band led by the Brazilian flautist and composer Joaquim Antônio da Silva Calado (1848-1880). A composer since childhood she wrote about a thousand dance tunes, and between seventy and eighty scores for burlesque, operettas and revues which were successful in her time.

63

64 Joaquim Francisco dos Santos (Quincas Laranjeiras) (1873-1935), Brazilian composer of popular music, guitarist and flautist. Son of a carpenter, he came to Rio de Janeiro from his native Olinda, in the state of Pernambuco, at the age of six months. When eleven years old, he worked in a garment factory called Alliança in the Laranjeiras district. This probably earned him his nickname Quincas Laranjeiras. He became a public servant in the Inspectorate for Hygiene and Assistance, later the Municipal Assistance Department. Here he is seen with João Pernambuco (1883-1947) *(left)* and Augustin Barrios *(centre)* during a visit on 5 July 1919 to the Cavaquinho de Ouro in the Rua Carioca, a place often frequented by Villa-Lobos and popular musicians.

64

65 Anacleto Augusto de Medeiros (1866-1907), Brazilian composer of popular music. Studied at the Conservatório Imperial de Música (today: Music School of the Federal University of Rio de Janeiro), and played many instruments, including the saxophone. Founded on 15 November 1896 the Fire Fighting Band and was its first conductor. He set to music poems by Catulo de Paixão Cearense, a contemporary poet, including *Rasga o Coração* (Rend the heart) which Villa-Lobos used as sub-title for his *Chôros No. 10* (composed in 1926).

65

66

66 Earliest known photograph of the composer which he dedicated to one of his sisters.

months before the inauguration of the Tunel Coelho Cintra, commonly known as Tunel Novo (New Tunnel) on 4 March 1906, the earliest known photograph of the composer was taken. This dates from November 1905 when the composer was eighteen years old. He appears well groomed with hat and coat and sporting an umbrella. His clothes, including a waistcoat, look rather heavy for the spring season but possibly it was his best 'Sunday attire' which also may have served him when playing in public for a living.

In those years Villa-Lobos had to contribute to the family budget. His mother Noêmia's income from a small widow's pension and her earnings as a washerwoman for the Confeitaria Colombo was insufficient for the upkeep of the whole family.

Because Villa-Lobos had learned no particular trade, he played the cello in vaudeville, cafés, cinemas and such places. One of these was the Café Assírio in the Avenida Central (today: Avenida Rio Branco) where a cup of coffee with musical entertainment by an orchestra cost one hundred reis (a few pence).

67   The Café Assírio in the Avenida Central was located where later would be the basement of the Teatro Municipal, built in 1909.

67

Villa-Lobos also played at the old Odeon Cinema which around 1910 was in the Avenida Central (today: Avenida Rio Branco) at the corner of the Rua Sete de Setembro (today: Eduardo Guinle Skyscraper). Walking towards the Largo São Francisco it was on the right-hand side before crossing Avenida Central. The orchestra was in the foyer. The cinema had two projection rooms. About 1927 the Odeon Cinema moved to the Cinelandia section of the city, almost facing the National Library and close to the Palácio Monroe, then the seat of the Brazilian Senate. But by then Villa-Lobos was already far away in Paris presenting his latest compositions to an enthusiastic audience.

Villa-Lobos played in the evening in the Café Assírio and in the afternoon in the orchestra that entertained guests at the famous Confeitaria Colombo which still exists today.

The Confeitaria Colombo opened on 17 September 1894. It was founded by a Portuguese immigrant Manuel José Lebrão, who called it Colombo because he had succeeded in reaching the Americas, which was the dream of many Portuguese at the time. The Colombo is located in the Rua Gonçalves Dias 32/36. The street was given this name in 1865 because at number 50 lived the Brazilian poet Antônio Gonçalves

68   Odeon Cinema in Cinelandia.

68

69

71

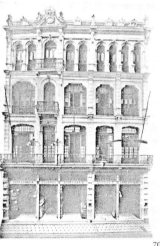

70

Dias. Nearby at the corner of the Rua Gonçalves Dias and Rua do Ouvidor was the point of departure for the first tramcars pulled by horses. The Colombo's walls are famous for the immense mirrors which, imported from Antwerp in 1912, were hand-framed in jacaranda wood. Remodelled, the Colombo re-opened in 1913 in Louis XVI style. Poets and the literary world met there and the place was often considered a branch of the Brazilian Academy of Letters, founded in 1896, some of whose members used to meet and chat in the afternoon at the Colombo's street entrance. The Colombo offers alcoholic beverages, meals and banqueting facilities and is renowned for its excellent service. It was the first Brazilian restaurant where, from its first opening, the prices on the menu included service.

71   The ground floor of the Confeitaria Colombo with its beautiful wall mirrors. The year was 1919, and men sported straw boaters.

72   Antônio Gonçalves Dias (1823-1864), Brazilian poet.

69   The remodelled façade of the Confeitaria Colombo in 1914, twenty years after its opening (1894).

70   Four years later, with the building next door incorporated to increase space.

72

Villa-Lobos's musical training

Around 1906-07, Villa-Lobos, principally a self-taught composer, sought advice from Agnello França, professor at the Instituto Nacional de Música (today: Music School of the Federal University of Rio de Janeiro). França also gave private lessons in his studio, located on the premises of the music firm Casa Vieira Machado, situated in the last block of the Rua do Ouvidor.

Villa-Lobos also sought advice from the Brazilian composer Antônio Francisco Braga who, some years later, in 1915, as conductor of an orchestra, performed a Villa-Lobos orchestral piece, *Suíte Característica for Strings*, to help him get started.

73

73 The Rua do Ouvidor at the time when the music publishing company Casa Vieira Machado was established at number 179 on the extreme right of the illustration. The firm has long since disappeared and the house has been demolished. But Agnello França's daughter, Geralda França, well remembered Casa Vieira Machado which published Villa-Lobos's first small compositions. In one of her letters to the author she

74

75

76

was professor of harmony at the Instituto Nacional de Música. Some of his pupils became well-known composers, conductors and scholars. His book *Arte de Modelar* (The Art of Modulation) was translated into French. His music was performed by Brazilian orchestras. When he taught Villa-Lobos, França lived in the Rua Pernambuco in the Encantado district of Rio de Janeiro.

76 Antônio Francisco Braga (1868-1945), Brazilian composer, conductor and teacher. Studied at the Conservatório Imperial de Música (today: Music School of the Federal University of Rio de Janeiro). With a government grant he went to Europe (in 1890) to study with Massenet (1842-1918) in Paris. In Germany (Dresden and Bayreuth) he came under Wagner's (1813-1883) influence, then went to Italy. After an absence of ten years he returned to Brazil (1900). From 1902 to 1938 he was professor at the Instituto Nacional de Música. He was conductor of the Sociedade de Concêrtos Sinfónicos in Rio de Janeiro from 1913 to 1933. On 31 July 1915 he gave the first performance of Villa-Lobos's *Suíte Característica for Strings* (with Villa-Lobos in the orchestra playing the cello) and on 15 August 1918 conducted the first performance of *Miremis* to promote his one-time pupil.

77 The 'Velho Casarão' of the old National Library in the nineteenth century to which the Instituto Nacional de Música moved in 1913. In the same year the cable car to Sugar Loaf mountain opened on 18 January.

generously offered her own reminiscences of what the place looked like in those years and what the firm offered the musicians who frequented it.

74 Excerpts from a letter from Geralda França to the author dated 11 November 1981, from Rio de Janeiro, reproduced in facsimile (published with her permission).

75 Agnello França in 1925 (1875-1964), Brazilian teacher and composer who came to Rio de Janeiro in 1897 from his native town of Marquês de Valencia in the state of Rio de Janeiro. For forty years (1904-1943) he

77

78 The building of the Instituto Nacional de Música in the Rua do Passeio 70 (today: 98).

79 The remodelled building, which was opened nine years later, in 1922.

80 The Largo da Sé in Rio de Janeiro in 1907 with its street markets where housewives regularly bought their supplies.

78

79

80

Agnello França had advised Villa-Lobos to enter the Music School to receive some regular music training. He was much interested in his pupil and wished him well. Villa-Lobos took this hint and entered the Music School, though we do not know the exact date. He did not remain there for long, however, and instead took private lessons with Agnello França as stated above.

The Instituto Nacional de Música was located in the Rua Luís Vaz de Camões 53. It was there that Villa-Lobos tried to pass the entrance examination, but (according to reports) he failed, although probably one of the most gifted applicants.

The original name of the Music School was Conservatório Imperial de Música, founded by Francisco Manuel da Silva (1795-1865), composer of the National Anthem of Brazil. It opened on 13 August 1848 in Rio de Janeiro, on 12 January 1890 changed its name to Instituto Nacional de Música and on 5 July 1937 to Escola Nacional de Música da Universidade do Brasil. On 13 March 1967 according to decree 60.455 it took the name of Escola de Música da Universidade Federal do Rio de Janeiro. First located in 53 Rua Luís Vaz de Camões (1517 or 1525-1580), it was transferred, in 1913, to the Velho Casarão of the old National Library in the Rua do Passeio 70 (today: 98). The remodelled building was opened on 9 November 1922.

Rio de Janeiro in those early years of the twentieth century was a beautiful city. The three-storeyed buildings with their wrought-iron balconies, broad streets where housewives bought their wares in the street markets, and the generously-proportioned thoroughfares lined with shady trees, with ample space for the horse-drawn carriages and public buses with open windows, so well suited to the warm climate, were a sheer delight. Handsome public buildings graced large squares where pedestrians could still walk unhampered by vehicles. It was a sedentary, placid life, in a period full of expectation, charm and serenity.

81

81 Rio de Janeiro's Praça da República in 1906. On the left can be seen the horse-drawn buses.

82 Rio de Janeiro's Largo de São Francisco after the remodelling by engineer Francisco Pereira Passos in 1905, with the Escola Politécnica (Photo: Marc Ferrez).

82

83 Rua Carioca in the centre of the city in 1908. The view features the three-storey houses and the unbustling streets.

84 The Praça José de Alencar (1829-1877), about 1909, showing the pretty gas lamps in the middle of the square, and the tramcars (no longer drawn by horses), still in use long after World War II. On the left can be seen, in a two-storey house, the foodstore with open windows which still existed in exactly the same fashion until after World War II (the author used to live a stone's throw away from this square and bought her food there). In the background are some of Rio de Janeiro's hills from which a cool breeze came down at night before the skyscrapers changed all this, and the air, clear and sparkling, was replaced by air-conditioning at home.

85 The Praça da Glória in 1908 depicts one of Rio de Janeiro's many gorgeous public squares. The landscaping with its tropical plants and flowers which blossom all year round in the favourable climate, the majestic palms and evergreen trees that line the square, are all a delight. It was equally lovely on warm summer nights when street lamps illuminated the paths where pedestrians strolled in the open air, richly scented by the surrounding floral displays. Wide streets separated the park from the two-storey houses in this residential section of Rio de Janeiro.

83

84

85

Villa-Lobos and the jungle

Villa-Lobos claimed that he had travelled much in Brazil during his adolescent years and that he had collected folklore material in the north of the country. He maintained he had made his first trip to Espírito Santo, Bahia and Pernambuco, as early as 1905-06, and, two years later, another journey to the south of Brazil. A third excursion, he alleged, took him to Minas Gerais, São Paulo and Mato Grosso, and from Santos, the harbour of São Paulo, he voyaged, once again, to Bahia from where he travelled, for three years, through all the northern states of Brazil, as well as the countries bordering her frontiers.

He told the author the most fantastic stories about his voyages up and down the tributaries of the great Amazon river, including the Rio Negro, Rio Tocantins, Rio Araguaia, Rio das Mortes, Rio Tabajós and São Francisco accompanied by just one friend and in a small home-made boat.[2]

It seems most unlikely that even a courageous young man, such as Villa-Lobos undoubtedly was, undertook all these adventurous trips in those days. Even today it would need considerable preparation and endurance of great hardship to undertake such strenuous travels. But Villa-Lobos liked to embellish his life. Especially in later years, when he lived in Paris and was asked about his native land, Villa-Lobos enjoyed dramatising and embroidering simple facts and he invented stories to put himself into the limelight and make himself attractive and interesting.

Two stories relating to his travels have, however, proved to be accurate. One concerns the time he once spent in Curitiba, in the southern Brazilian state of Paraná, when he worked in a match factory to make ends meet. The other concerns his trip to Manaos on the Amazon river. There he organised and played the cello in two concerts in the Teatro Amazonas. But this was as late as 7 September 1912, on Brazil's Independence Day or shortly before or after. On this occasion there was a performance of Villa-Lobos's *Japonesas,* op. 2 for voice and piano to words by Luís Guimarães Filho, which, according to the manuscript, was written on 5 March 1912 in Bahia and

2) 'Villa-Lobos's Brazilian Excursions', *The Musical Times,* Vol. 113, No. 1549, London, March 1972 and included in *Villa-Lobos: Collected Studies,* Scolar Press, Aldershot, 1992.

orchestrated on 12 July 1912. This indicates that his travels fell into a later period than the one he laid claim to.

Villa-Lobos, inquisitive and open to new impressions, was attracted by the magnitude of the Amazon river, the greatest waterway on earth with its immense width and grandeur and the splendour of the virgin forest lining its banks. He was undoubtedly impressed by the flora and fauna which he saw and the vastness of that region of Brazil. No-one as sensitive as the composer could fail to be impressed by the huge expanse, the overwhelming beauty and ferocity of such a phenomenon. On his travels there he also met people quite unlike those he had come to know in Rio de Janeiro. In all probability he came across some of the native peoples and their villages and observed the way in which they lived. Taken together, it must all have left a deep impression on the youthful mind of the twenty-five-year-old Villa-Lobos. He must also have watched the candomblés in Bahia and other similar ceremonies, witnessed native dances and heard indigenous songs which differed from those in the south of Brazil. Since he was without any academic training, a little primitive

86   Typical equatorial forest of the Amazon.

86

87

88

87 The dense equatorial
forest, impenetrable and
wild.

88 Northeastern Jaganda in
Ceará.

89 The beautiful *vitória
régia* often found on the
waters in the north.

89

himself at the time, and lacking any schooling or
formal education, he absorbed what he heard and saw
by instinct and without any intellectual interpretation:
the inhospitable wildness of the virgin forest, the
feeling of solitude, the noise of frightened animals, the
yells and screams of monkeys and other jungle animals
attacked by boa constrictors. The contrasts and
unpredictability of this immense area of water and
forest cannot fail to leave a profound impression.

90 One of the beautiful churches in the city of São Salvador, state of Bahia. Seen here is the Ordem Terceira de São Francisco.

91 Colonial building in Salvador, with its cobbled streets, old houses and nostalgic atmosphere of a past gone for ever but which Villa-Lobos had known during his travels in the north.

90

91

94

92

93

95

96

92 An Indian of the Amazon region such as Villa-Lobos must have seen during his travels.

93 A pretty Indian of the Amazon region attired in feathers.

94 Bahia women in their attractive dresses and headgear.

95 Eighteenth-century indigenous masks from the Amazon.

96 An iron-made *Exu*.

Villa-Lobos and the jungle 51

97

99

98

100

97 *Xangô*.

98 São Francisco river.

99 A collection of *Orixas* from Bahia in the last decade of the nineteenth century.

100 Some *Nhambiquaras* Indians from the *Serra dos Parecís* in the Mato Grosso.

101 Confluence of the Rio Negro with the Rio Solimões.

101

BRASILIEN.

103

102   Paranaguá in the
nineteenth century. Villa-
Lobos once spent some time
earning a living in a match
factory in nearby Curitiba.

103   Map of Brazil.

104 Map of the Amazon
river and its tributaries. Villa-
Lobos claimed he voyaged
on practically all of them
which is more than doubtful.

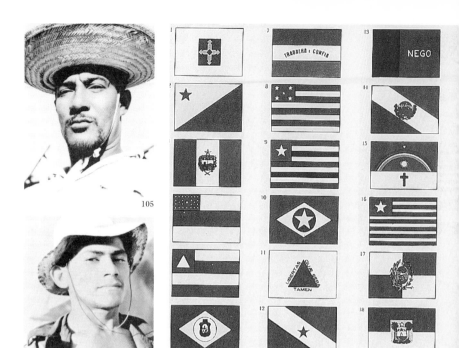

105 A fisherman from the Northeastern region of Brazil.

106 A cowboy from the island of Marajó on the Amazon river.

107 Map of Brazil divided into regions.

108

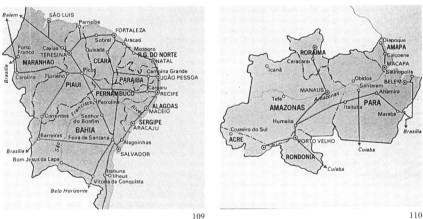

109

110

108   Flags of the Brazilian
Federal States. The former
territory of Rondônia was
added as the twenty-third
Federal state in 1981.

109   Map of the
Northeastern region.

110   Map of the Northern
region.

The Amazon region and its powerful atmosphere had left a great impression on Villa-Lobos. 'Here two-thirds of the total Amazon area is Brazilian: the rest is divided between Bolivia, Ecuador, Guyana, Columbia, Peru and Venezuela. The Brazilian regions consist of: Acre, Amazonas, North Mato Grosso, Pará, Goiás and part of Maranhão, as well as three territories Amapá, Rondonia and Roraíma. It is an immense area of almost five million square kilometres which encompasses about sixty per cent of Brazil. The distance of the Amazon region from east to west is almost 3,500 km, from north to south 2,800 km. More than one hundred times the area of Switzerland and twenty times that of West Germany yet with a population of only 9.3 million inhabitants.'[3]

3) *Neue Zürcher Zeitung*, Zurich, 27/28 October 1979.

111

111 Street in Manaos. The heavily cambered cobblestone street helps to drain away the torrential tropical rains. In the single-storey houses, stores or offices face the street and, as is customary in Latin American countries, living quarters are at the back in the part of the house that faces the patio or garden.

112 Interior of the Teatro Amazonas during the rubber boom at the end of the nineteenth century. Famous international artists performed here.

112

Rio de Janeiro at the time of Villa-Lobos's marriage

After Villa-Lobos had returned to Rio de Janeiro from his concerts in Manaos and possibly others in Bahia, he met Lucília Guimarães, a teacher and pianist, who, a year later, on 12 November 1913, became his wife. In her own words, she tells us about her first encounter with the young guitar-player and cellist and how it led to their marriage.

After his marriage to Lucília at the age of twenty-six, life for Villa-Lobos took a different turn. He had

113

113   Lucília Guimarães Villa-Lobos (26 May 1886-25 May 1966), Brazilian pianist, teacher and interpreter of Villa-Lobos's music who studied piano and singing at the Escola National de Música (today: Music School of the Federal University of Rio de Janeiro). She met Villa-Lobos on 1 November 1912 and married him a year later. They separated, childless, on 28 May 1936. Subsequently, she continued her musical activities as pianist and choral conductor. Villa-Lobos dedicated to her just one work: *A Prole do Bebé No. 1* for piano.

114   Memoirs by Lucília Villa-Lobos *(Visto da Platéia e na intimidada, 1912-1935* by Luiz Guimarães e Colaboradores: Oldemar Guimarães, Dinorah G. Campos, Alvaro de Oliveira Guimarães, Rio de Janeiro 1972, pp. 223/224). Since the book was published, the original Memoirs by Lucília Villa-Lobos cannot be found and are considered lost. It is even doubtful if they were

Eis como os fatos foram relatados do próprio punho, por Lucília, em "Minhas memórias", referendados por pessôas da família e pelo Dr. Lauro Sales de Oliveira (1), advogado, poeta e velho amigo da casa.

"Foi no dia de TODOS OS SANTOS (1/11/1912) que recebemos a visita de Villa-Lobos. Trazido por um amigo de meus Pais, Arthur Alves, o motivo era que iríamos ouvir um rapaz que tocava muito bem violão.

Moravamos, então, eu, minha Mãe e seis irmãos, n'uma vila, na rua Haddock Lobo (Vila Itala) hoje rua Domício da Gama.

Havia terminado meu curso de piano no INSTITUTO NACIONAL DE MÚSICA (hoje Escola Nacional de Música) e lecionava piano no COLÉGIO SACRÉ-COEUR, assim como também tinha algumas alunas particulares, de piano e de solfejo.

A noitada de música correu muito bem, extremamente agradavel, e, para nós, foi um sucesso o violão nas mãos de Villa-Lobos.

Terminando sua exibição, Villa-Lobos manifestou desejo de ouvir a pianista, e toquei, a seguir, alguns números de CHOPIN, cuja execução me pareceu ter impressionado bem, na técnica e na interpretação.

Villa-Lobos, porém, se sentiu constrangido; talvez mesmo inferiorizado, pois naquela época o violão não era instrumento de salão, de música de verdade, e sim instrumento vulgar, de chorões e seresteiros.

Súbitamente, vencendo como que uma depressão, declarou que o seu verdadeiro instrumento era o violoncelo, e que fazia questão de combinar uma reunião, em nossa casa, para se fazer ouvir em seu violoncelo. (2).

Ficou marcada nova reunião e combinado que enviaria, antecipadamente, as partes de piano para que eu as estudasse e pudesse acompanha-lo, logo no sábado seguinte.

No dia referido repetiu-se a audição, agora com Villa-Lobos ao violoncelo.

Outras reuniões se sucederam. Os contactos repetidos, a afinidade artística, e uma atração natural e crescente, culminaram em nosso noivado.

A 12 de Novembro de 1913 nos casámos. Continuei lecionando, e o Villa tocando, de dia, na Confeitaria Colombo e, á noite, no "Assírio" (3), restaurante localizado no Teatro Municipal.

Ficámos morando com minha família, já então em uma casa da Rua Fonseca Teles n.° 7, em S. Cristovão.

Apesar das dificuldades que atravessámos, o Villa (assim o chamava) começou a compor suas primeiras obras, com afinco e, como não tocasse piano ainda, era eu quem fazia as primeiras execuções, parciais".

(1) — Villa-Lobos musicou, inclusive, uns versos de Lauro Sales de Oliveira — "Crianças" — vide 5.ª audição — "O hino às Crianças" foi executado por um côro de 200 vozes, em 16-8-1918.

(2) — Villa-Lobos por essa ocasião (1912) integrava a orquestra da Sociedade de Concêrtos Sinfônicos, sob a regência de Francisco Braga.

(3) — O "Assírio" hoje é Museu dos Teatros do Rio de Janeiro — Lei 425 — 28-11-49. De costas para êle se acha um busto de Villa-Lobos, só identificado pelo nome gravado em bronze...

114

written except for the little pieces reproduced here. Possibly Lucília intended to write them but for reasons unknown, or possibly ill-health, she did not go

beyond those introductory sentences. (From a letter from Villa-Lobos's brother-in-law, Oldemar Guimarães to the author, Rio de Janeiro, 12 December 1979).

4) Francisco Pereira Passos (1836-1913), Brazilian politician. Mayor during the government of President Francisco de Paula Rodrigues Alves (1902-1906). Brought to fruition the redevelopment of the centre of the city, including tree-lined streets, which completely changed its appearance. Installed water, gas, a sewage system and electric lighting in the streets. Replaced horse-drawn trams with electric tramcars, built tunnels and laid out public parks.

5) André Gustavo Paulo de Frontin (1860-1933), Brazilian politician and engineer. During the government of President Francisco de Paula Rodrigues Alves (1902-1906) he excelled as an outstanding collaborator of Mayor Francisco Pereira Passos in remodelling the city of Rio de Janeiro. As chief of the construction commission, he laid out the Avenida Rio Branco in only twenty-two months, a tremendous feat at the time, considering that six hundred buildings were demolished. He was senator (1917) and Rio de Janeiro's mayor. During his administration he developed the city, created the Avenida Atlantica, Avenida Niemeyer, Avenida Rodrigues Alves and other boulevards and improved the city's urbanisation in many ways.

moved into her home, where she lived with her mother and six brothers and sisters. A more regular daily life, surrounded by loving relatives in an intellectual atmosphere – two of his brothers-in-law were about to become medical doctors – and encouraged by his wife to turn from popular to serious music, had its impact on the composer. He began to write smaller pieces for the piano and tried his hand at chamber music.

There were still further influences on him arising from the realisation of an immense urbanisation project, begun at the turn of the century. It modified the Avenida Central in Rio de Janeiro and gave the centre of the city a completely new appearance. It also included the construction of the Opera House at the entrance to the Avenida. This not only had an influence on the cultural life of the city but brought in its wake specific consequences for Villa-Lobos. He became a member of the Opera's orchestra and what he heard and played there would have a decisive influence on him as a composer.

The Avenida Rio Branco, originally called Avenida Central, was opened on 15 November 1905 to connect the port with the bay. To build the boulevard (1800 metres long and 30 metres wide), six hundred buildings were demolished. The entire project was realised during the administration of Mayor Francisco Pereira Passos[4] and the Presidency of Francisco de Paula Rodrigues Alves under the direction of engineer Paulo de Frontin.[5]

115 View of Avenida Rio Branco after reconstruction. On the left is the Hotel Avenida which was demolished after World War II. The view is looking towards the harbour.

115

116

117

118

119

116 117 Rio de Janeiro under construction during the urbanisation plan 1906-1910.

118 Palácio Monroe, opened in 1906 on the occasion of the Third Pan American Conference and which, for many years, served as the country's Senate. It was demolished in November 1976. *On the left:* the Obelisk, at the entrance to the Avenida Rio Branco.

120

119 The Largo da Lapa, not far from the Music School, in 1912. Seen here are the electric tramcars introduced as part of the urbanisation project.

120 Exterior view of the Opera House (Teatro Municipal).

Rio de Janeiro at the time of Villa-Lobos's marriage 61

121 View of the Teatro Municipal's foyer with its Louis XVI style furniture.

The Teatro Municipal, modelled in miniature on the Paris Opera, was part of the splendid urbanisation project. The Teatro was opened in the presence of President Nilo Peçanha on 14 July 1909 when the opera *Moema* by Delgado de Carvalho (1872-1921) was mounted, preceded by a dramatic performance and followed by a concert.

122

123

122   Nilo Peçanha (1867-1924), Brazilian politician;Vice President of Brazil (elected in 1906) who became President of Brazil upon the death (1909) of Afonso Augusto Moreira Pena who was President from 1906. Nilo Peçanha was President from 1909 until 1910.

123   Afonso Augusto Moreira Pena (1847-1909), Brazilian politician and President of Brazil (1906-1909).

First public performances of Villa-Lobos's music

124

In 1913, the year of Villa-Lobos's marriage, Diaghilev's (1872-1929) Ballets Russes with Nijinsky appeared for the first time in Rio de Janeiro and performed before an audience of 1500 at the Teatro Municipal, completed only a few years previously. The programme included excerpts from Borodin's (1834-1887) *Prince Igor*, Rimsky-Korsakov's (1844-1908) *Scheherezade*, Balakirev's (1837-1910) *Tamara* and Debussy's (1862-1918) *L'Après-midi d'un Faune* which influenced Villa-Lobos's musical development. He began to borrow French and Russian devices and used French titles.

Villa-Lobos now tried to get his works performed. The first opportunity presented itself in the mountain village of Nova Friburgo, near Rio de Janeiro, where he was holidaying in the home of his aunt, Leopoldina do Amaral – nicknamed Aunt Fifina. Together with his wife and a friend Agenor Bens, a flautist, he performed a programme that consisted mainly of his own music: a *Trio for flute, piano and cello*, some pieces for piano and cello, and a piano solo. The opening concert, in the Teatro D. Eugênia on 29 February 1915, was the first of a series of three concerts; the second and third concerts also included pieces for piano and the Trio.

Encouraged by having presented some of his music in public, Villa-Lobos immediately set about writing

124 Vaslav Fomitch Nijinsky (1890 [on his tomb is inscribed 1889] – 1950), Russian dancer, joined (1911-1914) the Ballets Russes. Travelled with his own group to England, North and South America (1914-1917). Mentally deranged (1917). His body was transferred to Montmartre cemetery in 1953.

125 Nova Friburgo.

125

another chamber work: the *String Quartet No. 1*, composed on his birthday – 5 March 1915 – but only given its première many years later, on 7 August 1946 in Rio de Janeiro. Whether the work was really written on the date mentioned in the manuscript is doubtful because of the date of the first performance. Villa-Lobos usually had his latest works performed immediately they were composed. Moreover, in *Villa-Lobos – Sua Obra*, Rio de Janeiro 1972, p. 84 it is stated that the work was first performed in the home of 'the Brazilian composer Homero Barreto (*c.* 1884-1924) in Nova Friburgo on 3 February 1915'. This is six weeks before it was supposedly written! Moreover, it was only published many years later by the Southern Music Publishing Company in New York City, whereas Villa-Lobos's *String Quartets No. 2* and *No. 3* which were performed before *String Quartet No. 1* were brought out by Éditions Max Eschig, his French publisher. It is likely that Villa-Lobos wrote the work shortly before it was actually published, except for a

126   The music performed here confirms Villa-Lobos's inclination towards French titles and his borrowing from the *Fables* of La Fontaine (1621-1695).[6] However, Villa-Lobos chose birds of his own country such as *Araponga* and *Irerê*.

6) *L'Oiseau blessé d'une flèche*, though finished in August 1913, was begun in May of that year.

PROGRAMMA

Segunda audição de composições de H. Villa Lobos, a

3 Fevereiro de 1917

N. 1 — Quartetto de cordas, n. 2 (op. 56) a 4 partes (1915)

a) — Allegro non troppo
b) — Scherzo
c) — Andante
d) X Allegro deciso
     X Presto
     X Prestissimo Final

O seguinte quartetto faz parte de uma collecção de quar-
tettos modernos obedecendo a seguinte nomenclatura, n. 1
(op. 50), n. 2 (op. 56) e n. 3 (op. 59). Este que será executado é baseado e desenvolvido sobre quatro themas que
em todos os tempos apparecem movidos por diversos ryh-
thmos.

VIOLINOS, Mlles. Judith Barcellos e Dagmar Noronha Gitahy.
VIOLA, Sr. Orlando Frederico.
CELLO, Sr. Alfredo Gomes.

N. 2

a) — L'oiseau — Fabula V de La Fontaine   X
b) — Les Mères — Poesia de Victor Hugo   X   CANTO E PIANO
c) — Fleur Fanée — Poesia de Gallait   X

L'oiseau blessé d'une fleche

Mortellement atteint d'une flèche empennée
Un oiseau déplorait sa triste destinée,
Et disait, en souffrant un surcroit de douleur :
Faut-il contribuer à son propre malheur !
Cruels humains, vous tirez de nos ailes
De quoi faire voler ces machines mortelles !
Mais ne vous moquez point, engeance sans pitié :
Souvent il vous arrive un sort comme le nôtre.

Musicada em Agosto de 1913

Les Mères

L'enfant chantait ; la mère au lit, extenuée,
Agonisant, beau front dans l'ombre se penchant:
La mort au dessus d'elle errait dans la nuée;
Et j'écoutais ce râle, et j'entendais ce chant.
L'enfant avait cinq ans, et, près de la fenetre,
Ses rires et ses jeux faisaient un charmant bruit.
Et la mère, à côté de ce pauvre doux être
Qui chantait tout le jour, toussait toute la nuit.
La mère alla dormir sous les dalles du cloitre ;
Et le petit enfant se remit à chanter...
La douleur est un fruit :
Dieu ne le fait pas croitre
Sur la branche trop faible encor pour le porter.

Musicada em Agosto de 1914

Fleur Fanée

Quand songeant au passé, son cœur devient morose,
Cherche, en un livre ancien que le temps a jauni,
L'ombre odorante encor d'un calice de rose,
Que l'oubli sans pitié de son souffle a bruni,

Souvenir d'un beau rêve, hélas ! trop tot fini !
Tandis qu'on le regarde, une larme l'arrose,
Mais, cruelle, pourquoi l'avoir mis dans la prose?
Peut-être dans les vers se fut-il moins terni !...

Pourtant la fleur se garde en sa forme derniere,
Tout le charme enchanteur de l'aube pritaniere
Où, fraiche de rosée, je la mis à son reveil.

Il semble lui rester sous son morne costume
Un parfum d'outre-tombe, une beauté posthume
Que la mort eut laissés par un secret dessein.

Musicada em Outubro de 1913
Sr. Frederico Nascimento Filho e Mme. Lucilia Villa-Lobos

N. 3
VIOLONCELLO   X a — Elegie – Op. 87 (1916)
E   X b — Preludio – Op. 20 – (A parte de piano é tratada com
PIANO   X   sonata em um tempo. (913)
Sr. Alfredo Gomes e Mme. Lucilia Villa Lobos

N. 4

a — Fabula op. 65 (n. 3) O GATO E O RATO

Piano Solo

b — Farrapos op. 47 (n. 1) DANSA INDIGENA
FABULA — escripta em 1916, faz parte de uma colletania de musicas exo-
ticas e descriptivas escriptas sobre a impressão de algumas fabulas de LAFON
e de outros fabulistas sendo na seguinte ordem : – N. 1 – O CUCO E O H
(op. 60); n. 2 – ARAPONGA E O IRIRE' (op· 64); n. 3 – O GATO E O
(od. 65) etc.
FARRAPOS — escripta 9/914, Kankukos em 4/915, pertencem a uma col
de 3 danças caracteristicas de Indios Africanos – FARRAPOS é a dança dos
Kankukos a dos moços e Kankikis a dos meninos.
Sr. Rubens de Figueiredo

N. 5
a – Il Nome di Maria – POESIA – Steechetti   CANTO E PIANO
b – Noite de Luar – POESIA – Baptista Junior CANTO E PIANO
c – Il Bove (o Boi) –   "   – Carducci   CANTO, PIANO E C

Il nome di Maria

Non per tempo che passi o lunga via
che da te mi divida o m'allontani,
non perrutassi de gli eventi umani
potrò dimenticarti, anima mia ;

e ne lo spasimar de l'agonia,
giunto a la sera che non ho domani,
pensando a questi di fatti lontani
il nome tuo singhiozzerò, Maria.

E diranno di mé: l'ora de l' pianto
ecco vince il ribelle : ecco il santo
chiese d'un nome benedetto e santo.

Ma no. Sul' letto funeral caduto
quel dolce nome io dirò soltanto
in memòria di' ben che m'hai voluto.

Musicada em 5 — 9

127

128

127   *Araponga.*

128   *Ireré.*

129   Frederico Nascimento Filho, Brazilian singer of Portuguese descent who gave concerts in South America; he was a teacher of harmony, to whom Villa-Lobos dedicated his *String Quartet No. 4.* The singer gave the first performance of Villa-Lobos's *Coleção Brasileira* under the composer's direction on 18 February 1925.

130   Alfredo Gomes.

few bars which he had composed as early as 5 March 1915.

After Antônio Francisco Braga, his former teacher and conductor of Sociedade de Concêrtos Sinfônicos, had sponsored his one-time pupil by performing Villa-Lobos's early orchestral work *Suíte Característica for Strings,* Villa-Lobos decided the time had come for him to organise some public concerts in Rio de Janeiro. The first took place on 13 November 1915, the second on 3 February 1917.

The programme also included artists who were to become some of his keenest interpreters in those early years: the singer Frederico Nascimento Filho, the cellist Alfredo Gomes (*d.* 1932) and the viola player Orlando Frederico to whom Villa-Lobos dedicated his *String Quartet No. 6.*

On 17 November 1917, Villa-Lobos organised a third concert at which his works were performed in the Salão Nobre of the *Jornal do Comércio* in Rio de Janeiro.

Ernani da Costa Braga (1888-1948), the Brazilian composer, pianist and founder of the Conservatório de Música of Pernambuco (1930) which he directed for a number of years, was to become one of Villa-Lobos's interpreters in the early years.

Villa-Lobos called one of the numbers from the *Suíte Floral: Idílio na Réde.* He thus acknowledged a well-known Brazilian custom. All through the centuries, especially in tropical areas, Brazilians have enjoyed resting or even sleeping in hammocks as noted by Hans Staden about fifty years after the discovery of Brazil, when travelling through the region.

Villa-Lobos made some progress in Rio de Janeiro in getting his works performed and being reviewed by the local press. São Paulo, on the other hand, which later would pay him more attention than Rio de Janeiro, at

129   130

First public performances of Villa-Lobos's music   65

PROGRAMMA

Terceirâ audição de composições de
H. VILLA-LOBOS
a 17 de Novembro de 1917

N? 1—SONATA II (Op. 46)
CÉLLO E PIANO
Sr. Gustavo Hess de Mello e Mme. Lucilia Villa Lobos

a) — ALLEGRO MODERATO
b) — ANDANTE
c) — SCHERZO
d) — ALLEGRO VIVACE SOSTENUTO e FINAL
A SONATA II (Op. 46) foi escripta no
anno de 1916, pertencendo a uma collecção de Sonatas modernas.

N? 2—CANTO E PIANO
Sr. Alberto Cabello Guimarães e Mme. Lucilia Villa Lobos

a) — SONHO (1917) — Soneto de A. Guimarães
b) — CHROMO (1917) — Soneto de Abilio Barreto
c) — JAPONEZAS (1912) — Soneto de Luiz Guimarães
Filho

CHROMO

Rescende o pomar. Laurita
Na redoiça se embalança,
De um jambeiro sob a trança,
Que levemente se agita.

Pedrinho outra linda criança,
Por perto corre, saltita.
Se encontra uma flôr bonita,
Traz e lhe engasta na trança.

Mas, emfim, eil-o que agora,
Colhendo uma rubra amóra,
Fita-a. Um idéa o provoca...

E diz-lhe a flôr dos pimpolhos :
— " Abre a bocca e fecha os olhos..."
E dá-lhe um beijo na bocca!

JAPONEZAS

Oh! Gheishas! bonecas vivas
De vestidos multicôres,
Sois lindas, frageis, esquivas
Como os gatos e os amores.

Tendes olhos zombadores
E attitudes pensativas,
Ora sois jarros de flôres,
Ora sois pombas captivas.

A noite, em doce abandono,
Moveis o alado Kimono
Ao triste som das guitarras.

O chá fuméga na esteira,
E na sombra hospitaleira
Morrem de frio as cigarras.

N? 3—SOLO DE PIANO
Sr. Ernani Braga

a) — IDYLLIO NA REDE (Op. 98) - (1917)
b) — KANKÍKUS (Op. 59) - (1915)
Da colleção de 3 danças caracteris-
cas de Indios Africanos, da qual faze
parte o FARRAPOS (executado na audiç
passado pelo Sr. Rubens de Figueired
e KANKIKIS, que irá no programma da
audição.

N? 4—VIOLINO E PIANO
Sr. Mario Camiuha e Mme. Lucilia Villa Lobos

a) — IMPROVISO N. 7 (1915) — Melodia
b) — A MARIPOSA NA LUZ (1916)

N? 5—CANTO E PIANO
Sr. Frederico Nascimento Filho e Mme. Lucilia Villa Lob

a) — MAL SECRETO (Soneto de Raymundo Corrêa) (191
b) — SINO DA ALDEIA (Uma quadra de Antonia Corre
de Oliveira) - (1915)
c) — LOUCO (Soneto de J. Cadilhe) - (1917)

131 Facsimile of the Concert Programme. (The composition dates and opus numbers do not always correspond with those mentioned in *Heitor Villa-Lobos, Leben und Werk des Brasilianischen Komponisten* by Lisa M. Peppercorn, Zurich 1972; I daresay that while I had checked them carefully with the manuscripts, it is possible that typographical errors may have been introduced in the programme published here).

132 Luís Guimarães Filho (1878-1940). When Villa-Lobos was in Bahia in 1912, he set to music Filho's sonnet in *Japonesas* op. 2.

133 Hammock from *Zwei Reisen nach Brasilien* (1548-

132

133

134

1555), by Hans Staden (*c.* 1525-c. 1576), Marburg 1557.

134 The habit of resting in a hammock is also recorded in *Mythes, Contes et Légendes des Indiens, Folklore-Brésiliene* by Gustavo Dodt Barroso (1888-1959), Paris 1930.

135

135   Rua 15 de Novembro,
São Paulo in 1915.

136   Panoramic view of the
Avenida São João, São Paulo
around 1915.

136

this time offered no such opportunities.

In 1918 Villa-Lobos was offered unexpected
opportunities. During Rio de Janeiro's winter season,
on 15 August, he was given an opportunity to conduct
a concert performance of the fourth act of his opera
Izaht. It made little impact. While the composer wrote
another more successful opera – *Yerma* – many years
later, which was performed posthumously, writing for
the stage was not something at which he excelled.

The great event in 1918 which was to have far-
reaching consequences for Villa-Lobos's career was his
encounter with the Polish-born American pianist
Arthur Rubinstein.

When Rubinstein visited Brazil on one of his first
South American tours, he sought out Villa-Lobos on
the advice of the Swiss conductor Ernest Ansermet.
Ansermet had travelled with Serge Diaghilev's Ballet
Russes from 1915 to 1923 and had heard of Villa-
Lobos during the ballet's two South American tours.

At a reception in Rio de Janeiro Rubinstein met Paul
Claudel, the new Minister at the French Legation in
Rio de Janeiro, and the young Darius Milhaud, his

137

138

137   Arthur Rubinstein
(1887-1982) to whom Villa-
Lobos dedicated *Rudepoéma*
and *Chôros No. 11* for piano
and orchestra.

138   Ernest Ansermet
(1883-1969).

139   Programme for the
performance of the fourth
act of *Izaht*.

140   The French Legation
at the Rua Paysandu in Rio
de Janeiro in 1917.

139

140

141

a dix ans, que tout cela c'est passé. Pendant mon séjour à Rio de Janeiro
entendu plusieurs fois le nom de Villa-Lobos que je ne connaissais pas
...'à ce moment. C'était un nom d'un musicien brésilien qui habitait à Rio.
.e trouvais tout de suite intéressé : il était pauvre, la vie le força de
.cher un emploi dans un orchestre de cinéma de troisième ordre. On avait
.ui de très différentes opinions. Il jouait le violoncelle et d'autres
.ruments. Il possédait une telle intuition musicale, qu'une fois lorsqu'il
.it remplacer un de ses amis qui jouait le violon, il prit cet instrument
.e un violoncelle, jouait le rôle de son ami. Mais j'étais plus étonné en
.ndant qu'il était un compositeur, qui possédait un style créateur tout a
. particulier. Tous les musiciens, avec qui j'avais l'occasion de parler de
., ne s'exprimaient de lui que d'une façon assez dédaigneuse. Mais, dans ce
.ls disaient, j'ai trouvé un peu de crainte, qui caractérise toujours nos
.ions sur des problèmes qui dépassent nos compétences.
.soir, que j'étais libre, je suis allé au cinéma où Villa-Lobos travaillait.
.rchestre jouait des pièces du répertoire international, comme on fait partout. Je
.mençais à m'ennuyer, lorsqu'une chose inattendue arriva : un des joueurs de
.rchestre regardant la salle m'aperçut parmi le public. Lorsque la seconde parti
.mmça, j'ai entendu une musique qui ne ressemblait pas du tout, à ce que j'avais
.ndu dans la première partie. C'était une danse exotique, très rythmique, et
.l expressive dans son harmonie. J'ai senti, tout de suite dans cette musique un
.nd talent qui ne se trouve pas tous les jours. Je me suis décidé de faire-
.mier pas et de faire la connaissance du compositeur. Je suis allé dans les
.lisses. Je l'ai trouvé, je me suis présenté et j'ai demandé des détails de
.oeuvre qui venait d'être exécutée. La réponse était tout à fait inattendue pour
.: "Ces choses ne peuvent pas vous interesser", Villa-Lobos répondit, me
.rnant me quitta.
.ques jours s'écoulèrent. Un certain matin je fus réveillé par un bruit dans
.ntichambre. Il était 9 heures et d'habitude à cette heure-ci c'était encore tout
.ait tranquille dans la maison. J'ai appelé les domestiques et j'ai appris avec

anxiété qu'une nombreuse délégation de l'orchestre demandait à me voir. Je me
suis habillé en grande hâte, très intéressé par cette affaire. Cette délégation
était tout à fait extraordinaire. J'ai remarqué dans l'antichambre plusieurs
musiciens avec leur instruments sous leur bras. Villa-Lobos se trouvait à leur
tête. Il me faisait part en quelques mots, qu'il réflechi et s'était décidé de
jouer pour moi quelques compositions. "Et voilà il me dit ce sont mes amis, des
braves gens, qu'ont bien voulu m'offrir leur seul moment libre dans la journée".
Nous nous sommes mis tous au travail. Pour que tout l'orchestre puisse trouver
place dans le salon, il fallut le transformer en une salle de concert. Nous avons
mis de côté l'armoire, les tables et les chaises. Enfin tout l'orchestre était
placé et on a pu commencer le concert. Je ne l'oublierai pas de toute ma vie.
Cette qualité était la parfaite particularité du style, qui caractérise
jusqu'à aujourd'hui la musique de Villa-Lobos. Elle était incomparable ! Elle avait
la sonorité et la forme, inconnue à nous, les européens. Il faudrait être sourd
pour ne pas sentir la profondeur de cette musique. J'étais tout à fait sous son
charme: je l'entendais avec plaisir et une grande joie... Villa-Lobos possède des
éléments qui correspondent avec les idées, de la beauté et avec les nécessités
esthétiques de nos temps.

142

141 Darius Milhaud (1892-1974), the French composer and one-time diplomat, is seen here in a group with Paul (Louis Charles) Claudel (1868-1955), the French poet and diplomat, at the French Legation in Rio de Janeiro. 'Nous arrivâmes à Rio de Janeiro le 1er février 1917, en plein été, par une chaleur intense' reported Darius Milhaud (*O Paiz*, Rio de Janeiro, 2 February 1917).

142 This text of Rubinstein's reminiscences about his encounter with Villa-Lobos (source unknown) was made available to the author by Éditions Max Eschig, Paris 1980.

First public performances of Villa-Lobos's music 69

143　From Arthur Rubinstein's *My Many Years*, London 1980, pp. 154-155.

144　Carlos Guinle (1882-1960), Brazilian industrialist and philanthropist from a well-known Brazilian family. His brother Guilherme (1882-1960) was founder of the Docas de Santos and the Banco de Boa Vista. Brother Eduardo was the builder of the Palácio de Laranjeiras (for some time seat of the Federal government); brother Otávio was owner of the Hotel Copacabana and brother Arnaldo an art patron and founder of the Fluminense Football Club. Many prominent guests were received on Carlos Guinle's estate in the nearby mountain village of Teresopolis.

145　Arnaldo Guinle (1884-1964), Brazilian industrialist and art patron with a great interest in sport. Sponsored, together with his brother Carlos, Villa-Lobos's second stay in Paris (1927-30). *Chôros No. 5* and *No. 7* are dedicated to him. Arnaldo, *seated*, is facing the camera.

private secretary from 1917 to 1919, whom he first mistook for the Brazilian composer. When the error was cleared up, Milhaud took Rubinstein to the Odeon Cinema where Villa-Lobos played the cello, and introduced the two musicians. Ten years later, Arthur Rubinstein reminisced about his encounter with Villa-Lobos. A few years later, Villa-Lobos appealed to his new-found friend to help him visit Paris for a chance to have his many works performed, as his own country had been slow to recognise his talents. Rubinstein, ever helpful, took the necessary steps as he recorded in his *Memoirs*.

> I suddenly asked my host, "Would you like to be celebrated after your death? Carlos," I continued, "the Archduke Rudolph, the Prince Lichnowsky, and Count Waldstein would have been forgotten if they hadn't had the good luck to understand and love the music of Beethoven and play a great role in his life as his benefactors. Their financial aid enabled the great genius to write his master works free from cares; these gentlemen and a few others like them now have a great name in the history of music. Carlos," I repeated again, "right here in Brazil lives an authentic genius, in my opinion the only one on the whole American continent. His country does not understand his music yet, but future generations will be proud of him. Like all great creators, he has no means of making his works known in the world unless he is helped by some great Maecenas. I thought of you first of all, knowing your understanding, your patriotism, and your great generosity. The composer is Heitor Villa-Lobos, a future famous name in the history of Brazil, and if you are ready to help him, your name will always be linked with his."
>
> Guinle was very impressed. "Your great opinion of him is sufficient for me and I shall be happy to do what I can for him."

143

144

145

First public recognition

The year 1919 was remarkable for Villa-Lobos in two ways: he was commissioned to write an orchestral piece, and he moved with his wife into their own home. Epitácio da Silva Pessoa, President of Brazil, had asked the Director of the Instituto Nacional de Música, Abdon Filinto Milanês, to organise a concert in celebration of the Peace Conference. Milanês commissioned three Brazilian composers – João Octaviano Gonçalves (1892-1962), Antônio Francisco Braga and Alberto Nepomuceno –, each of them to write a symphony about war, victory and peace, whose underlying text should be supplied by Luís Gastão de Escragnolle Dória. But Nepomuceno declined for personal reasons. Villa-Lobos was therefore entrusted with the commission instead. He wrote his *Symphony No. 3* and called it *'A Guerra'*.

By now Villa-Lobos's music had begun to receive some recognition. Even his greatest enemy, Oscar Guanabarino, the music critic of the prestigious *Jornal do Comércio,* occasionally found something good in his music, though more often than not he continued fiercely to attack Villa-Lobos.

Villa-Lobos now fell into the habit of dedicating his newest compositions to either his interpreters or his patrons who enabled him to perform his music. Among these were the cellist Newton de Menezes Pádua who gave the first performance of Villa-Lobos's *Cello Concerto No. 1* on 10 May 1919 at the Teatro

146 Epitácio da Silva Pessoa (1865-1942), Brazilian statesman, President of Brazil (1919-1922).

147 Abdon Filinto Milanês (1858-1927), Brazilian composer and politician. Studied engineering and composition and wrote music for the theatre. Director of the Instituto Nacional de Música (1916-22). During his administration the main building with its large and small concert halls was inaugurated.

146

147

148   149

148   Alberto Nepomuceno (1864-1920), Brazilian composer, conductor and teacher. He grew up in Recife, state of Pernambuco, and in 1884 came to Rio de Janeiro. 1888-1895 first European tour (Rome, Berlin, Paris). After his return to Brazil, he taught organ at the Music School. Head of the Sociedade de Concêrtos Populares (1896). Second European tour (1900-1902). Director of the Music School in Rio de Janeiro for a few months (1902-03). Third European tour (1910). Director of the Instituto Nacional de Música (1906-16). During his administration the Music School moved in 1913 from the Rua Luís Vaz de Camões to its present address at the Rua do Passeio, and plans for an extension of the building were made. He composed several works.

150

149   Luís Gastão de Escragnolle Dória (1869-1948), Brazilian writer and Director of the National Archives (1917-1922), a member of the Instituto Histórico e Geográfico Brasileira in Rio de Janeiro and various other national and international institutions. Contributor to many publications.

150   Villa-Lobos and his wife, Lucília, took up residence on their own and moved to Rua Didimo 10, ground floor, in the Tijuca district, the couple's home for about seventeen years until 28 May 1936.

152

151 A view of Praça 15 de Novembro, in 1920, at about the time when the Villa-Lobos's moved into their home. The photo was taken in 1920 by Augusto César Malta. On the left can be seen Morro do Castello already half-demolished. Here, the Esplanada do Castello – a new downtown district – would be built at a later date. In the background can be seen the Morro de Nova Cintra, Corcovado (still without the statue of Christ) and the Serra da Carioca.

154

152 The building of the *Jornal do Comércio* at the corner of Avenida Rio Branco and Rua do Ouvidor. Though the picture dates from 1905 the building remained the same until well after World War II. The name of the *Jornal* is seen at the top of the building facing Avenida Rio Branco.

153

153 Oscar Guanabarino (1851-1937), music critic of the *Jornal do Comércio*.

154 Newton de Menezes Pádua (1894-1966), Brazilian composer, cellist and interpreter of Villa-Lobos's music. Studied at the Escola Nacional de Música where, later, he taught harmony. Also professor at the Conservatório Brasileiro de Música.

First public recognition 73

//

//// ˙ *LES* MINIATURAS *DE VILLA LOBOS.*

M. Villa Lobos, dont Madame Vera Janacopulos ʀ chanté à l'un de ses si intéressants récitals les *Miniaturas*, est un compositeur brésilien, complètement inconnu, je crois, en Europe, et qu'on vient seulement de découvrir, d'ailleurs, dans son propre pays. Bien que jeune encore et ayant mené une vie fort agitée, Villa Lobos, qui a fait ses études musicales au Conservatoire de Rio de Janeiro où il fut l'élève de Braga et d'Oswald, a déjà écrit cinq symphonies, des quatuors, de nombreuses mélodies, pièces pour piano, etc. Les trois *Miniaturas*, admirablement exécutées par Mme Janacopulos-Stahl, *Chromo, Sino de Aldeia* et *Viola*, nous découvrent une âme extrêmement tendre, inquiète, vibrante. L'harmonie est relativement simple, mais fraîche, et réserve, parfois, des surprises très agréables ; la ligne mélodique, très souple, se maintient généralement dans des limites étroites ; extrêmement originale en est la vie rythmique, nerveuse, trépidante. Il se dégage de cette musique, fruste et raffinée en même temps, très sincère et qui paraît jaillir d'un seul jet, un charme très spécial et réellement exotique, étranger à toute formule. Il est certain que l'art de Villa Lobos, profond ment national, s'inspire des danses et des chants populaires.

B. DE S.

155

156

157

155 The first review of some of Villa-Lobos's music to appear in *La Revue Musicale,* Paris, No. 9, July 1921 featuring a few songs interpreted by Vera Janacópulos.

156 Aline van Barentzen (1897-1981), French pianist of American origin. At the age of nine she attended the Paris Conservatoire where she obtained a gold medal

and the grand prize at the age of eleven. Played in her teens with the Berlin Philharmonic Orchestra, concert tours with major European orchestras. New York debut (1915) at the age of eighteen. Played with leading American and Canadian orchestras. In Brazil she met Villa-Lobos and championed his music during the 1920s and 1930s in France where she was

professor of piano at the Paris Conservatoire. Villa-Lobos dedicated to her *A Prole do Bebé No. 2* of which she gave the first performance (5 December 1927). She was also one of the two pianists who performed *Chôros No. 8* with Leopold Stokowski and the Philadelphia Orchestra (12 and 13 April 1929) when the conductor pioneered the work of Villa-Lobos in the United States after he had, the previous year, sponsored the *Danças Características Africanas* for orchestra in Philadelphia (23/24 November 1928) and at New York's Carnegie Hall (27 November 1928).

157 Vera Janacópulos (1892-1955), Brazilian singer and teacher who studied violin and singing. She lived in France (1896-1936). At the height of her career, she retired in 1940 and devoted herself to teaching in Brazil. Arthur

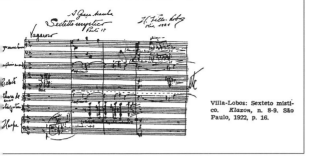

158 To José Pereira da Graça Aranha (1868-1931), was dedicated Villa-Lobos's *Sketches of the Sexteto Místico*. It remained a sketch of only a few bars in 1921 and was not finished until some time during World War II.

Villa-Lobos: Sexteto místico. *Klaxon*, n. 8-9. São
Paulo, 1922, p. 16.

158

Rubinstein commented on her in his autobiography *My Many Years*, London 1980, p. 47. '...a Greco-Brazilian singer, Vera Janacópulos...she had a dreadful husband, however, a bearded Russian who drank vodka in great quantities...'. Villa-Lobos dedicated to her the second movement of the *Suite for Voice and Violin* and the *Historietas*.

Abbaye de Royaumont
a. b. s. de Mme Gollin
Asnières-sur-Oise
95270 Luzarches

3 agosto de 1982

D. Lisa Peppercorn
Schulhaus Strasse 53
8002 Zurich
Suiça

Prezada Lisa

Conheci bem D. Laurinda Santos Lobo, destinatária de uma das cartas de Villa-Lobos. Estive muitas vezes em sua casa, em Santa Teresa. Era uma mulher de forte temperamento, que gostava de receber artistas em sua casa, como se fossem flores para enfeitá-la... Na realidade, aquilo em que ela acreditava, mesmo, era na indiscutível superioridade do dinheiro sobre todas as outras coisas... Arrastava, atrás dela, um marido sem vos no capítulo, dócil como un cãozinho doméstico.

Um abraço amigo do

L. H. Corrêa de Azevedo

159

159 Olivia Guedes Penteado (1872-1934), patron of the arts. Villa-Lobos dedicated to her *Tempos Atrás* from the *Coleção Brasileira* for voice and piano, given its first performance on 18 February 1925.

160

160 Facsimile of an extract from a letter from Luiz Heitor Corrêa de Azevedo (1905-1992) to the author, Paris, 3 August 1982.

First public recognition 75

161

162

Municipal, Aline van Barentzen who took a great liking to Villa-Lobos's music, Vera Janacópulos-Staal, the singer, who was first to introduce some of Villa-Lobos's *Miniaturas* in Paris, and José Pereira da Graça Aranha, the poet, to whom he dedicated the first sketches of his *Sexteto Místico* (see my article 'Ben trovato', *Tempo*, London, June 1991).

Of course Villa-Lobos also acknowledged those who enabled him to give concerts and who invited him to their homes and country estates. Besides the Guinle brothers, in Rio de Janeiro there was Madam Laurinda Santos Lobo. To her he dedicated his *Quatuor* (1921). The Brazilian scholar, Luiz Heitor Corrêa de Azevedo (1905-1992), often a guest in Madam Lobo's home, describes her in a letter to the author, dated 3 August 1982 (reproduced with his permission):

In the following year (1922) while Villa-Lobos was in São Paulo during 'The Week of Modern Art' he became in closer touch with Olivia Guedes Penteado and her family, where he would become a frequent guest.

On 13 June 1921 Villa-Lobos had an opportunity to present, in concert form, the third act of his opera *Izaht* in the Teatro São Pedro de Alcântara and the first performance of his piano piece *A Lenda do Caboclo*, in an orchestral version.

GOFFREDO T. DA SILVA TELLES
TELEPHONE 51-1635
RUA PIAUÍ, 703 - 2.o Andar - Oj. 6
SÃO PAULO

São Paulo, 18 de maio de 1981.

A última homenagem que Villa Lobos recebeu em São Paulo foi em 1957, na "Semana Villa Lobos", organizada por meu filho Goffredo Telles Junior, então titular da secretaria de Cultura da Prefeitura, sendo Prefeito Dr. Adhemar de Barros.

Prezada Senhora:

Essa Semana constou de conferencias sobre o home nageado e diversos concertos de suas obras, no Teatro Munici-pal. Villa Lobos pessoalmente regeu, com brilho excepcional, o concerto de encerramento da Semana. Foi sua última aparição em público na cidade de São Paulo.

Remeti-lhe esta semana as fotografias pedidas em sua carta. São de minha mãe, Olivia Guedes Penteado; de meu marido, Goffredo Teixeira da Silva Telles, e de mim própria, Carolina Penteado da Silva Telles.

Espero que essas pequenas informações lhe possam ser de alguma valia e lamento não poder lhe dar mais detalhes sobre a vida desse grande homem.

Essas fotografias foram feitas nos anos 20, em que Villa Lobos estava sempre conosco em São Paulo e na nossa fazenda. Espero que sejam de seu agrado.

Permaneço a sua disposição para qualquer informa ção que eu lhe possa fornecer e aqui fico anciosa a espera des da biografia de sua autoria, que deve ser muito interessante.

Na nossa fazenda, ele passou várias temporadas na década de 20, participando de nossa vida familiar, a dar ex pansão a sua jovialidade, brincando com meus filhos, como se fosse um verdadeiro menino. Ensinou-lhes a arte da capoeira e a tecnica de construir enormes pipas e balões de São João.

Queira receber, prezada Senhora, minhas muito cordiais saudações.

Alí também ele iniciou, no velho piano Erard, a composição de algumas de suas obras celebres.

Carolina Penteado de Silva Telles
Carolina Penteado da Silva Telles

Em São Paulo, no piano de cauda Steinway da casa de minha mãe, ele ficava, esquecido, a tocar e a compor até altas horas da noite.

163

PROGRAMMA

1.ª Parte
Cantos Brazileiros

I – H. VILLA-LOBOS – (1920) – "Lenda do caboclo" ORCHESTRA. Reg. *Maestro Soriano Robert,*

II – FRANC.co BRAGA – "Catita" – (Poesia de Ovidio de Mello). CANTO – *Alberto Guimarães,*

III – NEPOMUCENO – "Medroso de Amôr" – (Poesia de Juvenal Galeno). CANTO – *Maria Emma,*

IV – VILLA-LOBOS – (1916) – "Viola" – Poesia de Silvio Romero). CANTO – *Nascimento Filho.*

V – ADALBERTO DE CARVALHO – "Recordando" Trecho para orchestra dedicado á Villa-Lobos, regida pelo auctor.

VI – VILLA-LOBOS – (1919) – "Sertão no estio" – (Poesia de Arthur Lemos) – CANTO – *Vicente Celestino*

VII – VILLA-LOBOS – (1912) – "As creanças" – (Poesia de Lauro Salles). CANTO – *Nicia Silva* – acompanhada por um côro de vozes femininas.

Os numeros de canto serão regidos pelo maestro **Soriano Robert.**

2.ª Parte

I – VILLA-LOBOS – PRELUDIO SYMPHONICO da opera *"Izaht"* – Orchestra reg. por *Villa-Lobos.*

II – VILLA-LOBOS – (1914) – Terceiro acto da opera *Izaht.*

3.ª Parte
Quarto acto da IZAHT

IZAHT . . . . . MARIA EMMA—Soprano
ENIHT . . . . . . NICIA SILVA—Soprano.
GÁMERT . . . . . ALBERTO GUIMARÃES—Tenor.
CONDE MAKIAN VICENTE CELESTINO—Tenor.
PERRUCHE . . . NASCIMENTO SILVA—Baritono.
HADAN . . . . . FRANKLIN ROCHA—Baixo cantante.
FOURN . . . . . IGNACIO GUIMARÃES—Baixo.
PAULO . . . . . GUIMARÃES—Baixo.

NO CONJUNCTO:

Senhorinhas: Antonietta Leite de Castro, Heloisa Caribé da Rocha, Idelzuith Galvão, Elzy Alvarenga, Valentina Bandeira Goveia, Aurora Alves Vieira, Iracema Nazareth.

Senhores: Vilmar, Salema, Olivieri, Echevarria, Mario Schubxe, Lima e Silva, Manoel Gomes, Palmieri, Djalma.

REGENCIA DO AUCTOR
— H V M —

164

161 Carolina Penteado da Silva Telles, daughter of Olivia Guedes Penteado, a patron of the arts and socialite in São Paulo. Villa-Lobos dedicated to her *Tristeza* from the *Coleção Brasileira.*

162 Goffredo Teixeira da Silva Telles (*d.* 1980), lawyer and poet, husband of Carolina Penteado da Silva Telles. Villa-Lobos set some of his poems to music, including *Tempos Atrás* from the *Coleção Brasileira.*

163 Facsimile letter from Carolina Penteado da Silva Telles to the author, São Paulo, 18 May 1981, in which she reminiscences about Villa-Lobos as a frequent guest at her mother's country estate (published with her permission).

164 Concert programme.

165 Amazon *caboclo.*

165

166 The theatre was originally called Teatro Real de São João and opened on 12 October 1813. It was demolished by fire on 25 March 1824 and rebuilt. By decree of 15 September 1824 it was called Imperial Teatro de São Pedro de Alcântara and reopened on 16 April 1827. On 3 May 1831 it was renamed Teatro Constitucional Fluminense and kept this name until 2 June 1838 when it was again called Teatro São Pedro. On 9 August 1851 another fire destroyed the theatre; it reopened on 18 August of the following year. A third fire broke out on 26 January 1856; the theatre reopened on 3 January 1857. By decree of 24 August 1923 it was called Teatro João Caetano, named after the producer and impresario João Caetano de Santos (1808-1863). Later it was demolished and in its place was built another theatre with the same name which was opened on 28 June 1930. (The illustration is a design by Jacques Arago (1790-1855) from 1817. In the background, *on the left*, is seen a person in a carriage carried by hand and *on the right* some Negroes carrying water.)

The Week of Modern Art, São Paulo

167 Rua 15 de Novembro, São Paulo, in 1922.

168 The Teatro Municipal in São Paulo where the concerts were held.

The University of Rio de Janeiro was inaugurated on 7 September 1922. It was subsequently renamed the University of Brazil and is now the Federal University of Rio de Janeiro. The occasion offered Villa-Lobos a splendid opportunity to be heard and seen and to be in contact with other artists. This happened in São Paulo between 11 and 18 February when painters, poets and composers presented their works at the Municipal Theatre. The event was called 'The Week of Modern Art'. It came into being through the efforts of Mário Raúl de Morais Andrade, a versatile intellectual who exercised great influence on his contemporaries and the younger generation. He encouraged others to help him organise this extraordinary affair which was held in the year of Brazil's centenary celebration of her independence from Portugal. The spiritual stimulus behind the idea was to break with tradition and the past in cultural terms.

Artists who participated during 'The Week of Modern Art' and performers who took part in Villa-Lobos's three concerts included some of Brazil's most

168

1.ª PARTE

CONFERENCIA DE

GRAÇA ARANHA

A emoção esthetica na arte moderna, illustrada com musica executada por Ernani Braga e poesia por Guilherme de Almeida e Ronald de Carvalho.

MUSICA DE CAMERA

VILLA - LOBOS

1. — SONATA II DE VIOLONCELLO E PIANO — (1916).

A) — Allegro Moderato.
B) — Andante.
C) — Scherzo.
D) — Allegro vivace sostenuto e final.

ALFREDO GOMES E LUCILIA VILLA-LOBOS.

2. — TRIO SEGUNDO — (1916) — VIOLINO E PIANO.

A) — Allegro Moderato.
B) — Andantino calmo (Berceuse-Barcarola).
C) — Scherzo-Spiritoso.
Molto Allegro e final.

Paulina d'Ambrosio, Alfredo Gomes e Fructuoso de Lima Vianna.

2.ª PARTE

CONFERENCIA DE

RONALD DE CARVALHO

A pintura e a esculptura moderna do Brasil.

3. — SOLOS DE PIANO — Ernani Braga.

(1917) A — Valva Mystica — (Da simples collectanea.
(1919) B — Rhodante (Da simples collectanea).
(1921) C — A Fiandeira.

4. — OTTETTO — (Tres dansas africanas).

A — Farrapos — (Dança dos moços) 1914.
B — Kankukus — (Dansa dos velhos) 1915.
C — Kamkikis — (Dansa dos meninos) 1916.

VIOLINOS: — Paulina d'Ambrosio — George Marinuzzi.
ALTO: — Orlando Frederico.
VIOLONCELLOS: — Alfredo Gomes — Basso — Alfredo Carazza
FLAUTA: — Pedro Vieira.
CLARINO: — Antão Soares.
PIANO: — Fructuoso de Lima Vianna.

1.ª PARTE

VILLA-LOBOS

1 — Trio terceiro
Violino, Cello e piano — 1918.
a) Allegro con moto.
b) Moderato.
c) Allegretto spirituoso.
d) Allegro animato.
Paulina D'Ambrosio, Alfredo Gomes e Lucilia Villa-Lobos.

2 — Canto e piano.
Maria Emma e Lucilia Villa-Lobos.
1920
HISTORIETTAS
DE
RONALD DE CARVALHO
a) Lune d'octobre.
b) Voilà la vie.
c) Jenia sans retard, car vita s'escula la vie.

3 — Sonata Segunda
Violino e piano — 1914.
a) Allegro non troppo.
b) Largo.
c) Allegro Rondó — Prestissimo Final.
Paulina D'Ambrosio — Fructuoso Vianna.

2.ª PARTE

VILLA-LOBOS

4 — Solos de Piano
Ernani Braga.
a) Camponeza Cantadeira — Da Suite Floral — 191?
b) Num berço encantado — Da Simples Collectanea 1?
c) Dansa infernal. — 1920.

5 — Quarteto symbolico
(Impressões da vida mundana).
Flauta, Saxophonico, Celeste e Harpa ou Piano
Com vozes femininas em côro occulto — 921.
a) Allegro non troppo.
b) Andantino.
c) Allegro — Final.
Pedro Vieira — Antão Soares — Ernani Braga e Fructuoso de Lima Vianna.

169 170 171 Works by Villa-Lobos were heard in three programmes during the Festival. First programme (169); second programme (171); third programme (170).

172 Paulo Menotti del Picchia (1892-1988), Brazilian poet who studied law. He was a rancher and journalist and Federal Deputy. Together with Mário Raúl de Morais Andrade he was the principal initiator of 'The Week of Modern Art'. (Drawing by Giannino Carta).

172

PROGRAMA DO SEGUNDO FESTIVAL
4.ª FEIRA, 15 DE FEVEREIRO

1.ª PARTE

1. Palestra de Menotti del Picchia

   ilustrada com poesias e trechos de prosa por Oswaldo de Andrade, Luiz Aranha, Sérgio Milliet, Tácito de Almeida, Ribeiro Couto, Mário de Andrade, Plínio Salgado, Agenor Barbosa e dança pela senhorinha Yvonne Daumerie.

2. Solos de piano: Guiomar Novaes:

   a) E. R. Blanchet: *Au jardin du vieux Serail* (Andrinople).
   b) H. Villa-Lobos: *O Ginête do Pierrozinho*.
   c) C. Debussy: *La soirée dans granade*.
   d) · C. Debussy: *Minstrels*.

INTERVALO

Palestra de Mário de Andrade no saguão do Teatro.

2.ª PARTE

1. Renato Almeida
   Perennis Poesia

2. Canto e piano
   Frederico Nascimento Filho e Lucília Villa-Lobos

   1919 — a) Festim Pagão.
   1920 — b) Solidão.
   1917 — c) Cascavel.

3. *Quarteto Terceiro* (cordas 1916)
   a) Allegro giusto.
   b) Scherzo satirico (pipocas e patócas).
   c) Adagio.
   d) Allegro con fuoco e finale.

   Violinos: Paulina d'Ambrósio — George Marinuzzi.
   Alto: Orlando Frederico.
   Violoncelo: Alfredo Gomes.

171

173

174

175

173 Mário Raúl de Morais Andrade (1893-1945), Brazilian poet, critic, musicologist and public servant. Studied at the Conservatório Dramático Musical in São Paulo where he later taught piano and history of music. He played a prominent part in São Paulo's 'Week of Modern Art' (1922). From 1934 to 1938 he was head of the Cultural Division of the Municipality of São Paulo. Responsible for the foundation of a chorus and quartet, he set up lending libraries, children's libraries and a public record library, furthered free admission to concerts, devised plans for a new library, organised expeditions to collect Brazilian folklore and the convocation of the Congresso da Língua Nacional Cantada (1937). He lived in Rio de Janeiro (1938-1940), was a literary critic and taught aesthetics at the University of the Federal District. He was the most influential, versatile, cultured intellectual personality of the modern movement of his time and influenced the younger generation of poets, composers and intellectuals.

176

Author of scholarly books on music and Brazilian folklore, he also wrote poems and essays. *Chôros No. 2* is dedicated to him. (Reproduction of a painting by Lasar Segall (1891-1957).

174 Paulo da Silva Prado (1869-1943), Brazilian historian and sociologist, participated in 'The Week of Modern Art' in São Paulo (1922). The principal analyst of Brazil's social life during the pre-revolutionary period. President of the National Coffee Council (1931-32). *Chôros No. 10* is dedicated to him.

175 Carlos Drumond de Andrade (1902-1987), Brazilian poet and writer and son of a plantation owner. Studied first in his home town, Itabira in the state of Minas Gerais, then Belo Horizonte and later in Nova Friburgo near Rio de Janeiro, finally settling in Rio de Janeiro. Villa-Lobos set some of his texts to music in his *Serestas*.

176 Guilherme de Andrade e Almeida (1890-1969), Brazilian poet, essayist and journalist. Studied law in São Paulo, was editor of various publications, member of the Brazilian Academy of Letters and other institutions. Supported the modern trends of his time and participated in São Paulo's 'Week of Modern Art' in 1922.

177 Manuel Carneiro de Souza Bandeira Filho (1886-1968), Brazilian writer, poet, journalist and university professor. Studied at Rio de Janeiro's Colégio Pedro II (1938-43), and at the University of Brazil (1943-56). Member of the Brazilian Academy of Letters (1940). Villa-Lobos set some of his poems to music and used his text for the second movement of the *Bachianas Brasileiras No. 5 (Dança/Martelo)*.

178 Ronald de Carvalho (1893-1935), Brazilian poet and critic. Studied law (1912), diplomat in various South American countries, Mexico, United States and Paris. Began his literary career in 1910 and participated in 1922 in 'The Week of Modern Art' in São Paulo. He died in a motoring accident. His works include *Pequena História da Literatura Brasileira and Epigramas Irónicos e Sentimentais* which Villa-Lobos set to music.

179 Title page of Ronald de Carvalho's *Epigrammas Irónicos e Sentimentaes* (with the old Brazilian spelling) which Villa-Lobos began to set to music in 1921. Première of the first piece *(Voilà la Vie)* took place on 21 October 1921 in Rio de Janeiro with Maria Freire, a frequent interpreter of Villa-Lobos's music. The work is dedicated to her. Lucília Villa-Lobos was the accompanist.

177

178

RONALD DE CARVALHO

EPIGRAMMAS IRONICOS E SENTIMENTAES

EDITORES
ANNUARIO DO BRASIL — RIO DE JANEIRO
SEARA NOVA — LISBOA
RENASCENÇA PORTUGUESA — PORTO

179

180 José Oswald de Souza Andrade (1890-1954), Brazilian poet, essayist and journalist, who studied law. In 1917 he met Mário Raúl de Morais Andrade; together they championed the modern movement in Brazil, which led to 'The Week of Modern Art'. In 1924 he participated in the literary movement *Pau Brasil* (Brazil Wood). Visited Europe where he met the literary avant-garde. Lectured at the University of São Paulo (1945). *Chôros No. 3* is dedicated to him and his wife, the painter Tarsila do Amaral.

180a Not illustrated Paulina d'Ambrosio (1890-1976), Brazilian violinist and teacher. She studied in Brazil and Belgium. In 1907 settled in Rio de Janeiro. Participated at the opening of Rio de Janeiro's Municipal Theatre (1909) and during 'The Week of Modern Art' (1922) in São Paulo. Teacher at the Escola Nacional de Música (1917-1959) and at the Academia de Música Oscar Lorenzo Fernandez (1897-1948) which she co-founded. Many famous Brazilian composers dedicated works to her.

distinguished figures of the time.

The three concerts during 'The Week of Modern Art' and the attention Villa-Lobos received from the audience and the press, helped him find a well-disposed publisher to get some of his works into print. The music publishing house of Casa Arthur Napoleão, which also maintained a music store on Avenida Rio Branco 122 near the corner of Rua Sete de Setembro, offered Villa-Lobos three contracts, on 2 and 3 June and 16 August 1922, to publish some of his piano pieces, including *Carnaval das Crianças Brasileiras, Simples Coletânea, Suíte Floral op. 97* and the *Suíte Infantil No. 1* and *No. 2,* some other smaller piano pieces, and some music for violin and piano.

180b Not illustrated Renato Costa Almeida (1895-1980), Brazilian teacher, writer and musicologist who participated in 'The Week of Modern Art' at the age of twenty-seven. He was Director of the Colégio Franco-Brasileiro, professor at the Conservatório Brasileiro de Música, Secretary of the National Commission of Folklore, member of numerous institutions and author of several works, including *História da Música Brasiliera*, Rio de Janeiro 1942 (second edition).

181

181 Tarsila do Amaral (1897-1973), Brazilian painter who first studied in Brazil then went in 1920 to Paris. In the same year held her first exhibition. In 1926 organised her first one-woman show. In 1923 returned to Brazil. She illustrated books, and poems by the writer José Oswald de Souza Andrade whom she later married. (The artist is seen here in front of one of her paintings).

182

183

184

182 Anita Malfatti (1896-1964), Brazilian painter who studied in São Paulo, Berlin and the United States. Her exhibitions prepared the way for 'The Week of Modern Art' in which she took part. Her paintings were included in São Paulo's Biennale exhibitions (1951 and 1963). She had shows in Argentina, Chile and Peru.

183 Another early photo of Villa-Lobos, taken only a year after 'The Week of Modern Art', in 1923 and dedicated to Mário Raúl de Morais Andrade 'who always observes him with much faith'.

184 Villa-Lobos is seen here (on the right) with friends (from l. to r.), in 1919: the violinist Pery Machado (1898-1955), the viola player Orlando Frederico, Nascimento Filho and (in the centre) Fructuoso de Lima Viana (1896-1976), the Brazilian composer and pianist who studied in Brazil and Paris and who, from the 1940s, lived in Rio de Janeiro. He also participated in 'The Week of Modern Art' in São Paulo.

185

185   Guiomar Novais Pinto
(1895-1979), eminent
Brazilian pianist of
international repute who
toured Europe, the United
States and Canada. Recipient
of the Legion of Honour.

186   The charming three-
storey building in later years
was squeezed between
skyscrapers and finally had to
give way and was
demolished. The firm itself
also disappeared and was
taken over by Fermata do
Brasil Ltda. in São Paulo.

186

187   A close-up of the
ground floor shows that the
Casa Arthur Napoleão also
sold pianos. The trees seen
here on Avenida Rio Branco
have long since disappeared
to make room for the
enlargement of the
boulevard. The store was
originally founded by Arthur
Napoleão.[7]

7) Arthur Napoleão (1843-
1925), Brazilian pianist,
composer and teacher. His
mother was Portuguese, his
father Italian. He made his
concert debut at the age of six.
First concert in Rio de Janeiro in
1857. Settled in the city in 1886
during heyday of concert life in
Rio de Janeiro with many visiting
virtuosi. With José White,
Napoleão established the
Sociedade de Concêrtos
Clássicos. In 1878 founded the
publishing house Arthur
Napoleão and Miguez which was
established in the Rua do
Ouvidor 89. Later the firm
moved to the Avenida Rio
Branco 122. Upon the
demolition of the building the
firm moved to Rua Marrecas 46
and eventually was taken over by
the firm Fermata do Brasil Ltda.
of São Paulo.

187

First visit to Paris

188

188   The Chamber of Deputies met in the Velha Cadeia (Old Prison) building from 3 May 1826 to 2 September 1914.

189   The Chamber of Deputies was located at the Palácio Monroe (built on the occasion of the Third Pan American Conference in 1906) from 3 September 1914 to 18 June 1922.

190   The Chamber of Deputies moved to the National Library on the Avenida Rio Branco on 19 June 1922 and remained there until 5 May 1926, while awaiting the completion of its new building – the Palácio Tiradentes. This was begun in 1922 and opened on 6 May 1926 to commemorate the centenary of the installation of the legislature in a building which was named after Joaquim José da Silva Xavier (1746-1792), known as Tiradentes, a martyr and leader of a conspiracy to establish a Republic (he was executed on 21 April 1792).

Since 1921 Villa Lobos had tried to have a trip to Europe funded by the Brazilian government. Brazilian composers before him, like Alberto Nepomuceno, Alexandre Levy (1864-1892), Antônio Francisco Braga, Antônio Carlos Gomes (1836-1896) and others, had spent some time in Europe. Villa-Lobos aspired to do likewise. While 'The Week of Modern Art' had accorded him some *succès d'estime*, the ensuing concerts, organised by himself and partly sponsored by well-meaning friends in Rio de Janeiro and São Paulo, were often given before half-empty houses, a discouraging situation because the much sought after government grant for a trip to Europe made only slow progress when discussed in the Chamber of Deputies. When the project was submitted by some deputies on 21 August 1921, the Chamber of Deputies was still in the Palácio Monroe. When the project was finally approved on 22 July 1922 it had moved to the National Library.

189

190

191   Palácio Tiradentes to
which the Chamber of
Deputies moved on 6 May
1926. It remained there until
it transferred to the Palácio
do Congresso, Brasília on 21
April 1960.

192   Facsimile concert
programme of 30 May 1924.

On 30 June 1923, about twelve months after the
Chamber of Deputies had approved a grant for a visit
to Europe, Villa-Lobos embarked on the S.S. *Croix*. In
Europe Villa-Lobos busied himself principally with
organising and giving concerts in Lisbon, Paris and
Brussels, with music by Latin American composers.
Only on 30 May 1924 was it possible to present a

▨▨▨ ŒUVRES DE VILLA LOBOS.

Nous ne connaissions jusqu'ici de Villa Lobos, le jeune compositeur brésilien, que quelques mélodies, différentes petites pièces de piano et aussi ce *Trio*, très stravinskien, que nous avait fait entendre Jean Wiéner. Mais dernièrement un concert consacré entièrement à ses œuvres, admirablement interprétées par Vera Janacopulos, Arthur Rubinstein, la Société Moderne d'Instruments à vent et le Chœur Mixte de Paris sous la direction de l'auteur lui-même, nous fit connaître quelques-unes de ses compositions les plus importantes, entre autres un *Quatuor* pour grande flûte, saxophone, celesta et harpe, avec voix féminines, un poème, *Pensées d'enfant*, pour chant, grande flûte, clarinette et violoncelle et un *Nonetto*, pour flûte hautbois, clarinette, saxophone, basson, celesta, harpe, piano et batterie, avec voix féminines.

La simple énumération de ces instruments nous montre déjà que les préoccupations de sonorités de timbre jouent un rôle primordial dans l'art du compositeur ; c'est en effet une musique de timbres et aussi de rythmes. L'élément mélodique n'est pas très saillant et la plupart des thèmes se réduisent en somme à des formules rythmiques ou bien à des combinaisons et des oppositions de sonorités ; mais la diversité et la complexité métriques de ces œuvres est extraordinaire et le jeu des timbres atteint à une richesse et un raffinement exquis. Le talent, la faculté d'invention de Villa Lobos me paraissent indéniables ; on peut aimer plus ou moins cet art, si particulier, mais quels que soient les goûts et les idées du critique, il ne peut s'empêcher d'être frappé et saisi par cette fougue, cette puissance, cette abondance.

Mais ce qui fait la saveur de la musique de Villa Lobos, son « primitivisme », constitue aussi un certain danger pour le développement de cet art qui découle directement des chants et des danses des Indiens du Brésil ; cette musique « sauvage » exerce, on le sent bien, une sorte de hantise sur le compositeur. Il paraît que le *Trio* d'allure si stravinskienne fut composé à une époque où Villa Lobos ne connaissait encore Stravinsky que de nom. Il y aurait donc un rapprochement intéressant à établir entre la métrique du *Sacre* et celle des indigènes sud-américains. Dans le *Nonetto* il semble avoir pourtant réussi à dominer sa matière en lui imposant une certaine forme européenne ; mais c'est là précisément que réside la difficulté : si Villa Lobos se contente de verser sa pâte exotique dans le moule des formes européennes, son art s'étiolera, dans un « scholisme » analogue à celui de ces compositeurs roumains dont j'ai eu l'occasion de parler. La culture européenne lui est indispensable, mais elle doit lui servir de discipline : il ne s'agit pas de copier les modèles européens, mais d'adopter les méthodes européennes et d'acquérir ainsi une maîtrise, une liberté qui permettent de créer des formes nouvelles, adéquates à la matière traitée. La tâche est difficile ! Mais ses dons exceptionnels permettront sans aucun doute à Villa Lobos de réussir.

B. DE SCHLŒZER.

193

193　*La Revue Musicale,*
Paris, 5ième année, No. 9,
July 1924.

concert devoted exclusively to his own works. This attracted B. de Schloezer to review it at length in *La Revue Musicale,* Paris.

In Paris, Villa-Lobos was also anxious to find a publisher for his works. It may well be assumed that it was the singer Vera Janacópulos and her husband, A. Staal, who directly or through some friends were able to interest the music publishing house of Éditions Max Eschig in Villa-Lobos, since the first of his works which the music firm published – *Suite for voice and violin* – was precisely the music which Janacópulos had sung in Paris (23 October 1923) during the composer's stay (albeit without the third movement). It was written shortly before the concert and, probably to please his interpreter and friends, Villa-Lobos dedicated the second movement to the singer and the first movement to her husband.

Max Eschig who had given the publishing house its name, signed the first contract with Villa-Lobos on 8 October 1924. This was the beginning of a business

194 Éditions Max Eschig, located until the end of 1990 at 48 Rue de Rome, Paris, not far from the Gare St Lazare.

195 Max Eschig (1872-1927), French music publisher of Czech origin, founded the music publishing company Éditions Max Eschig which he directed from 1905 to September 1927.

196 Eugène Cools (1877-1936), Director of Éditions Max Eschig, Paris from September 1927 to August 1936.

194

195

196

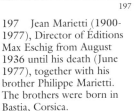

197

198

197 Jean Marietti (1900-1977), Director of Éditions Max Eschig from August 1936 until his death (June 1977), together with his brother Philippe Marietti. The brothers were born in Bastia, Corsica.

198 Philippe Marietti (1915-1993), Director of Éditions Max Eschig from 1936 to 1985, together with his brother Jean.

relationship and friendship which deepened as the years went on and lasted throughout the lifetime of Max Eschig and his successors: Eugène Cools, Jean and Philippe Marietti. After World War II other firms, particularly in Italy and the United States, published some of Villa-Lobos's music. But Éditions Max Eschig and its American representative, Associated Music Publishers, remained Villa-Lobos's principal publisher.

Rio de Janeiro to which Villa-Lobos returned some time in 1924 and where he was to perform many of his latest works during the next two-and-a-half years, looked as beautiful as ever. Grand buildings had been constructed in the (then) capital, and generous squares with attractive plants and scented flowers in public gardens, landscaped in the French manner, graced the city. Avenida Rio Branco featured along its beautiful boulevard lined with trees a completed row of handsome buildings. Guanabara Palace, residence of the President of the Republic in Rua Pinheiro Machado, was a sumptuous building not far from the Rua Paysandu, lined with palm trees, and one of the city's loveliest streets. Botafogo Bay at Avenida Beira Mar still included at that time the Mourisco Pavilion, long since demolished to make way for skyscrapers. And the Canal de Mangue with its majestic palm-trees

199 (*Top left*) the Canal de Mangue, (*top right*) Ilha Fiscal. (*Bottom left*) is the Praça da Glória with the Outeiro da Glória Church in the background, *right*. In the foreground on the wide thoroughfare is a tramcar with open windows and the generously landscaped garden leading to the Bay. (*Bottom right*) Botafogo Bay with the Mourisco Pavilion in the foreground, and the open vista before skyscrapers obscured the view.

199

and wide footpaths and thoroughfares embellished that part of the city until, some time after World War II, it also disappeared to accommodate the increasing traffic. Never was Rio de Janeiro more beautiful than in the 1920s and 1930s.

São Paulo had a different look altogether. It lacked the overwhelming natural beauty of Rio de Janeiro. It was the business city, the centre where South America's largest industrial complex was destined to develop.

Some concerts which Villa-Lobos gave in São Paulo in 1925 were performed not at the Teatro Municipal – as was the case during 'The Week of Modern Art' in 1922 – but at the Teatro Santana.

The years following his return to Brazil until his second departure for Europe in early 1927 were the most fruitful and most significant in Villa-Lobos's development as a composer. For the first time in his life, he created his own style. This was the result of his experience in Paris. Europe had definitely not influenced him in the sense of persuading him to adapt something European or French. Villa-Lobos had been much too busy organising concerts of Latin American music, including some of his own, and looking for a publisher. He could not occupy his mind with anything else. He was not even interested in meeting Stravinsky

200 (*Top left*) the Palácio Monroe, (*top right*) the City Hall. Rio de Janeiro's streets, practically all lined with trees at that time, were wide and spacious and gave the city an aspect of generosity. (*Bottom left*) is the Guanabara Palace, the long-time residence of Brazil's President. (*Bottom right*) a further view of Avenida Rio Branco with its completed row of buildings.

200

201 View of São Paulo's
Rua Direito in the centre of
the city.

202 Aerial view of São
Paulo in the middle of the
1920s.

203 The Theatre was
originally called Teatro
Provisório and was located in
the Travessa Boa Vista. The
foundation stone was laid in
March 1873. It opened on
23 August 1873. Afterwards
it was called in succession
Minerva and Apolo. At the
beginning of 1899 it was
demolished. At the same
location the industrialist
Antônio Alvares Leite
Penteado (later: Count
Romano) began – in April
1899 – the construction of
the Teatro Santana, which
opened on 18 May 1900. It
was in use until 1911 and
was demolished in 1912. The
second theatre under this
name was opened on 25
April 1921 in the Rua 24 de
Maio by Leite Penteado's
successor. It was demolished
in 1959.

201

202

203

204

204　The Brazilian bird Uirapurú lives in the Amazon region and is known to sing beautifully. According to legend he brings luck to those who own him, dried or stuffed. Further legends can be found in *Mythes, Contes et Légendes des Indiens; Folklore Brésilien* by Gustavo Dodt Barroso, Paris, 1930.[8]

8) Gustavo Dodt Barroso (1888-1959), Brazilian writer and journalist, participated in international congresses, was a member of many associations, including the Brazilian Academy of Letters and the Instituto Histórico e Geográfico Brasileiro. Was the first Director of the Museu Histórico Nacional. Wrote numerous volumes on many subjects.

(1882-1971) or Diaghilev or any of the other prominent musical figures who lived in Paris. Nor was he keen to be invited to the literary salon of Gertrude Stein (1874-1946) to meet the 'lost generation', the self-styled exiled American writers and poets, nor the painters in Paris. He was not interested in absorbing any fresh ideas. The Louvre and the other cultural treasures in Paris held no attraction for him. Most likely he never visited any of them, nor did he attend theatrical performances or be touched or fascinated by the cultural atmosphere which Paris, Brussels, Liège and Lisbon offered in such rich variety. He was only mindful to discover what would 'sell' and how he could make a name for himself. The answer, he discovered, was to be original and distinctive in order to attract attention.

Returning to Brazil, he decided to become just that: distinctive and very original. For Villa-Lobos this meant offering something specifically Brazilian. And once he had set his mind to something, there was nothing that could deter him from his goal. He pursued his objective with all the ambition he could muster. It is true that he had written some time before a few works with Brazilian titles, such as *Amazonas* and *Uirapurú* – which, though begun in 1917, was only orchestrated in 1934 – but the music was impressionistic.

Villa-Lobos's studies

It is a widely held but completely erroneous opinion that Villa-Lobos – in order to give his music a Brazilian flavour – roamed through virgin forests in the Amazon region, mingled with natives, collected folk material in the interior of Brazil, and used it all in his music. He did not collect one single melody and therefore no such tunes are used in his compositions.

So, what did he do to give his music a specifically Brazilian characteristic? His approach was intellectual. He went about it like any researcher in any field. He bought and read books, consulted chronicles, annals, records and documents in libraries and archives, examined lithographs, drawings and photographs, visited museums to study indigenous instruments and listened to recordings of native tunes collected by others. He studied not music, but the ancient history and culture of his country, Brazil's past and present customs and habits, the sound of Indian languages, the legends of the Indians. The rich literature and iconography, old and new, all easily available in Brazil, offered unlimited opportunities to an eager mind like that of Villa-Lobos. At some time in life, the date is not known, he admitted to having 'sought to document himself as much as he could'. It was Villa-Lobos's careful investigation of the immense archive of information available from Pre-Columbian times until his own day that was largely responsible for the Brazilian spirit which his music transmits. The relish which his music often communicates, the sensuousness of certain melodic lines or the hilarious sound combinations and tone colours in some smaller works, may well be the result of his diligent scrutiny of the origins and traditions of his country.

Villa-Lobos thus set out to learn for himself the things he ought to know, to seek in the great works of the past the advice he needed. This in turn posed the problem of how to find a way to assimilate these elements naturally and without effort, of how to approach the world around him with ingenuity and inventiveness. His persistence helped him to achieve the appropriate means of expression.

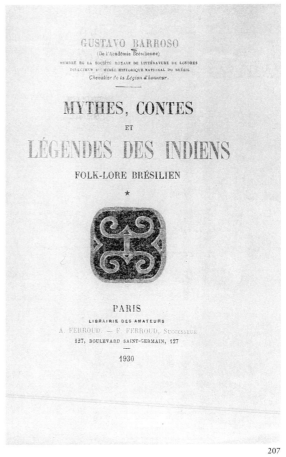

205   Facsimile of Villa-Lobos's statement concerning his researches which enabled him to write compositions with a Brazilian flavour.

206   João Barbosa Rodrigues (1842-1909), Brazilian botanist, anthropologist, archaeologist and ethnologist who was one of the great authorities in his field. Director of the Botanical Garden in Rio de Janeiro (1889-1909). He wrote about sixty works.

207   Title page of Gustavo Dodt Barroso's book on Brazilian legends.

§ IV. — OUIRAPOUROU

Le génie protecteur des oiseaux vit incarné sous la forme d'un petit oiseau de l'Amazonie, dont le chant est très agréable. Lorsqu'il chante tous les autres oiseaux se taisent pour l'entendre.

Ceux qui réussissent à se procurer le corps empaillé ou quelques plumes même de Ouirapourou auront du bonheur toute leur vie. C'est le meilleur des talismans[1].

On raconte aussi que l'Ouirapourou, le petit oiseau, est un chef, un cacique exilé et que les autres oiseaux le respectent et l'aiment car ils sont leurs sujets. Tous ont été transformés en bêtes par des mauvais génies[2].

208

§ V. — SACI-PERERÉ

Saci-Pereré, Saci-Cereré ou Mati-Taperé[3], génie des champs et des bois, espiègle et moqueur comme les korrigans et les farfadets, c'est le lutin du Brésil. Il se montre généralement sous la forme d'un petit Indien boiteux ou même avec une seule jambe[4], coiffé d'un bonnet rouge.

Dans des légendes plus primitives, il apparaissait parfois sous la forme d'un oiseau, le Coculus-Cornutus que les Indiens croient être un oiseau-fée.

1. D'après M. Couto de Magalhaens.
2. D'après M. Raymundo Moraes.
3. Saci ou Çaci, mère des âmes, du Toupi-Sa ou Çá, âme, et Ci, mère. Taperé (corrompu en Pereré ou Cereré), dans la même langue, de Taperebé : Tape, sur, l'e, chemin, et Ce, particule dont le C se change en R par euphonie. Ainsi Saci-Taperé, qui est le vrai nom, signifie, d'après le savant brésilien, M. Baptista Caetano, La mère des âmes qui apparaît sur le chemin.
4. Le Saci rappelle les sciapodes de Pline, dont on trouve l'image dans la Chronique de Nuremberg, manuscrit de la Bibliothèque Nationale de Paris. Quelquefois le troll scandinave n'a, lui aussi, qu'une seule jambe (Lescure, Histoire des Fées, et Ed. Pilon, Contes anciens du Nord).

209

XI. L'ORIGINE DU FLEUVE DES AMAZONES

(Conte des Indiens du fleuve Solimoëns.)

Il y a longtemps, la lune était fiancée au soleil, mais si ce mariage avait lieu le monde finirait, car l'ardent amour du soleil le brûlerait et les larmes de la lune l'inonderaient. Alors ils se résignèrent à ne pas se marier.

Ils se séparèrent, mais la lune pleura jour et nuit. Ses larmes coulèrent sur la terre jusqu'à la mer. Ainsi naquit la Grande Rivière[2].

1. D'après M. Barbosa Rodrigues.
2. Idem.

210

§ XIII. — JOUROUPARÍ[1]

Les Indiens Toupis n'avaient pas une vraie conception d'un esprit du mal. Leur diable n'était que le créateur des cauchemars. La nuit il s'approchait des hamacs où dormaient les hommes et surtout les enfants et il leur serrait la gorge pour gêner leur sommeil[1]

Il y avait une idole de Jouroupari en bois sculpté qu'on cachait dans le fleuve. Certains jours on allait la chercher et on la déposait sur le sable de la rive suivant des rites consacrés. C'était un jour de fête et de réjouissance. Mais seuls les hommes pouvaient voir et toucher l'idole. Cette faveur était interdite aux femmes. Si, poussée par la curiosité, une épouse ou une jeune fille voyait ou touchait le Jouroupari, elle était condamnée à mort.

On la paraît comme pour une grande cérémonie et on la conduisait au son d'une musique primitive jusqu'au centre d'un cercle de guerriers qui dansaient. Alors le chef de la tribu s'avançait, hiératique et solennel, et la tuait d'un coup de sa Noviba[3].

1. Du Toupi-Jouroupoarí qui signifie, selon le jésuite Montoya : main sur la bouche; et selon M. Baptista Caetano : être qui vient à notre hamac.
2. D'après M. Couto de Magalhaens.
3. La Noviba est une sorte de marteau qui sert aux sacrifices rituels et qui rappelle le merlin des abattoirs français.

211

§ VIII. — COURROUPÍRA[2]

Génie des bois, qui protège les arbres. Il ressemble à un petit Indien aux pieds tournés en arrière comme les enotocètes de Mégasthènes, mais son corps est bâti tout d'une pièce sans la moindre ouverture.

Quand on entend du bruit dans les bois, c'est le Courroupíra qui frappe le tronc des arbres pour voir s'ils sont en bon état, où s'ils sont pourris ou rongés par les vers.

Il châtie ceux qui font du mal aux arbres en les faisant s'égarer dans la forêt[1].

1. D'après M. Couto de Magalhaens.

212

208   Legend of *Uirapurú*.

209   Legend of *Saci-Pereré*.

210   Legend of the 'Origin of the Amazon'.

211   Legend of *Jurupari*.

212   Legend of *Currupira*.

214

213

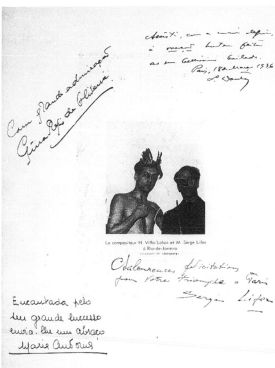

215

213   Parecis Indian.

214   Engraving of
Currupira from Jean de
Léry's *Histoire d'un voyage...'*
op. cit. La Rochelle, 1578.

215   Serge Lifar[9]
with Villa-Lobos in Rio de
Janeiro after the performance
of *Jurupari*.

Villa-Lobos also familiarised himself with Brazilian legends. In 1930 some were also published in French, in Paris, by Gustavo Dodt Barroso.[8] They include those about Uirapurú, Saci-Pererê and 'The Origin of the Amazon River'. The latter Villa-Lobos used as a basis for his composition *Erosão* (composed in 1950) to fulfil a commission given him by the Louisville Orchestra to which the work is dedicated. Other such works were *Jurupary*, a title which he later applied to *Chôros No. 10* written in 1926 when Serge Lifar[9] choreographed and danced this work in Paris (17 March 1936), and *Currupira* which, allegedly, was written and then went missing.

Villa-Lobos also consulted the first book ever published about Brazil. It is by the German Hans Staden and is rich in documentary source material.

Villa-Lobos also studied Jean de Léry's work. Jean de Léry (1534-1613), French Calvinist pastor, traveller and writer, was born in Burgundy where he earned his living as a shoemaker. As a student in Geneva (1550)

9) Serge Lifar (1905-1986), French dancer and choreographer of Russian origin who came to Paris in 1923 and joined Diaghilev's Ballets Russes. Villa-Lobos dedicated *Uirapurú* to him and *O Papageio do Moleque*. He also danced *Jurupary*, based on Villa-Lobos's *Chôros No. 10* in Paris and Rio de Janeiro.

216 Paris concert programme for *Jurupary*, 17 March 1936.

217 Portrait of Hans Staden (*c.* 1525-*c.* 1576), German traveller and chronicler. Little is known about his life. He made two trips to Brazil (*c.* 1548 and 1500-1555). His book *Zwei Reisen nach Brasilien* (1548-1555), translated into several languages, is an important source for the study of the early history of Brazil.

218 Title page of first edition published in Marburg 1557, which also includes an illustration of a native resting in a hammock, a motif used by Villa-Lobos in his *Idílio na Rêde* from the *Suíte Floral* (see illustration 133). It also shows how the Indian is savouring the delicacy of a human leg while other legs roast over a fire. The Indians were cannibals and Hans Staden was almost a victim himself.

II.

L'ŒUVRE DE POUCHKINE,
par M. PAUL VALÉRY, *de l'Académie Française.*

BORIS GODOUNOV, *scène du couronnement* MOUSSORGSKY
Orchestre et chœur.

JURUPARY

(CRÉATION)

*Ballet en un acte de M. Serge Lifar et de M. de Carvalho,
inspiré de la légende indienne du Brésil, chorégraphie
de M.* SERGE LIFAR, *musique de M.* VILLA-LOBOS.

Jurupary (l'esprit) .... X...

Yacina .... MME SURIA MAGITO

Yauar .... M. SERGE LIFAR

Pagé .... M. LEBERCHER

et le corps de Ballet de l'Opéra

216

217

Hiſtoria vnd beſchreibung eyner Landt=
ſchafft der Wilden/Nacketen/Grimmigen Menſchfreſſer
Leuthen/in der Newenwelt America gelegen/vor vnd nach
Chriſti geburt im Land zů Heſſen vnbckant/biß vff diſe ÿ.
nechſt vergangene jar/Da ſie Hans Staden von Homs
berg auß Heſſen durch ſein eygne erfarung erkant/
vnd yetzo durch den truck an tag gibt.
Dedicirt dem Durchleuchtigen Hochgebornen herrn/
H.philipſen Landtgraff zů Heſſen/Graff zů Catzen-
elnbogen/Dietz/Ziegenhain vnd Nidda/ſeinem G.H.
Mit eyner vorrede D.Joh. Dryandri/genant Eychmann/
Ordinary Profeſſoris Medici zů Marpurgk.
Inhalt des Büchlins volget nach den Vorreden.

Getruckt zů Marpurg/im iar M. D. LVII.

218

10) Nicolas Durand de Villega(i)gnon (1510-1775), a French coloniser who was the leader of an attempted French settlement in the Bay of Guanabara with both Catholic and Protestant support. He left Le Havre with settlers and convicts on 12 July 1555 for Brazil where Brazil wood traders had been active for three or four decades.

he joined a group of Huguenots. On 19 November 1556 he left for Brazil to join Admiral Nicolas Durand de Villega(i)gnon (1510-1575)[10] who tried to establish a Huguenot colony in Brazil. Léry arrived in Brazil on 10 March 1557, stayed ten months and left again on 4 January 1558, arriving in France on 20 May 1558. Léry described his observations of and experiences in Brazil in his now famous book *Histoire d'un voyage faict en la terre du Brésil autrement dite Amérique* which appeared after 1578 in several editions and translations in the sixteenth and seventeenth centuries. The third edition, published in 1585 by Antoine Chuppin in Geneva, contains for the first time five melodies of the *Tupinambá* Indians. These melodies are, however, missing in the first two editions and in modern editions the tunes are not always identical. Villa-Lobos's *Canidé-Ioune-Sabath* (Song of the Yellow Bird) – 'canidé-ioune' means yellow bird; 'sabath' means elegiac song – the first of three songs from the

**Wahrhaftiger kurzer Bericht
über Sitten und Gebräuche der Tupinambás,**

deren Gefangener ich gewesen bin. Sie wohnen in Amerika.
Ihr Land liegt 24 Grad südlich der Äquinoktiallinie
und grenzt an das Mündungsgebiet eines Flusses,
der Rio de Janeiro heißt.

33. Tupinambás mit Keule und Federschmuck

219

219 Two *Tupinambá* Indians with club (*left*) and feather gear. Many travellers arriving in Brazil in the early period believed that what in reality was Guanabara Bay was the mouth of a river called Rio de Janeiro, because the locality had this name (Hans Staden, op. cit.).

220 Seen here is the vessel on which early explorers like Hans Staden and others travelled across the Atlantic to Brazil (Hans Staden, op. cit.).

220

HISTOIRE
D'VN VOYAGE
FAIT EN LA TERRE
DV BRESIL, DITE
Amerique.

CONTENANT LA NAVIGATION, & choses remarquables, veuës sur mer par l'Autheur...

AVEC LES FIGVRES, REVEVE, CORrigee & bien augmentee par l'Autheur.

QVATRIEME EDITION.

DEDIEE
A MADAME LA PRINCESSE D'ORANGE.

PSEAVME CVIII.
Seigneur, ie te celebrerai entre les peuples, & te diray Pseaumes entre les nations.

POVR les Heritiers d'Eustache Vignon.
1600.

221

222

221 Title page of the 1600 edition of Jean de Léry's book *Histoire d'un voyage ...* (op. cit.)

222 Reproduction of the *Canidé-Ioune-Sabath* melody from Jean de Léry's 1600 edition of his book (op. cit.)

223 There is an excellent erudite study by Luiz Heitor Corrêa de Azevedo [11] about the five melodies found in the various editions of Jean de Léry's book and the variations and amendments. Reproduced here are extracts from this study and one of five versions of *Canidé-Ioune-Sabath* as they appear in the French, Latin and Brazilian editions.

11) Luiz Heitor Corrêa de Azevedo, 'Tupinambá Melodies in Jean de Léry's *Histoire d'un Voyage faict en la Terre du Brésil*', *Papers of the American Musicological Society*, Annual Meeting, 1941, Minneapolis, Minnesota; edited by Gustave Reese, printed by the Society, Richmond, Virginia, 1946, pp. 85-96.

The five melodies in this book were collected among the Tupynambá Indians near Rio de Janeiro. The first, in Chapter 11, is the *Song of the Yellow Bird*, *Canidé Ioune*; the second, in Chapter 11, refers to a large fish, *Camourou-pouy-ouassou*; the others, in Chapter 16, were sung by the Indians in a very important ceremony, which Léry witnessed.

As I have mentioned before, these melodies differ among the several editions. In some cases, these differences are considerable; but in others they entail only the wrong placing of the clef on the staff. It must be mentioned that their presentation in all these old editions is very poor, so that the clef, the accidentals, or even the notes are sometimes wrongly placed. In these otherwise carefully made and beautifully illustrated editions, the music was neglected and some examples were included merely as additional illustrations. After the third edition, they were never seriously revised, and appear exactly as they were arranged by an artisan poorly qualified for this work.

The first melody, *Song of the Yellow Bird*, appeared in three different versions in the five old editions that are considered in this study: 1) The version of the French editions of 1585 and 1600, with the difference that in the version of 1600 the two notes before the last are quarter-notes; 2) that of the French edition of 1611; 3) those of the Latin versions of 1586 and 1594. In groups 1 and 2 it is very probable that the C clef should be on the first line. This would eliminate the differences among the three groups. The current version, in Brazil, however, is still different, because of the addition of the F as the next to the last note, which gives it a rhythmic symmetry that is not found in the other versions.

MELODY 1

French edition, 1585
French edition, 1600
French edition, 1611
Latin edition, 1586
Latin edition, 1594
Brazilian version

223

224 *Tupinambá* ceremonial dance from Jean de Léry's book. The illustration by Theodor de Bry (1528-1598) appeared in *Americae Tertia Pars,* Frankfurt/Main 1592 and was, together with the other excellent engravings, later often reproduced. It is also included in the works by Hans Staden.

225 The dance ceremony by the *Camacans* is from an engraving by A. Seyffer and J.P. Bittheuser in Maximilian Prince of Wied-Neuwied (1782-1867)*Reise nach Brasilien in den Jahren 1815-1817,* Frankfurt/Main 1820.

cycle *Três Poemas Indígenas* (Three Native Poems), composed in 1926, is based on an Indian song which was collected by Léry. Villa-Lobos again studied Léry's book in his preparation for the score of his composition *Descobrimento do Brasil* (Discovery of Brazil), composed between 1936 and 1942.

Villa-Lobos particularly valued the book *Reise in Brasilien 1817-1820* by Johann Baptist von Spix and Carl Friedrich Philipp von Martius because it contained a supplement of Brazilian folk songs and Indian melodies.

Jean Baptiste Debret also offered pictorial insights to Villa-Lobos which enabled him to study Brazil's history and culture.

226 Johann Baptist von Spix (1781-1826), German zoologist and research traveller. Together with Carl Friedrich Philipp von Martius, he went to Rio de Janeiro, Goiás and the north as far as the São Francisco river. Together they published a book *Reise in Brasilien 1817-1820*. Spix died while the book was still being set into type.

226

227

227 Carl Friedrich Philipp von Martius (1794-1868), son of a court pharmacist whose family came from Umbria and emigrated via Hungary to Germany. Studied medicine at the age of sixteen. King Maximilian Joseph I (1756-1825) planned to send a scientific expedition to South America. He was able to realise this idea when Archduchess Leopoldina of Austria married Brazil's Crown Prince, later the Emperor Dom Pedro I. The King made it possible for two Bavarian naturalists to join the ships which escorted the Archduchess and her entourage to Brazil. The zoologist Johann Baptist von Spix and the botanist Martius were selected for the purpose. On 7 April 1817 two frigates *Austria* and *Augusta* left Trieste. On the first vessel were the two scientists who arrived in Rio de Janeiro on 15 July. They stayed in Brazil for two years and eleven months (until 18 June 1820) and described the fauna and flora of Brazil based on their expeditions in a book, *Reise in Brasilien 1817-1820*.

228 Title page of *Reise in Brasilien 1817-1820*, Munich 1823-1831.

R e i s e

in

B r a s i l i e n

auf Befehl Sr. Majestät

MAXIMILIAN JOSEPH I.

Königs von Baiern

in den Jahren 1817 bis 1820 gemacht und beschrieben

von

Dr. Joh. Bapt. von SPIX,

Ritter des k. baier. Civil-Verdienstordens, ord. wirkl. Mitgliede d. k. b. Akademie d. IV.,
Conservator der zool. zoot. Sammlungen, der Car. Leop. Akad. d. Naturforsch., der Edinb.,
Mosk., Marb., Frankf., Niederrhein. naturf. Gesellschaft Mitgliede,

und

Dr. Carl Friedr. Phil. von MARTIUS,

Ritter des k. baier. Civil-Verdienstordens, ord. wirkl. Mitgliede d. k. b. Akademie d. IV.,
Mitvorstand u. zweit. Conservator d. k. bot. Gartens, d. Car. Leop. Akad. d. Naturforsch. der
Frankf., Nürnb., Niederrhein., Erl., Regensb. naturf., d. London. Hort. Ges. Mitgliede.

Erster Theil.

München, 1823.
Gedruckt bei M. Lindauer.

228

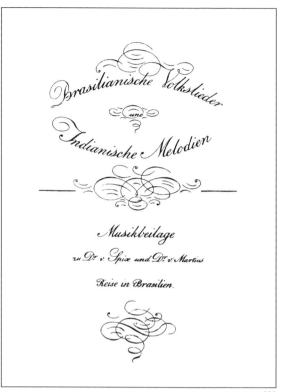

229

229　Title page of
*Brasilianische Volkslieder und
Indianische Melodien
Musikbeilage zu Reise in
Brasilien 1817-1820.*

230　The *Baducca*
(*Batuque*) dance in São Paulo
from *Bilder aus dem
Menschenleben,* engraving by
Nachtmann in the Atlas to
Reise in Brasilien 1817-1820.

230

231　Reproduction of the
fourteen melodies from the
musical supplement to *Reise
in Brasilien 1817-1820.*

231

232

233

234

235

232   Indians from different tribes with interesting headgear, ornaments and body paintings (J.B. von Spix and C.F.P. von Martius, op. cit.).

233   This example of female types from sixteen different African nations, chosen by Jean Baptiste Debret, gives some idea of the ethnic complexity of the cross-breeds and people of mixed race in Rio de Janeiro (Jean Baptiste Debret, op. cit.).

236

234   Jean Baptiste Debret (1768-1848), French painter who joined the team of French artists and craftsmen who travelled to Brazil in 1816 under Joachim Lebreton (1760-1819) and remained there until 1831. He played a key role in organising the Academy of Fine Arts in Rio de Janeiro, set up in 1826. Debret trained a generation of Brazilian painters and in 1829 organised the first exhibition of fine arts in Brazil. He was one of the most perceptive observers of Brazilian colonial life, recording scenes from daily life, landscapes, customs and habits ranging from the activities of noblemen to those of the common people.

His illustrations have the verisimilitude of actual photographs because of their great attention to detail. He left three volumes of *Voyage pittoresque et historique au Brésil, ou Séjour d'un artiste français au Brésil depuis 1816 jusqu'en 1831 inclusivement* (Paris 1834-1839) which depict Brazil and its people.

235   The *Sertanejos* – the 'hillbillies' who lived in the wilderness (the *Sertão*) – in the state of Piaui (J.B. von Spix and C.P.F. von Martius, op. cit.).

236   *Danse des sauvages de la Mission de St José,* engraving by Ch. Matte, in Jean Baptiste Debret, op. cit.

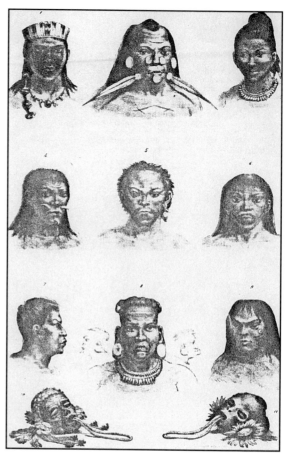

237

238a

237   Heads of Indians (Jean Baptiste Debret, op. cit.).

238a,b   Travelling barber (*below left*) and Barber's shop (*right*) from Jean Baptiste Debret, op. cit.

239a,b   Basket salesman (*top*) and Negroes selling poultry, from Jean Baptiste Debret, op. cit.

238b

239a

239b

240 Title page from
Malerische Reise in Brasilien:
here his name is given as
Moritz Rugendas whereas
nearly all the reference books
add his first name 'Johann'.

241 *Batuque* dance.

242

242 Two Negroes on a plantation.

Villa-Lobos received excitement and stimulus from the engravings of Johann Moritz Rugendas (1802-1858), the German painter who left an important documentary survey of Brazil's landscapes, customs and population. In 1821 he joined the expedition of Baron Georg Heinrich Landsdorff to Brazil. He returned to Europe after several years away (1821-

243 Two Negro women in Rio de Janeiro.

1825) with one hundred illustrations which eventually appeared as lithographs in his *Malerische Reise in Brasilien* (Paris 1835), published by Engelmann with German and French texts. Later Rugendas travelled through South America.

In addition to the illustrations of people of mixed race which Villa-Lobos was able to study in Debret's account, Rugendas offered illustrations of negroes and their way of life.

Rugendas also provided Villa-Lobos with

244

244   Indians on the
Solimões river, in the Amazon
regions, about 1865.

245   *Lundu* dance.

comparisons between Indians and negroes.

There were other complementary sources which enabled Villa-Lobos to study Brazil's racial mixture.

Of particular interest to Villa-Lobos were the details of the two Brazilian dances: *batuque* and *lundu* in Rugendas's work.

Rugendas was a rich source of historical material, and his lithographs gave Villa-Lobos an understanding of the life, work and customs of Brazil in times past.

Rugendas and other sources also described pictorially the home life of both Indians and negroes during the colonial period.

One of Villa-Lobos's principal sources of inspiration was Rio de Janeiro's National Museum at Quinta da Boa Vista.

The National Museum offered Villa-Lobos ample opportunities to study various native instruments. But he also consulted other sources such as the details recorded in the beautifully illustrated volumes mentioned above. He later employed some of these instruments in his own compositions, and tried to capture the sounds of others by using conventional

245

246

247

248

249

246 Preparation and
processing of sugar cane.

247 Coffee harvesting in
the state of Rio de Janeiro.

248 A beautiful landscape
in the state of Minas Gerais.

249 Negro housing.

250

251

252

253

254

250   Indian homes at Monte Alegre.

251   Founded on 6 June 1808 by Prince Dom João, the National Museum, a great research centre, has been located since 1892 at the Quinta da Boa Vista in Rio de Janeiro. Villa-Lobos often frequented it, together with his wife, Lucília. There he heard the *Nozani-ná* melody (registered No. 14,597), which he used in his *Chôros No. 3*, composed in 1925, and as the second piece in his song cycle *Chansons Typiques Brésiliennes*. He also heard at the Museum the indigenous tune *Teiru* (registered No.

14,598). This melody Villa-Lobos incorporated as the second item in his three-piece-song-cycle *Três Poemas Indígenas* (Three Native Poems) and which was expanded and enlarged in a similar fashion as *Canidé-Ioune-Sabath*, the first song in the cycle. In 1946 the National Museum was incorporated into the University of Brazil. One of its most eminent Directors was Edgard Roquette-Pinto under whose administration (1926-1935) many innovations took place.

252   Edgard Roquette-Pinto (1884-1954), Brazilian anthropologist, studied

medicine in Rio de Janeiro. Participated in the 1907/08 expedition by Cândido Mariano da Silva Rondon in the northeast of Mato Grosso state. In 1913 he travelled to Goiás and the Amazon through scarcely populated Indian regions where he collected material about *Parecís* Indians and made recordings and photographs described in the ethnological work *Rondonia*. He founded (1937) and directed – until 1947 – the National Institute of Educational Cinema where he was responsible for, in 1937, the historical parts of the film *Descobrimento do Brasil* (Discovery of Brazil)

FONOGRAMA 14.597
(índios parecis)

FONOGRAMA 14.598
(índios parecís)

TEIRU'
(índios parecís)

255

256

257

produced by the Brazilian Cacao Institute of Bahia with music by Villa-Lobos. He was a member of the Brazilian Academy of Letters and the Brazilian Institute of History and Geography and was Director (1926-1935) of Rio de Janeiro's National Museum.

253   Edgard Roquette-Pinto and Villa-Lobos in later years.

254   General Cândido Mariano da Silva Rondon (1865-1958), Brazilian army officer and the explorer. Built telegraph lines in Mato Grosso, Goiás and the Amazon regions and, at the same time, undertook important research work. He led scientific expeditions (the Rondon Commission) which made great contributions to the development of natural history in Brazil. Director of the Indian Protection Service (1910).

255   The *Nozani-ná* melody from Roquette-Pinto's work, op. cit.

256   The *Teiru* melody and other tunes which Villa-Lobos listened to on recordings in the National Museum and which are reproduced in the book by Roquette-Pinto (op. cit.).

257   Title page of Edgard Roquette-Pinto's *Rondonia*, 5th edition, São Paulo.

Villa-Lobos's studies   119

Some of the principal instruments Villa-Lobos must have come across in the National Museum or in other places:

258

1. *Puíta* or *Cuíca* (friction drum).

2. *Atabaques* (drums) used in *candomblé*, in Bahia.

3. *Zabumba* (drum) used in Paraíba.

4. *Atabaque* used in the locality where *Macumba* takes place.

5. *Xere de Ogum* (*chocalho*) used in *Xangô* in Recife.

6. Various types of *guaiás* (*chocalhos*).

7. *Ganzá* (*chocalho*) used in Paraíba.

8. *Pifes* (flutes): *above*, from Paraíba; *below*, from Pernambuco.

9. *Agogô* and iron stick (percussion instrument in *candomblé*), in Bahia.

10. *Gonguê* or *agogô* used in *xangô* in Recife.

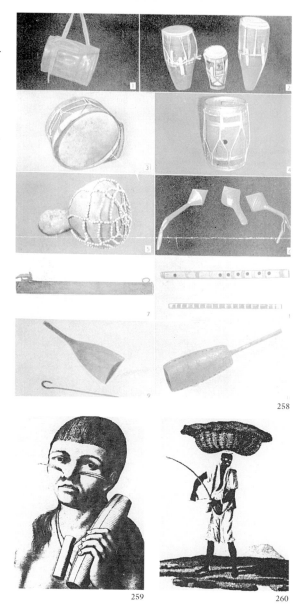

258

259 Indian with whistle.

260 Street vendor playing the *berimbau*.

261

1. Different types of drums, *at extreme right: Tambu* (drum) *de jongo*, a Brazilian rural dance with songs.

2. and 3. *Quinjengue* (drum) - *Tambu* used in *batuque* in São Paulo.

4. Top: *Caxíxis* (*chocalhos*); *below, left* and *centre:* *Angóias* (*chocalhos*); *right:* *Guaxaguaio* (*chocalho*).

5. Various types of *Reco-reco* and *pandeiros*.

6. Drum.

7. *Agogó.*

8. Triangle.

9. *Candongueiro* (drum) *de jongo* in São Paulo.

10. *Adufe* (tambourine).

11. *Rabeca* (fiddle).

12. Viola.

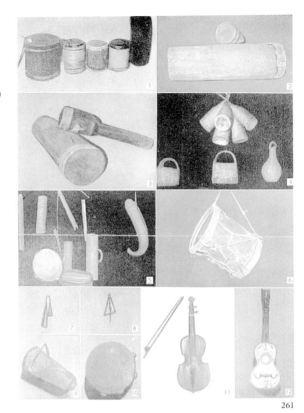

261

262

262   *L'Aveugle chanteur* with *berimbau* by Jean Baptiste Debret.

263 *Buzina* (horn).

264 An Indian using a horn in the Amazon region.

265 *Candongueiro.*

266 Indigenous flutes used in the National Park of *Xingú.*

267 Indian with flute.

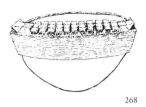

268

269

268 Marimba.

269 *Sunday Walk with Reco-reco and Marimba Players* about 1826 from Jean Baptiste Debret, op. cit.

270 Indian manufacturing a *maracá*, with text from Jean de Léry, op. cit.

In jenem Lande gibt es auch eine Baumsorte, die eine Frucht von der Größe eines Straußeneies, dessen Form sie übrigens auch hat, hervorbringt. Die Wilden durchbohren diese Frucht in der Mitte, höhlen sie aus und füllen sie mit kleinen runden Steinen oder auch mit Körnern ihrer groben Hirse, von der an anderer Stelle berichtet wird. Dann setzen sie einen anderthalb Fuß langen Stock ein und erhalten ein Instrument, das sie »Maraka« nennen und das mehr Lärm als eine mit Erbsen gefüllte Schweinsblase macht. Unsere Brasilianer tragen dieses Instrument meistens in der Hand. Wenn ich auf ihre Religion zu sprechen komme, werde ich erzählen, wie sie über diese Maraka und die von ihr erzeugten Laute denken, nachdem sie mit schönen Federn verziert und dem für sie bestimmten Zweck,

270

271 A sort of viola which the Negroes play in Pará, eighteenth century, from Alexandre Rodrigues Ferreira op. cit.

272 The first map of Rio de Janeiro, correctly scaled, from the Archivo Ultramarino, Lisbon. It was produced by João Massé.

273 Eighteenth-century map showing port and location of São Salvador, capital of Brazil from 1549 to 1763 when the capital was transferred to Rio de Janeiro.

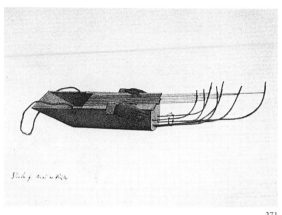

271

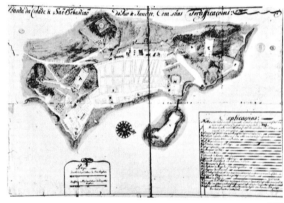

272

273

274

274 Earliest known map of Brazilian interior, made in 1628 by Luís de Céspedes Xeria, governor of Paraguay. It shows São Paulo village and the City Hall. (The original is in the Archive of the Indies, Seville, Spain).

275 Another map of Rio de Janeiro.

276 Dance masks of the Tucuna Indians from Alexandre Rodrigues Ferreira, op. cit.

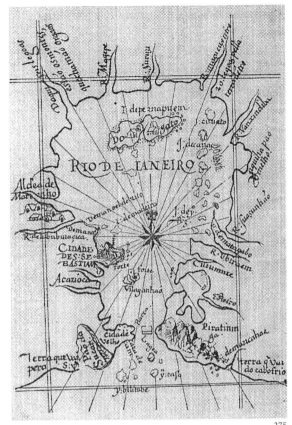

275

276

instruments in particular ways. In all probability, this added to the peculiar effects and the extraordinary tone colours which he often achieved in his music.

Villa-Lobos also examined old maps and masks. His interest turned particularly to Rio de Janeiro, his home town, São Salvador, the first capital of Brazil, and the country's interior.

277

278

279

280

277   Goldwashers.

278   *Garimpeiros* (diamond searchers), drawing by Percy Lau, IBGE, Rio de Janeiro.

279   A Negro woman in Bahia, drawing by Percy Lau (1908-1972), Instituto Brasileiro de Geografia e Estatística (IBGE), Rio de Janeiro.

280   In the southwestern Mato Grosso oxen are often used as a means of crossing the swampy region, drawing by Percy Lau, IBGE, Rio de Janeiro.

281 *Seringueiro* (rubber tapper) in the Amazon region, drawing by Percy Lau, IBGE, Rio de Janeiro.

282 A *gaúcho* (or cowboy) from the vast plains of Rio Grande do Sul, who likes to drink *chimarão*, a sort of mate-tea, drawing by Percy Lau, IBGE, Rio de Janeiro.

283 *Maracatú* in the streets of Recife in the northern state of Pernambuco, drawing by Percy Lau, IBGE, Rio de Janeiro.

284 Scene from *Samba* Schools in São Paulo during carnival time.

Villa-Lobos's research not only concentrated on Brazil's ancient culture and history, indigenous tunes, the instruments, maps and masks. He was as much affected by the people around him and those in other parts of the country. He was fascinated not merely by the inhabitants of the big cities, such as Rio de Janeiro and São Paulo, but also by those dwelling in the Sertão (Wilderness), as well as coffee pickers, gold washers, diamond searchers, rubber-tree tappers, cattle drivers in the south, gatherers of mate-tea, in short, everyone closely linked with the soil and land of Brazil. Their ways of life differed from one another, as did the climatic conditions in which they eked out their existence. By acquainting himself directly with people from all these backgrounds, if opportunities presented themselves, or by studying them in illustrations and

285

286

285 *Pica-Pau*
(woodpecker), Museu de
Caça e Pesca.

286 A cricket

historical texts, Villa-Lobos was able to perceive and
detect the quintessential atmosphere and flavour of
Brazil which he intended should filter through into his
music. At times they did, and sometimes, too, he
added special titles or explanations to his compositions
to ensure that his audiences were aware of the sources
of his music. On occasions, though, the explanations
were rather involved but often they added a special
touch to his music, or, at least, that's what he hoped
they would do. At any rate, his music gradually
reflected a more personal style that was to become his
trademark.

Bahia held a special fascination for Villa-Lobos. It
was the ancient capital, a city whose inhabitants were
decked out prettily in traditional Bahian costume, and

where the *candomblé* and other Brazilian dances and music were particularly cultivated.

After Villa-Lobos had taken into account his studies, research in libraries and archives, and numerous visits to the National Museum, and digested all that he had discovered, he decided no longer to name his new compositions in the traditional manner – symphonies, quartets, trios, etc. True, he had already given slightly unusual titles to some of his compositions, but he now deliberately chose titles which were intended to emphasise the Brazilian character of his music. Although one such piece for piano was called *Sul America* to provide 'spiritual impressions based on the folklore of the South American countries' many of his compositions were now called *Chôros,* whether the work was for orchestra with or without chorus, instrumental ensembles or solo piano. He had written one such *Chôros* for guitar in his youth. But this was rather intended as an example of the popular *chôros* that was in vogue amongst his musician friends with whom he mingled at the time. Now it appeared to him to be the appropriate name to give to his compositions, a title which would surely, at least, attract attention at home and possibly abroad too: he had renewed aspirations to travel abroad once again. To *Chôros No. 5* he even added the subtitle *Alma Brasileira* to emphasise its Brazilian atmosphere. *Chôros No.3* was subtitled *Pica-Pau* (woodpecker). Here again he employed a Brazilian ornithological name as he had done before with birds such as *Irerê, Araponga* and *Uirapurú.*

Incidentally, Villa-Lobos wrote another piece in those years, *Martírio dos Insetos,* whose three movements also borrow titles from the world of natural history (the cricket, the glow-worm and the butterfly).

Três Poemas Indígenas, Chansons Typiques Brésiliennes and *Serestas,* all for voice and piano or orchestra, were products of the few years Villa-Lobos spent in Brazil between his first and second visits to Paris. Even the two songs *Tempos Atrás* and *Tristeza* were eventually joined under the title *Coleção Brasileira* to show once again how concerned he was to stress the idiom of his country. Though he also wrote other compositions during those years in which no evidence of his intention to write typically Brazilian music is revealed in the title, this music too uses pseudo-folklore devices and the flavour is unmistakably that of Villa-Lobos's newly-discovered style.

Second visit to Paris

287

Villa-Lobos's great opportunity came in 1927, the same year in which Charles Lindbergh (1902-1974) reached Paris on the first transatlantic flight (21 May 1927). Carlos and Arnaldo Guinle, the Brazilian industrialists and philanthropists, had finally decided to sponsor a visit to Paris for Villa-Lobos and his wife, Lucília, and to help finance the publication of some further works with Éditions Max Eschig. Settled at 11 Place St Michel in Paris, Villa-Lobos busied himself at once with getting his latest compositions into print and, following Eschig's advice, in getting these performed. For the two concerts on 24 October and 5 December 1927 featuring his latest works, Villa-Lobos was fortunate enough to enlist the participation of some well-known artists. It also offered him the opportunity to which he had aspired: the press took

= BUREAU DE CONCERTS MARCEL DE VALMALÈTE =
45, Rue La Boëtie (Maison Gaveau)
Téléphone : Elysées 06-72 — — — Télégrammes : Valmaletav - Paris 47

MAISON GAVEAU (Salle des Concerts)
45-47, rue La Boëtie - Paris-8'

Lundi 24 Octobre 1927 à 21 h. précises
(Ouverture des Portes à 20 h. 30)

PREMIER CONCERT
ŒUVRES de VILLA-LOBOS

Interprétées par

Arthur **RUBINSTEIN**
Elsie *HOUSTON*
avec le concours de
Aline *VAN BARENTZEN*
Tomás *TERÁN*
Orchestre composé exclusivement d'Artistes des
CONCERTS COLONNE
sous la direction de
VILLA - LOBOS

⚹ PIANOS GAVEAU ⚹

PRIX DES PLACES (droits compris) : Loges (la place) 50 frs. - Parterre 1ʳᵉ série,
50 frs. - 2ᵉ série, 40 frs. - Pourtours, 25 frs. - 1ᵉʳ Balcon, 1ᵉʳ série, 30 frs. - 2ᵉ série,
20 frs. - Pourtours, 15 frs. - 2ᵉ Balcon, 1ᵉʳ eᵗ 2ᵉ 20 frs. - 2ᵉ eᵗ 3ᵉ, 15 frs. - Pourtours, 10 fr.
Billets : Maison GAVEAU, 45, Rue La Boëtie, chez ESCHIG, 48, Rue de Rome, DURAND, 4, Place
de la Madeleine et GUIDE-BILLETS, 20, Avenue de l'Opéra.

Œuvres de VILLA-LOBOS *(1ᵉʳ concert)*

PROGRAMME

I. - *1923* - Chôros (n° 4) *pour trois cors et trombone.* Dédié à Carlos Guinle.
(Ed. MAX ESCHIG et Cie)

II. - *1924* - Chôros (n° 2) *pour flûte et clarinette*
Dédié à Mario de Andrade
(Ed. MAX ESCHIG et Cie)

III. - *1924* - Chôros (n° 7) *pour flûte, hautbois, clarinette. saxophone, basson, violon et violoncelle.*
Dédié à Arnaldo Guinle
(Ed. MAX ESCHIG et Cie)

IV. - *1921 à 1926* - Rudepoême *p' piano solo*
Dédié à Arthur Rubinstein
(Ed. MAX ESCHIG et Cie)

Arthur RUBINSTEIN
•••••

V. - *1925* - Chôros (n° 8) *pour orchestre*
Dédié à Tomás Terán
aux pianos : Aline VAN BARENTZEN et Tomás TERÁN

VI. - *1925* - Seréstas *pour chant et orchestre*
(Ed. A. Napoleão (Rio)
a) Abril.
b) Desejo.
c) Realejo (*dédié à Elsie Houston*).
d) Cantiga do viuvo (*dédié à Mauricio Gudin*).
e) Canção do carreiro.

Elsie HOUSTON

L'Orchestre sous la direction de VILLA - LOBOS

288

Le deuxième Concert consacré aux Œuvres de Villa-Lobos aura lieu à la Salle Gaveau le Lundi 5 Décembre 1927 à 20 h, 30 *avec le concours de* Vera JANACOPULOS, *Aline* VAN BARENTZEN *et Tomás* TERÁN.

⁂

L'Orchestre composé uniquement d'Artistes des CONCERTS COLONNE *et* L'ART CHORAL, *seront dirigés par* VILLA-LOBOS *et* Robert SIOHAN. *(300* Exécutants*).*

289

ŒUVRES DE VILLA-LOBOS

Publiées ou en cours de publication

chez MAX ESCHIG & Cⁱᵉ. Editeurs

48, Rue de Rome - Paris

SUITE .. .. *pour chant et violon*

A PROLE DO BEBE N° 2 (La Famille de Bébé N° 2) « Os Bichinos (*Les Petites Bêtes*) .. *pour piano*

SAUDADES DAS SELVAS BRASILEIRAS *pour piano*

TROIS POÈMES INDIENS .. *pour chant et orchestre*
   I. — Teirú.
   II. — Canide Ioune Sabatii.
   III. — Iará.

GRAND CONCERTO .. *pour violoncelle et orchestre*

DEUXIEME TRIO .. *pour piano, violon et violoncelle*

TROISIEME TRIO .. *pour piano, violon et violoncelle*

TROISIEME QUATUOR A CORDES

NONETTO .. .. *pour orchestre*

NA BAHIA TEM .. .. *pour chœur et capella*

CHÔROS N° 10 .. .. *pour orchestre*

CHÔROS N° 2 .. .. *pour flûte et clarinette*

CHÔROS N° 7 .. .. .. *pour orchestre de chambre*

DEUXIEME SONATE .. .. *pour violoncelle et piano*

CHÔROS N° 4 .. .. .. *pour trois cors et trombone*

CHÔROS N° 8 .. .. *pour orchestre*

RUDEPOEME .. .. *pour piano*

POÊMA DA CRIANÇA E SUA MAMÂ
   Poème de l'enfant et sa mère. .. .. .. *pour chant et piano*

290

287 Villa-Lobos in 1927.

288 Programme of the concert on 24 October 1927.

289 Announcement of the concert on 5 December 1927.

290 Works by Villa-Lobos which Éditions Max Eschig & Cie had published or were about to publish, as announced in the concert programme.

Chôros

Le Chôros représente une nouvelle forme de composition musicale, dans laquelle sont synthétisées les différentes modalités de notre musique indigène et populaire, ayant pour principaux éléments-le Rythme et n'importe quelle Mélodie typique de caractère populaire, qui apparaît de temps à autre accidentellement, toujours transformée selon la personnalité de l'auteur

Les procédés harmoniques sont, eux aussi, presque une stylisation complète de l'original.

Le mot Sérénade peut donner une idée approximative de la signification du Chôros et de la Seresta.

III III III

Seresta

La' Seresta. est une nouvelle forme de composition pour chant qui rappelle, dans une forme raffinée, tous les genres de nos sérénades traditionnelles, toutes les chansons de nos mendiants, musiciens ambulants, et différentes chansons des charretiers, bouviers, campagnards, maçons, etc... originaires de nos régions les plus lointaines de la Capitale Fédérale.

291 Villa-Lobos's explanations of *Chôros* and *Serestas*, included in the concert programme of 24 October 1927 to impress upon his audience the distinctive Brazilian origins of his music. His explanations are, as usual, somewhat confused and exaggerated, trying to be original and without much meaning. Neither *Chôros* nor the *Serestas* are 'a novel form of composition'. In plain language one would call a *Chôros* – written for any type of instrumental combination – a symphonic poem.

ample notice of the concerts and wrote admiring reviews.

Other composers had taken popular dance forms – allemand, gaillard, bourrée, gigue – and transformed them into sophisticated pieces for the classical repertoire. This was not the case with the *Chôros*. For Villa-Lobos *Chôros* was simply a name he gave to assorted series of compositions each of which could just as well be called symphony, trio, duo, etc.

In Paris Villa-Lobos also met Florent Schmitt, the music critic, who became a great admirer of the composer and whose reviews in both *La Revue de France* and, later, *Le Temps,* were of considerable assistance to Villa-Lobos in establishing his reputation in Paris.

Florent Schmitt had given significant space to all the concerts, large and small, at which Villa-Lobos's music was played before and during his visits to Paris. These reviews with my comments were reprinted in *Latin American Music Review,* Vol. 1, No. 2, 1980, Austin, Texas, USA, (*La Revue de France,* 1 October 1927, 1 January and 1 July 1928 and *Le Temps,* 28 December

292

293

Heitor grabbed his manuscript out of my hands after the big hug I gave him, and rushed to the piano to play it for me. It was a very long and very complicated piece of music. The "Rude" of the title did not have the English meaning. In Brazil it meant "savage." When I asked him if he considered me a savage pianist, he said excitedly, "We are both savage! We don't care much for pedantic detail. I compose and you play, off the heart, making the music live, and this is what I hope I expressed in this work." We read it, playing it in turn with great difficulty, but I did recognize that it was a most original and in places a very beautiful work. It certainly made me want to learn it, I spent that whole day with Villa-Lobos, took him out for dinner, and we parted late at night.

On my return home, I put the *Rudepoêma* back on the piano stand and read it through again, this time undisturbed by the presence of the composer. It appeared to me to be a monumental attempt to express the origins of the native Brazilian *caboclos*, their sorrows and joys, their wars and peace, finishing with a savage dance.

294

295

296

292 Elsie Houston (1902-1943), one of Villa-Lobos's interpreters at the first concert. A Brazilian singer, she had studied in Rio de Janeiro, made her debut in Paris in 1924 and had given concert performances in Europe and the United States. A well-known interpreter of Brazilian folk music.

293 Another interpreter was Tomás Terán – here seen in a self-portrait from the collection of the Brazilian pianist Arnaldo Estrella. Terán (1896-1964), a Brazilian pianist and teacher of Spanish origin, had lived in Brazil since 1929 and exercised great influence on the younger Brazilian

generation. Villa-Lobos dedicated his *Chôros No. 8* to him. Terán premièred the *Cirandas* for piano on 13 August 1929 in the Teatro Lyrico in Rio de Janeiro.

294 Arthur Rubinstein premièred Villa-Lobos's *Rudepoêma* which is dedicated to him. The virtuoso pianist describes with humour and understanding his first encounter with the composer when he learned the story behind the work and tells how he tried to perceive and play the music. (From *My Many Years* by Arthur Rubinstein, London 1980, p. 252).

295 On 5 December 1927 Robert Lucien Siohan (1894-1985) conducted a concert in Paris, which included Villa-Lobos's *Chôros No. 3*. The French composer, conductor and musicologist founded the Association des Concerts Siohan (1929-1935) which performed many new works. He was also chorus-master of the Opéra Chorus and professor at the Conservatoire (1948-1962).

296 Florent Schmitt (1870-1958), French composer and music critic of *Le Temps*, Paris.

Les Concerts

ŒUVRES, de VILLA-LOBOS

Le jeune compositeur brésilien Villa-Lobos n'était jusqu'ici connu à Paris que par ses mélodies, ses pièces de piano et sa musique de chambre. Les concerts de *la Revue musicale*, les récitals de Véra Janacopoulos et d'Arthur Rubinstein avaient révélé son nom, mais on peut affirmer que l'on ignorait jusqu'ici le véritable Villa-Lobos. Ces compositions en effet témoignaient d'une habileté technique des plus remarquables et d'une délicate sensibilité, mais elles ne nous apportaient rien de bien nouveau. Ce n'était qu'un reflet coloré de la musique européenne.

Les deux concerts avec orchestre et chœurs donnés à la Salle Gaveau les 24 octobre et 5 décembre nous ont fait connaître des compositions d'une tout autre originalité. C'est la première fois qu'en Europe on entend des œuvres venues de l'Amérique latine et qui apportent avec elles les enchantements des forêts vierges, des grandes plaines, d'une nature exubérante, prodigue en fruits, en fleurs, en oiseaux éclatants.

Villa-Lobos après de solides études musicales a, durant quatre années, parcouru le Brésil en tous sens, recueillant de la bouche des indiens des chants dont les uns remontent à une antiquité reculée, les autres portent déjà traces de l'influence européenne, mais qui, tous, par leurs rythmes variés, leurs modes, leurs contours mélodiques, présentent le plus vif intérêt musical.

Villa-Lobos ne s'est pas contenté de mettre en œuvre ces matériaux précieux, il s'est refait au contact de la nature et des indigènes une âme de primitif. Les œuvres qu'il a construites au moyen de ces éléments stylisés pourraient être comparées aux tableaux et aux sculptures d'un Gauguin à Tahiti.

Il ne faut pas y chercher des développements logiques selon l'esprit de la musique européenne, c'est une sorte de chaos sonore, mais qui s'ordonne néanmoins selon un sens très raffiné de l'équilibre et des proportions. L'art sauvage ignore la symétrie rigoureuse comme la perspective linéaire, il crée néanmoins des œuvres d'une beauté indiscutable.

Dans les trois poèmes indiens *Canine-ioune-sabaléi*, *Teïrû*, *Iára*, ce sont surtout les instruments à percussion qui servent d'accompagnement, de temps à autre les chœurs poussent un cri bref et dur, pour marquer le rythme. Dans le magnifique Chôros *Pica Paô*, les vocalises éperdues des ténors se déroulent au-dessus du refrain obstiné des basses, scandé sur un rythme dansant, tandis que font rage les instruments de la batterie augmentés de quelques instruments indiens.

A ces concerts, les chôros, « nouvelle forme de composition musicale qui synthétise les différentes modalités de la musique brésilienne, indienne et populaire » ont été une révélation. Ces morceaux sont construits sur un thème populaire qui disparaît et reparaît plus ou moins déformé. La polyphonie ou est très originale, et s'inspire de la curieuse polyphonie de timbres des Indiens. Villa-Lobos se joue avec aisance des combinaisons et des superpositions de rythmes les plus compliquées. Les instruments

à percussion indigènes jouent un grand rôle à la batterie : calebasses secouées raclées, xylophones de toutes natures : Xucalho, Càràcàchà, Réco-réco, Pu, Caxambú, Matràca, etc.

Le Choros 8 pour orchestre et deux pianos est sans doute avec le Nonetto, trois chants indiens, et le Choros 10, ce que nous avons entendu de plus frappe. Par moment un vent de folie se déchaîne, les voix hurlent de surprenantes ono topées, la batterie, véritable orchestre d'instruments à percussion, martèle les ryth. avec une fureur dyonisiaque, l'orchestre se surpasse en violence frénétique, c'est cataclysme sonore, une éruption volcanique, un cyclone...

On peut avoir une autre conception de l'art musical, on ne saurait rester ind rent à des œuvres de cette puissance et l'on doit reconnaître avec Florent Scha que « le véritable grand souffle a passé ».

A ces concerts, Mme Véra Janacopoulos chanta avec grand art les trois ma, fiques *Poèmes indiens*, tâche ardue, car l'accompagnement, loin de soutenir la ve ne fait que poser de loin en loin un accord violemment dissonant pour marque rythme. Arthur Rubinstein et Aline van Barentzen interprétèrent avec une splenc virtuosité les compositions pour piano de Villa-Lobos, d'une difficulté diabolic

L'Art Choral de Robert Siohan se tira à son honneur de cette entreprise pérille Ce groupement choral a accompli d'immenses progrès depuis un an. Les élémε médiocres ont été éliminés, les amateurs solidement encadrés entre des profession de valeur. C'est maintenant l'une des meilleures, sinon la meilleure chorale dont c dispositions à Paris.

L'orchestre et les chœurs dirigés par Villa-Lobos, d'une part R. Siohan, exécutè fort bien l'ensemble des deux programmes. Ce furent deux belles séances et qui, c la médiocrité des concerts quotidiens produisirent une impression profonde sur auditeurs : révélation d'un nouveau monde sonore.

Henry PRUNIÈRE

297

297 The two concerts were extensively reviewed in the next issue of *La Revue Musicale*, Paris (9th year, No. 3, January 1928) by Henry Prunières (1886-1942). Unfortunately, however, he let himself be carried away (not knowing any better, of course) by what Villa-Lobos must have intentionally but erroneously put about in Paris 'that for many years he had scoured Brazil in all directions'.

298 Arthur Rubinstein relates wittily what he learned when meeting the composer after the concert and also how the pianist felt embarrassed at luncheon shortly afterwards when hearing from Carlos Guinle of Villa-Lobos's 'gaffe'. (From *My Many Years* by Arthur Rubinstein, London 1980, p. 172-173).

Villa-Lobos had a brilliant debut at the Salle Gaveau. He presented some of his larger things for orchestra, some with voice, but I don't remember the titles. This concert was a great success without any doubt. The somewhat savage quality of his music, the unorthodox development of his ideas, and the novel treatment of his songs and solo instruments intrigued and pleased the Parisians. There were many important musicians in the hall—Prokofiev and Ravel, I remember, among them. These two showed a respectful interest in the music of the Brazilian, but Florent Schmitt, who was also an influential critic, became a staunch follower of Villa-Lobos.

Carlos Guinle and his wife were present in a box. At the end of the concert Heitor received an ovation from an audience consisting of many Parisians and a large number of South Americans—among them, the same Brazilians who had booed him in their capital but had changed their minds in Paris.

When I went to embrace him, I found him happy and proud of having had the good idea of coming to Paris.

... At lunch with Carlos Guinle, a few days after Heitor's debut, I said, smiling and very pleased with myself, "You see, Carlos, I was right, wasn't I? Villa-Lobos will leave a great name behind him." Guinle listened, not very convinced. "Do you doubt it?" I asked him, quite alarmed. "No, no," he replied, "you were right about him, of course, but he annoyed me a little. I made a special effort to be here for his debut and asked him for a box and you know what he did? He sent me a bill for it." I blushed for my friend's big blunder.

298

En une séance tumultueuse à la salle Gaveau, M. Gaston Poulet nous révélait deux œuvres de marque. Je vous ai souvent parlé d'Heitor Villa-Lobos. Aux admirables *choros* s'ajoute à présent un poème symphonique, *Amazones*, inspiré d'une légende indienne (les Indes de Christophe Colomb). Légende de la forêt inextricable de Marajo et du plus long des fleuves à son embouchure, elle fournit au musicien un merveilleux scénario :

« Une vierge indienne, consacrée par les dieux des forêts enchantées, avait l'habitude de saluer l'aurore en se baignant dans les eaux de l'Amazone, fleuve des Marajos qui ressentait encore les effets de sa colère contre les filles de l'Atlantide, mais qui, en hommage à leur beauté, apaisait parfois les ondes de son courant éternel. La jeune sauvage s'amusait allègrement, parfois invoquant le soleil de ses poses religieuses, parfois tordant son corps divin dans une coquetterie maléfique, afin que son image pût être contemplée par l'astre et réfléchie dans l'ondulante surface. Plus elle voyait son ombre dessinant sur cette toile morbide et froide les traits de l'esthétique féminine, idéalisée comme par aucun peintre, plus elle s'enorgueillissait dans un sensualisme brutal. Pendant que la vierge rêvait à cette vie éthérée, le dieu des vents tropicaux la parfumait d'un souffle caressant et amoureux. Mais elle, sans écouter ses supplications, se livrait éperdument à ses plaisirs comme une enfant ingénue, dansant et folâtrant. Le dieu des vents, jaloux, indigné de ce mépris, conduisit le chaste parfum de la fille des Marajos vers les régions profanes des monstres.

» De très loin l'un d'eux le sent. Dans l'anxiété de la posséder, détruisant tout sur son passage, il s'avance et, à pas feutrés, s'approche de la vierge. A une faible distance il se met à ramper. Tout près il la contemple en extase et la convoite.

» Sans être aperçu, il cherche à se coucher dans un endroit d'où son image sera réfléchie par le soleil sur la tache grise de l'ombre de la jeune fille.

» En voyant son image transformée, elle se précipite pleine d'horreur, sans but, et suivie par le monstre, dans l'abime de son désir... »

Ce poème symphonique, qui est en réalité un poème chorégraphique, commente la légende avec une sensualité et une violence auxquelles nous pouvions nous attendre de la part de ce génial tortionnaire. Dès les premières mesures, on ne s'y trompe pas. C'est bien toujours le même Villa-Lobos. Il ne renie aucune de ses frénésies, de ses impétuosités, voire de ses outrances, d'ailleurs toujours sympathiques. Et si souple en même temps, si félin! Il a toutes les grâces et toutes les férocités de l'habitant de la jungle. C'est une force de la nature malaisément disciplinée. Mais peut-il être question de discipline pour le tigre! Il faut ou s'en faire un ami ou le détruire. Il n'y a pas de milieu. Villa-Lobos est à jamais inapprivoisable — et tant mieux.

299

1929 and 8 March 1930), and in *Villa-Lobos: Collected Studies*, Scolar Press 1992. There is, however, one review of the concert on 30 May 1929 which appeared in *La Revue de France* on 1 January 1930, eight months after the concert. I had overlooked it at the time but it is now reproduced here. It concerns the first performance of Villa-Lobos's *Amazonas*.

In the summer of 1929 Villa-Lobos holidayed in Brazil and arranged some concerts which included his music. The violinist Maurice Raskin, whom he brought from Paris, took part.

300

301

300   Gaston Poulet who conducted the concert on 30 May 1929. French violinist and conductor (1882-1974) who founded the Gaston Poulet Concerts (1912). Also conducted the Concerts Colonne in Paris (1940-1945) and was a teacher at the Paris Conservatoire (1944-1964).

301   Avenida Rio Branco in Rio de Janeiro in 1929.

301a **Not illustrated** Maurice Raskin (1906-1985), Belgian violinist who studied at the Royal Conservatoire in Liège and in Paris. Gave performances in South America (1929-30), Germany and France and other European countries in 1933-35. Teacher at the Royal Conservatoire at Brussels from 1936 onwards, and in 1940 founded a string quartet.

302   Programme of the concert in honour of Villa-Lobos's patrons, the Guinle brothers.

RIO DE JANEIRO, 26 DE AGOSTO DE 1929.

3.' e ultimo CONCERTO, (Orchestra) as 17 horas
Em homenagem aos meus amigos
ARNALDO E CARLOS GUINLE

no THEATRO LYRICO

1 —(1914) — Dansas africanas — (reducção para pequeno conjuncto)
    a)—Farrapós
    b)—Kankukús
    c)—Kankikis
2—Canto e conjuncto—(1920)—Epigrammas ironicos e sentimentaes
    Poesia de Ronald de Carvalho

a)—Eis a vida...   e)—Perversidade
b)—Inutil epigramme   f)—Pudor
c)—Sonho de uma noite de verão   g)—Image
d)—Epigramme.   h)—Verdade

ELSIE HOUSTON

3—(1918)—Folia de um bloco infantil—(N. 8 do Carnaval das crianças brasileiras)
    Conjuncto sob a regencia do autor
4—(1925) - a)—Choros (N. 2)—para Flauta e Clarinetta
    b)—Chôros (N. 7) (Setimino) para Flauta, Oboé, Cla-
    rinella, Saxophones, Fagotte, violino e violoncello.
    Dedicado a Arnaldo Guinle
5)—1920) — Serenidade — (N.' 2 da Fantasia dos movimentos mixtos)—Violino e conjuncto

MAURICE RASKIN

6) —(1929)--Suite Suggestiva—(Cinemas)—Poêma en francez de Oswaldo de Andrade, René Chalupt e Manoel Bandeira.
    Dedicado ao Dr. Carlos Guinle
    a)—Ouverture de l'homme tel.
    b)—Prélude, choral et funebre— (Cine-Journal)
    c)—Croche-pied au flic -(Capueira)-(Comedia) }O. Andrade
    d)—Le récit du peureux—(Drame)........
    e)—Charlot aviateur –(Comique)........ René Chalupt
    f)—L'enfant et le Youroupari (Tragédie).... M. Bandeira
    g)—Surprise de l'opportunité — (Marche finale)

**ELSIE HOUSTON e ADACTO FILHO
Ao piano LUCILIA VILLA-LOBOS
e BRUTOS PEDREIRA**

302

303　Magda Tagliaferro
(Petropolis, near Rio de
Janeiro, 1893-1986).
Brazilian pianist of
international repute who
lived in Paris as teacher and
gave concert performances
there. She also gave master
courses in Brazil.
Mômoprecóce is dedicated to
her.

304　Edgard Varèse (1883-
1965) (*left*) and Villa-Lobos
on the balcony of Villa-
Lobos's apartment in Paris,
1930.

303

304

305

305　Programme for the
concert given, at Salle
Chopin on 14 March 1930,
in which Janine Cools, eldest
daughter of Eugène Cools
(1877-1936), Director of
Éditions Max Eschig,
premièred *Saudades das
Selvas Brasileiras*. She died
before the outbreak of World
War II.[12]

12) In the biography *Heitor
Villa-Lobos, Leben und Werk des
brasilianischen Komponisten*,
Zurich, 1972, p. 121, the
première of *Saudades das Selves
Brasileiras* is erroneously given as
25 November 1930 which was
not the world première but the
date of the first performance in
Brazil.

In the programme for his concert
Poème de l'enfant et de sa mère is
shown as being given its
première. However, the first
performance took place on 30

May 1924 in the Salle des
Agriculteurs, Paris, under the title
Pensées d'enfant (see the biography
referred to above, p.54).

Ualaloce later disappeared from
Chansons Typiques Brésiliennes.

306

M.r IRVING SCHWERKE

18 rue Juliette Lamber
Paris XVII.e

Voir au verso.

Cher ami   Paris, 17/4/1929

Pendant la journée de 18(Jeudi)
prochain, je serais libre
seulement de midi a 2 h.½
d'après midi. Par consequent
je pourrais accepter avec plaisir
votre dejeuner si ne vous
derrange pas.
    Donc à demain sans faute

                Bien a vous

                Villa-Lobos

307

306 *Standing (from left to right)*: Oscar Fried (1871-1942), the German composer and conductor who, in 1934, went to Tiflis; Magda Tagliaferro, Leopold Stokowski, Edgard Varèse, Villa-Lobos. *Front row:* Conrad Becker, Lucília Villa-Lobos, Maurice Raskin and the cellist Tony Close, who together with André Asselin, premièred *Chôros Bis* in the Salle Pleyel on 14 March 1930.

307 Facsimile letter from Villa-Lobos to Irving Schwerké, 17 April 1929. It seems that Villa-Lobos preferred to communicate by pneumatic post rather than using the telephone.[13] Reproduced here for the first time in facsimile by courtesy of The Library of Congress, Music Division, Washington, DC, with the consent of Arminda Villa-Lobos. Another letter in which Villa-Lobos speaks of being overworked probably refers to the preparations for previous concerts (14 March and 3 April) and another to come on 7 May 1930.

13) The Paris 'pneumatic tube' postal service, installed in underground tubes during the Second Empire under Napoleon III for the dispatch of Special Delivery Mail in the French capital, ceased operating on 1 April 1984, replaced by modern means of communication such as telephone and telex.

308 Leopold Stokowski (1882-1977).

Back in Paris, his Brazilian compatriot, the internationally renowned pianist Magda Tagliaferro, premièred Villa-Lobos's *Mômoprecóce* on 23 February 1930 with the Orchestre Symphonique under the Spanish conductor Enrique Fernández Arbós (1863-1939).

Another concert took place on 14 March 1930 in which Villa-Lobos's new friend Edgard Varèse (1883-1965), the American composer of French origin, participated.

Villa-Lobos's circle of friends in Paris in 1928 included a number of celebrities of the time:

Villa-Lobos also maintained close friendships with three Americans based in Paris: Irving Schwerké, Leopold Stokowski and Hugh Ross. The two conductors were soon to perform some of his music in the United States, the first time that his compositions were brought before an American audience. To Irving Schwerké (1893-1975), the pianist and writer on music, Villa-Lobos wrote a dozen letters, four of them during his stay in Paris (1927-1930),[13] the others (between 1949 and 1952) from Rio de Janeiro apart from one in 1953 from New York. Schwerké, the American pianist, went to Europe in 1920, studied at Madrid University and finally settled in Paris, at 18 Rue Juliette Lamber, where he taught and wrote. He was

308

drama critic and correspondent for various American publications, organised the first European festival of American music in Bad Homburg (Germany) in 1931 and only returned to the United States in 1941 to teach and write. He received many awards in Europe. Villa-Lobos and Schwerké shared quite a few interests. In addition, Villa-Lobos cherished Schwerké's reviews of his concerts in American journals, as the composer already aspired to conduct in America.

During the 1928/29 season of the Philadelphia Orchestra Leopold Stokowski (1882-1977), the American conductor of British birth, who became a close friend of the Brazilian composer in Paris, wanted to be helpful. He introduced Villa-Lobos's *Danças Características Africanas* in New York City's Carnegie Hall on 27 November 1928 after the orchestra with

SEASON 1928-1929

The
PHILADELPHIA ORCHESTRA
LEOPOLD STOKOWSKI, Conductor

CARNEGIE HALL
Third Concert
TUESDAY EVENING, NOVEMBER 27, 1928
at 8.45

PROGRAM

BACH	Suite No. 2, in B minor

    I. Overture—Grave. Allegro. Lentement
    II. Rondo
    III. Sarabande
    IV. (a) Bourrée I
        (b) Bourrée II
    V. Polonaise
    VI. Badinerie. Rondo
             Flutes:
      Solo: William M. Kincaid
      Ripieni: Joseph La Monaca
               John A. Fischer
               Hans Schlegel

BACH	Prelude in E-flat minor
BACH	Toccata and Fugue in D minor

INTERMISSION

VILLA-LOBOS	Dansas Caracteristicas De Indios Africanos

    I. Farrapos
    II. Kankukus
    III. Kankikis

CASINIÈRE	"Hercule et les Centaures"
WAGNER	Vorspiel und Liebestod,—"Tristan und Isolde"

The Steinway is the Official Piano of The Philadelphia Orchestra

Any of the works on this program can be obtained for home study at the 58th Street Branch of the New York Public Library, 121 East 58th Street.

ARTHUR JUDSON, Manager
LOUIS A. MATTSON, Assistant Manager
PACKARD BUILDING, PHILADELPHIA

309 Programme for the Philadelphia Orchestra's concert at Carnegie Hall. Villa-Lobos's composition was performed after the Intermission.

308

Friday Afternoon
April 12

Saturday Evening
April 13

1929

The
PHILADELPHIA ORCHESTRA
LEOPOLD STOKOWSKI, Conductor

Assisting Artists: ALINE VAN BÄRENTZEN } *Pianists*
HARRY KAUFMAN

TANSMAN	Ouverture Symphonique
EICHHEIM	Japanese Nocturne
VILLA-LOBOS	Choros No. 8

INTERMISSION

BACH	Fantasia and Fugue in G minor
BACH	Choralvorspiel, "Ich rufe zu dir, Herr Jesu Christ"
BACH	Passacaglia in C minor

The Steinway is the Official Piano of The Philadelphia Orchestra

1106

310 Programme of the Philadelphia Orchestra and Stokowski, for concerts on 12 and 13 April 1929.

310

the same conductor had given the American first performance a few days earlier in Philadelphia on 23 and 24 November.

Stokowski was more ambitious the following year. He presented with the same orchestra, on 12 and 13 April 1929, Villa-Lobos's *Chôros No. 8.* The concerts were given at the Academy of Music at Broad and Locust Streets in Philadelphia, and Lawrence Gilman wrote the analytical notes. He observed – the information was probably supplied by the composer – that in his music it is said that 'all hitherto accepted laws are utterly ignored' and that 'by the time Villa-Lobos was twenty-five years old he found himself the most conspicuous composer in South America'. (In

Carnegie Hall Program

SEASON 1929—1930

FIRE NOTICE—Look around *now* and choose the nearest exit to your seat. In case of fire walk (not run) to *that* Exit. Do not try to beat your neighbor to the street.
John J. Dorman, *Fire Commissioner*

CARNEGIE HALL
Wednesday Evening, January 15, at 8:45

Schola Cantorum

HUGH ROSS, *Conductor*

Assisted by

JEANNE LEVENTHAL, *soprano*
EDWARD MURCH, HAROLD HEITZMANN, *Sopranos Grace Church Choir*
DEWORA NADWORNEY, *contralto*
DAN GRIDLEY, *tenor*
FRASER GANGE, *barytone*
DAVID McK. WILLIAMS *at the organ*
COLIN McPHEE *at the piano*
PHILHARMONIC-SYMPHONY ORCHESTRA
J. AMANS, *solo flute*
RENE POLLAIN, *solo viola*

I

Requiem Mass in C-minor. . *Joseph Haydn*
For chorus, soprano, alto, tenor and barytone solos, solo viola, orchestra and organ
(*First performance in America*)

II

Pastoral . . . . *Arthur Bliss*
For chorus, solo flute and orchestra
(*First performance in America*)

INTERMISSION

III

Taillefer . . . . *Richard Strauss*
For soprano, tenor and barytone solos, chorus and orchestra

IV

Chorus No. 10 . . . . . .*Hector Villa-Lobos*
For chorus and orchestra
(*First performance in America*)

Rose A. Held, *Manager*
333 Fourth Ave.

(*Knabe Piano*)

Important Concert Announcements on Inside Back Cover, Page 11.

See Page 8 for SCHRAFFT'S Announcement

INFORMATION BUREAU FOR LOST AND FOUND ARTICLES AT SUPERINTENDENT'S OFFICE

Ladies' Parlor on Every Floor Except Parquet

311

311 Programme for the first American performance of *Chôros No. 10* by Hugh Ross and the Schola Cantorum of New York, in Carnegie Hall, on 15 January 1930.

312 Hugh Ross (1898-1990), American choral conductor born in England. From 1929 conductor of the Schola Cantorum in New York City. From 1941 to 1962 head of the choral department at Tanglewood. Extensive American and foreign travels as choral conductor. He also participated with the Schola Cantorum in the first performance of *Mandú-Çarará* – the version for two pianos, percussion instruments, mixed and children's chorus – on 23 January 1948.

313 Concert programme for *Mandú-Çarará*, 23 January 1948.

THIRTY-NINTH SEASON   1948

Schola Cantorum of New York

HUGH ROSS, Conductor

•

Assisting Artists:

PIERRE
LUBOSHUTZ   and   GENIA
NEMENOFF

•

CARNEGIE HALL

Friday Evening, January 23, 1948

LUBOSHUTZ AND NEMENOFF USE BALDWIN PIANOS
THE STEINWAY IS THE OFFICIAL PIANO OF THE SCHOLA CANTORUM

313

1912, at the age of twenty-five, Villa-Lobos was still unable to write well for the piano!)

The following year, on 15 January 1930, Hugh Ross, another friend of Villa-Lobos from his Paris days, endeavoured to present Villa-Lobos's *Chôros No. 10* in New York's Carnegie Hall. 'It was the success of Villa-Lobos's *Chôros No. 10'* – Hugh Ross wrote to the author on 16 November 1973 – 'which finally established me as a ranking choral conductor on the New York scene.'

At the end of May 1930 Villa-Lobos and his wife Lucília left Paris and returned to Brazil. This meant the end of the Guinle brothers' financial support. Shortly after Villa-Lobos's arrival in Brazil, he tried, once again, to secure their sponsorship for yet another European visit. But to no avail. From the 13 letters

14) An English translation and comments are found in Lisa M. Peppercorn, 'A Letter of Villa-Lobos to Arnaldo Guinle', *Studi Musicali*, Anno X, No. 1, Rome, 1981.

exchanged between Villa-Lobos and the Guinle brothers, only a single letter still survives, the others having mysteriously disappeared. The surviving letter was found in Lucília's estate and is presently in the possession of her brothers and sister. Dated 24 February 1930, it was written just one day after Magda Tagliaferro had premièred the composer's *Mômoprecóce* in Paris.[14]

Mandu-Carara   .   .   .   .   .   .   **HEITOR VILLA-LOBOS**
(1889-)

A symphonic poem or ballet

For two pianos, percussion, large chorus and *children's chorus

"Mandu-Carara" is a legend of the Nheengatu people, a Brazilian Indian tribe. The work is named for a famous young Indian dancer, and the climax is a triumphal dance led by Mandu-Carara in celebration of the happy ending of the story.

The legend concerns the adventures of two children and parallels in a Brazilian setting the story of Hänsel and Gretel. Two greedy children have been left by their poor father in the woods as he is unable to feed them any longer. In their wanderings they come upon an ogre "Currupira" who lures them to his hearth. They ask him the way home but he detains them and his wife begins stuffing them with food.

A musical interlude then describes how the children outwit Currupira telling him how they had just seen two fat monkeys near his hut. He goes in search of them and meanwhile the children kill his wife and run away.

Currupira comes home and rushes madly about the wood crying with fury. The children save themselves from him by swimming across a river and with the help of forest creatures, find their way home. There they find Mandu-Carara with their father. This is the signal for a general celebration, culminating in the dance of Mandu-Carara.

The story has elements both of symphony and ballet. The one-eyed Currupira with reversed ears and feet and his wicked Indian wife, the cotias and monkeys of the jungle, the children, Mandu-Carara and the Indians, all find their musical embodiment in Villa-Lobos' score.

The percussion instruments emphasize the rhythms of Mandu-Carara's dance. A heavy stumbling ostinato, soon after the entry of the chorus, represents the frightened children wandering in the jungle.

The work was composed in two forms, as a symphonic poem either for chorus and full orchestra or with two pianos and percussion.

*Girls Ensemble from the High School of Music and Art.

314

314   Programme note for the 23 January concert includes the legend of the *Mandú-Çarará*.

315   Pierre Luboshutz and Genia Nemènoff. Luboshutz (1894-1971), American pianist of Russian origin, who came to the United States in 1926, together with his wife Genia Nemènoff (1908-1989), American pianist of French origin, gave concerts at two pianos following their debut in 1937.

315

Villa-Lobos the music educationalist

15) The facsimiles appeared for the first time in *Villa-Lobos, Visto da Plateia e na Intimidade,* ibid. Translations of all letters with the author's comments are published in *Music and Letters,* Vol. 61, No. 3/4, July/Oct., Oxford, 1980 and *The Villa-Lobos Letters* by Lisa M. Peppercorn, Toccata Press, 1994.

316   Villa-Lobos and his wife Lucília seen with the pianist João de Souza Lima and Magda Tagliaferro.

Upon his return to Brazil, Villa-Lobos immediately went to São Paulo where he organised a number of concerts which offered interesting programmes, including works by French composers. This was a novelty for Brazil and though disappointing artistically, the concerts often met with success. Lucília had meanwhile remained in Rio de Janeiro. The first three of nine letters exchanged between the composer and his wife date from this period.[15]

Various factors contributed to a complete transformation of Villa-Lobos's career during the following months. Artistically satisfied with his success in São Paulo but financially still as insecure as before, Villa-Lobos longed to return to Paris with the financial assistance of the Guinle brothers. They, however, emphatically refused any further help. Instead they drew Villa-Lobos's attention to the possible consequences that the political changes that occurred in Brazil with the October 1930 Revolution might have in store for him. President Washington Luíz Pereira de Souza was deposed on 24 October 1930 –

317

317

318

319

317 Lucília Guimarães Villa-Lobos in 1931.

318 Washington Luíz Pereira de Souza (1870-1957).

319 Getúlio Dornelles Vargas (1883-1954), Brazilian politician, chief of the provisional government (1930-1934), President of Brazil (1934-1937), Dictator (1937-1945) and again President of Brazil (1951-1954); he committed suicide on 24 August 1954.

he had been President of Brazil since 1926 – and Getúlio Dornelles Vargas came to power on 3 November 1930.

A further contributing factor in Villa-Lobos's existence was his ability to adapt quickly to new situations whenever they occurred in his life. He possessed uncanny ingenuity in devising new ideas for composition (*Chôros, Serestas* and others) or other novelties in his intense desire to succeed in life.

He was quick to seize on new musical opportunities which would be in tune with an idea, trend or scheme that was already in vogue or looked as though it soon would be. He somehow had a flair for anticipating future requirements.

Villa-Lobos devised a programme to be offered to small towns in the state of São Paulo. It was to consist of good music, including his own, since these places were otherwise deprived of any form of cultural entertainment. To realise this plan he and a group of musicians had to undertake the implementation of the idea themselves of course. These musical tours happened around the time when the statue of the Christ the Redeemer was inaugurated on top of the Corcovado mountain in Rio de Janeiro (on 12 October 1931).

The musical tours were arranged in financial cooperation with the respective municipalities. Some documentary illustrations are available from this period.

In the city of São Paulo Villa-Lobos tried out one more idea with far-reaching consequences. Its outstanding results eventually landed him a permanent position as a civil servant on a secure financial basis in Rio de Janeiro. Villa-Lobos devised a project to organise and conduct massed choirs in the belief that these would attract a wide range of people to music. It would also attract the participants' families and relatives to concerts. With good contacts and the support of persons with influence Villa-Lobos aimed to interest the authorities in São Paulo, but more especially those in Rio de Janeiro, in his plans by introducing mandatory singing in schools. One of those who supported Villa-Lobos's endeavours was João Alberto Lins de Barros.

Another backer was Anísio Spinola Teixeira (1900-1971), a Brazilian politician who had graduated from Columbia University in New York City. He was director of the Department of Education (1932) in Rio de Janeiro, belonged to the Secretariat of Education

320   Statue of Christ the Redeemer on top of the Corcovado mountain in Rio de Janeiro.

320

321

322

321   *Left to right:* Villa-
Lobos, Nair Duarte Nunes,
the Brazilian singer,
Antonieta Rudge (1886-
1974), the Brazilian pianist,
and Lucília.

322   Villa-Lobos (*fourth
from right*), Magda
Tagliaferro (*third from right*),
João de Souza Lima (*second
from right*), and Lucília (*third
from left*).

323 João Alberto Lins de Barros (1899-1959) (*centre*), Brazilian politician who studied engineering and participated in the revolutionary movement (1922-1924) and the revolution (1930). In 1932 he was Governor by appointment of the state of São Paulo, Deputy of Pernambuco (1933) and after the creation of the New State (Estado Novo) in 1937, held various posts abroad and in Brazil. Villa-Lobos dedicated *String Quartet No. 5* to him.

323

324

324 Villa-Lobos is seen clad in a colourful tunic which could easily be seen by members of the massed choirs.

and Culture of the (then) Federal District and exercised much influence in Rio de Janeiro's educational life.

These supporters, together with the nationalist tendencies of the Vargas regime, led to the foundation of SEMA – Superintendência de Educação Musical e Artística do Departamento de Educação da Prefeitura do Distrito Federal – by decree 18.890 of 18 April 1931. It ensured that choral singing became mandatory in municipal schools. Villa-Lobos was appointed head of this department and thus, for the first time in his life, no longer had financial worries.

At once Villa-Lobos began to train teachers and then to present his teachers' chorus, the Orfeão dos Professores, in public concerts.

Self-assured in his position, Villa-Lobos had also

327

325   Villa-Lobos in 1932
when he was appointed head
of SEMA.

326   Portrait of Villa-Lobos
in the 1930s.

327   Villa-Lobos's office
was in the Andorinha
building in the Avenida
Almirante Barroso 81, in
Room 504 on the fifth floor.

secured a good post for his wife, Lucília. His letter to
Lucília of 5 May 1932 provides evidence for this.

Whenever an opportunity presented itself Villa-
Lobos organised and conducted massed choirs, always
with the same idea in mind: to interest relatives of the
members of the choir in music, in the faint hope that
some of them would eventually listen to and like his
own music.

Villa-Lobos's choral and teaching activities in Rio de
Janeiro also offered engagements elsewhere, as can be
seen from a note and letter he wrote to his wife Lucília
on 4 July 1934 from Bahia and 7 July 1934 from
Recife in the state of Pernambuco.

In the following year Villa-Lobos visited Buenos
Aires in May and June and gave concerts of his own
works at the Colón Theatre.

328

329

328 A programme from
one of his many massed choir
demonstrations, 7 July 1935.

329 Bahia's new modern
district with high-rise
buildings.

330 Villa-Lobos in Buenos
Aires in 1935.

330

Villa-Lobos the music educationalist 151

331

332

333

331   By contrast, Bahia's old city with its narrow streets and old-world charm.

332   Recife, a view of the old city.

333   Teatro Santa Isabel, Recife where Villa-Lobos participated in a concert on 5 July 1934, at the invitation of the Pernambuco state government.

334   Colón Theatre in Buenos Aires.

334

Villa-Lobos in the 1930s

335 The Martinelli skyscraper built between World Wars I and II, is seen here towering over the enchanting small houses from the colonial period.

336 In São Paulo's residential district the old single-storey houses were still dominant in 1937.

337 Map of Rio de Janeiro state and surrounding states of Espírito Santo, São Paulo and Minas Gerais.

In the 1930s São Paulo and Rio de Janeiro took on a new appearance. Modern architecture was introduced, skyscrapers sprung up everywhere and although some parts of both cities still retained their charming atmosphere from the past, the change was noticeable and irreversible.

Gradually schools began to be named after the Brazilian composer who, by now, was generally recognised as an outstanding music educationalist, more particularly as he had previously had neither administrative, pedagogical nor musical training.

The Conservatório Nacional de Canto Orfeônico came into being on 26 November 1942, and, for some time, was installed in the Piaui Building, Avenida Almirante Barroso 72, Rio de Janeiro. On 22

335

336

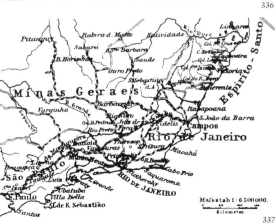

337

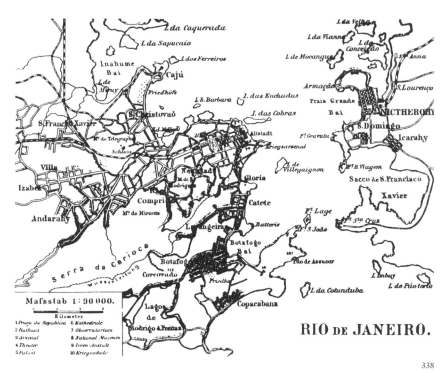

338

339

340

341

338   Map of Rio de Janeiro.

339   School children in Rio
de Janeiro vividly illustrate
Brazil's racial diversity.

340   Rio de Janeiro's
Copacabana district still had
only a few high-rise buildings
in the second half of the
1930s. The sea breeze could
still reach all the streets and
houses that stretched
between the ocean and the
mountains before the
building of skyscrapers acted
as a barrier to the refreshing
sea-air.

341   Escola Villa-Lobos.

342

342   In March 1960 the
Escola de Música Villa-Lobos
was established in Rio de
Janeiro.

343 One of the
programmes to which the
letter refers.

344 Leo Kestenberg (1882-
1962) *(Left)*, Israeli music
educationalist of Hungarian
origin, seen here with Felix
Weingartner (1865-1942). In
1918 chairman of the music
department of the Prussian
Ministry of Art and Science.
In 1929 counsellor of that
music department. In 1933
he left for Prague where he
founded the International
Society for Music Education
which held three congresses
(1936-38). Went to Palestine
in 1938. From 1939 to 1945
Music Director of Palestine
(now Israel) Philharmonic
Symphony Orchestra. On
retirement founded and
taught at Israel's First Music
Teachers' Training College.
(From *Die Musikgeschichte
Israels,* Peter Gradenwitz *b.*
1910), Kassel 1961, by kind
permission of the author).

345 Walter Burle Marx
(1992-1990), Brazilian
composer, conductor and
pianist. Studied in Brazil,
London and Berlin. Gave
performances as a pianist in
Europe. Returned to Brazil,
founded (1931) the
Philharmonic Orchestra in
Rio de Janeiro. 1947 Director
of the Teatro Municipal in
Rio de Janeiro. After 1952
lived in Philadelphia where he
taught piano and
composition. On 23
November 1932, he
premièred Villa-Lobos's
unfinished *Caixinha de Boas
Festas* (*Vitrina encantada*),
which is dedicated to him, in
one of his children's concerts.
On 8 December 1932 he
conducted the completed
version.

TEATRO MUNICIPAL

(ENTRADA FRANCA)

CONCERTO CULTURAL POPULAR DO *ORFEAO DE PROFESSORES* do
Distrito Federal organizados pela SEMA (Superintendencia de Educação Musical e
Artistica do Departamento de Educação).
Sob a regencia do *Maestro Villa-Lobos*

SABADO, 18 DE DEZEMBRO DE 1937, AS 20 ½ HORAS

1.ª PARTE

(Classico)

a) Preludio n.º 22 (x) (Sem palavras) — Côro mixto a capela   *J. S. Bach*
b) Preludio n.º 14 (x) (Sem palavras) — Côro mixto a capela   " " "
c) Fuga n.º. 21 (x) (Sem palavras) — Côro mixto a capela..   " " "

(Romantico)

a) Reverie (x) — Côro mixto a capela — (Vocalismo) ......   *Schumann*
b) Serenata (x) — Côro mixto a capela — (Vocalismo) .....   *Schubert*
   Letra de X X X
2 c) Ay-Ay-Ay (x) — Côro mixto a capela ....   *Popular Chileno*
   Letra — popular traduzida
d) Lamento (x) — (Sem palavras) — Côro mixto a capela... *Homero Barreto*
e) Iphigenia en Aulide (x) — Opera antiga — C. mixto a capela   *Gluck*

2.ª PARTE

(Folclóre infantil antigo, ambientedo)
a) Manquinha (x) — 1.ª audição ....   *Folclóre Brasileiro*
   Letra anonima
3 b) O Gato (x) — 1.ª audição ....,.............   "
c) Você diz que sabe tudo (x) — 1.ª adição ....   " "
   Letra anonima

a) Casinha pequenina (Folclóre ambientado) ....,.......   *L. Fernandez*
   Letra — Guimarães Passos
b) Jupira — Opera Nacional (côro interno) ....,.   *Francisco Braga*
c) O Ferreiro — Original ....,.........,..   *Barrôzo Netto*
   Letra — Paulo' Gustavo

a) Jaquibau (Folclóre ambientado) ....,..............   *H. Villa-lobos*
   Letra anonima
b) Bazrum — (Original) ....,...,.....,..   " " "
   Letra — Domingos Magárinos
c) Patria — (Civico-artistico) ....,..   " " "
   Letra — P. Haroldo

(x)   arranjo de H. V. L.

343

344

September 1967 it was renamed Instituto Villa-Lobos. Within the framework of SEMA activity Villa-Lobos organised a number of interesting concerts with unusual programmes, including works never before – or seldom – heard in Brazil. To secure support from all levels of society and thus have as diverse an audience as possible, Villa-Lobos remembered old friends who had helped him at the start of his career. He now turned to them once more. One letter preserved from that period (1937) is to his one-time sponsor Laurinda Santos Lobo in Rio de Janeiro, which refers to concerts at popular prices. In these concerts Villa-Lobos not only directed symphonic music but also choral compositions involving his choir of music teachers.

International recognition of Villa-Lobos as music educationalist came with an invitation to participate in

345

346   Excerpts from a letter – excerpts reproduced here with the writer's permission – from Walter Burle Marx to the author dated 3 May 1981. It offers an interesting insight into Villa-Lobos's method of composing and also hints at some revealing shortcomings in a very talented composer whose fertile source of ideas sometimes makes him too lazy to polish a work once it is finished.[16]

16) Luiz Heitor who is mentioned in this letter is Luiz Heitor Corrêa de Azevedo, the Brazilian musicologist.

```
                                        Caracas, Venezuela
                                           May 31, 1981
     Dear Lisa,
          Your letter of March 9th reached me delayed through various
     detours.
          IN answer to your questions:

          I don't know that a program of that world premiere was ever printed
     I remember that the program was in in early December, 1932, previous
     to my departure (Dec. 10) to Europe on the "Cap Arcona".  I recollect
     also that the concert was on a Saturday.  I visited him about two
     days before around 7 p.m. when he was living near the Central Police.
     I think they called the district Morro do Castelo.  Villa-Lobos had
     just finished dinner and the table was being cleared when I said:
     "V. L.,you promised me a work for my youth concert."  He answered:
     "I will have it ready on Friday morning at 4 a.m."  "And the parts?"
     I said, "My rehearsal starts at 9 a.m.:"  He continued, "I will do
     them myself and I have some friends who will help me."  I said,"Then
     I will let you alone:  He said, "You don't disturb me:"  He con-
     tinued at once orchestrating the work, writing in ink, and conversing
     with me.  IN the next room Viera Brandão, V-L tone poem, "Amazonas".
     From time to time V-L was shouting and/correcting,"G-flat in the bass:
     It was unbelievable, but I had the score and parts the next morning:
                                                was playing
          Luiz Heitor was my speaker at these youth concerts that I
     introduced in Brazil.  Since the premiere of the Caixinha de Boas
     Festas V.L. started to add to the score, losing some of its trans-
     parency.
          Very often I used to tell him what I thought of certain instru-
     mentation and also about his forms.  In the Caixinha for example,
     I told him that the last number was too short and ended too abruptly.
     And in order to tie this work together he should bring back some of
     the more important themes as or motives.  His answer was,"I'm not
     a classical composer and a modern composer would not use such a
     device."  To my surprise, I saw repeat sign at the end of the last
     number in the printed score.  He also added some additional instru-
     ments to the original ones.  This he may have done to cover weaknesse:
     of some local performers.  Also, it might have been a temptation to
     me employ certain new instruments in new passages, as he played all
     the instruments:
          A typical example of V-L temperament and way of thinking concern
     the Bachianas #5.  I did the U.S premiere in New York at the Worlds
     Fair on May 4th, 1939 with the New York Philharmonic and Bidú Sayão,
     using the manuscript of V-L.  Later on when I saw the manuscript
     again, there was a repeat sign in the first introductory measure in
     5/4.  I asked him why he did that and he replied that he felt that
     the introduction was too short.  I asked him why he didn't compose
     two different measures--he who had so much imagination--he smiled
     and said, "Para dizer a verdade, eu tive preguiça!" (To tell the trut
     I felt lazy!)  This was one of his faults; once a work was finished
     he very rarely went back to polish it, much less to change it.

                    For the present, um abraço do velho amigo,
                                                  Walter

         1530 Locust Street
         Apt. 3-F
         Philadelphia, Pa.  19102
         U.S.A.     Tel. (215)735-5953
```

346

Villa-Lobos in the 1930s   157

Another cup-, libation-, wine-bearer was our good friend the United States of Brazil. Under the leadership of Burle Marx, the brilliant conductor from Rio de Janeiro, its concert in the Music Hall at the Fair Grounds and succeeding broadcasts over WQXR presented, among other unfamiliar pieces, three of the improvisation-like compositions by Heitor Villa-Lobos, to which their prolific author has given the common name of Choros. They were numbers 7 and 8, for instrumental ensembles, and number 10 for voices with orchestra. Three of his curious fusions of Bach-style and folk style entitled *Bachianas Brasileiras*, were also played. These performances showed us the reason for Villa-Lobos's fame. (Hitherto his North American reputation largely had been a matter of hearsay.) They revealed an amazing involuntary force.

The abundance of his ideas was plain from the compositions (ideas, indeed, seemed to tumble into his works as from a cornucopia) as well as his not mean capacity for thematic development. Both were doubly striking in view of the fact that the pieces performed were selections from a body of work comprising almost a thousand compositions–selections which, for all their grandeur of proportion and

recency, are apparently quite representative of this enormous output. Evident too was the exuberance and the vitality of his rhythms and his gift for interweaving them. The hotly colored Choros No. 8 in more than a single mind excited comparisons with the earlier music of Stravinsky. "A *Sacre du Printemps* of the Amazon!" was the recurrent excited phrase. It was not at all unhappy. Together with enormous rhythmic vitality and intricacy this monumental piece, like other of Villa-Lobos's major compositions, has drive, primitive vehemence, earthly lyricism. If we do not immediately apply the term of "genius"–the meed of great involuntary forces–to its profoundly gifted author, it is merely for the reason that there persists in us the suspicion that his powers are not as yet the *perfect* match for the larger forms. The unreassuring aspect of both Choros 8 and Choros 10 is their opacity and turbidness, a consequence, possibly, of the composer's tendency–evinced equally by other compositions –towards lush and overelaborate instrumentation. Idiomatic as his orchestration is, and rich in color effects, unnecessary doublings of the orchestral voices oftentimes thicken it. Villa-Lobos is an autodidact–possibly the most talented since Musorgsky. Probably not only the pedants will be tempted to presume that it is from his lack of readily acquirable science that his clumsiness flows.

In the smaller forms, however, and in the instances wherein he has restricted himself to smaller, less multicolored ensembles–the first *Bachiana Brasileira* for eight 'celli is one of them–his musical instinct and fantasy seem infallible and at home. He has a gift for extracting orchestral effects from a few instruments. His harmonic progressions, which verge at times on vulgarity, are most distinguished in some of the small pieces played over the radio–the *Cirandas* for example. (These "Round Games" are arrangements and original harmonizations of popular Brazilian tunes. No. 7 beautifully exhibits a favorite, rich harmonic device. It consists in a sort of *glissando*, made up of abruptly sounded chords that slide suddenly into remotely related and sustained ones.) Noteworthy also is the circumstance that many of the more lucid and readily appealing of his longer pieces, Choros 7 and the *Bachianas Brasileiras* for example, are combinations of short movements. What alone diminishes one's enjoyment of certain of these most lyrical works are their occasional lapses from taste. We do not refer to the mixtures of music in the Bach style with music of New World folk color and

inspiration, presented to us by some of these works, fantastic though the mixtures may be. (The contrapuntal passages inspired in Villa-Lobos by his naïve enthusiasm for Bach are pervaded by a soft romantic glow, a drowsy luxuriant color, that both individualizes them and often renders them perfectly congruous with the music by which they are surrounded. Probably a desire to tweak solemn noses, as much as anything else, is at the base of the title *Bachianas Brasileiras*.) What we do refer to are phenomena of the sort of which the second *Bachiana* supplies an instance. It has its prelude, aria and dance, followed by the *toccatina* on the shuffling figure suggesting the rotation of wheels, "The Little Back-Country Train." This *Trenzinho do Caipira* is a gay bit of program music. But it is vulgar and altogether slighter in substance than the rich, deeply moved preceding sections. The mere circumstance that it broadly exploits the flutter-tongue device, which is intermittently used in the other movements, is not enough to tie all the sections together.

Invariably, none the less, Villa-Lobos casts that possibly most potent of the artist's spells, the one born of perfect spontaneity. Quantities of his compositions possess the characteristic Latin gaiety; no sort of strain makes itself felt in any of them. One is aware only of their author's enjoyment of his gifts and satisfaction in giving them free rein. The works set one perfectly at ease, as do all aesthetic expressions that bloom out of and satisfy entirely inner impulses. And a feeling new to music, indubitably an intimate feeling of the tropics (very different from Milhaud's), pierces through them. Sometimes it is a feeling of wild tanglewoods, fantastic vegetation and animal life, damp and drowsy heat. Momentarily we are in "the dank arboreal gloom", while, on the other hand, the *Trenzinho*– it is in love, the little thing, and merrily sings its music-hall ditty as it climbs–carries us among the coffee-plantations of the high tropics. In other instances, the feeling seems to comprehend the essence of a humanity without either intellectuality or constructive ability, but earthfast and still in possession of primitive passion, sweetness, and *joie de vivre*. Naturally, this feeling is in part the consequence of the composer's frequent use of barbaric melodies, rhythms, and sonorities, derived from the Negroes and Indians of Matto Grosso and the Amazon as well as from the masses of the larger cities. Still, it flows from music of his that is bare of ethnological associations and folk color: for example, from the chaste

Little Song" and the jovial fugue in the first *Bachiana Brasileira*. In other words, it is essential to him. The optimistic Villa-Lobos must thus be reckoned in the first rank of those composers of the two Americas–today in process of approaching one another–who, like Ives and Harris in the United States and Chavez in Mexico, are robust voices of their countries' lives.

the First International Congress for Musical Education in Prague in April 1936, organised by Leo Kestenberg. There Villa-Lobos gave a lecture, in French, describing his method.

Villa-Lobos composed less during his SEMA years because his time was taken up with administrative work, teaching and arranging music for choirs. Nevertheless, he did compose. He also fulfilled requests to provide works for special occasions, such as the *Caixinha de Boas Festas* which he wrote for the composer-conductor Walter Burle Marx and one of his children's concerts that he organised at the beginning of the 1930s with the Philharmonic Orchestra –which Burle Marx had also founded – in Rio de Janeiro.

Also Stravinsky could also do two things at the same time when making corrections on proofs of his compositions.[17]

A few months before the première of the *Caixinha de Boas Festas,* Burle Marx had given Villa-Lobos an opportunity to conduct two movements from his *Bachianas Brasileiras No. 1* composed in 1930, at the Sixth Concert of the Philharmonic Orchestra on 12 September 1932.

It was largely due to Burle Marx's efforts that the United States became better acquainted with Villa-Lobos's music during the late 1930s and the early 1940s. During the 1939 World's Fair in New York from 4 to 9 May, Burle Marx performed some of Villa-Lobos's music to which he also refers in the above-mentioned letter to the author. Paul Rosenfeld reviewed these concerts for *The Musical Quarterly* in New York.

The following year offered another more ample opportunity to perform Villa-Lobos's music in the United States. A Festival of Brazilian Music was held in New York's Museum of Modern Art in the autumn of 1940. The President of the Museum at the time was Nelson A. Rockefeller whom Franklin D. Roosevelt (1882-1945) had appointed Coordinator of Inter-American Commercial and Cultural Affairs and who, in the interest of the 'Good-Neighbor' policy, had promoted the Festival with the help of Armando Vidal, Brazilian General Commissioner at the World's Fair. Numerous prominent figures from Brazil and especially North America had supported and promoted these undertakings.

The Festival of Brazilian Music was held in

17) '…. The evenings which he (Stravinsky) liked to prolong very much served him mostly to correct proofs and do the instrumentation. For this type of work he needed no seclusion although it required careful attention. In these moments he developed an extraordinary gift to be able to do two things at the same time; while he was working he liked somebody to read aloud to him and he listened attentively. Only from time to time did he request silence for a minute; then a particularly exacting problem required his undivided attention...' (*Igor Stravinsky, Mensch und Künstler* by Théodore Stravinsky, B. Schott's Söhne, Mainz, n.d., p. 65)

347 *The Musical Quarterly,* Vol. XXV, No. 4, 1939.

348　Nelson A. Rockefeller (1909-1979) at a press conference in Rio de Janeiro in 1942 while he was Coordinator of Inter-American Commercial and Cultural Affairs.

349　Cândido Torquato Portinari's (1903-1962) *First Mass in Brazil*. The painting is in the main office building of the Banco Boa Vista in Rio de Janeiro.

348

349

18) He studied at the Escola Nacional de Bellas Artes (1918), spent some time in Europe (1928) and in 1936 began to paint murals, including one for the United Nations (War and Peace). Exhibited in Brazil and abroad. Abroad, he is the best-known Brazilian painter of the modern movement.

conjunction with an exhibition of paintings by Cândido Torquato Portinari (1903-1962), the Brazilian painter.[18]

Villa-Lobos was always lucky in life. Notwithstanding his own efforts there always appeared to be help from somewhere to assist him in realising his plans and dreams. He met his wife Lucília when he needed personal encouragement, a helpmate who understood his struggle to find his style, and his need for artistic recognition – she was also an interpreter of his music. The Brazilian government came to his support and granted him funds to spend a year in Europe in 1923-24. The Guinle brothers sponsored a three-and-a-half year stay in Europe (1927-1930) and financed the first publication of his works by Éditions Max Eschig. Returning to Brazil, he found in São Paulo understanding, support and backing from João Alberto Lins de Barros, the future governor of the state of São

FESTIVAL
OF
BRAZILIAN
MUSIC

SPONSORED BY THE COMMISSIONER-GENERAL FROM BRAZIL TO THE NEW YORK WORLD'S FAIR AND THE MUSEUM OF MODERN ART OCTOBER 16 TO 20, 1940 IN THE AUDITORIUM OF THE MUSEUM, 11 WEST 53 STREET, NEW YORK

350

350   Title page of the Festival programme.

351   Press release from The Museum of Modern Art, New York City, regarding the three concerts between 16 and 20 October 1940.

FOR RELEASE SATURDAY, OCTOBER 5, or
SUNDAY, OCTOBER 6, 1940.

NINE PREMIERES TO BE PRESENTED

ON FESTIVAL OF BRAZILIAN MUSIC PROGRAMS

The Festival of Brazilian Music at the Museum of Modern Art, 11 West 53 Street, from October 16 through October 20 will present nine premiere performances of works by contemporary Brazilian composers. The premieres are equally divided among the three programs of the Festival.

On the first program, October 16 evening and October 17 afternoon, will be presented three of the Villa-Lobos Choros not heard in this country before. These are Choros II for violin and cello; Choros IV   for three horns and trombone; and Choros VII for chamber orchestra. Burle Marx will conduct. This same program will also present Romeo Silva and his orchestra, Elsie Houston, Bernardo Segal and Candido Botelho in folk and contemporary Brazilian compositions.

A group of Folk Songs arranged for chorus and pianoforte by Luciano Gallet, and the Nonetto by Villa-Lobos will be presented for the first time in this country on the second program, October 18 evening and October 19 afternoon. They will be sung by members of the Schola Cantorum directed by Hugh Ross. On this program there will also be the first presentation here of a group of violin solos—Serenedade, Canto do Cysne Negro and Mariposa na Luz— by Villa-Lobos. They will be played by Pery Machado. Elsie Houston and Romeo Silva will appear again on this program.

The last program of the Festival, October 20 afternoon and evening, will be devoted entirely to the works of Villa-Lobos and will have first performances in North America of his piano solo, Rudeooema, which Artur Rubinstein will play and of his Bachiana Brazileira No. I for eight celli, and his arrangement of folk songs for chorus a cappella. Mr. Marx will conduct the Bachiana and Mr. Ross will direct members of the Schola Cantorum in the Folk Songs. On the program will also be the Aria from Villa-Lobos' Bachiana No. 5 for soprano and celli. It will be sung by Virginia Johnson..

351

Paulo, which facilitated his musical tours into the hinterland of that state. His work with massed choirs, his idea of giving schoolchildren a musical education and his proposals to organise popular concerts for adults in Rio de Janeiro all met with encouragement from Anísio Spinola Teixeira, who in 1932 was director of the Department of Education.

In the name of the (then) mayor Pedro Ernesto do Rego Batista (1886-1942), Teixeira created an entirely new post for Villa-Lobos as head of SEMA. Thus, for the first time in his life, the composer achieved financial security. And a few years later, as a result of the changing world situation arising from World War II which brought still closer ties between the United

ARTUR RUBINSTEIN, PIANIST
BURLE MARX, CONDUCTOR
HUGH ROSS, CONDUCTOR
VIRGINIA JOHNSON, SOPRANO
CANDIDO BOTELHO, TENOR
MEMBERS OF THE SCHOLA CANTORUM OF
NEW YORK
CONSTANTINE CALLINICOS, ACCOMPANIST
FOR MR. BOTELHO

PROGRAM 3
VILLA-LOBOS

SUNDAY AFTERNOON AND
SUNDAY EVENING, OCTOBER 20

Notes for this program will be found on pages 15 to 16

1. BACHIANA BRASILEIRA NO. 1 (for orchestra of eight celli)   Heitor Villa-Lobos
MR. MARX AND ORCHESTRA

2. FOLK SONGS (for chorus a cappella and tenor)   Heitor Villa-Lobos
A. O Ferreiro   B. Canção de Saudade   C. As Costureiras
MR. ROSS AND MEMBERS OF THE SCHOLA CANTORUM

D. Sertao no Estio   E. Teiru
MR. BOTELHO

F. Jaquibau
MR. ROSS, MR. BOTELHO, MEMBERS OF THE SCHOLA CANTORUM
ALTO OBBLIGATO, LORAINE ELEY; TENOR OBBLIGATO, ALLAN ADAIR

3. ARIA FROM BACHIANA NO. 5 (for soprano and celli)   Heitor Villa-Lobos
MR. MARX, MISS JOHNSON AND ORCHESTRA

4. PIANO SOLOS
A. Rudepôema   Heitor Villa-Lobos

TEN-MINUTE INTERMISSION

The correction occurs in the following section:

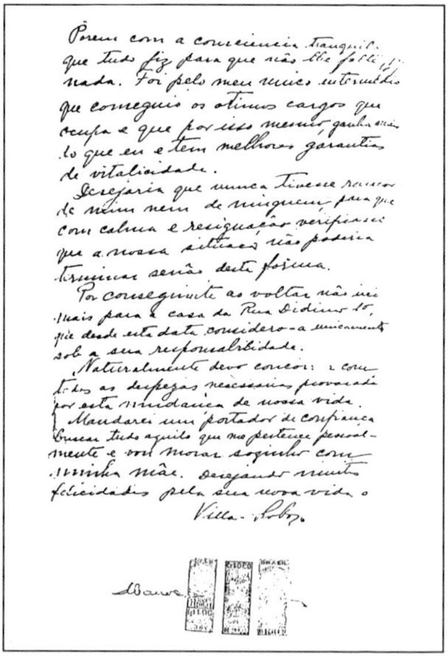

B. Prole do Bebê   Heitor Villa-Lobos
1. Branquinha
2. Moreninha
3. Bruxa
4. Negrinha
5. Caboclinha
6. Pobresinha
7. Polichinel

C. Alegria Na Horta (Impressions of a rural fiesta)   Heitor Villa-Lobos
MR. RUBINSTEIN

352

352 The third concert programme, entirely devoted to the works of Villa-Lobos.

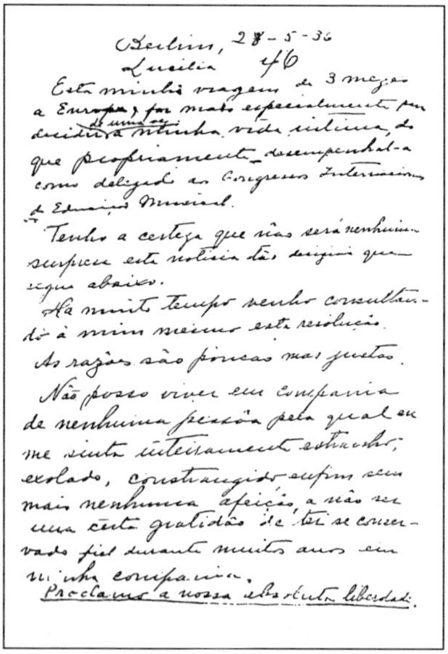

353 Letter from Villa-Lobos to Lucília, 28 May 1936.

Berlin, 28-5-36

Lucília

[handwritten letter in Portuguese]

353

354

355

354 Villa-Lobos in 1936, at the time when his private life was undergoing profound changes.

355 The composer, who had settled into his new home at Rua Araújo Pôrto Alegre 56, Apt. 54, is seen here with his Gaveau piano in 1937.

States and Brazil through Roosevelt's 'Good-Neighbor Policy', Villa-Lobos was offered an unexpected opportunity to win over American audiences as composer-conductor. Eventually these developments were to bring Villa-Lobos much hoped for artistic and financial success in the Americas and Europe.

When he was nearly fifty years old, however, in 1936, a crisis occurred in his life. Although professionally settled and financially secure, Villa-Lobos's private life was suddenly in turmoil. He had fallen in love, and his marriage was threatened. He revealed his intention to leave Lucília in a letter written in Berlin on his return trip from the First International Congress for Musical Education in Prague.

Lucília was a brave companion and a fine interpreter of Villa-Lobos's music during the composer's difficult and crucial years when he was becoming a composer of serious music, trying to develop his proper style and struggling for recognition. Villa-Lobos's marriage to Lucília had lasted about twenty-three years.

Arminda Neves d'Almeida (1912-1985), Villa-Lobos's new companion, was much younger than the composer. She had once been his student, and was to share the rest of the composer's life. She and Villa-Lobos were unable to marry, however, as Lucília outlived the composer by six-and-a-half years and divorce was not possible in Brazil until 1977. Much later Arminda changed her name legally to Arminda Villa-Lobos and was in effect the second Mrs Villa-Lobos. She became the organising mind behind the composer, helping to copy his works and dealing with his correspondence – after she had learned and mastered French and English of which she was ignorant when first they met – acting as his hostess and generally ministering to his needs.

Settled at Rua Araújo Pôrto Alegre

356

19) See detailed description in *Heitor Villa-Lobos, Leben und Werk des brasilianischen Komponisten* by Lisa M. Peppercorn, Zurich, 1972, pp. 213-217.

356 Manuel Araújo Pôrto Alegre (Barão de Santo Ângelo) (1806-1879), Brazilian diplomat, writer, architect and painter. Pioneer of the romantic movement in Brazil. At an early age he went to Rio de Janeiro from his home town São José do Rio Pardo and became a follower of Jean Baptiste Debret. In 1831 he went to Europe (Italy, Paris) for six years and returned again to Rio de Janeiro. Founder, in 1837, of the Conservatório Dramático and the Academia de Opera Lírica. A member of many institutions. From 1859 served as a diplomat abroad. On 9 May 1874 he was made a baron.

Villa-Lobos had now made his home in a modest three-room apartment, his last residence in Rio de Janeiro. It was downtown, in the Esplanada do Castello district, in a street named after Manuel de Araújo Pôrto Alegre.

Happily settled in his new home, Villa-Lobos began to compose a number of new works, each very different from the others. He began the year 1937 by writing religious music: the *Missa São Sebastião,* dedicated to Frei Pedro Sinzig, OFM.

Another work of that period, begun in 1936 though only finished in 1942, was the four suites entitled *Descobrimento do Brasil* whose individual movements are not all original compositions but partly rearrangements and instrumental arrangements of pieces composed previously.[19] Nevertheless the work is characteristic of Villa-Lobos. Whatever his musical ideas might be, he gave his compositions a specifically Brazilian flavour, if he so desired, either by writing pseudo-folk music or by adapting his style to the narrative on which his music is based. In the case of *Descobrimento do Brasil* a long description is provided to illustrate his intentions. The ideas are based principally on a letter written by Pero Vaz de Caminha to Manuel I, his King in Portugal, in which he describes his voyage, arrival and short stay in Brazil when he accompanied Pedro Álvares Cabral, the discoverer of Brazil.

The first performance of Villa-Lobos's *Bachianas Brasileiras No. 5* (first movement only), on 25 March 1939, in Rio de Janeiro, had far-reaching consequences. This piece (together with the second movement, premièred on 10 October 1947) was to become Villa-Lobos's best known composition throughout the world and was to contribute much to his international reputation. An opinion expressed, many years later, in 1952, by Irving Fine in *The Musical Quarterly,* when reviewing the piece, shows excellent judgement:

'Villa-Lobos's piece is too well known to need comment. Saved by its virtuosity, it barely escapes *café concert* material. That it succeeds in being something

VILLA-LOBOS: *Mass of Saint Sebastian,* for three voices, *a cappella.* Chorus of the University of California at Berkeley, cond. Werner Janssen 12" LP. Columbia ML 4516.

Villa-Lobos's *Mass of Saint Sebastian,* written in 1937, is a work of great religious fervor, composed with technical skill. It seems incredible that so great a number of diversified musical elements can be placed next to each other without making a jumble, or that they appear in good taste; but here they are united in a three-part counterpoint deriving its spirit (rather than its actual practices) from 16th-century vocal music. The music relates itself more to the Spanish and Portuguese composers of this period, with their humanly intense music, than to the less emotional Lassus and Palestrina.

Villa-Lobos has a great deal to say in his contribution to the notes on the "sleeve" about which parts belong more to the sacred style and which are more "Villalobian." Actually all of it sounds like sacred music, and all of it reflects the composer's unique ability to integrate primitive and folk elements with those of Renaissance counterpoint. Villa-Lobos really has a wide variety of styles rather than one. He has in many works borrowed materials from the Baroque and Classical periods as well as from modern French models, and he has been equally interested in Indian, Negro, and Portuguese tunes and rhythms. His way of putting these things together in a convincing unit is his music's most characteristic feature.

The choral writing in the Mass is most effective, and interestingly enough is made so by means employed by our own Sacred Harp singers—the doubling of all parts by men and women. The Mass is written as for three women's voices, but with instructions to double all parts an octave lower with men. The resulting interlocking parts make a richly-woven fabric of sound. The rhythm is usually very close to that of 16th-century music, except that there are some dramatic pauses and *sforzandi,* and some staccato passages in the Credo. Tonally there is great variety. It is mainly diatonic, but with some telling chromaticism; it gives the impression of being modal and uses all diatonic tetrachords freely, but does not employ the known modal cadences very often. It modulates from mode to mode, and from mode to key and back. It does not sound wandering, however, because one mode or key is usually confirmed before there is a change. Changes therefore come as surprises. Perfect intervals are preferred at cadences, and there are many ingenious approaches to them; here for example is the final cadence of the Kyrie:

All varieties of triads are used freely, including many diminished triads in root position, and some based on perfect fourths. Dissonant tones do not always resolve conjunctly.

The Credo (from which the words *Credo in unum Deum* have been omitted) is perhaps the most unusual movement. There is a long string of short sentences, each ending very definitely, and each different in style and character. Some are primitive-sounding (Villa-Lobos says the tunes are from the Macumbas—followers of fetishlike religions of Brazil). Some are like simple folk tunes, some are complex and chromatic. In one spot melodic tritones predominate while in another there is what appears to be a quotation from Puccini's *Vissi d'arte,* with the same block-chord harmonization. All very un-16th-century. The Sanctus is in conjunct modal motion with increasing chromatic passing tones, which develop still further in the Benedictus. In the Agnus Dei there is sudden accent, and there is a dramatic tone, leading to a gripping final cadence into an unexpected major triad.

The Mass throughout contains a moving quality, perhaps because it retains the high spirituality of Renaissance vocal music while employing the emotional powers of drama, discord, and chromaticism of Villa-Lobos's own times.

HENRY COWELL
358

357

357   Frei Pedro Sinzig OFM (1876-1952), who died during a trip to Germany but was buried in Brazil. Brazilian monk of German origin who arrived in Brazil, aged thirty, with other Franciscan monks. He encouraged and developed the use of music in the Brazilian Catholic liturgy, wrote a music dictionary, edited a review of sacred music and was responsible for encouraging music in general and church music in particular. He also translated and composed and was extremely active in Rio de Janeiro's musical life.

358   Henry Cowell's (1897-1965) review of a recording of the *Missa São Sebastião,* in *The Musical Quarterly,* Vol. XXXIX, April 1953.

359

360

more than a *tour de force* is a tribute to the composer's phenomenal musicality and overwhelming naturalness.' (*The Musical Quarterly*, Vol. XXXVIII, No 3, July 1952).

Ruth Valadares Corrêa who wrote the libretto for the first piece *Aria* (*Cantilena*) also sang at the première.

As ties between Brazil and the United States strengthened as a consequence of World War II, a

---

RESUMÉ HISTORIQUE

— 2 —

I — Periode de 1500 à 1579

Vasco da Gama venait de découvrir l'Inde par la voie maritime, en doublant la pointe méridionale de l'Afrique. Aussitôt après le retour du célèbre navigateur à Lisbonne, en 1499, le roi de Portugal, Dom Manuel le Fortuné, voulant s'assurer le commerce des épiceries de l'Orient, fit équiper une deuxième flotte plus nombreuse, dont il donna le commandement à Pedro Alvares Cabral.

Parti du Tage avec treize vaisseaux, le 9 Mars 1500, cet amiral aperçut les Canaries le 14 du même mois ; le 22, il passa devant les Iles du Cap Vert et poussa ensuite fort avant vers l'Ouest. Le 21 Avril, des indices annoncèrent aux marins portugais la proximité de la terre.

Dans l'après-midi du lendemain (22 Avril), la flotte arriva en vue d'une grande montagne inconnue, dont les contreforts se prolongeaient vers le Sud, et qui reçut le nom de Mont Paschoal. C'est ainsi que fut découvert le Brésil.

Le 23, la flotte se rapprocha de la côte et la longea lentement vers le Nord, à la recherche d'une rade où elle pût mouiller en sûreté. A dix lieues (1) environ plus haut, on trouva un port, où la flotte jeta l'ancre, et auquel Cabral donna le nom de Porto-Seguro (Port-Sûr), que conserve encore une localité voisine.

Le 26 Avril, dimanche de Quasimodo, l'amiral fit célébrer une messe sur un autel dressé dans un îlot du port. Le 1ᵉʳ Mai, une autre messe fut célébrée sur le continent, et à cette occasion Cabral, qui avait fait élever une grande croix de bois portant les armes de Dom Manuel, prit solennellement possession de la nouvelle contrée, au nom de la couronne de Portugal.

Le pays découvert reçut d'abord le nom d'Ile de Vera-Cruz (Vraie Croix), puis successivement ceux de Terre de Vera-Cruz et Terre de Santa-Cruz (Sainte-Croix) ; ce ne fut que plus tard qu'on lui donna le nom de *Brasil* (Brésil), qui lui est resté.

Le 2 Mai, Cabral expédia à Lisbonne un de ses vaisseaux, chargé de porter cette bonne nouvelle au roi de Portugal ; puis, avec le gros da sa flotte, il poursuivit sa route vers le Cap de Bonne Espérance, à destination de l'Inde.

(1) La lieue portugaise était d'environ 6.000 mètres.

Centro Industrial do Brasil

Aussitôt qu'il apprit cette découverte, Dom Manuel en donna connaissance à tous les souverains de l'Europe et résolut de faire explorer sa nouvelle possession. Vers le milieu de l'année 1501, une flotille portugaise visita le Brésil, depuis le Rio Grande do Norte jusqu'au littoral de l'Etat de São Paulo actuel ; elle se dirigea ensuite vers le Sud jusqu'au cap Santa Maria, donnant dans ce voyage à différentes localités des noms, dont la plupart sont encore conservés. Plusieurs autres expéditions se succédèrent, mais elles furent surtout équipées par des particuliers et n'eurent aucun résultat au point de vue du peuplement du pays ; leur seul but était de prendre de grands chargements de bois de Brésil, qui avait à cette époque une grande valeur mercantile. L'arbre qui le produit (*Casalpinia echinata*) était alors très abondant dans les forêts voisines du littoral.

361

362

359   The statue of São Sebastião, patron saint of the city of Rio de Janeiro, which stands on the Place Baden-Powell.

360   *Foundation of the city of São Sebastião do Rio de Janeiro,* painting by Rodolfo Amoedo.

361   Description of the voyage and arrival in Brazil from *Le Brésil, ses richesses naturelles, ses industries,* Waldemiro Potsch, Rio de Janeiro, 1908.

362   Pedro Álvares Cabral (1467 or 1468-1520), Portuguese navigator and discoverer of Brazil. He sighted the coast of South America on 22 April 1500 while sailing to India and claimed the territory for Manuel I, King of Portugal. The land was first called Vera Cruz, then Santa Cruz and finally Brazil after the red wood which was a valuable export commodity and which Europe up to that time, had imported from Asia. He sailed on 9 March 1500 with 1,500 men.

363   Pedro Álvares Cabral's fleet.

364   One of Cabral's vessels from his fleet of 13 ships.

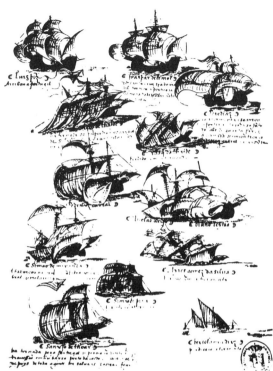

a esquadra de Cabral, tirado do Livro das Armadas. Academia de Ciências de Lisboa

363

364

365   *Cabral sees the coast of America* (Painting by Aurélio de Figueiredo).

366   Loading *Pau-Brasil* timber for export to Portugal.

367   As Jean de Léry remarked (op. cit.): 'The Indians walk around completely naked, adorning themselves only for ceremonies'.

368   *'Pau-Brasil'* tree from whose red wood the cross is made that marks the site of the first mass.

369   *Jequitibá* tree of whose wood the Cross for the First Mass in Brazil was made.

370   *Cascavel* (rattlesnake) which Villa-Lobos describes in the third piece of the Second Suite of *Descobrimento do Brasil*.

371   The first and last page of the letter which Pero Vaz de Caminha (1450-1500) wrote to Dom Manuel, King of Portugal (1469-1521).

365

366

367

jequitibá

368

369

370

371

372   Ruth Valadares Corrêa (*b.* 1904), Brazilian singer and teacher, studied at the Instituto Nacional de Música, gave concert performances in Rio de Janeiro, Buenos Aires, Montevideo and the United States. Taught at the Conservatório Nacional de Canto Orfeônico (today: Instituto Villa-Lobos) and at the Conservatório Brasileiro de Música, founded by Oscar Lorenzo Fernandez (1897-1948).

372

373

373   Villa-Lobos in full evening dress around 1940.

374   Nicolas Slonimsky (*b.* 1894), American lexicographer of Russian birth who came to the United States in 1923. Editor of *Baker's Biographical Dictionary of Musicians* and one-time editor of *The International Dictionary of Music and Musicians.*

375   Oscar Borgerth (*b.* 1906), Brazilian violinist. After studies in Rio de Janeiro, he was concert master in Rio de Janeiro with the orchestra of the Sociedade de Concêrtos Sinfônicos. Toured Europe, founded the Borgerth Trio with Tomás Terán (pianist), and Iberê Gomes Grosso (cellist). Subsequently concert master of the orchestra of the Teatro Municipal in Rio de Janeiro, and professor at the Escola de Música. Gave concert performances as a soloist with foreign orchestras. Premièred many compositions by Brazilian composers, who dedicated their works to him.

374

375

376   Albert Wolff (1884-1970), French conductor at the Paris Opéra (1922-24), chief of Concerts Lamoureux (1928) and Concerts Pasdeloup (1934).

376

377 *The New York Times,*
11 October 1942, paid
attention to Villa-Lobos's
latest compositions – *Chôros
Nos. 6, 9 and 11* – which
were given their first
performances in Rio de
Janeiro.

378 On both sides of the
spacious boulevard high-rise
buildings appeared in rapid
succession.

NEW VILLA-LOBOS WORKS

RIO DE JANEIRO.

A NUMBER of orchestral works by Villa-Lobos were recently presented for the first time, directed by the composer, at the Rio Municipal Theatre this Summer. The programs consisted of two orchestrations of piano works (Rudepoêma and Bachianas Brasileiras, No. 4), the Third Suite of the Descobrimento do Brasil (the First Suite was given in New York last year), Chôros, Nos. 6 and 9, and Chôros No. 11 for piano and orchestra. According to the programs the three Chôros were composed between 1926-29, but the musical style of Chôros Nos. 6 and 11, like the first number of the Third Suite, suggests that if these works were conceived at that time the actual writing must have been done recently.

The greatest success was achieved by Chôros No. 6, a piece that lasts thirty minutes. Despite polyrhythms, percussion and brass effects and other elements that have always prevailed in the Villa-Lobos music in which the Brazilian tendency dominates, Chôros No. 6 is conceived on a more universal basis. The work is inspired, profound and one of his best compositions to date. In the lyrical passages, which are very impressive, Villa-Lobos continues the style of some of the Bachianas Brasileiras. The structure is clear and

tight, the treatment of the subject-matter interesting and the orchestra, which includes some little known percussion instruments, said to be of Indian origin, is less overloaded than in other works of that kind.

Chôros No. 11, a work which takes more than an hour to perform, is not a piano concerto in the usual sense. The difficult piano part, played by the Brazilian pianist, José Vieira Brandão, is treated rather like an orchestral solo voice. Stylistically, the work is not unlike Chôros No. 6, but less balanced and very long. However, Chôros No. 11 is quite dramatic and impressive and has some highly inspired passages, including those where the piano is accompanied by the string section.

LISA M. PEPPERCORN.

377

378

number of American musical celebrities paid a visit to Brazil in 1940. They included Arturo Toscanini (1867-1957) with the NBC Symphony Orchestra and Leopold Stokowski with the All-American Youth Orchestra. Both gave concerts in Rio de Janeiro. At the same time the American lexicographer of Russian birth Nicolas Slonimsky, who at that time wrote music articles for *The Christian Science Monitor* in Boston, was on a trip through Latin America researching a book on the music of South America. He called, of course, on Villa-Lobos. Some time later, they exchanged a couple of letters. Villa-Lobos's letters to Nicolas Slonimsky date from 29 April 1940 and 6 February 1941. This last letter speaks of the difficulties, at the time of establishing dates for first performances of Villa-Lobos's works, as the composer kept no records. These difficulties have also been experienced by the present author.

379 A view of Copacabana with its twelve-storeyed residential properties and the much enlarged Avenida Atlantica providing improved facilities for the circulation of ever-increasing traffic.

380 An aerial view of Leme in the foreground and Sugar Loaf mountain in the background. On the left is Botafogo Bay.

379

380

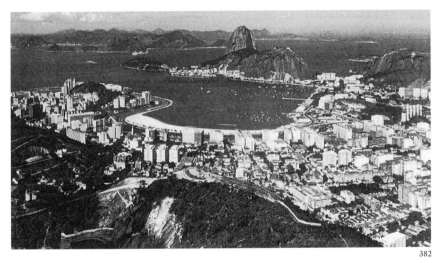

381 Downtown Rio de Janeiro in the early 1940s.

382 Flamengo Bay (*far left*) and Botafogo Bay (*in full view*) with the Sugar Loaf (*centre background*) and the open ocean. Skyscrapers, scattered at first, were gradually to take hold of the entire city.

A fresh encounter in Buenos Aires with the French conductor, Albert Wolff, a friend from Villa-Lobos's Paris days, and the prospect that he would conduct some concerts in Rio de Janeiro, including a composition by the Brazilian composer, made Villa-Lobos finally complete his previously unfinished composition *Fantasia de Movimentos Mixtos* which Wolff premièred in Rio de Janeiro on 23 April 1941, with Oscar Borgerth as soloist.

Meanwhile Rio de Janeiro had burgeoned into a mass of modern skyscrapers and had lost forever its once idyllic atmosphere by demolishing old buildings in all parts of the city, downtown and at the sea shore. In 1943 the Avenida Presidente Vargas, 200 metres in width, was opened.

Villa-Lobos's debut in the United States 1944-1945

With Villa-Lobos's music played at the New York's World Fair in 1939, his compositions performed at the Museum of Modern Art in New York in 1940, articles about his music published in *The New York Times*, visiting American scholars, composers and conductors calling on him in Rio de Janeiro, the 'Good-Neighbor' policy between the United States and Brazil under way, all these developments had prepared the way, ever since

383   Occidental College, Los Angeles, California, view towards Thorne Hall.

384   Érico Veríssimo (1905-1976), Brazilian novelist who spent most of his life in his home town Pôrto Alegre, writing and acting as editorial consultant to the Globo publishing house. He also taught at the University of Wisconsin and the University of California at Berkeley.

383

384

the beginning of World War II, for Villa-Lobos's eventual appearance in person in the United States. He seems to have received offers from various American orchestras and there were other orchestras too which he would have been happy to conduct, as is evident from a letter that he addressed to his old friend Serge Koussevitzky on 24 May 1944.

Villa-Lobos's first public appearance in the United States occurred in Los Angeles. On 21 November 1944 the Occidental College awarded him an honorary Doctorate in Law at the suggestion of Raymond G. McKelvey, Professor of Political Science at Occidental College and Executive Director of the Southern California Council. Walter E. Hartley, Professor of the Music Department, introduced him and the President of the College, Dr Remsen Bird, conferred the distinction.

As the composer spoke no English, Érico Veríssimo, the Brazilian writer, who happened to be in Los Angeles before returning to the University of California at Berkeley, where he was lecturing on Brazilian literature, acted as interpreter.

Villa-Lobos's first American appearance as composer-

385 Programme for Villa-Lobos's concert debut in the United States on 26 November 1944 in Los Angeles.

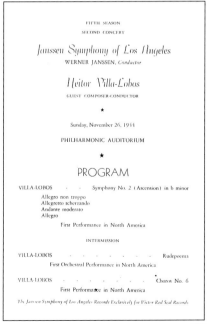

386

387

20) *Pacific Coast Musician,* Los Angeles, 2 December 1944.

386   Werner Janssen (1899-1990), American conductor, founded the Janssen Symphony of Los Angeles and guested with major orchestras in the United States and Europe.

387   Villa-Lobos (*left*) and Arminda Villa-Lobos (*centre*) with family members of the poet Raúl Bopp (1898-1984) during Villa-Lobos's first visit to the USA.

conductor was likewise scheduled for Los Angeles, on 26 November 1944, when he led the Janssen Symphony of Los Angeles which had been founded four years earlier by his friend Werner Janssen. The two had first met in Rio de Janeiro where Janssen had conducted a few concerts during World War II.

The audience showed little interest in Villa-Lobos's programme which the composer directed 'in the Philharmonic Auditorium before an audience that only partly filled the room, much smaller than the important standing of the South American composer might have been expected to draw'.[20]

At one of the innumerable receptions given for him on the West Coast, Villa-Lobos also met some old friends, the Brazilian diplomat and poet Raúl Bopp and his family.

Three weeks later Villa-Lobos was in New York City. His conversation with Olin Downes, music critic of *The New York Times,* was published and thus catapulted the Brazilian composer into the limelight. At the end of the conversation (see last paragraph of 388) Villa-Lobos emphasised that he had never written a 'pot-pourri of folk-melodies' and stressed his comprehensive study of Brazilian sources including history, customs and social background to equip and prepare himself to compose music with a Brazilian flavour.

A reception at the Waldorf Astoria, where the composer was staying, soon followed, attended by

HECTOR VILLA-LOBOS

Visiting Brazilian Composer Discusses Sources of Nationalism in Art

By OLIN DOWNES

VERY gradually, in the course of the last two decades, the music of Hector Villa-Lobos, the leading composer of Brazil and of South America, has become known in our concert halls. In a period of prevailing musical sterility it has served significantly to refresh our orchestral programs.

Today Mr. Villa-Lobos is in New York. Three weeks ago he made his first personal appearance as conductor in the United States in a program of his orchestral compositions, listed as first performances in this country, with the Werner Janssen Symphony of Los Angeles. The works performed were his Second symphony; his "Rudepoema" and Choros No. 6. On the 23d of February he will appear at the invitation of Dr. Koussevitzky with the Boston Symphony.

It is to be hoped that before he ends a visit which was not planned far in advance that an opportunity may be found for a program of Villa-Lobos' music in New York. They would merit some special attention, because, while we have not yet had an opportunity to make any near estimate of the value of his enormous production of music as a whole, there is no question that he is one of the greatest creative figures in the field of contemporaneous composition.

Enlightened Nationalist

As a composer Villa-Lobos, a man in his late fifties, with eyes that flash, and a singularly vigorous personality, is a nationalist, but not a patrioteer. "The distinction," he said, "is most important. Patriotism in music and capitalizing upon it, is very dangerous. You cannot produce great music in that way. You will have instead propaganda. But nationalism—power of the earth, the geographic and ethnographic influences that a composer cannot escape; the musical idioms and sentiment of a people and environment—these origins, in my opinion, are indispensable to a

you what I had done. If you don't like what I do, I'm going away. If you do like it, I shall remain for a time"—and would that some of our smart neophytes had had as much creative conviction.

"This imitativeness of so much art, especially of the most publicized aspects of foreign art, proceeds, I think, from an inferiority complex. It is a defensive mechanism, and of course becomes snobbery of the most sterile and destructive kind," said the composer.

Musical Insecurity

"It also proceeds, in a majority of cases, from musical insecurity. For very few musicians in South America, at least, are really well trained. Oh, yes, they are taught the rules, usually by accredited masters resident in the land or situated overseas. Where music is concerned a majority are taught paper rules. They are not taught to hear, or to heed the inalienable instinct of the ear for what is good and fresh and what is not. Only if you can trust your ear can you possibly become a real musician and composer; you must be able to express yourself instinctively in the language of music. The rest follows. Some of my friends seem surprised that I play a number of instruments. I play these instruments readily because I do not study them as matters of fingering and technic to be understood before the music is understood.

"In Brazil, at one time or another, most of us played in small bands, and had to change from instrument to instrument when we were short-handed. Usually I was 'cellist in the orchestra, but when we produced Strauss' 'Salome' in Rio de Janeiro I played interchangeably the 'cello and the third clarinet.

"In Los Angeles the men in the orchestra were nonplused by the technical requirements of my scoring. I assured them it could be done. A very fine oboist was in the orchestra who had played under me in Paris. He reassured the

vital and genuine art.

"So I say that race and environment must inhere in a composer's expression, and I see very little of that today—even in Brazil, where we are in one respect particularly fortunate. For standardized musical education and precedent are not well established in my country. Indeed, our people have a better chance, perhaps, than those farther north, to be themselves in their musical conceptions. But the disease of acceptance and domination by a foreign idea, a foreign tradition and theory of art, is, I believe, widespread.

"It is curious. We are people enamored of liberty, yet we are content to be slaves of musical conventions, slaves hardly aware of their abject obedience to rules which neither they nor their direct ancestors created.

Advice Given

"True, it is not easy for a composer to find his way. He is variously told that he is ignorant, an amateur, a dilettante, a lazy student who will not master his classwork; that he is deceiving himself about his own aims and talent. But I was always asked by the musical falsity I saw about me. The professors who could not write harmony, much less create it, but who passed on their dilettantism and their lack of a genuine musical perception to their pupils! Who looked up the textbook when they heard a new chord. Aha! It isn't here! That is not permissible! There is no possible growth of music with such men; no organic, fruitful development of the art where its development is fearfully suppressed, or in the classroom where they arbitrarily administer platitudes. What could be done with these people? And why were we, of a new world, incredibly rich in resources, in powers, in fresh spiritual horizons, if only we would lift our eyes to them—why were we so willing, as artists, so willing to sell our birthright, and to be liveried slaves?"

Here one recalled the statement of Mr. Villa-Lobos to certain colleagues in Paris, where he went in the early Twenties with his music. The supposition seemed to be that he had come to these self-appointed mentors as a student, or supplicant, with his talent. But that was their impression, it was quickly removed. "Did you think I came here," he said, "to absorb your ideas? I came here to show my

others. 'You may believe him,' he said. 'In Paris,' he said, 'they had great trouble until they did just what he told them. Ça va—don't worry.'"

In 1930 Villa-Lobos went to the head of the Brazilian Government. "You find it hard here to establish discipline among the people in our elections, don't you? I have a proposal. I can accomplish this discipline, and with it civic-social understanding and responsibility. I can accomplish by means of my art that which you cannot produce with your soldiers."

He was given permission to proceed. In four months he had a chorus of 12,000 voices from different centers, comprising among its elements the upper class, the military and the plain people. The 12,000 sang in four parts, a cappella. Came the revolution.

Villa-Lobos went to the Vargas Government, receiving again permission to proceed, and authority with the Prefectures of cities and other places to form his choral hosts and educate them. Now great choruses, with a repertory principally of the folk-kind, perform in all centers of Brazil on the 7th of September, which is Independence Day.

Ennobling Power

Mr. Villa-Lobos said that he did not believe in music as "culture," or "education," or even as a device for amusement or for quieting the nerves, but as something more potent, mystical and profound in its effect. Music has this power to communicate, to heal and to ennoble, when it is made a part of man's life and consciousness. We asked him if he used Brazilian folk-tunes as such in his music. He said never. "I compose in the folk-style, I utilize thematic idioms in my own way, and subject to my own development. An artist must do this. He must select and transmit the material given him by his people. To make a potpourri of folk-melody, and think that in this way music has been created, is hopeless. But it is only nature and humanity that can lead an artist to the truth. Do you think that as a composer I spend my time in technical exercises? I study the history, the country, the speech, the customs, the background of the people. I have always done this, and it is from these sources, spiritual as well as practical, that I have drawn my art."

388 *The New York Times* of 17 December 1944 published an interview with Villa-Lobos and the music critic Olin Downes.[21]

21) Olin Downes (1886-1955), American music critic and author. From 1924 music critic of *The New York Times*, lecturer at Boston University, Harvard and Brooklyn Academy of Music in New York. Villa-Lobos's Symphony No. 8, written in 1950, and premièred on 14/15/17 January 1955 in Philadelphia, with Villa-Lobos conducting, is dedicated to Downes.

389 Guests at the Waldorf Astoria Hotel reception included Aaron Copland (1900-1990), the American composer (*left*), seen here with Villa-Lobos (*centre*).

390 *From left to right:* Villa-Lobos, Henri Leiser (1899-1973) of New York's William Morris Agency and the composer's agent at the time of his American debut and Marion Anderson (1897-1993), the American singer who made her Metropolitan Opera House debut in 1935 and retired from her career in 1965. The Howard University, Washington DC conferred an honorary doctorate on her (1938).

391 Villa-Lobos with Jascha Heifetz (1901-1987), the American violinist of Russian origin.

389

390

391

distinguished figures from the musical world and other prominent personalities.

Soon other honours followed. The League of Composers invited Villa-Lobos to attend a chamber music concert of his works in which the celebrated Brazilian artist Olga Praguer Coelho took part, and a reception was held at the Museum of Modern Art to celebrate the composer.

Villa-Lobos's great opportunity came in early February when he was invited to conduct two of his works – *Chôros Nos. 8* and *9* – in New York as guest of the Philharmonic-Symphony Society, otherwise under the direction of Arthur Rodzinski. The programme notes to the concert by Louis Biancolli contain some interesting explanations of the native instruments used in both works.

A few days later, another opportunity presented itself. An old friend from his Paris days, Leopold Stokowski, invited Villa-Lobos to share a concert with him and conduct some of his works with the New York

The League of Composers
cordially invites you to attend
an evening in honor of
the celebrated Brazilian composer
HECTOR VILLA-LOBOS
at the Museum of Modern Art
11 West 53rd Street

Sunday Evening, January 28th
at eight thirty

A program of chamber music by
Mr. Villa-Lobos to be followed by
a reception in his honor

Assisting Artists
Olga Coelho, soprano   Jeanne Behrend, piano
The Albeneri Trio
Alexander Schneider, violin - - Benar Heifetz, cello
Erich Itor Kahn, pianist

As the space is limited, in case you are unable to accept this invitation kindly return it to the League of Composers 130 West 56th Street, New York
Kindly present this invitation at the door.
Admit Two.

392   The League of Composers' Invitation to attend a concert and reception at the Museum of Modern Art on 28 January 1945 in honour of Villa-Lobos.

392

At the Auditorium of
MUSEUM OF MODERN ART
11 West 53rd Street

Sunday Evening
January 28th, 1945
8:30 P. M.

THE LEAGUE OF COMPOSERS

Presents an Evening
In Honor of

HEITOR VILLA-LOBOS

Assisting Artists

OLGA COELHO, *Soprano*   JEANNE BEHREND, *Pianist*
CAROL LONGONE, *Pianist*

The Albaneri Trio

ALEXANDER SCHNEIDER, *Violin*   BENAR HEIFETZ, *Cello*
ERICH ITOR KAHN, *Pianist*

PROGRAM

TWO CHOROS (bis) for violin and 'cello
Moderé
Lent

ALEXANDER SCHNEIDER
BENAR HEIFETZ

GROUP of Piano Solos
The Three Maries
Alnitah
Alnilam
Mintika
Two Cirandas (folk-song)
"Senhora Dona Sancha"
"A Condessa"
Danza do Indio Branco

JEANNE BEHREND

GROUP of Songs
*Canção do Marinheiro
*Lundú da 'Marqueza de Santos
Modinha - Seresta No. 5
Serenata - Seresta No. 13
Canção do Carreiro
* First New York performance.

OLGA COELHO
At the piano CAROL LONGONE

SECOND TRIO for violin, cello and piano
Allegro moderato
Berceuse barcarolla-Andantino calmo
Scherzo - Allegro vivace spiritoso
Final - Molto allegro

ALEXANDER SCHNEIDER
BENAR HEIFETZ
ERICH ITOR KAHN

A reception to Mr. Villa-Lobos will follow the program, in the lounge.

Miss Behrend appears through the courtesy of Concert Bureau AACIM.

Office of the League of Composers
130 West 56th Street
New York City

Steinway Piano

393

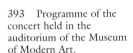

393 Programme of the concert held in the auditorium of the Museum of Modern Art.

394 Olga Praguer Coelho (*b.* 1909), Brazilian soprano, who specialised in a folk music repertoire. Debut in Rio de Janeiro (1928) followed by worldwide concert tours. She is a Brazilian artist of international fame and resided in New York.

394

City Symphony Orchestra on 12/13 February 1945. The concert was announced well in advance, on 6 January. However, the honorary degree from New York University mentioned in the article was only bestowed on Villa-Lobos many years later, on 3 December 1958.

About one week later, another friend from his Paris days, Serge Koussevitzky, offered Villa-Lobos the possibility of conducting his Boston Symphony

PHILHARMONIC-SYMPHONY SOCIETY
1842 OF NEW YORK 1878

CONSOLIDATED 1928

ARTUR RODZINSKI, Musical Director

| 1944 | ONE HUNDRED THIRD SEASON | 1945 |

CARNEGIE HALL

THURSDAY EVENING, FEBRUARY 8, 1945, AT 8:45
FRIDAY AFTERNOON, FEBRUARY 9, 1945, AT 2:30

4205th and 4206th Concerts

Under the Direction of

ARTUR RODZINSKI

Assisting Artist:
ZINO FRANCESCATTI, Violinist

PROGRAM

HAYDN   "Toy" Symphony
    I. Allegro
    II. Minuet
    III. Finale

VILLA-LOBOS   (a) Choros No. 8, for Orchestra
                        and Two Pianos
RAOUL SPIVAK and IGNACE STRASFOGEL, Pianists
(First performance by the Society)
             (b) Choros No. 9, for Orchestra
(First performance in North America)

Conducted by the Composer

INTERMISSION

PAGANINI   Concerto for Violin and Orchestra
                        in D major, Opus 6
    I. Allegro maestoso
    II. Adagio
    III. Rondo: Allegro spiritoso
          ZINO FRANCESCATTI

LISZT   "Mephisto Waltz"

ARTHUR JUDSON, Manager   **BRUNO ZIRATO, Associate Manager**
THE STEINWAY is the Official Piano of The Philharmonic-Symphony Society
———— COLUMBIA AND VICTOR RECORDS ————
ORCHESTRA PENSION FUND—*It is requested that subscribers who are unable to use their tickets kindly return them to the Philharmonic-Symphony Offices, 113 W. 57th or to the Box Office, Carnegie Hall, at their choice either to be sold for the benefit of the Orchestra Pension Fund, or given to the uniformed men through the local organizations instituted for this purpose. All tickets received will be acknowledged.*

"Buy War Bonds and Stamps" .

These concerts will end on Thursday at approximately 10:40 p.m., and on Friday at approximately 4:25 p.m.

395

395 Programme of concert by the New York Philharmonic-Symphony Society on 8/9 February 1945.

"Choros" Nos. 8 and 9 call for a huge assortment of native percussion instruments. Among them are the *reco-reco* (notched stick); the *chocalho* (a rattle made by natives either with gourd seeds inside, or with strung and netted gourd seeds on the outside; in' this performance metal and wooden rattles filled with stones will be used); the *pios* (used only in No. 9), a thin wooden stick producing a whistling sound when rubbed with a piece of folded cloth; the *puita* ("small animal roar"), described by ·John N. Burk, Boston Symphony annotator, as "a tin cylinder about 15 inches deep and 10 inches in diameter with a drum-head on one end and a gut string rubbed with rosin which extends from the center of the drum-head through the cylinder—it is played by tightly pulling the hand over the strings; the *matraca* ⟨ratchet⟩, the *caxambu*, a glass bottle filled with gravel; and the *camisao grande* and *camisao pequeno* (literally "large shirt" and "little shirt," terms used for box-like drums struck with the hand). In this performance a big snare-drum will replace the *caxambu*, as well as the *camisao grande* and *camisao pequeno*, which are used only in "Choros No. 9." Three additional native drums are called for in "Choros No. 9"—the *tartaruga*, the *tambor surdo* (muted drum) and the *tambourine de samba*. The snare-drum will be substituted for the first two, and a tambourine without jingles for the third.

396

HEITOR VILLA-LOBOS WILL CONDUCT HERE

Brazilian Composer Is to Join Stokowski in Programs at City Center Feb. 12, 13

Heitor Villa-Lobos, South America's most famous composer and conductor, will make his first personal appearance in New York next month, when he will lead the New York City Symphony at the City Center of Music and Drama, it was learned yesterday. Mr. Villa-Lobos, who is visiting this country for the first time on a semi-official tour, will direct the orchestra on Monday evening, Feb. 12, and Tuesday afternoon, Feb. 13, sharing the podium with Leopold Stokowski, the orchestra's permanent conductor.

Though details of the program have not yet been announced, it was revealed that Mr. Villa-Lobos will direct the orchestra during half of each concert, playing some of his works that have not been heard before in this country.

Besides his appearances with the City Symphony the Brazilian composer will direct several radio concerts for the Columbia Broadcasting System and will appear as guest conductor of the Boston Symphony Orchestra on Feb. 23 at the invitation of Dr. Serge Koussevitzky. He also is having discussions with music educators and Government officials here and is expected to receive an honorary degree from New York University.

Mr. Villa-Lobos, who is an official of the Department of Education of the Brazilian Government, arrived in this country early last month and made his first appearance in the United States with the Janssen Symphony of Los Angeles. He is expected to remain here until the end of February, when official duties will necessitate his return to his native country.

397

396 Extract from the programme notes explaining the nature of the Brazilian native instruments.

397 Announcement of the programme in *The New York Times*, 6 January 1945.

Orchestra. This was in response to Villa-Lobos's inquiry made on 24 May 1944. Villa-Lobos presented the programme three times. First, at the Sanders Theatre, Harvard University, Cambridge, Mass., scheduled as the fifth concert of that series, and again on 23 and 24 February 1945 as the seventeenth programme in Boston.

Villa-Lobos's *Chôros No. 12* which bears the

VILLA-LOBOS GUEST AT THE CITY CENTER

Shares Baton With Stokowski —Latter Conducts Orchestra in Beethoven 'Pastoral'

By OLIN DOWNES

Heitor Villa-Lobos was the guest of Leopold Stokowski and the New York Symphony Orchestra last night in the City Center, conducting the performances of two of his own works. Mr. Stokowski's half of the program included his interpretations of Henry Cowell's "Fanfare for the Forces of Our Latin-American Allies" and that of the Beethoven "Pastoral" Symphony.

This account of the occasion must begin with the bearing of the symphony. The performance was one of much beauty and prevailingly fine proportion. There was an occasional over-accentuation, a phrasing too studied, or a tempo a little livelier than is customary. But this was amply within the bounds of the legitimate conception of a remarkable conductor, and by the same token there were places that Mr. Stokowski gave uncommon significance. Not the least of these was the music of thanksgiving after the storm. His tempest was dramatic and not overdone. Nor, for a moment, did the long symphony fail to engross the audience. The beauty of the orchestral tone was striking, and it may be said at once that in the difficult and unusually scored compositions of Villa-Lobos the players also comported themselves brilliantly.

Villa Lobos' symphonic poem, "Uirapuru," was heard for the first time in North America. It is a highly imaginative and fascinating score, brilliantly colored. The Uirapuru is the bird of love, sought by a band of hunters. With the appearance of an Indian maiden he turns into a beautiful youth, but is transfixed by the arrow of an envious watcher. Slain, he becomes again a bird, whose song haunts the forest.

The program is enough for the composer to portray Brazilian nature and its colors and sounds; to intersperse these passages with the music of savage dances, the flute-calls of the Uirapuru's enemy, and outbursts of sensuous song. There are superb pages, pages not merely photographic, or ventriloquistic, but of a genuine and highly individual impressionism. It was once said of Rimsky-Korsakoff's orchestration that his coloring was so sensuous that one not only heard, but tasted the instrumental tone. It may be said of Villa-Lobos' scoring that in places one scents as well as hears the forest, sees the play of light, is aware of the tropical night and its strange enchantment.

Not all the pages are of equal distinction, and if one sought for "sonata form" he would not find it here. He might detect measures not imitated but assimilated from composers whose idioms had come near the kind of expression desired by Villa-Lobos. As a whole it is richly creative writing. The living stuff of music is in it.

The Seventh of the Bachianas Brasilieras completed the concert. It is a suite in four movements, a kind of "Homage" to the universal spirit, as Villa-Lobos puts it, of the great Bach, as that spirit is reflected in the consciousness of a Brazilian artist, and the nature of the Brazilian land. There is a certain naiveté in the music. It has its disproportions; the idioms are those of Brazilian and Latin-American folk-music. The counterpoint of rhythmic as well as linear. Some of the movements are too long; some of them astonishingly popular for the Bach idea. All of them are real, living, sincere and produced by impulsion from within. Mr. Villa-Lobos conducted with admirable simplicity and authority and the orchestra responded in kind.

398

composition date 1929, was given its first performance at the Boston concert. It is questionable if it was written in that year, because Villa-Lobos used to première all his works shortly after they were composed. It must be assumed, therefore, that though some sketches or ideas may date from 1929, it was written much later, and presumably only completed for the above performance to take advantage of a world première with the Boston Symphony Orchestra.

Villa-Lobos's contact with Serge Koussevitzky did not end with the Boston concert. The American conductor included Villa-Lobos's *Rudepoéma* –

399 Programme of the concert at Cambridge, Mass.

400 Villa-Lobos (*right*) in the company of Serge Koussevitzky and Arminda Villa-Lobos in Boston.

401 Serge Koussevitzky (1874-1951), American conductor of Russian birth.

402 Iberê Gomes Grosso (1905-1983), Brazilian cellist who studied with his uncle, Alfredo Gomes, and Pablo Casals (1876-1973). He was an orchestral and chamber music player and teacher. Gave concert performances in Europe and the Americas.

Sanders Theatre · *Harvard University* · Cambridge

Boston Symphony Orchestra

SIXTY-FOURTH SEASON, 1944–1945

SERGE KOUSSEVITZKY, *Conductor*

FIFTH CONCERT

WEDNESDAY EVENING, FEBRUARY 21

Programme

HEITOR VILLA-LOBOS *Conducting*

VILLA-LOBOS....Two Movements from "Bachianas Brasileiras" No. 7
   Toccata ("Desafio" – "Challenge")
   Fugue ("Conversa" – "Conversation")

VILLA-LOBOS.......................................Chôros No. 12
      (*First performance*)

INTERMISSION

VILLA-LOBOS .... Rudepoêma

BALDWIN PIANO

399

400

401   402   403

403 Eleazar de Carvalho
(1912 - 1996), Brazilian
conductor and composer. At
an early age he came to Rio
de Janeiro from his native
Fortaleza in the state of
Ceará. Played the tuba in the
band of the marines. In 1941
he became assistant
conductor of the Orquestra
Sinfônica Brasileira in Rio de
Janeiro. Continued his
studies at Tanglewood in
1946 with Koussevitzky who
sponsored him
internationally. Conductor of
major orchestras in the
United States, Europe and
since 1963 conductor of the
St Louis Symphony
Orchestra. Considered the
best known Brazilian
conductor at the time.
Premièred Villa-Lobos's
Bachianas Brasileiras No. 9
on 17 November 1948 in
Rio de Janeiro and the *Piano
Concerto No. 3* with Arnaldo
Estrella in the Teatro
Municipal in Rio de Janeiro
on 24 August 1957.

404 Programme of the first
American performance of
Madona.

Tenth Program

FRIDAY AFTERNOON, December 26, *at* 2:30 *o'clock*

SATURDAY EVENING, December 27, *at* 8:30 *o'clock*

ELEAZAR DE CARVALHO *Conducting*

GUARNIERI . . . . Prologo e Fuga
            (First performance)

VILLA-LOBOS . . . . "Madona," Symphonic Poem
            (First performance)

DE FALLA . . . . Suite from "El Amor Brujo,"
                                                    "Love, the Sorcerer"
Introduction and Scene — The Gypsies (Evening) — The Homecomer
— Dance of Terror — The Magic Circle (Narrative of the Fisherman)
— Midnight (Sorceries) — Ritual Dance of Fire (To dispel Evil
Spirits) — Pantomime — Dance of the Game of Love — Finale
(Morning Chimes).

INTERMISSION

DVOŘÁK . . . . Symphony No. 5, in E minor, "From the
                                        New World," *Op.* 95
    I.   Adagio; Allegro molto
    II. Larghetto
    III. Scherzo: Molto vivace
    IV. Allegro con fuoco

BALDWIN PIANO   VICTOR RECORDS

[521]

404

Villa-Lobos's debut in the United States 1944-1945   185

405

405 Natalie Koussevitzky, born Ouchkoff (1882-1942), American of Russian origin, first wife of Serge Koussevitzky. Educated in Moscow and Paris. Met Serge Koussevitzky in 1900 in Moscow and married him on 8 September 1905. She was a talented sculptress. Her busts include one of Jean Sibelius (1865-1957) and another of Serge Koussevitzky which are both in Symphony Hall, Boston. In 1942 the Koussevitzky Music Foundation established in her memory commissioned works by composers of all nationalities (courtesy Olga Koussevitzky).[22]

22) Olga Koussevitzky (*b.* Naumow, 1901-1978) whom Serge Koussevitzky married on 15 August 1947 was the niece of Natalie Koussevitzky. On her husband's death in 1951 she succeeded him as President of the Koussevitzky Music Foundation which was established in memory of his first wife, Natalie. A member of the United States Commission to UNESCO, she also held numerous other posts.

presented by Villa-Lobos in Boston during his visit to that city in February – in a concert given at New York's Carnegie Hall by the Boston Symphony Orchestra under his baton on 14 March 1945. To show his gratitude, Villa-Lobos dedicated his *Fantasia for Cello and Orchestra*, written in 1945, to Serge Koussevitzky. It was premièred in Rio de Janeiro (8 October 1946) with Iberê Gomes Grosso (1905-1983) as soloist under the composer's direction.

In May 1946 Villa-Lobos once more approached his friend Serge Koussevitzky, this time on behalf of a young Brazilian conductor, Eleazar de Carvalho, whom he was trying to help.

He wrote to Koussevitzky on 13 May 1946 and cabled on 4 July 1946 to which Koussevitzky replied on 5 July 1946. An undated letter from Villa-Lobos to Koussevitzky ended the correspondence in that year.

Under Koussevitzky's guidance Carvalho made a career for himself and it was he – not Villa-Lobos – who conducted the Boston Symphony Orchestra the following year, on 26 and 27 December 1947, presenting amongst other works, Villa-Lobos's *Madona*, a symphonic poem, erroneously announced as first performance instead of first US performance. The world première had already taken place in Rio de Janeiro the previous year, on 8 October 1946, with the Municipal Orchestra under the direction of the composer.

Villa-Lobos had previously sounded out Koussevitzky in a letter dated 27 June 1947 as to whether another opportunity would be presented to him to conduct the Boston Symphony Orchestra, as the composer intended to be back in the United States from December 1947 until April 1948. However, Koussevitzky decided to give Carvalho the chance to conduct instead.

Madona was commissioned by the Serge Koussevitzky Music Foundation in the Library of Congress. The score, written in December 1945, is dedicated to the memory of Natalie Koussevitzky, first wife of Serge Koussevitzky.

The last available evidence of Villa-Lobos's relationship with Koussevitzky's Boston Symphony Orchestra was a commission sent him on 29 October 1954, three years after Koussevitzky's death, inviting Villa-Lobos – together with a number of other leading composers from the United States, South America and

Boston Symphony Orchestra
CHARLES MUNCH, *Music Director*
THOMAS D. PERRY, JR., *Manager*
G. W. RECTOR *and* N. B. SHIRK, *Assistant Managers*
SYMPHONY HALL, BOSTON 15, MASSACHUSETTS

October 29, 1954

Mr. Heitor Villa-Lobos
Villa-Lobos Music Corporation
221 West 47th Street
New York, New York

Dear Mr. Villa-Lobos:

The Boston Symphony Orchestra will observe its 75th Anniversary during the season 1955-56. To celebrate the occasion, the Serge Koussevitzky Music Foundation in the Library of Congress and the Boston Symphony Orchestra jointly are inviting a number of the leading composers of the United States, Europe and South America to accept commissions to compose works for the Orchestra. The Foundation and the Orchestra wish to invite you to accept one of these commissions to take part in the celebration.

The conditions of the commission are outlined on the attached sheet. If you accept, please sign the enclosed copy of this letter and return it to the Boston Symphony Orchestra, Symphony Hall, Boston 15, Mass. by December 1, 1954. Upon receipt of your acceptance, the initial check of $1,000 will be sent you. Your acceptance of the commission implies acceptance of the conditions on the attached sheet.

The Foundation and the Orchestra will be much honored if you are free to undertake this work which we believe will constitute an important addition to the contemporary orchestral repertoire.

Faithfully yours,

For the Boston Symphony
Orchestra:

CHARLES MUNCH, Music Director

HENRY B. CABOT, President

For the Serge Koussevitzky
Music Foundation in the
Library of Congress:

MRS. SERGE KOUSSEVITZKY
Chairman, Advisory Board

I accept this commission:

HEITOR VILLA-LOBOS   Date: *November 29th, 1954*

406

406   Facsimile of the Boston Symphony Orchestras's invitation to Villa-Lobos, 29 October 1954.

Europe – to compose works to celebrate the seventy-fifth anniversary of the Boston Symphony Orchestra.

Villa-Lobos accepted and composed *Symphony No. 11*. The première took place in 1956.

Returning to events in 1945, after the Boston engagement, on 24 February, Villa-Lobos had another concert scheduled, at the University of Chicago in the Composers Concert Series. There Remi Gassmann, the director, had devoted the third concert exclusively to the music of the Brazilian composer. The performance took place at Leon Mandel Assembly Hall on 27 February 1945.

Upon his return to Brazil, Villa-Lobos learned of the death, on 25 February 1945, of Mário Raúl de Morais Andrade, the great advocate of his music and an eminent pioneer who exercised an important influence on the younger generation. The loss of this prominent figure in Brazilian intellectual circles and the approaching end of World War II brought a marked

Seventeenth Program

FRIDAY AFTERNOON, MARCH 2, at 2:15 o'clock

SATURDAY EVENING, MARCH 3, at 8:30 o'clock

TCHAIKOVSKY..............."Romeo and Juliet," Overture-Fantasia

VILLA-LOBOS.................................Symphony No. 11
    I.   Allegro moderato
    II. Largo
    III. Scherzo: molto vivace
    IV. Molto allegro
    (Composed for the 75th anniversary of the Boston Symphony Orchestra;
                      First Performance)
    CONDUCTED BY THE COMPOSER

INTERMISSION

BEETHOVEN..............Piano Concerto No. 4, in G major, Op. 58
    I.   Allegro moderato
    II. Andante con moto
    III. Rondo vivace

SOLOIST
EUGENE ISTOMIN
Mr. ISTOMIN uses the Steinway Piano

These concerts will end about 4:00 o'clock on Friday Afternoon;
10:15 o'clock on Saturday Evening.

BALDWIN PIANO   RCA VICTOR RECORDS

407

407 Programme of the concert by the Boston Symphony Orchestra on 2/3 March 1956 in Boston.

turning away – in Brazil – from folk themes and Brazilian source material and a leaning towards universalism, human and social topics. This also had its repercussions for Villa-Lobos and his choice of themes for compositions. He no longer wrote *Bachianas Brasileiras* nor *Chôros* but gave many of his works the traditional titles used in chamber and orchestral music, especially when he was preparing works that had been commissioned. With this in mind and pleased and grateful for the reception and success accorded him during his three-month stay in the United States, Villa-Lobos decided upon his return to Rio de Janeiro to found a Brazilian Academy of Music. This was inaugurated on 14 July 1945. It consists of forty members, twenty members each drawn from performers and corresponding members. The opening session was duly celebrated.

At some later date, the Academy gave a reception in honour of Arthur Rubinstein, a corresponding

Music: New Symphony

Villa-Lobos' Eleventh Has Premiere Here

BOSTON SYMPHONY ORCHESTRA,
Charles Munch conducting. At Carnegie
Hall.
Romeo and Juliet Overture..Tchaikovsky
Symphony No. 11 (first New York
performance) ...., Villa-Lobos
Symphony No. 7 ....Beethoven

By HOWARD TAUBMAN

HEITOR VILLA - LOBOS, Brazil's best-known man of music, may well be the most prolific composer alive. His total output must be close to 2,000 pieces, and it is not surprising that his latest symphony, introduced to New York at Carnegie Hall last night, is his eleventh. Presumably there are ten predecessors, though one cannot recall hearing any of them in many years.

•

The Eleventh was played last night by the Boston Symphony under Charles Munch. This symphony is one of fifteen scores commissioned jointly by the Koussevitzky Music Foundation and the Boston Symphony in observance of the orchestra's current seventy-fifth season. Seven of these pieces have now been heard in New York, and the others should be along next season.

The Villa-Lobos work is marked by its energy and luxuriant use of orchestral colors. The composer pitches in with enthusiasm and the expertness of a man who knows he can make use of the full orchestral apparatus. He is good at building up climaxes, and he knows how to bring a movement to an end decisively. In fact, a couple of the four movements close so precipitately that you wonder if the composer did not exclaim suddenly, "Enough of this movement, on to the next!"

Mr. Villa-Lobos once said, "I do not walk in company with routine." This symphony is clearly an effort at individual expression. But the uncomfortable fact must be recorded that its essential material is superficial, even banal, suitable for some popular medium, not for a symphony. Mr. Villa-Lobos' scoring generates sufficient excitement to make one forget that the work does not add up to much of a communication.

Mr. Villa-Lobos paid the Boston Symphony the compliment of providing all of its sections, and many of its soloists, with opportunities to show their virtuosity. They played the piece with brilliance under Mr. Munch's rousing direction.

•

The evening began with a dramatic reading of Tchaikovsky's "Romeo and Juliet" Overture-Fantasy. Mr. Munch, an intense man, poured a lot of feeling into this product of late romanticism. He and his orchestra ended the evening with a solid work, Beethoven's Seventh Symphony, whose Dionysian moods they know how to convey.

Heitor Villa-Lobos

408   *The New York Times,* 22 March 1956, reviewed a repeat performance of *Symphony No. 11* with the Boston Symphony Orchestra under Charles Munch's (1891-1968) direction in New York's Carnegie Hall on 21 March 1956.

408

The University of Chicago
The Department of Music

COMPOSERS CONCERTS

REMI GASSMANN, *Director*
1944–1945

THIRD PROGRAM

MUSIC BY HEITOR VILLA-LOBOS

LEON MANDEL ASSEMBLY HALL
TUESDAY, FEBRUARY 27, 1945 · 8:30 P.M.

MUSIC BY HEITOR VILLA-LOBOS

HEITOR VILLA-LOBOS, *Composer-Conductor*
JOHN WEICHER, *Violin*
DUDLEY POWERS, *Violoncello*
PERRY O'NEIL, *Piano*
CECIL LEESON, *Mus 2/c Saxophone*
INSTRUMENTALISTS FROM THE CHICAGO SYMPHONY ORCHESTRA:
HARVEY NOACK, *Flute*   JOSEPH VITO, *Harp*
ROBERT LINDEMANN, *Clarinet*   CLARKE KESSLER, *Celesta and Bassoon*
FLORIAN MUELLER, *Oboe*
JENSKA SLEBOS, RICHARD WAGNER, THEODORE RATZER, RICHARD BEIDEL, NICOLAI ZEDELER, RUSSELL HENDRICKSON, ALOIS TRNKA, *Violoncelli*
ENSEMBLE OF WOMEN'S VOICES FROM THE UNIVERSITY OF CHICAGO CHOIR, GERHARD SCHROTH, *Director*

PROGRAM

Quatuor, for harp, celesta, flute, and alto saxophone, with chorus of women's voices (1921)
Allegro con moto.
Andantino (calme).
Allegro deciso.

Bachianas Brasileiras No. 1, for orchestra of violoncelli (1930)
Introdução (Embolada): Animado.
Preludio (Modinha): Andante.
Fuga (Conversa): Un poco animado.

INTERMISSION OF TEN MINUTES

Trio No. 3, for violin, violoncello, and piano (1918)
Allegro con moto.
Assai moderato.
Allegretto spirtuoso.
Allegro animato.

Chôros No. 7, septet for flute, oboe, clarinet, alto saxophone, bassoon, violin, and violoncello (1924)

409

410

409   Programme for Chicago University Concert, 27 February 1945.

410   *Left to right:* José Cândido de Andrade Muricy (1895-1984), João Itiberê da Cunha,[23] a representative of the government, Villa-Lobos, two unknown persons, Oscar Lorenzo Fernandez,[24] Luiz Heitor Corrêa de Azevedo.[25]

23) João Itiberê da Cunha (1869-1953), Brazilian diplomat and music critic. His articles appeared in the *Correio da Manhã* under the initials JIC.

24) Oscar Lorenzo Fernandez (1897-1948), eminent Brazilian composer, poet and teacher. Founded in 1936 the Conservatório Brasileiro de Música and was its first director. In 1938 represented Brazil at the quatercentenary of Bogotá, Colombia.

25) Luiz Heitor Corrêa de Azevedo, Brazilian musicologist who was librarian of the Instituto Nacional de Música (1932) where he edited the *Revista Brasileira de Música* (1934-

1942) and founded the Chair of Musical Folklore in 1939. He was consultant to the Music Division of the Pan American Union, Washington, DC (1941). From 1947 until retirement, he held an important position with UNESCO in Paris. He is the author of many scholarly books and contributor to music journals and dictionaries.

member, who was once Villa-Lobos's principal sponsor at the start of his career. The celebration took place in the Auditorium of the Ministry of Education.

The year 1945, which signalled the end of World War II and brought Villa-Lobos unexpected public success in the United States and Brazil, held yet another honour in store for the composer that summer: a commission from the Elizabeth Sprague Coolidge Foundation[26] at the Library of Congress, Washington DC.

Villa-Lobos responded with a *Trio for violin, viola and cello* and sent it, together with the parts, before 1 October 1945, to be ready for the performance by the

26) Elizabeth Sprague Coolidge (1864-1953), patroness of music who, in 1925, established the Elizabeth Sprague Coolidge Foundation at the Library of Congress which organises festivals of chamber music and offers commissions to composers.

THE LIBRARY OF CONGRESS

THE ELIZABETH SPRAGUE COOLIDGE FOUNDATION

Founder's Day Concert

THE ALBENERI TRIO

ALEXANDER SCHNEIDER, *Violin*   BENAR HEIFETZ, *Violoncello*

ERICH ITOR KAHN, *Piano*

AND

MILTON KATIMS, *Viola*

THE COOLIDGE AUDITORIUM

TUESDAY EVENING, OCTOBER 30, 1945

At 8:30 o'clock

411

411 Programme of the concert, 30 October 1945. The Albeneri Trio premièred the commissioned Trio.

Albeneri Trio at the Founder's Day Concert on 30 October 1945 in the Coolidge Auditorium at the Library of Congress.

Villa-Lobos's two cables, one received in Washington on 17 August and the other sent by the composer on 8 October, and one letter (12 October 1945), all addressed to Harold Spivacke (1904-1977), chief of the Music Division, The Library of Congress, Washington DC, refer to this commission.

In August 1949 Villa-Lobos resumed his correspondence with Irving Schwerké and continued to exchange letters with him until March 1953. The letters give evidence of the composer's strong character and willpower. In spite of two serious operations for the removal of a cancerous bladder which, twice, necessitated long hospitalisation in New York's Memorial Hospital, he only lightly touched on this subject in two letters to Schwerké. He was not complaining at all, on the contrary, he appreciated the 'life that was given him again' by his surgeon, and in the same sentence switched immediately to his favourite subjects – his career, his travels in Europe and in the United States to conduct his music. This positive attitude and love of life probably aided his recovery and enabled him to live another eleven years following his

412   Rio de Janeiro between mountains and ocean.

412

413   414

413   Brazilian Press Association Building (Associacão Brasileira de Imprensa – ABI), at that time an ultra-modern steel and glass structure built on columns.

414   The Serrador Hotel with its beautiful exterior.

415   At the Praça de Republica the Ministry of War and (*left*) the Central Station were both constructed in the modern style.

415

first operation in July 1948.

In the 1950s Rio de Janeiro and São Paulo burgeoned into highly modern cities and were fast becoming well-known abroad for their bold and beautiful architecture. Old buildings were torn down everywhere and skyscrapers, sometimes with daring designs, replaced them.

It should be remembered, of course, that Brazil is not only Rio de Janeiro and São Paulo. Brazil is a vast country consisting of various regional divisions each with its own characteristics.

One of these regions in the Amazon valley – *Marajó* Island, which is very large – held a special fascination for Villa-Lobos. It is here that he sets his story which

416

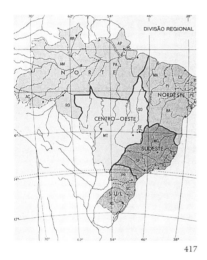

417

418

416 An aerial view of São Paulo which had grown into the country's leading industrial centre, and which reveals even more adventurous constructions than Rio de Janeiro.

417 Regional divisions.

418 Southern Region.

provides the theme for the orchestral piece *Rudá*, composed in 1951 and premièred on 30 August 1954 at the Théâtre des Champs Elysées, Paris.

Such thematic matierial, however, was a rather isolated instance following Villa-Lobos's visit to the United States.

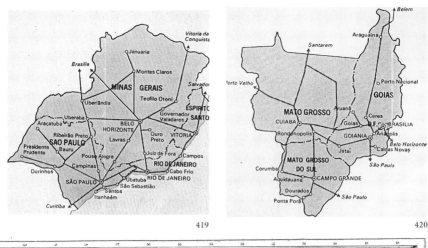

419   420

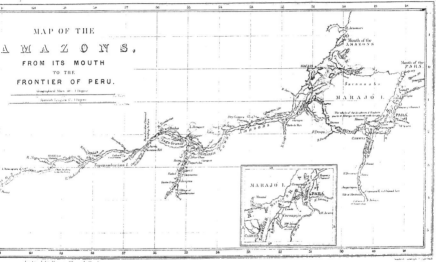

421

419   Southeastern Region.

420   Central Western
Region.

421   The map shows (*far
right*) Marajó Island.

Commissions for piano concertos

The large number of commissions which the Brazilian composer received following his American debut and which extended over a period until shortly before his death probably made him rethink the nature of his compositions. He turned again to more classical titles for his pieces, either in accordance with the artists' wishes or to secure greater acceptability on the concert circuit.

Such works included three concertos for piano, one each for cello, harp, guitar and harmonica, stage works, two ballets, orchestral works and chamber music. These were all given their first performance during Villa-Lobos's life with the exception of the opera *Yerma* first performed posthumously in 1971.

The *Piano Concerto No. 1* was commissioned in 1945 by Ellen Ballon to whom the work is dedicated.

Not long after the première of the *Concerto,* Villa-Lobos and Ellen Ballon began to exchange letters and the correspondence continued until September 1947. Visiting New York himself once more around Christmas 1952 Villa-Lobos sent best wishes for the holiday season to her New York address.

The *Piano Concertos No. 2* and *No. 3* were not commissioned. Villa-Lobos dedicated his *Piano*

422 One of the letters, dated 26 July 1947, from Arminda Villa-Lobos to Ellen Ballon, in Arminda Villa-Lobos's handwriting but written as though it were from Villa-Lobos himself, reveals her delightful manner of coping with the English language (as did also the previous letters which she wrote in Villa-Lobos's name). The last letter also tells of the composer's busy concert schedule in Europe and the prestige he enjoyed in the Old World, a consequence of his success in the United States following his debut there in 1944-45. The opportunity to present his own compositions in quick succession in Paris, Rome, Lisbon and London was, for a composer-conductor from faraway Brazil, most encouraging. (The facsimile letter to Ellen Ballon is published here for the first time by courtesy of the University Archives, Dalhousie University Library, Ellen Ballon papers, Halifax, Nova Scotia, Canada). The last letter (9 September 1947) mentions for the first time 'the difficult situation in Europe', which probably refers to the conditions after the war. This may also explain why Villa-Lobos was much in demand, since Europe had been starved of new musical experiences during the war.

Very bad English! ....?

HOTEL ROBLIN
6 Rue Chauveau Lagarde
PARIS (8°)

Paris, July, 26, 1947

My dear friend Miss Biston

It was a very great pleasure to hear from you.

We have in Paris until 31, day that we go to the Rome, when I shall conduct at 6 in August. After we go to the Lisbon and my concert is 14. Of the Lisbon, we come back to Paris and I will conduct 21 in the Theatre of Champs Elysées. Perhaps we go to London, but we don't know yet

the date. It was very good if you was with us playing your concert piano, but we hope sooner it was possible.

I think it was a good idea and you were very kind to me mention of my works to Mr. Werse-mann and Defauw to play them. Descobrimento do Brasil (1st suite) is a duration 13 minutes, but Bachianas n° 4 about 25 minutes.

We liked very much the choice that you did of my piano soli. Thank you for all.

We hope we can hear the Piano Concert in October 28th next.

It was very nice to see the picture in the Musical Courier

of New-York, and we hope to receive a copy of the Montreal Standard too.

I'm the hoping to see you and your good friend Mr. Gus-Tapson very soon, we send you our "Saudades".

Most cordially, yours friends

Villa-Lobos

(L'Adress: Ambassade du Brésil
Av. Montaigne, 45
Paris - France

(I hope you can understand what I wrote in English and without "typewriter". I did many efforts to write with a calligraphie that you can read.
Love

423

424

423 & 424   In appreciation
of Ellen Ballon's
interpretation of his *Piano
Concerto No. 1* on several
occasions, Villa-Lobos mailed
her some of his own photos
with dedications. One dates
from 30 September 1947
and the other was sent
several years later, on 9
February 1955. (Both
reproductions appear here
for the first time by courtesy
of The University Archives,
Dalhousie University Library,
Ellen Ballon Papers, Halifax,
Nova Scotia, Canada.)

425

425   Villa-Lobos discussing
the new concerto with Ellen
Ballon (1898-1969),
Canadian pianist of Russian
parentage. A child prodigy,
she studied at McGill
University, Toronto. New
York debut in 1910, toured
Europe for the first time in
1927, settled in England
until World War II. A
longtime friend of Villa-
Lobos and interpreter of his
works, she gave the first
performance of the *Piano
Concerto No. 1* at Rio de
Janeiro's Teatro Municipal on
11 October 1946 under the
composer's direction. She
also gave the first
performance in the United
States in Dallas under Antal
Doráti (1906-1988), the
Canadian première on 28
October 1947 under Désiré
Defauw (1885-1960) and
recorded the work with the
Orchestre de la Suisse
Romande under Ernest
Ansermet in 1949.

426

427

426　Arnaldo Estrella (1908-1979), Brazilian pianist and teacher, toured the world and from 1952 lived in Paris. Well-known interpreter of Brazilian music. Professor at the Escola de Música da Universidade Federal do Rio de Janeiro and at the Instituto Villa-Lobos in Rio de Janeiro.

427　João de Souza Lima (1898-1982), who premièred the work on 21 April 1950 in Rio de Janeiro under Villa-Lobos's direction.

428　Programme for the première of the *Piano Concerto No. 4* on 9 and 11 January.

The Pittsburgh Symphony Orchestra

WILLIAM STEINBERG, Conducting
HEITOR VILLA-LOBOS, Guest Conductor
BERNARDO SEGALL, Piano Soloist

SYRIA MOSQUE

Friday Evening, January 9, 1953
Sunday Afternoon, January 11, 1953

PROGRAM

Villa-Lobos . . . . Choros No. 6

Villa-Lobos . . . . Concerto No. 4 for Piano and Orchestra*
　　Allegro non troppo
　　Andante con moto
　　Scherzo — Allegro vivace
　　Allegro moderato — Lento — Allegro moderato
　　　　　　　　Mr. Segall

Both Works Under the Direction of the Composer

INTERMISSION

Schumann . . . . Symphony No. 1 in B-flat major, Op. 38
　　Andante un poco maestoso
　　Larghetto
　　Molto vivace
　　Allegro animato e grazioso

*UNITED STATES PREMIÈRE

STEINWAY PIANOS　　　　　　　　　　　　CAPITOL RECORDS
(13)

428

429

429 Bernardo Segáll (*b.* 1911), Brazilian pianist and composer who studied in Brazil and toured the United States. He premièred the *Piano Concerto No. 4* with the Pittsburgh Symphony Orchestra on 9 January 1953, with Villa-Lobos conducting.

430 Programme for the première of the *Piano Concerto No. 5* on 8 May 1955.

431 Felicja Blumental (1915-1991), Brazilian pianist of Polish origin who emigrated to South America in 1942. From 1955 performed with European orchestras. Known for her recordings of rarely-heard piano works. Villa-Lobos was impressed with her interpretation of *Bachianas Brasileiras No. 3* and wrote the *Piano Concerto No. 5* for her in response to her commission. She premièred the work on 8 May 1955 with the London Philharmonic Orchestra under Jean Martinon.

430

431

432

432 Jean Martinon (1910-1976), French composer and conductor. Pupil of Albert Roussel (1869-1937) and Charles Munch (1891-1968), director of the Lamoureux Concerts, associate chief of the London Philharmonic Orchestra, artistic director of the Israel Philharmonic Orchestra, musical director of the Chicago Symphony Orchestra and others. Premièred Villa-Lobos's *Piano Concerto No. 5* with Felicja Blumental.

433 Felicja Blumental and Heitor Villa-Lobos following the performance of the composer's *Piano Concerto No. 5* by the Vienna Symphony Orchestra (25 May 1955).

433

Concerto No. 2 to his great friend João de Souza Lima. It was composed in 1948, three years after the work for Ellen Ballon.

The *Piano Concerto No. 3*, begun in 1952 but only finished in 1957 when the composer was seventy years old, is dedicated to the Brazilian pianist Arnaldo Estrella who premièred the work on 24 August 1957 in Rio de Janeiro under Eleazar de Carvalho.

The *Piano Concerto No. 4* was commissioned in 1952 and is dedicated to Bernardo Segáll.

The *Piano Concerto No. 5* was commissioned by and is dedicated to Felicja Blumental.

Commissions for other solo instruments

Villa-Lobos also received commissions from his artist friends, all virtuosi on their particular instruments – guitar, harp, cello and harmonica – to whom he dedicated the respective works. The *Guitar Concerto*, written in 1951, was premièred by Andrés Segovia, the Spanish virtuoso guitarist of international repute and the Houston Symphony Orchestra, on 6 February 1956.

Also composed in 1953, like the *Harp Concerto*, was the *Cello Concerto No. 2*, commissioned by and dedicated to Villa-Lobos's countryman Aldo Parisot.

THE HOUSTON SYMPHONY ORCHESTRA

LEOPOLD STOKOWSKI
MUSIC DIRECTOR

MAURICE BONNEY
Associate Conductor

SEASON 1955-56

FIFTEENTH SUBSCRIPTION CONCERT

HEITOR VILLA-LOBOS, Conducting

ANDRES SEGOVIA, Guitarist

MONDAY EVENING, FEBRUARY 6, 1956, 8:30 P.M.
MUSIC HALL

434

434 Programme for the première of the *Guitar Concerto* on 6 February 1956.

435 Andrés Segovia (1893-1987) seen here during an interval in rehearsal involving the Philharmonic Orchestra and the Spanish harp virtuoso Nicanor Zabaleta (1907-1993) for the première of Villa-Lobos's *Harp Concerto* on 14 January 1955. Others in the photo include Villa-Lobos, Nicanor Zabaleta, Arminda Villa-Lobos, Walter Burle Marx, Bernardo Segáll and Arthur Cohn (*b.* 1910).

435

Mindinha

Anós e anos consecutivos o grande Amigo Andrés Ségovia insistia com Villa-Lobos para que compusesse um concerto para violão e orquestra.

E a história se inicia: Villa-Lobos só concordaria em escrevê-lo se pudesse utilizar um microfone.

Apaixonado pelo violão, Villa-Lobos ainda o preferia como instrumento íntimo, que ecoasse com caráter recôndito.

Verdadeiro enlevo para Villa-Lobos: à sua mesa, trabalhando sem cessar ao lado de Segovia, quando este preparava seus programas de concertos nos Estados Unidos e na Europa. Estamos convencidos, foram estas suas mais intensas emoções artísticas.

O nosso Segovia sempre apelando para nos: — "Mindinha, lembra ao Heitor (assim Segovia o chamava) que componha o meu Concerto".

E essa tarefa não nos era fácil de cumpri-la. Além de enriquecer a obra violonística de Villa-Lobos proporcionava alegria ao nosso grande artista e aumentava-lhe o repertório vilalobístico.

Eis que o dia é chegado. Villa-Lobos, meio adoentado, pede-nos o violão e diz-nos que sente cócegas nos dedos, com idéias para colocá-las na pauta.

Villa-Lobos afinal conclui uma Fantasia para violão e orquestra, que envia a Segovia e surpreende-se mais tarde que não haja sido apresentada em concerto. A verdade, porém, surge: Segovia desejava uma Cadência para a obra, a fim de que revestisse a forma de Concerto.

Villa-Lobos, assim mesmo, reluta em escrever a Cadência e eis que, por ocasião da primeira audição mundial, em Filadelfia, do Concerto para harpa e orquestra, encomendado por Zabaleta, fomos surpreendidos com a presença de Segovia no Teatro, que viera especialmente para ouvir esse Concerto e sentir como a obra soava.

Aí então, Villa-Lobos não soube fugir à pretensão de Segovia e escreveu a Cadência, que o grande violonista e Amigo lhe cobrava.

Chega finalmente a oportunidade da execução do Concerto em Houston a 6 de fevereiro de 1956, cinco anos após ser composto.

Segovia não escondia sua apreensão com o possível peso da orquestração. E pudemos compreender o susto: havia um trombone na partitura!...

Antecedendo o ensaio, Villa-Lobos pede-nos que, corrigindo as partes de orquestra, acrescentassemos em todas as indicações pianíssimo. Chegamos ao exagero de colocar — pppp.

Assistimos ao primeiro ensaio do Concerto, sob a regência do próprio Villa-Lobos, e Segovia com sua peculiar doçura, amizade e confiança que nos devota, indagou-nos: "Mindinha, consegue-se ouvir o violão?" Retrucamos: — "O que não se ouve é a orquestra". E isso foi o resultado do excesso de zelo de Villa-Lobos, com tanto **pianíssimo.**

Após o ensaio, de volta ao Hotel, em tom jocoso insinuamos: — Por que não eliminar a orquestra e deixar apenas o solista, já que é tão bonita a parte do solo?"

Essa brincadeira não teria qualquer efeito, e o importante foi o sucesso entusiástico na noite da "première", consagrando os dois artistas. A orquestra aliás soou lindamente, na proporção devida.

436

436 Arminda Villa-Lobos, nicknamed by the composer 'Mindinha', reminisces about the origins of the *Guitar Concerto* (*Presença de Villa-Lobos*, Vol. 11, 1980, MEC/SEAC/MVL, Rio de Janeiro).

437   Programme for the world première of Villa-Lobos's *Harp Concerto*, written in 1953 and premièred on 14, 15 and 17 January 1955 by the Philadelphia Orchestra with Nicanor Zabaleta (1902-1993), and the composer conducting. The programme also included the première of Villa-Lobos's *Symphony No. 8* which is dedicated to Olin Downes, the music critic of *The New York Times* who reviewed the work after its New York performance at Carnegie Hall, on 18 January 1955.

438   Aldo Parisot (*b*. 1918), Brazilian cellist who went to the United States in 1946 where he was principal cellist with the Pittsburgh Orchestra and who also performed as soloist in the United States and Europe. He premièred the *Cello Concerto No. 2* with the New York Philharmonic Symphony Orchestra on 5 February 1955 under Walter Hendl.

439   Walter Hendl (*b*. 1917), American conductor and teacher who taught at Sarah Lawrence College (1939-1941), pianist and conductor at the Berkshire Music Center (1941-1942), associate conductor of the New York Philharmonic Symphony Orchestra (1945), conductor of the Dallas Symphony Orchestra (1949). Toured the Far East (1955), director of the Eastman School of Music, Rochester, NY (1964).

440   Olin Downes's review of Villa-Lobos's *Harp Concerto* and the *Symphony No. 8, The New York Times*, 19 January 1955.

THE PHILADELPHIA ORCHESTRA
Fifty-fifth Season—1954-55

FOURTEENTH PAIR OF CONCERTS
Friday Afternoon, January 14, at Two
Saturday Evening, January 15, at Eight-Thirty

FIFTH MONDAY CONCERT
Monday Evening, January 17, at Eight-Thirty

HEITOR VILLA-LOBOS Conducting
NICANOR ZABALETA, Harpist

VILLA-LOBOS PROGRAM

Bachianas Brasileiras No. 8 (1944)
I Preludio
II Aria (Modinha)
III Tocata (Catira Batida)
IV Fuga
(First performances at these concerts)

Sinfonia No. 8 (1950)
I Andante; allegro
II Lento assai
III Allegretto scherzando
IV Allegro justo
(First performances anywhere)

INTERMISSION

Concerto for Harp and Orchestra (1953)
I Allegro
II Andante moderato
III Scherzo: Allegretto quasi allegro
IV Allegro non troppo
NICANOR ZABALETA
(First performances anywhere)

Choros No. 6 (1926)
(First performances at these concerts)

The LESTER PIANO is the official piano of The Philadelphia Orchestra
Columbia Records   Victor Records
333

437

438

439

Music: Villa-Lobos Leads Own Works

Composer's Symphony and Concerto Bow

PHILADELPHIA ORCHESTRA, Heitor Villa-Lobos conducting. Nicanor Zabaleta, harpist. At Carnegie Hall. Villa-Lobos program: Bachianas Brasileiras No. 8; Symphony No. 8 (first New York performance); Harp Concerto (first New York performance); Choros No. 6.

By OLIN DOWNES

TWO important works by Heitor Villa-Lobos were heard for the first time in New York when the Brazilian composer conducted a program last night consisting exclusively of his compositions in Carnegie Hall.

These were Villa-Lobos' Eighth Symphony and his concerto for harp and orchestra, with a superb harpist, Nicanor Zabaleta, as soloist.

The symphony proved the most compact and in some respects the most advanced music on the program. It is not in Villa-Lobos exotic vein.

Exotic colorings in other music heard during the evening were present in splendor and abundance. The symphony is austere rather than sensuous in its character. It leans in the direction of the neo-classic rather than the romantic and coloristic. A large orchestra is used, but economically as regards "doubling" and effects merely of color.

The symphony is remarkably integrated in its material. Thus the first movement, all of which emanates from the motif announced at the beginning by the brass, is virtually nonthematic. The introductor motif also is the generator of ideas that recur in later movements of the symphony, and these ideas germinate remarkably in the score, one leading to another, which is nearly related to the theme that went before. There is what we might call chain invention, and structure rather than drama emphasized through the whole score.

●

This is not a symphony, then, to be jauntily assessed and pronounced upon at a single hearing. The movements that stood out last night were the first and the second. The first is of a somber and powerful character, its working out from a single thematic source being especially consistent and in a way ruthless. It is done with a big sweep.

The second movement is tragical, with now and again

Heitor Villa-Lobos

revealing vistas that make the more striking the generally dark nature of the thought. Of the last two movements, the third being very fantastic, one wants to wait before speaking.

●

Concerning the harp concerto, this writer has his reservations. He thinks it too long, and finds, to his surprise, that the writing for the harp is less distinguished and telling than he had anticipated. It was as if Mr. Villa-Lobos, whom we have heard use the harp wonderfully in some of his most orchestral scores, was less interested in scoring for a solo concerto. He writes for the most part for the upper half of the instrument, which he is often content to have play long stretches of quite ordinary figuration as accompaniment for the orchestra. And writing for the orchestra, he keeps the instruments way down in order not to overwhelm the harp. They surely could be used with more audacity and variety of color, and the harp would not lose by this. The concerto was played superbly, so far as its opportunities permitted.

Mr. Zabaleta was recalled many times, with the composer. One's personal opinion being what it is, the question arises as to what occasioned the immense enthusiasm—the harpist or the concerto?

The program, as originally

Zabaleta Is the Soloist at Carnegie Hall

constituted, would have been too long. Mr. Villa-Lobos wisely played but one of the four movements of his Eighth "Bachianas Brasileiras." This was the second movement, the "Aria." It is a beauty, with its warm caltilena, its singular fusion of a Bach-like melody and a southern, rhapsodic and emotionally intense expression. It also is notable for its simplicity and for the breadth of the line that is maintained principally by the 'cellos of the orchestra.

They sang it impressively under the composer's direction. Mr. Villa-Lobos conducts, not as a professional conductor, but as a composer interested solely in projecting his musical ideas. He does this very naturally, spontaneously and well. The men understand him, and the Philadelphia Orchestra has never been remiss in the care and attention that it gives to the guest conductors, and the compositions that they offer the public.

Last on the program was the Sixth "Choros," which plunged the listener into a primitive scene. He hears primitive sounds, and pulsatile instruments; he thinks of the cries of villagers, their rude dances, their wild rhythms and gyrations in the forest. Mr. Villa-Lobos hears with his own ears —not those that a conservatory told him to listen with. He has the keen aural sense, one would say, almost of a wild animal, and puts down his aural sensations without anything that is conventional coming between him and the chord that lands on the music paper.

●

His prevailing sin is lengthiness. This Sixth "Choros" would be more effective if one-quarter of it was lopped off. This is true also of the harp concerto. Nevertheless here is perhaps the most original composer writing music today; one with too many ideas, rather than too few; of an immense creativeness, vitality and inspiration, which carry home.

The audience applauded everything last night, with obvious approval. They had had an unusually extended experience of Villa-Lobos' too-seldom heard music.

440

441

Concerto for 'Cello and Orchestra, No. 2, in A minor
HEITOR VILLA-LOBOS
(Born in Rio di Janeiro, March 5, 1887 (?); now living there)

(First performance anywhere)

The second 'cello concerto of Villa-Lobos (the first dates from 1916) was written at the suggestion of and on commission from the present performer, Aldo Parisot. A compatriot of Villa-Lobos (though born in Natal), Parisot first became acquainted with the composer in 1940. Soon after, as a member of the Yacozino Quartet, he took part in the first performance of the Villa-Lobos quartet No. 7, at which time the idea of a 'cello concerto first occurred to him.

However nothing came of the thought until 1953, when Villa-Lobos wrote it within a period of a month and a half. It is thus contemporary with the Concerto for Harp recently heard (January 18) at a Philadelphia Orchestra concert with the composer conducting and Nicanor Zabaleta as soloist. It is, as noted, of clear tonality, though the designation is not included in the composer's superscription which reads, simply: "Concerto (No. 2) para violoncelo e orquestra."

Villa-Lobos is notably adept in writing for almost any instrument that invites his attention, but the 'cello has a special place in his affection. It was the first instrument he learned to play (at the age of six, when his father made a suitable-sized instrument for him out of a viola). After experiments with various other means of music making, he settled down to the serious study of the 'cello in his late 'teens, and made his living as a touring performer while struggling for recognition as a composer. In addition to several sonatas for 'cello and piano, and the concerto No. 1 previously mentioned, he has been partial to the instrument in other characteristic works, including the famous "Bachianas Brasileiras No. 5" in which the soprano solo line is supported by an ensemble of 'celli.

According to Mr. Parisot, Villa-Lobos uses folk-like material at various points in this work, though nothing he can identify as actually of folk origin

441 Programme for the world première of the *Cello Concerto No. 2*.

442 Comments on the *Cello Concerto No. 2* published in the programme for the première.

206

442

New York

Heitor Villa-Lobos's fecundity is well known, but it is still rather striking when two concertos written by him within the past year or so are given their first performance during the same season. These are his Concerto for Harp (played by the Philadelphia Orchestra) and his Concerto No. 2 for Violoncello and Orchestra, which was given a world première by the New York Philharmonic-Symphony Orchestra in an especially good performance conducted by Walter Hendl, and with Villa-Lobos's compatriot Aldo Parisot, for whom it was written, as soloist.

Probably no other composer born in the Western Hemisphere possesses a greater international reputation than Villa-Lobos. He has written a large number of works (although it is freely rumored that many he has listed are incomplete) in many media, and in styles which at times differ from each other so much that it is hard to realize they are by the same composer. His many years in Paris resulted in a strong French influence (his Trio for piano, violin, and violoncello seems purely French); but many of his best-known works are firmly built of characteristic Brazilian elements. In them he uses Afro-Brazilian folk instruments, tunes, and rhythms, and enhances these with original composed but similar materials. In his early *Amazones* he employs a large orchestra, uses Portuguese, African, and Indian-Brazilian themes, and builds up curious super-chord structures (usually with high minor seconds plus open fourths on more conventional underpinnings) that fit the exotic elements. Some critical young Brazilians then taxed him with being merely a folkish composer, with no relationship to the whole world of music. Other anti-Villa-Lobos young men admitted his ability to write in French style; but since this group used exclusively the Viennese twelve-tone row, which they called "international," he still felt the need to do something about the criticism. He then announced that according to his belief, the greatest and most international music would be forthcoming if the Bach style were applied to the diversified Brazilian folk elements. He then proceeded to write his famous series *Bachianas Brasileiras*.

These points are all by way of introducing the Concerto No. 2 for Violoncello and Orchestra; for some knowledge of this history is needed to understand its style. There is an obvious attempt to make a further integration between the styles of Bach and Brazil.

The Concerto is excellently written for 'cello; Villa-Lobos's first instrument was the 'cello; as a young man he toured as a soloist on this instrument, and the writing displays an intimate knowledge of the sort that comes only by playing oneself. This does not mean that the writing is unconventional; only in one or two spots in the cadenza of the last movement are there highly unusual double-stop glissandos. On the other hand, surprisingly little use is made of harmonics, pizzicatos, or other special effects. It is as though the composer wished to prove that he could write in a straightforward melodious manner without recourse even to mildly strange sounds on the instrument. The orchestra, also, is treated much less colorfully than has been the custom with Villa-Lobos; it is for the most part sedate even to the point of being somewhat boring. Only here and there are there flashes of the powerful and colorful Brazilian instrumentation and rhythm. Even the sounds of *timbales* in the Scherzo were used in a subdued way. Furthermore, rather thick and unLatin-American orchestration often obscured the solo 'cello. It was clear that this was the fault neither of the soloist nor of the conductor.

The work is tonal throughout, mostly in A minor. The melodic lines are built on fragments all of which may be found in Bach, and are treated in Bach-like sequences; often with the familiar device of having the melodic outline limn a seventh, and be resolved in sequence a step lower. The fundamental chords are simple ones, with dissonant seasoning high above on rare occasions.

In some respects the building on Bachian style falls down. The music does not make much use of dominant chords, and is not built on dominant-tonic structure; and listen as one would, no planned substitute or other diatonic organization seemed to take the place of such structure. Thus the chord sequences seemed rather formless, without designed harmonic plan. There was a feeling of aimlessness rather than of any arrival at an inevitable point. The music often remained in the same key for over-long periods, while still studiously avoiding chromaticism. This contributed to a sense of inertia. Bach's lack of chromaticism is fully compensated for by the constant key shifts in his developments, and the organic round of keys contributes mightily to the drive towards a conclusion that is so powerful an aspect of the Bach style. There is a warmth and richness in the melodic flow and its harmonic support in the Concerto; but it lacks the variety of chromaticism, of key modulation, or of modal change; it lacks counterpoint almost completely, and it lacks harmonic structure. So it would seem that Villa-Lobos is giving us his impressions of Bach rather than adopting Bach-like musical form. The result failed to convince at least one listener who is in general a genuine admirer of the composer.

HENRY COWELL

443   Reproduction of Henry Cowell's (1897-1965) review of the *Cello Concerto No. 2*, published in *The Musical Quarterly*, Vol. XVI, No. 2, April 1955.

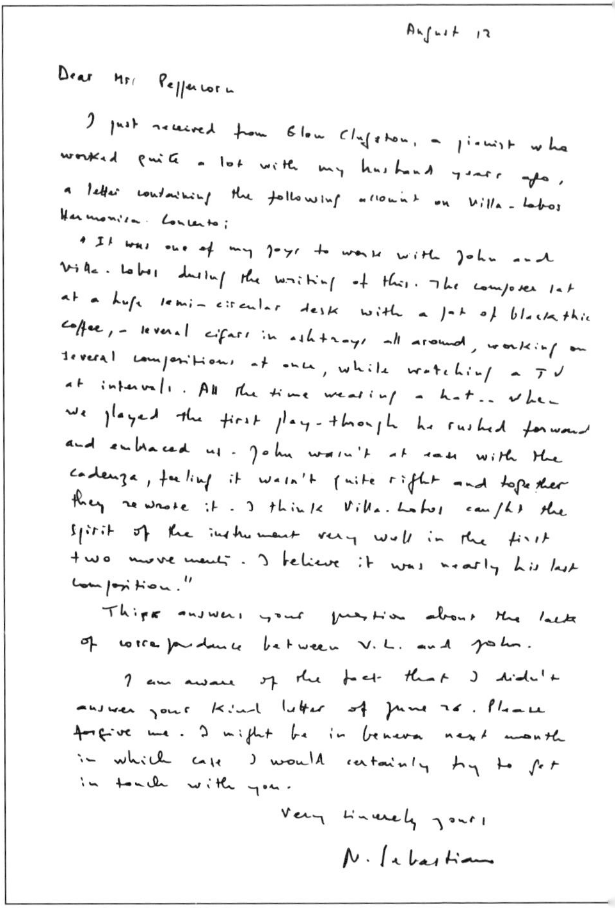

444

[Facsimile handwritten letter]

August 12

Dear Mr. Peppercorn

I just received from Glen Clugston, a pianist who worked quite a lot with my husband years ago, a letter containing the following account on Villa-Lobos Harmonica Concerto:

"It was one of my joys to work with John and Villa-Lobos during the writing of this. The composer sat at a huge semi-circular desk with a jar of black thick coffee, - several cigars in ashtrays all around, working on several compositions at once, while watching a TV at intervals. All the time wearing a hat... when we played the first play-through he rushed forward and embraced us. John wasn't at ease with the cadenza, feeling it wasn't quite right and together they rewrote it. I think Villa-Lobos caught the spirit of the instrument very well in the first two movements. I believe it was nearly his last composition."

This answers your question about the lack of correspondence between V.L. and John.

I am aware of the fact that I didn't answer your kind letter of June 26. Please forgive me. I might be in Geneva next month in which case I would certainly try to get in touch with you.

Very sincerely yours

N. Sebastian

444 Facsimile letter from Nadia Sebastian to the author, 12 August 1981, in which she quotes an interesting comment on the *Harmonica Concerto* by Glen Clugston, one-time accompanist of John Sebastian (published with her permission).

445 First page of the score of the *Cello Concerto No. 2*.

Two years after the *Cello Concerto No. 2*, Villa-Lobos accepted a commission from yet another internationally known virtuoso, the harmonica player John Sebastian.

Nadia Sebastian, widow of the virtuoso, corresponded with the author from her home in St Vincent de Cosse, France, to which she and John Sebastian had moved in 1977.

To fulfil Eugene List's commission in 1953, Villa-Lobos hit on a different idea. He composed and dedicated to the American pianist the *Fantasia Concertante for piano, clarinet and bassoon*. In a letter written from Finland to the author on 30 June 1981, Eugene List recalls how he came to commission Villa-

445

Lobos to write a composition for him which was
premièred on 19 November 1968 in the Sala Cecília
Meireles in Rio de Janeiro.

MUSICAL DIARY

'Unfinished' Works

Concert by Israel Composers, sponsored by the League of Composers, Kol Yisrael and the Milo Artists Club (Tel Aviv, October 26). Yitzhak Barzam: Elegy for Strings, Sinfonietta for Strings. Yehezkiel Braun: Piano Sonata, Song cycle for voice and piano, to words by Leah Goldberg, concerto for Flute and Orchestra.

I BARZAM (b. 1922) is undoubtedly a gifted man but still lacks a good deal of craftsmanship and stylistic originality. He writes in a post-romantic style and the striking features of his works are strong and deeply felt emotional values.

His string scores sound well, yet he does not explore the possibilities of modern string orchestration. The Elegy, written in memory of Aviasaf Barnea, the late Haifa composer, is quite effective and speaks to the heart but sounds banal in places. The Sinfonietta has a simple but good formal basis but often sounds shallow and the development of the material is not interesting enough.

An astonishing fact is the total absence of Israel elements in Barzam's music. This is indeed surprising for a man who came to this country as a boy.

Yehezkiel Braun (b. 1922) speaks a quite different language. His music is much more rooted in the atmosphere of the country and sometimes influenced by eastern European Jewish melodies and rhythms.

Of the works performed, we found the songs and the concerto the best. The songs betray a delicate and sensitive soul and fit the words very well. In the concerto he demonstrates an excellent treatment of the solo instrument and good scoring for the orchestra, but a much too long, and sometimes wearying last movement.

Braun has still yet to develop a more personal and homogenous style, especially in his harmonic language. Braun's songs were sung by Esther Sorokin, soprano, and the sonata was played by Malka Mevorach. The orchestral work's were tape recorded. **B. BAR-AM**

Ambitious Programme

The Kol Yisrael Orchestra, Georg Singer, conductor; John Sebastian, harmonica. (Edison Hall, Jerusalem, October 27). Rolf Liebermann : Symphony (1949); Cimarosa: Concerto for Oboe and Orchestra; Vaughan-Williams: Overture "The Wasps"; Villa-Lobos: Concerto for Harmonica and Orchestra.

The enlargement and the indisputable improvement of the Kol Yisrael Orchestra seems to be inducing the organizers of these programmes to a more and more ambitious programme policy. This concert even included two First Perform-ances of quite demanding works. The Symphony by Rolf Liebermann was given a concise and spirited treatment bringing out the Swiss composer's inherent vitality and dynamic, if sometimes a bit harsh, writing. Georg Singer conducted with enthusiasm and inspiring energy and led a very creditable performance of the orchestra, which also played the Vaughan-Williams Overture soundly and efficiently.

John Sebastian, the Harmonica virtuoso, had already given a most impressive account of his technical and musical abilities in his interpretation of the Tscherepnin Concerto with the same orchestra and conductor the week before in Tel Aviv. Here again, he proved the great value of cooperation between a performing artist and a composer in the creation of new works. Villa-Lobos seems to have written this concerto not only for Sebastian, but actually together with him: although this is a fine opus in its own right, the possibilities of the harmonica were exploited to the maximum extent, enabling Sebastian to display his sweet *cantilena* as well as his breath-taking aerobatics (especially in the *cadenza* of the third movement) to the best advantage of player and work alike. An encore of his own writing made one look forward to his solo recital with great expectations.

M.

446

447

448

446   Review of the world première of the *Harmonica Concerto,* The *Jerusalem Post,* 1 November 1959.

447   John Sebastian (1914-1980), American harmonica virtuoso, studied law in Philadelphia, literature in Rome and Florence, specialising in the seventeenth and eighteenth centuries. A self-taught harmonica player, he returned to the United States and gave some 600 performances in the United States and Canada in the following years. Soloist with many international orchestras. Prominent composers wrote for and dedicated their works to him. Villa-Lobos's *Harmonica Concerto* is dedicated to him. He premièred the work with the Kol Israel Orchestra in Jerusalem on 27 October 1959.

448   Eugene List (1918-1985), American pianist who gave concert performances internationally and taught at Eastman School of Music, Rochester NY.

449   Excerpts from a facsimile of Eugene List's letter to the author, 30 June 1981 (published with his permission).

310 W. 83 St.
New York, N.Y.
10024
Written from Finland
30 June 81

Dear Mr. Peppercorn,

... I met Villa-Lobos through my good friend, Joseph Battista, the pianist, who had met Villa-Lobos in Brazil while on a concert tour there. Joseph Battista died prematurely, unfortunately, many years ago. It was at a small gathering at the Battista apartment in New York that I met Villa-Lobos, and it was at that time that I commissioned the "Fantasie Concertante"

Sincerely,
Eugene List

449

Commissions for orchestral works and chamber music

Works for virtuosi were not the only pieces Villa-Lobos wrote on commission. Others included symphonic poems, symphonies, ballets and works for wind ensembles. The Louisville Orchestra gave him two commissions, after deciding in the spring of 1948 that 'instead of engaging expensive soloists' it would use its budget for soloists to 'commission composers of world renown to write pieces especially for the orchestra'.

Villa-Lobos was fortunate to be included in this new endeavour. The first commission was received in 1950. He wrote *Erosão*, a symphonic poem on 'The Origin of

THE LOUISVILLE PHILHARMONIC SOCIETY

PRESENTS

The Louisville Orchestra

ROBERT WHITNEY, Conductor
DOROTHEA ADKINS & ANN MONKS, Duo-Pianists
HEITOR VILLA-LOBOS, Composer

Program

OVERTURE: The Wildwood Troubadour, or the Dawning of
Musical Inspiration in a Log House in Kentucky—
An Autobiography ....Heinrich
Revised by Robert Whitney

SYMPHONIC POEM: THE ORIGIN OF THE AMAZON
RIVER ....Villa-Lobos
(World Premiere)

CONCERTO IN D MINOR FOR TWO PIANOS................Poulenc
Allegro ma non troppo
Larghetto
Finale. Allegro molto

DOROTHEA ADKINS AND ANN MONKS, Soloists
(Steinway Pianos)

INTERMISSION

SYMPHONY No. 5 IN D MINOR, "THE REFORMATION".......Mendelssohn
Andante—Allegro con fuoco
Allegro vivace
Andante—
Choral: A Mighty Fortress is Our God—Allegro vivace

The Steinway is the Official Piano of The Louisville Orchestra

450　Programme for the world première of *Erosão* on 7 and 8 November 1951.

450

THE LOUISVILLE ORCHESTRA
by Robert Whitney

In the spring of 1948, Charles P. Farnsley was elected president of the Philharmonic Society. He invited Conductor Whitney to visit him in his law offices and offered a number of imaginative proposals for the future of the Louisville Orchestra.

He pointed out that the Orchestra, with a deficit of $40,000 "was broke, and always had been," and offered a new approach to its problem of gaining adequate public support. Instead of engaging expensive soloists, he recommended using the budget for soloists to "commission" composers of world renown to write pieces especially for the Orchestra. "The composer is the forgotten man of music," he said, "yet without him music would die. Follow the practice of the 18th century, where every concert offered a brand new piece of music. Let concert going be an adventure — an occasion to hear something new and challenging. Make concert going fun!"

He also urged that the number of players in the Orchestra be limited to 50 and that its name be changed to The Louisville Orchestra; and that it move from the Memorial Auditorium to smaller Columbia Auditorium, seating 1,100 people. The smaller hall, with better acoustics, would be ideal for a classical-sized orchestra. And 50 players would be adequate for recording, broadcasting, for travelling by bus in the State, or by air, if that should be necessary.

The long-playing phonograph record had only that year come on the market, but Mr. Farnsley foresaw that it would revolutionize the world of music. He compared its effects to that of the printing press on the written word.

For the season of 1948-9, the Orchestra commissioned new works from Darius Milhaud, Virgil Thomson, Roy Harris, Joaquin Rodrigo of Spain and Gian-Francesco Malipiero of Italy. Louisville's own Claude Almand completed the list. Composers Thomson, Almand and Harris conducted their own works and Louisville audiences for the first time realized that living composers could lend new note of excitement to a concert. . . .

Of course, opinion was mixed regarding the new departure. Some took violent exception to the new music and went so far as to refer to the plan as a cheap publicity trick to attract national attention at the expense of the Louisville audiences. Attract attention it certainly did, for composers all over the world hailed the idea with delight and offered to compose works for the Louisville Orchestra.

For the season 1949-50, the Orchestra commissioned works by Paul Hindemith, William Schuman, David Diamond, Robert Russell Bennett and Claud Almand. The composers names were given the headlines instead of the soloists as in the pas . . .

The season of 1951-2 brought Martha Graham back to Louisville in another commissioned work for the dance, *The Triumph of St. Joan*, by Norman Dello Joio. On March 13, 1952 the Orchestra recorded this work for Columbia Masterworks. Coupled with this was another commissioned work, *Erosion. The Origin of the Amazon River* by the Brazilian master, Villa Lobos.

452   The story which inspired Villa-Lobos to write the work, as found on the fly-leaf of the score.

453   The recording of *Erosão* by the Louisville Orchestra, conducted by Robert Whitney, reviewed by Rudolph Reti in *The Musical Quarterly*, Vol. XXXIX, No. 2, April 1953.

454   Robert Whitney (1904-1986), American conductor who was born in England of American parents. Music director of the Louisville Orchestra and guest conductor of other orchestras.

On the fly-leaf of the score commissioned by the Louisville Philharmonic Society this explanation of the Symphonic Poem is typed, written by the composer:

"A long time ago the moon was engaged to the sun who wanted to marry her but if that would happen, if they got married, the earth would be destroyed, the blasting love of the sun would burn the world and the moon with its tears would flood the earth. For that reason they didn't get married. The moon would extinguish the fire and the fire would evaporate the water. They got parted. The moon cried all day and all night long. It was then that the tears ran over the earth until reaching the ocean. The sea became tempestuous and for that reason the moon was unable to mix its tears with the sea. During half the year they go up during the other half they go down. The tears of the moon gave the origin of the Amazonas River. (This story concerns the cataclysm of the Amazonas valley and the uprising of the Andes.)" It is added that the story was collected by Barbosa Rodrigues.

In listening to the music do not follow the text, expecting a musical equivalent of this strange legend, with representational sounds. In the majority of his works, even his symphonies, Villa-Lobos has supplied a program, but he seems to use it only as a source of inspiration, a sort of diving-board from which he plunges into the great reservoir of his musical expression.

452

Villa-Lobos's *Erosion*, which is on the other side of the record, is a colorfully orchestrated piece that attempts to depict the various phases of the course of the great Amazon River, and thus is perhaps a kind of South American counterpart to Smetana's *Moldau*. Like the latter it voices the rippling of the water, dancing from valley to valley, forcing its way through rocks and mountains—of course, all this expressed in an idiom derived from Debussy, Delius, Sibelius, and others, but molded into the characteristic Latin-American vernacular which is Villa-Lobos's very own domain and which has made his music popular all over the world.

RUDOLPH RETI

453

454

the Amazon River' which was premièred on 7 and 8 November 1951 by the Louisville Orchestra conducted by Robert Whitney.

Three years after the first commission, Villa-Lobos was again approached by the Louisville Orchestra. He responded with the overture *Alvorada na Floresta Tropical* (Dawn in a Tropical Forest), about which he exchanged letters with the Louisville Orchestra between 22 July 1953 and 15 July 1954.

In 1955 Villa-Lobos, who could neither conduct nor be present when his new work was performed by the Louisville Orchestra, thought, nevertheless, that he might be in demand to conduct some of his other compositions with that orchestra. He therefore addressed two letters (5 March 1955 and 2 January 1956) to the Louisville Orchestra from which it is evident that he had meanwhile changed his concert agent to Arthur Judson in New York. But the management of the Louisville Orchestra politely declined Villa-Lobos's offers.

The orchestral works commissioned during this period were *Symphonies Nos. 10* and *11*. For *Symphony No. 10,* subtitled 'Sumé Pater Patrium', composed in 1952, a monumental composition for soloists, mixed choir and orchestra, written to celebrate the

455 Father José de Anchieta (1534-1597), Jesuit priest, poet, teacher and dramatist who arrived in Brazil in 1553. Apart from missionary work which earned him the title of 'Apostle of Brazil', he wrote a considerable amount of poetry.

456 Facsimile letter from Robert Austin Boudreau to the author, 17 August 1981 (published with his permission), in which he recalls his encounter with the composer. Although Mr Boudreau believes that Villa-Lobos was present at both world premières, he was, in fact, unable to attend the 1959 performance because of ill-health. He died four-and-a-half months later.

Quatercentenary of the city of São Paulo, Villa-Lobos used verses from the Beata Virgine of the Jesuit Father José de Anchieta who lived in Brazil in the sixteenth century and exercised a considerable influence there. The other work, *Symphony No. 11*, written for the seventy-fifth anniversary of the Boston Symphony Orchestra has already been discussed earlier in this book (see pages 187, 189).

In 1958 and 1959, shortly before his death, two very interesting commissions reached Villa-Lobos from Robert Austin Boudreau, founder and director of the American Wind Symphony Orchestra (AWSO) in Pittsburgh. The instrumental combination which the Brazilian composer was able to choose for these commissions was very much of the kind in which he excelled, involving the creation of tone colours of unusual beauty.

The American Wind Symphony Orchestra (AWSO), founded by Robert Austin Boudreau in 1957 with

456

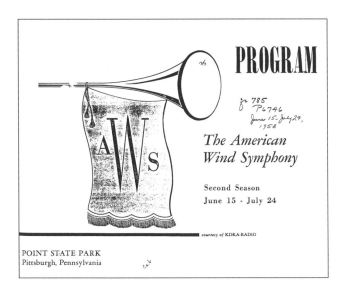

PROGRAM

The American Wind Symphony

Second Season
June 15 - July 24

courtesy of KDKA-RADIO

POINT STATE PARK
Pittsburgh, Pennsylvania

P R O G R A M

JUNE 15

**THE STORY OF THE SYMPHONY
OF WINDS *** .... *George Kleinsinger*
Commissioned by: The Mary & Leland Hazard Trust
Narrator: George Kleinsinger
WORLD PREMIERE

PETITE SYMPHONIE .... *Charles Gounod (1818 - 1893)*
Adagio-Allegretto   Scherzo
Andante Cantabile   Finale

WATER MUSIC .... *George Frederick Handel (1685 - 1759)*
Allegro   Hornpipe
Air   Allegro
Bourree

**CONCERTO FOR 3 PERCUSSIONISTS AND
WIND ORCHESTRA *** .... *George Kleinsinger*
Commissioned by: Mrs. Clifford S. Heinz
WORLD PREMIERE

JUNE 19

THE TOPS IN POPS

JUNE 22

SONATINE .... *Nicholas Tcherepnine (1873 - 1945)*
(for wind orchestra, tympani, xylophone; Op. 61)
Andantino Commodo   Allegretto Scherzando
Andante   Allegro Risoluto
AMERICAN PREMIERE

SONATA PIAN e FORTE .... *Giovanni Gabrieli (1557 - 1612)*
Brass Choir

MASS in e minor .... *Anton Bruckner (1824 - 1896)*
Kyrie   Sanctus
Gloria   Benedictus
Credo   Agnus Dei
Mendelssohn Choir of Pittsburgh
Director: Russell G. Wichmann

Published by C. F. Peters Corp.

JUNE 26

CHILDREN'S CONCERT – (Songs by Robert Schmertz)

JUNE 29

FOLKSONG SUITE .... *Ralph Vaughn Williams (1872 -*

SUITE FOR WINDS, Opus 4 .... *Richard Strauss (1864 -*
Allegretto   Romanze
Introduction and Fugue

MORGENMUSIK .... *Paul Hindemith (1895 -*
Brass Choir
I Moderato   III Allegro
II Lied

FANTASIA EM 3 MOVIMENTOS .... *Heitor Villa-*
Andante   Molto Allegro
Allegretto

Commissioned by: Mrs. S. J. Anathan
to be dedicated to the Rivers of Pittsburgh
WORLD PREMIERE

JULY 4

FOURTH OF JULY CELEBRATION (Fireworks Display)

JULY 6

FANFARE FOR THE COMMON MAN .... *Aaron Copland (1900*

FANFARE FROM "LA PERI" .... *Paul Dukas (1865*
Brass Choir

SERENADE FOR WINDS, Op. 44 .... *Anton Dvorak (1841 -*

CONCERTINO FOR CELLO .... *Jacques Ibert (1890*
Pastorale   Romance
Soloist: Theodore Salzman

**CONCERTO GROSSO FOR WIND QUINTET AND
WIND ORCHESTRA *** .... *Robert Russell Bennett (1894*
WORLD PREMIERE

JULY 10

ALL REQUEST PROGRAM

458

457 Programme for the world première of Villa-Lobos's *Fantasia in three movements* on 29 June 1958.

458 Robert Austin Boudreau (*b*. 1927), founder and music director of the American Wind Symphony Orchestra (AWSO), the floating art centre, and captain of Point Counterpoint II. Studied at Boston University (1947) and the Juilliard School of Music. Obtained a Fulbright scholarship (1954) for study in Paris. Associate professor of music at Duquesne University (1955), director of Wind Instrumental Music Programme and conductor of the Wind Ensemble. He commissioned Villa-Lobos to write *Fantasia em tres Movimentos* (in the form of a *Chôros*), sponsored by Mrs S.J. Anathan and dedicated to the 'Rivers of Pittsburgh'. This was premièred on 29 June 1958 in Pittsburgh, and *Concerto Grosso*, sponsored by Mrs Clifford S. Heinz was premièred on 5 July 1959.

459 Programme of the world première on 5 July 1959 of Villa-Lobos's *Concerto Grosso* for flute, oboe, clarinet, bassoon and wind orchestra.

grants from private corporations and local government, has since visited hundreds of American cities and in 1981-82 Puerto Rico and some of the Caribbean islands. The concerts are given free of charge. The orchestra plays music especially written by composers from all over the world. Three hundred such works had been commissioned and performed by 1981. They are published as a series by C.F. Peters, with Boudreau as editor. On the Silver Jubilee Anniversary of the orchestra on 7 July 1981, Villa-Lobos's *Concerto Grosso* was again performed.

The commissions for ballets included *Genesis* and *The Emperor Jones*. The first was commissioned by Janet Collins (b. 1917), the American dancer who appeared as a soloist before becoming première danseuse at the Metropolitan Opera in New York from 1951 to 1954. After retirement she taught dancing and devoted

---

JULY 5th—SUNDAY   II
CONCERTO FOR PIANO AND WIND ORCHESTRA........
                                    Igor Stavinsky
    Largo Allegro   (1882-)
    Largo
    Allegro
        Soloist: RUSSELL SHERMAN
        Presented in cooperation with the Edgar M. Leventritt
        Foundation
CONCERTO GROSSO FOR FLUTE, OBOE, CLARINET,
BASSOON AND WIND ORCHESTRA........*Heitor Villa Lobos*
                                    (1887-)
    Allegro non troppo
    Allegretto Scherzando
    Andante
            (World Premiere)
    Commissioned by Mrs. Clifford S. Heinz
MUSIC FOR THE ROYAL FIREWORKS.....*George Frideric Handel*
                                  (1685-1759)
                                Edited: R. A. Boudreau
    Ouverture (Larghetto and Allegro)
    Bourree
    La Paix
    La Rejouissance
    Menuet I
    Menuet II
    Finale

The American Wind Symphony is most grateful to those who have made the commissioned works possible:
    "SYMPHONY OF THE WINDS"..........By George Kleinsinger
                (Mary and Leland Hazard Trust)
    "FANTASIA EM 3 MOVIMENTOS"..........By Heitor Villa-Lobos
                (Mrs. S. J. Anathan)
          Dedicated to the Rivers of Pittsburgh
    "CONCERTO FOR 3 PERCUSSIONISTS AND
        WIND ORCHESTRA"..........By George Kleinsinger
                (Mrs. Clifford S. Heinz)
    "CONCERTO GROSSO FOR WIND QUINTET AND
        WIND ORCHESTRA"..........By Robert Russell Bennett
           (Mr. and Mrs. Oliver M. Kaufmann)
    "CONCERTO GROSSO"..........By Heitor Villa-Lobos
                (Mrs. Clifford S. Heinz)
    "OHIO RIVER SUITE"..........By Robert Russell Bennett
        (Wherrett Memorial Fund Through the Pittsburgh Foundation)

459

Evangeline Residence #215
1215 Seneca Street
Seattle, Wash., 98101
U. S. A.

Ms. Lisa M. Peppercorn
Schulhaus-Strasse 53
8002 Zurich, Switzerland

Dear Ms. Peppercorn:

Thank you for your kind letter of March 16th. All of the material and information you desire is to be found in the Dance Collection at Lincoln Center in New York City. The person and address you write to are:

... The theme of "Genesis" is God's creation of man — and man's evolving — consciousness — into complete awareness of his Creator. My name is on Mr. Villa-Lobos score. He wrote "Argument — Janet Collins." He composed the work from a detailed dance libretto I wrote for him. This is also in the archives.

I choreographed the work, but never performed it professionally. This music has been recorded, I was informed by Malvina Leshock, a friend of Mr. Villa-Lobos; though, unfortunately, I have never heard it in full symphonic form. I am only familiar with the duo-piano version — which in itself is a small masterpiece! It is beautiful music — and worthy of this great Brazilian composer.

For your information, I was born March 2, 1917 in New Orleans, Louisiana. In closing, I would like to wish you great success in your book on Mr. Villa-Lobos, and I do hope this letter has been of helpful for you.

Sincerely yours,
Janet Collins

460

218 *The World of Villa-Lobos*

461

460 Extract from an undated facsimile letter from Janet Collins (*b.* 1917) to the author, received on 8 April 1981, published with her permission, in which the dancer explains the events which led to the commission, her own and Villa-Lobos's ideas on the subject.

461 Basil Langton (*b.* 1912), the English-born dancer, actor, theatre and opera director. Performed in repertory theatres in England. He was director of the Empire State Music Festival (1955-1959). Associated himself with the John Brownlee (1901-1969) Opera Theatre at the Manhattan School of Music. For the Mexican-born dancer and choreographer José Arcadio Limón, he commissioned Villa-Lobos in 1956 to compose the dance-drama *The Emperor Jones* based on the play by Eugene O'Neill (1888-1953). The ballet was first performed on 12 July 1956. Limón also directed the première (1971) of Villa-Lobos's opera *Yerma*, composed in 1955-56 to words by Federico García Lorca.

Presenting THE WORLD FAMOUS

SYMPHONY OF THE AIR

(ARTURO TOSCANINI, Conductor-Emeritus)

PROGRAM—1956

─── FIRST WEEK ───

July 4—CARLOS CHAVEZ, Conducting
Buxtehude-Chavez: Chaconne; Shostakovich: Symphony No. 5;
Falla: Three dances from "The Three-Cornered Hat"
Ravel: "Pavane pur une Infante defunte"; Chavez: "Sinfonia India"

July 5 & 7—BALLET THEATRE DANCERS
NORA KAYE, JOHN KRIZA and cast of 14
Lupe Serrano, Ruth Ann Koesun, Scott Douglass
Thure. July 5: Designs with Strings; The Combat;
Pas de Deux (The Black Swan); Fancy Free
Sat. July 7: Streetcar Named Desire; Coppelia;
Interplay; Designs with Strings
Conductor: JOSEPH LEVINE   Piano Soloist: IRVING OWEN

July 8—CARLOS CHAVEZ, Conducting
Vivaldi: Concerto Grosso in D minor, Op. 3, No. 11;
Mozart: Symphony in G minor, No. 40 (K550);
Debussy: Two Nocturnes, "Nuages," "Fetes";
Barber: Essay for Orchestra, Stravinsky: The Firebird

─── SECOND WEEK ───

July 11—TIBOR KOZMA, Conducting
Weber: Overture to "Oberon"; Schumann: Symphony in D minor, No. 4,
Op. 120; Wagner: "A Siegfried Idyl";
Milhaud: "Saudades do Brasil"; Bartok: Hungarian Peasant Songs

July 12 & 14—WORLD PREMIERE
Dance-Drama after the play of Eugene O'Neill
"EMPEROR JONES"
Music Composed and Conducted by
HEITOR VILLA-LOBOS
Choreographed and Danced by
JOSE LIMON and Company
with LUCAS HOVING
and Symphony Concert—VILLA-LOBOS, Conducting
Bach—Villa-Lobos: Fantasy and Fugue No. 6; Villa-Lobos: Alvorada na Floresta
Tropical; Concerto for Piano and Orchestra No. 4,
Wagner: Prelude to "Die Meistersinger"
BERNARDO SEGALL, Piano Soloist

July 15—LUKAS FOSS, Conducting
MARVIN HAYES, Baritone-Narrator
Berlioz: "The Roman Carnival"; Foss: "Song of Anguish"; Copland: "A
Lincoln Portrait"; Beethoven: Symphony in A major No. 7, Op. 92

─── THIRD WEEK ───

July 19, 20 & 21—AMERICAN PREMIERE
New Music by CARL ORFF
For full stage production of Shakespeare's comedy
"A MIDSUMMER NIGHT'S DREAM"
Conducted by LEOPOLD STOKOWSKI
Starring BASIL RATHBONE • RED BUTTONS
with a noted Broadway Cast — Staged by Basil Langton
Settings: Kim Edgar Swados   Costumes: David Ffolkes
with Members of the Schola Cantorum, Direction: Hugh Ross

July 22—MILTON KATIMS, Conducting
Weber: Euryanthe; Dvorak: Symphony No. 2 in D Minor
Enesco: Roumanian Rhapsody No. 1; Tschaikowsky: Concerto in B flat minor

462

462 Programme for the première of the ballet *The Emperor Jones* on 12 July 1956.

463

464

463 José Arcadio Limón
(1908-1972), American
dancer and choreographer of
Mexican origin who lived in
the United States from 1915
onwards. Dancer in and
choreographer of various
Broadway shows; college and
university lecturer, including
the Juilliard Institute of
Music. Toured South
America, Mexico and Canada
and Paris. Choreographed
Villa-Lobos's *The Emperor
Jones* (1956) and *Yerma*
(1971).

465

464 Scene from *The
Emperor Jones.*

465 José Arcadio Limón
(*left*) with Arminda Villa-
Lobos and the composer.

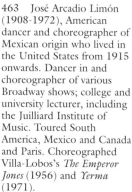

466

466 Villa-Lobos during the
première of his ballet *The
Emperor Jones.*

herself to painting. In 1954 she commissioned Villa-
Lobos to compose *Genesis,* a symphonic poem and
ballet for which she provided the story and created the
choreography. The concert première took place in Rio
de Janeiro on 21 November 1969.

Four letters from Villa-Lobos to Janet Collins (kept
at the New York Public Library), 9 February, 5 May,
31 May and 2 July 1954 relate to this commission.
Encouraged by the many commissions Villa-Lobos had
received previously for which the usual fee was $1,000,
the composer now chanced his arm and asked Janet
Collins for a fee of $2,000. Whether Janet Collins
agreed is not evident from the correspondence.

To write a ballet of a complete different type was the
commission he received from Basil Langton. In 1956
he asked Villa-Lobos to compose music based on
Eugene O'Neill's play *The Emperor Jones.* It was
premièred the same year during the Empire State
Music Festival at Ellenville, NY.

Ballet: 'Emperor Jones'

Premiere of Work by Limon at Ellenville

Special to The New York Times.

ELLENVILLE, N. Y., July 12 —The world première of José Limon's "The Emperor Jones" was the featured event on the program of the third week of the Empire State Music Festival, which opened tonight.

This was the second dance event to be presented by the festival this season. Mr. Limon and his company danced in Ellenville last year, but nothing so ambitious as the première was presented at that time.

"The Emperor Jones" is the third work that Mr. Limon has created for his group of male dancers and the second to have a dramatic basis. The choice of the story in this case was the play by Eugene O'Neill. The plot is a powerful one and one that is, in many ways, admirably suited to choreographic interpretation.

•

A self-made "Emperor" rules tyrannically over the natives of a West Indian island. In time they revolt, plotting his downfall, and he tries to escape only to be so haunted by fear for the sins he has committed that he dies in panic, the victim of his fright.

Although the stage of the tent in Ellenville is not the best for viewing dance—it is small and lacking in depth—Mr. Limon succeeded in creating a work of much power and, at times, of gripping intensity.

In his own role of the protagonist he was a poignant figure. Bold and swaggering at the beginning, as he sat on his gaudy throne, he tried to convince himself of his own

José Limon

confidence.

The most effective scenes came with two of his visions of the past, not merely a personal but a racial past. There was the episode of the chain gang, moving like the cry of a Negro spiritual, as Jones recalled the fury that had made him murder a guard. And there is an exciting African ritual of magic, which O'Neill himself had designated to be choreographed, filled with vibrating hands and savage rattles.

•

As the white man who, in various guises, continually hunts the nightmarish visions, Lucas Hoving was appropriately cold and sinister. As he sat at the end, relaxed and fanning himself on the throne of the dead emperor, he was the picture of a malicious victor.

The six men who assisted Mr. Limon in their various roles of rebellious natives and helpless co-sufferers all deserve commendation. They were Richard Fitzgerald, José Gutierrez, Michael Hollander, Harlan McCallum, Martin Morginsky and Chester Wolenski.

"The Emperor Jones," however, had its weak spots. There were elements of motivation, especially at the beginning, that were never completely clarified. It was a difficult task to convey through movement the cause of revolt against the emperor; the urgency of Jones' need for escape was also a problem.

But these were difficulties inherent in adapting the plot. There were weaknesses in timing also—a slow beginning before the suspense got under way and a too brief handling of the final moments of panic. But, on the whole, this was an effective dance-drama.

The music, by Heitor Villa-Lo-Bos, was especially composed for the dance and was commissioned for it by the Empire State Festival. Judging strictly as an enhancement of the choreography, it served its function admirably, building up to a stunning climax in the scene of primitive incantation. But one rather wondered why O'Neill's specification of gradually accelerating drum beats, which he asked to be heard throughout the play, were ignored.

Pauline Lawrence's striking costume for Mr. Limon—gold, blue, and scarlet—followed the dramatist's direction, and it was just right. The set was designed by Kim Edgar Swados.

The orchestral portion of the program consisted of works by Senhôr Villa-Lo-Bos and Wagner. Senhor Villa-Lobos conducted the Symphony of the Air.

The program will be repeated on Saturday.   S. J. C.

467

467 Review of *The Emperor Jones*, *The New York Times*, 13 July 1956.

Stage works

468 *Izaht's* cast before going on stage. *From left to right:*
João Carlos Ditter (*b.* 1935), Brazilian bass who came to Rio de Janeiro in 1957 from his native city of Curitiba. He sang in various Brazilian theatres and won several prizes (as *Alexandre*).
Maria Henriques (*b.* 1917), Brazilian mezzo-soprano, studied in Brazil and made her debut in Pôrto Alegre (1945), giving concert performances in Brazil, Venezuela and Portugal. Winner of several prizes and awards (as *Condessa La Perle*).
Alfredo Colósimo (*b.* 1923), Brazilian tenor who sang in all the Brazilian opera houses and at Colón in Buenos Aires (1959), Colombia (1964), Italy and Munich. Teacher at the Academia de Música Lorenzo Fernandez in Rio de Janeiro (as *Visconde Gamart*).

Villa-Lobos was also commissioned to write music for stage works. This was not exactly his favourite occupation. He had composed an opera before, *Izaht,* but it was not altogether successful. The overture, the third and fourth acts had each been performed separately in the concert hall without too much notice being taken. A concert performance of the entire opera was presented on 6 April 1940. Only about a year before the composer's death, on 13 December 1958, the work was eventually given a stage performance in Rio de Janeiro with Edoardo di Guarnieri conducting.

There are three more members of the cast of the *Izaht* who are not shown in illustration 468. They appear individually in illustration 469, 470 and 471.

In the 1940s Villa-Lobos was commissioned by Edwin Lester, President of the Los Angeles Civic Light Opera Association, to compose a work of a very different kind: *Magdalena* which the composer called a 'musical adventure'. Written between January and March 1947, it was premièred on 26 July 1948 at the Philharmonic Hall in Los Angeles, and after performances at the Curran Theatre in San Francisco, it opened at the Ziegfeld Theatre in New York on 20 September 1948. George Forrest and Robert Wright, the American producers, worked with Villa-Lobos on

468

Aracy Bellas Campos (*b.* 1923), Brazilian soprano who made her debut at the Teatro Municipal in Rio de Janeiro (1950). Concert performances in Europe, the United States and South America and holder of various prizes (as *Enith*).

Edoardo di Guarnieri (1899-1968), Brazilian conductor and cellist of Italian origin. Studied in Venice and Paris. Founded (1920) a quartet and gave concert performances in Europe. From 1929 onwards opera and concert conductor. Lived in Brazil from the end of the 1930s. Artistic director and conductor of the Pro-Arte of Rio de Janeiro and one of the conductors of the Municipal Orchestra in São Paulo. Recipient of many prizes. Premièred Villa-Lobos's *Magnificat Aleluia* on 8 November 1958 with the Associação de Canto Coral and *A Menina das Nuvens* on 29 November 1960, both in Rio de Janeiro.

Maria Sá-Earp (*b.* 1915), Brazilian soprano who sang in Brazil, the United States and Europe. Winner of several medals (as *Izaht*).

Paulo Fortes (*b.* 1924), Brazilian baritone, teacher at the Escola do Canto Lírico of the Teatro Municipal in Rio de Janeiro. Recipient of many prizes and medals (as *Perruche*).

Esther Nelly (as *Mena*).

469

470

471

472

469   Armando Assis Pacheco (*b.* 1918), Brazilian tenor (as *Conde Makian*).

470   Glória Queiroz Costa, Brazilian mezzo-soprano who made her debut (1951) at the Teatro Municipal in Rio de Janeiro. Recipient of many prizes (as *Barnar*).

471   Guilherme Damiano (*b.* 1912), Brazilian bass of Argentine origin who made his debut at the Colón in Buenos Aires before he moved to Brazil (as *Hadan*).

472   Edwin Lester (1895-1990), founded the Los Angeles Civic Light Opera Association in 1938. He presented 106 shows and as he remarked developed the nation's biggest subscription audience. As a youngster he played the piano in vaudeville and wrote songs.

473   George Forrest (*b.* 1914 (*right*), American promoter, producer, writer and composer who worked from an early age with Robert Wright. Robert

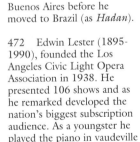

473

Wright (*b.* 1915) (*left*), American producer, director of musicals, who, together with George Forrest, wrote the music and lyrics for stage works and songs for musicals, and also made recordings and published more than 300 songs.

A VILLA-LOBOS OPERA

RIO DE JANEIRO.

THE four-act opera "Izaht," by Villa-Lobos, the Brazilian composer, was given its first performance at the Municipal Theatre in Rio de Janeiro on April 6 and executed as a private presentation for musicians and the staff of the music-educational department of the municipality. The house was packed and the composer, who conducted, had a great success. This event took place shortly before the actual music season began in South America. The almost thirty-year-old work was heard in its entirety for the first time in Brazil, although not staged, but given as oratorio; the overture and occasionally the last two acts have been played before. Outside this country "Izaht" has remained unknown.

Only in his youth did Villa-Lobos confine himself to opera writing (he wrote five altogether). In later years he abandoned the idea of dramatic composition entirely and turned to other forms. Nevertheless, "Izaht" (the only opera of the five which is completely orchestrated) belongs to his favorite works, as he has realized herein his idea of being original. The music, written during 1912 and 1914 (the first and third acts being orchestrated in 1918 and the two others in 1920) when the composer was in his middle twenties, is a typical product of his youth.

* * *

In spite of a strong Puccini influence, one of his models at the time, "Izaht" indicates willful characteristics of Villa-Lobos's more mature style and reminiscences of Brazilian folk motives. The music of the third and fourth acts is more dramatic, contrasting and more elaborate than the first two, in which the lyric tendency prevails. In the final act various combinations of instrumental colors are already typically his own, a special characteristic which comes to perfection in his later works.

For the flute as well as for the 'cello—the latter used elaborately, for instance, in the "Bacchianas Brasileiras," played in New York last year—he seems to have had a predilection in those early days. The flute, a favorite and much used instrument among the Brazilian natives, must have attracted his attention during his extended stay in the interior which had preceded the conception of "Izaht." And the 'cello he likes best of all the instruments he plays himself.

On the whole, the music of "Izaht" keeps pace with the romantic and complicated plot and reflects the composer's idea of and attitude toward opera writing: to omit dullness and boredom. This may be the reason for the quickly changing motives, the brisk transitions and the rapid alterations of arias, ensembles and chorus. However, the chorus plays a prominent role, and the fine and expressive setting of the voices clearly shows Villa-Lobos's outstanding ability in this direction, of which he has taken full advantage in the choral works written during the last ten years.

The libretto of "Izaht," signed by Azevedo Junior and E. Villalba, is actually by the composer himself; the subject and layout are so typically Villa-Lobos that they leave no doubt as to the originality of its text-writer. In the decidedly romantic plot with castles and taverns turn up viscounts and other nobility, gypsies, gangsters and Parisian apaches. Villa-Lobos says the opera is of an "essentially psychological character" and gives full and detailed descriptions of each character. This explanation brought about considerable controversies when parts of "Izaht" came to light many years ago, as it was maintained that every dramatic work necessarily has a psychological basis.

The unusual story is as follows: Izaht, a depraved gypsy girl, belongs to a gangster band in the suburbs of Paris and has to entice rich people. For the first time in her life she falls in love with a viscount who rescues her from the slaps of her father. In the meantime, the gangsters plan to rob the house of the viscount's fiancée, and later on that of the viscount. Izaht rescues him from the gangsters. Izaht dies when the gangsters are about to kidnap the count's fiancée. Finally the leader of the band, a decayed nobleman, recognizes in the viscount's fiancée his own natural daughter.

Unlike many other stage composers Villa-Lobos approaches opera writing with an idée fixe; For him it is the lowest class of serious music, a music essentially meant for the great public and the masses which want to be entertained. In his opinion one has, therefore, to meet the public's taste and sacrifice one's own ideals even to such an extent that tuneful and almost vulgar melodies should take the place of proper ones. This makes the extraordinary plot understandable.   LISA M. PEPPERCORN.

474 *The New York Times,* 28 April 1940, published a review of the performance of *Izaht* given in the concert hall in Rio de Janeiro on 6 April 1940.

475 The title page of *Magdalena* from the programme of the San Francisco performance.

476 Costumes from *Magdalena.*

SAN FRANCISCO CIVIC LIGHT OPERA ASSOCIATION
PRESENTS

MAGDALENA

CURRAN THEATER
9TH ANNUAL SEASON
1948

STARRING **IRRA PETINA**
JOHN RAITT
DOROTHY SARNOFF
HUGO HAAS

475

PICTURE ON COVER BY SHARAFF

476

Music by **HEITOR VILLA-LOBOS**

Pattern and Lyrics by
ROBERT WRIGHT
and
GEORGE FORREST

A MUS

STARRING   **IRRA PETINA**

JOHN R

CAST OF CHARACTERS
(IN ORDER OF APPEARANCE)

PADRE JOSEF	GERHARD PECHNER
MANUEL	ARMANDO GARCIA
SOLIS	MELVA NILES
SIMON	HENRY REESE
MORE	DOROTHY SARNOFF
	JOHN RAITT
SEÑOR BLANCO	FERDINAND HILT
DOCTOR LOPEZ	JOHN ARTHUR
GENERAL CARABANA	HUGO HAAS
CHANTEUSE	BETTY HUFF
CIGARETTE GIRL	CHRISTINE MATSIOS
WINE STEWARD	LEONARD MORGANTHALER
ZOGGIE	JOHN SCHICKLING
DANSEUSE	LORRAINE MILLER
TERESA	IRRA PETINA
THE OLD ONE	GENE CURTSINGER
CHICO	PATRICK KIRK
JUAN	LEONARD MORGANTHALER
CONCHITA	BETTY BRUSHER

Setti

UNDERSTUDIES

For Miss Petina.......Vera Bryner	For Miss Sarnoff....Glorya Curran	For Mr. Pechner.....Roy Raymond
For Mr. Raitt .....Tommy Gleason	For Miss Niles........Betty Huff	For Master Garcia......Peter Fields

SINGERS

LUCY ANDONIAN, MARION BEGIN, JOAN BISHOP, BETTY BRUSHER, TRUDY DE LUZ, SOFIA DERUE, JEANNE EISEN, VERA FORD, MARTHA FLYNN, AUDREY GARDNER, AUDREY GUARD, BETTY HUFF, PHYLLIS KRAMER, GWENN LAKIND, CHRISTINE MATSIOS, THERESA PIPER, MARY WOOD.

ARTHUR BREY, STEPHEN ESAIL, KAHLER FLOCK, TOMMY GLEASON, JOHN HUCK, JOHN KING, ROSS LYNCH, JOE MAZZOLINI, ANGELO RAFFAELLI, ROY RAYMOND, STANLEY ROSE, RICHARD SHARRETTS, LEONARD TAYLOR.

DANCERS

LIBBY BURKE, RITA CHARISE, NORMA DOGGETT, MARIE GROSCUP, JUDY LANDON, MARY MENZIES, LORRAINE MILLER, JOAN MORTON, SUE REMOS.

DALE LEFLER, MATT MATTOX, BILL MILLER, VERNE MILLER, MICHAEL SANDIN, MICHAEL SCRITTORALE, RALPH SMITH, PAUL STEFFEN, ROBERT THOMPSON.

CHILDREN

RED CURL, PETER FIELDS, PATRICK KIRK, FRANK SAUCEDO, ROSARITA VARELA.

---

477   The cast of characters from the programme of the first performance in Los Angeles. The work had about thirty-two performances in Los Angeles, an equal number in San Francisco and approximately seventy performances in the Ziegfeld Theatre in New York City.

LENA

TURE

SARINOFF
HUGO HAAS

Book by
FREDERICK HAZLITT BRENNAN
and
HOMER CURRAN

g by

y

y

THE SCENES

ACT I   TIME: ABOUT 1912

SCENE 1....The courtyard of Padre Josef's chapel near the Magdalena River.

SCENE 2....A private dining room in the Little Black Mouse Cafe in Paris. Two weeks later.

SCENE 3....The boat landing at the Muzo village. Ten days later.

SCENE 4....At the Shrine of the Madonna. The same evening.

ACT II

SCENE 1....At the Singing Tree. A few hours later.

SCENE 2....The kitchen of General Carabana's hacienda. The next afternoon.

SCENE 3....A terrace of the General's hacienda. That evening.

SCENE 4....The floor of a canyon near General's hacienda. A few....

SCENE 5....The chapel courtyard. Next....

MUSICAL NUMBERS

ACT I

SCENE 1: The Jungle Chapel
  A. *Women Weaving* . . . . ENSEMBLE AND PADRE
  B. *Peteca!* . . . . . SOLIS, RAMON, DANCERS AND ENSEMBLE
  C. *The Seed of God* . . . . . PADRE, DANCERS AND ENSEMBLE
  The Omen Bird (Teru, Teru) . . . . MARIA, DANCERS AND ENSEMBLE
  My Bus and I . . . . PEDRO AND ENSEMBLE
  The Emerald . . . . MARIA AND PEDRO

SCENE 2: *The Civilized People* . . . CARABANA, ZOGGIE, DANSEUSE AND ENSEMBLE
  Food For Thought . . . . TERESA AND ENSEMBLE
  Colombia Calls
  A. *Come to Colombia* . . . . . . TERESA, CARABANA AND BLANCO
  B. *Plan It by the Planets* . . . . . TERESA, ZOGGIE AND ENSEMBLE
  C. *Bon Soir, Paris* . . . . TERESA
  D. *Travel, Travel, Travel* . . TERESA, CARABANA, BLANCO, ZOGGIE AND ENSEMBLE

SCENE 3: Magdalena
  A. *Magdalena* . . . . THE OLD ONE AND ENSEMBLE
  B. *The Broken Pianolita* . . . . . . DANCERS AND ENSEMBLE
  The Festival
  A. *The Children* . . . . CHILDREN
  B. *The Omen Bird* . . . . MARIA AND GIRLS
  C. *River Song* . . . . ENSEMBLE
  D. *Chivor Dance* . . . . DANCERS
  My Bus and I (Reprise) . PEDRO, TERESA, CARABANA, BLANCO, LOPEZ AND ENSEMBLE

SCENE 4: *The Forbidden Orchid* . . . . MARIA AND PEDRO

ACT II

SCENE 1: *Ceremonial* . . . . . THE OLD ONE, DANCERS (MARIA GROSCUP, NORMA DOGGETT, LORRAINE MILLER), DANCE AND ENSEMBLE

  The Singing Tree . . . . RAMON, SOLIS AND ENSEMBLE
  Lost . . . . MARIA AND PEDRO
  Freedom! . . . . PEDRO AND ENSEMBLE

SCENE 3: *Vals de Espana* . . . A SPANISH DANCER (MARIA GROSCUP) AND DANCERS
  The Emerald (Reprise) . . . . PEDRO
  Piece de Resistance . . . . TERESA AND CARABANA

SCENE 5: *The Seed of God* . . . . PADRE, MARIA, PEDRO, RAMON, SOLIS AND ENSEMBLE

477

MAGDALENA – HOW IT CAME ABOUT
by Edwin Lester

It was nearly three years ago that Homer Curran conceived the idea which has now become *Magdalena*. It was his feeling that South America—particularly the Magdalena River locale with its wonderful variety of color and atmosphere, would be something new for the musical theatre. Toward that end, he created a basic story and our next task was to find a composer who could bring the color and authenticity to match the locale. The perfect choice was the distinguished Brazilian, Heitor Villa-Lobos, South America's foremost composer. We extended the invitation to Maestro Villa-Lobos with much more hope than confidence. The musical world was as amazed as we when Villa-Lobos accepted our proposal. It was part of our arrangement that Wright and Forrest would write the lyrics and pattern the music to the requirements of the story.

Arrangements were made to send Wright and Forrest to Rio de Janeiro to meet Maestro Villa-Lobos, discuss story and gather material. Twice their scheduled flights to Rio were forced back to New York because of mechanical difficulties. By now Wright and Forrest had lost their enthusiasm for flying. So we asked Villa-Lobos to come to America instead. He arrived in New York late in January, 1947. With him came Senora Villa-Lobos and Jose Brandao, a top-ranking Brazilian pianist who had spent several years lecturing on South American music in American universities. Since Villa-Lobos spoke only Portuguese, Spanish, and French and no English, Senor Brandao acted as interpreter. At many of the conferences, Henri Leiser, another friend of Villa-Lobos, interpreted in French.

Happily, Villa-Lobos and Wright and Forrest "hit it off" from the very first. The lyricists had so steeped themselves in Villa-Lobos' music that their knowledge of his idiom amazed the composer. At the end of their first two days together, the collaborators were in complete rapport.

Villa-Lobos could remain only a few weeks but so great was his enthusiasm that he was determined to finish his "operette" within that time. What had started out to be a preliminary get-together had suddenly become the real thing. The book was at best in skeleton form and Wright and Forrest had to work from the few musical situations which existed at the time and invent enough additional ones to give Villa-Lobos material upon which to complete a score. By some still unaccountable miracle, the basic score was finished in less than eight weeks and Villa-Lobos returned to South America. Wright and Forrest came to California to write the lyrics.

Magdalena was now a tangible thing on which production could proceed. It was at this point that Frederick Hazlitt Brennan, distinguished author with a formidable list of credits as novelist and writer for stage and screen, was so impressed by the project that he accepted Mr. Curran's invitation to work on the book. Thus another important creative collaborator became a part of *Magdalena*.

With the decision to premiere *Magdalena* as the closing event of the 1948 Season of the Los Angeles and San Francisco Civic Light Opera Associations, the endless conferences between the collaborators included the necessity for bringing Villa-Lobos to New York again (this time from Paris) for a final session with Wright and Forrest. It is of interest that the orchestrations were done by Villa-Lobos in Paris, New York, and Rio.

The members of the Production Staff were engaged to bring a particular brand of distinction to the production. Each outstanding in his respective field, their records described elsewhere in this book, are: Jules Dassin, Stage Director; Jack Cole, Choreographer; Howard Bay, Designer of Settings and Lighting; Sharaff, Costume Designer; Arthur Kay, Musical Director; and Robert Zeller, Choral Director. Undoubtedly no finer production staff has ever been assembled. Each of these Artists was called upon to do enormous research and study for many weeks before his actual work on *Magdalena* began. But to each, it has been a labor of unbounded enthusiasm.

The personalities and events mentioned in the foregoing notes give the reader some idea of the "behind-the-scenes" story of *Magdalena*. That the Stars, supporting Artists, and individuals of the Singing and Dancing ensembles, have been chosen with equal care, goes without saying. They too have had their weeks of study and rehearsal, and once the curtain is raised, it is they who become the active medium for interpreting to the audience all the work which has gone before.

And it is the audience which becomes the final collaborator. This world premiere for our California audiences is without benefit of "out-of-town" experimentation. While it is inevitable that there will be changes for the better as public reaction indicates where such changes shall be made, we hope that you will find a special pride in your own part in the birth of this new musical adventure.

478

THE STORY OF "MAGDALENA"

The background of *Magdalena* is the fabulous Magdalena River country. No river in the world more picturesque than the Magdalena, which flows from high up in the Andes through Colombia to the Gulf of Mexico. Its rambling course is a study in contrasts. Peopled mostly by native Indian tribes, som of them are lowly, others are descended from the highest Pagan culture. Here we find the beautif ranchos of the Spanish ruling class along side decadent fishing villages. Here among barren mountair and impenetrable jungle are the richest emerald mines in the world.

Our story deals with one of these great emerald mines, owned by General Carabana and worke by the Muzo Indian tribe whose leader is the beautiful Maria. Padre Josef, a Franciscan missionar has had a fine influence over the Muzos, all but Pedro, self-styled "the best damned bus driver in Sou America." Pedro's bus makes him a very important person in the community but his unwillingness to becom a convert has created a rift between him and Maria since Maria became the trusted ally of Padre Jose Pedro blames all of his troubles with Maria on the prized Madonna which stands outside the chapel ar which to him is the symbol of gentleness unbecoming to the Muzo tradition. Pedro and Maria have on thing in common, their desire to relieve the Muzos of the burdens put upon them by the absentee landlor General Carabana. Pedro, the typical "insurrecto", would use force. But Maria believes that th Christian principle of brotherly love can better accomplish their purpose.

To far away Paris, Blanco, aide to Carabana, comes to tell the General that he must return South America to protect his mining interests. Leaving Paris is sad news for Carabana, whose love fe food has made him the greatest gourmet and gourmand on the Paris scene. It means also that he mu leave his beloved "lady" Teresa, whose wonderful art as a cook has made her Little Black Mouse Cat a famous rendezvous. Carabana, using all the wiles at his command, including the promise of a pricele emerald necklace, induces Teresa to accompany him to South America.

Their arrival in Colombia is the scene for a grand pageant prepared by Maria for the General as display of the affection of the Muzos. Pedro makes a dramatic attempt to break up the pageant b Maria's hold on the Muzos is too strong. Pedro, still believing that force is the only solution to the problems, determines to steal the Madonna and remove this symbol of pacifism.

From this point, the conflict between Pedro and Maria grows until it forces Maria into an allian with Carabana. The development from here on concerns the resource by which the tempestuous Tere punishes her General, the amusing "miracle" by which Pedro is regenerated and peace and prosper are once more restored to the Muzo village.

479

MUSICAL THEATRE

Fine Score Not Enough To Carry the Day

By HOWARD TAUBMAN

AT the Ziegfeld Theatre, where "Magdalena" opened last Monday night, a lady was heard murmuring to her neighbor during the second act, more in bewilderment than disappointment, "I thought this was a musical."

Well, there were a lot of reactions to "Magdalena," many of them unflattering, but the one thing you could not doubt about the work was that it had a great deal of music, on the stage and in the pit. Heitor Villa-Lobos, Brazil's most gifted and original composer, has lavished a remarkably rich and varied score on the show. How come that anybody could question its being a "musical"?

The explanation is only partly in semantics, for words have to be played with when certain attitudes and prejudices of the public have to be confronted. The one word that causes Broadway to shudder almost as much as the ugly four-letter opera, probably because they are regarded as synonymous.

No matter how much Broadway showmen may distrust opera one exception is the temerarious Billy Rose, who appears ready not only to embrace it but to take on the Metropolitan Opera to prove that it is negotiable it is creeping steadily into the Broadway theatres.

Choose a Name

Of course, it is not called opera. It has such names as "musical adventure," the term used to describe "Magdalena," or it is called "musical play" or "play with music" for what you will. No matter what name you give it, there has been the flowering of a kind of lyric theatre on Broadway for which "musical comedy" is not a sufficient descriptive.

It is a theatre in which music does more than provide tunes for the leads and the comics to sin and for the dancers and the chorus line to do a few routines to. It is a theatre in which the music is occasionally integrated into the story and action, sometimes serving to further the movement of the plot and to comment on and reveal the characters of the people in it.

That, in essence, is the business of opera. When story, characters and music are indivisible you have good opera. There is a tradition

Heitor Villa-Lobos.

that unless every word in the piece is sung, either as aria or recitative, it is not technically opera; but even at the Metropolitan, where there is no intention to produce anything but opera, there are works like "The Magic Flute" by Mozart and "Fidelio" by Beethoven, to name only two, in which spoken dialogue alternates with singing.

Story Counts

Furthermore, the opera in countries like Italy is the principal theatre form. People there go to the opera not merely because they are aficionados of singing and lovers of gaudy stage spectacles but because they expect to be moved by the fate of the people in the story. You may say that after one has seen "Rigoletto" a dozen times, how can one work up any interest in the characters of the drama the thirteenth time? But many of us get involved with "Hamlet" and "The Cherry Orchard" and the other great plays even after a dozen performances.

If the old-style musical comedy has been undergoing changes on Broadway it is because the well-established formulas have become wearisome to authors, players and producers. New styles in lyric theatre are being created because the adventurousness of the creators is being matched by the patronage of a growing public. And what has been happening in shows like "Oklahoma!", "Allegro," "Finian's Rainbow," "Brigadoon," "Street Scene" and "The Medium," whatever one may think of the individual merits of each production, is valuable.

It may be that on Broadway, rather than at the Metropolitan, an indigenous American lyric theatre will be developed. Who cares whether it will be called opera or something more palatable to the average Broadway ticket-buyer? This does not mean that every show with a lot of music is necessarily a step forward. For all the color and imagination of the score that Villa-Lobos has written for "Magdalena," a pretentious production of this caliber may be a setback rather than an advance. For if music is not employed wisely, it will, through no fault of its own, evoke antagonism.

Villa-Lobos' score for "Magdalena" is unquestionably one of the most complex and fanciful a Broadway show has ever had. It is a rare thing for so brilliant and imaginative a craftsman to be called upon to do the whole score for a Broadway show. And Villa-Lobos has written with a subtlety and variety—for principals, chorus and orchestra—almost unparalleled on a Broadway stage.

His restless imagination evidently would not permit him to turn ut just a few tunes. Even in the songs that were meant to be the equivalent of the hit tunes of the average presentation, he could not resist the temptation to write with freshness and boldness in the sketching of a melodic line. His harmonies and rhythms have not only the exotic flavor of South America but the personal profile of a composer of originality.

Songs to Remember

There are many delightful things in this score. In "The Emerald" Villa-Lobos has written a love song of haunting beauty that avoids the clichés of the Broadway theatre. In "Food for Thought," which serves as a tour de force for Irra Petina, a fine singing comedienne, the composer proves that he can write with wit. One had the feeling that in this number Villa-Lobos was also doing a take-off on the "Habanera" in "Carmen."

There is a fiesta for which Villa-Lobos has written music of exotic rhythms and flaming colors. He has created striking effects with his contrapuntal writing for chorus and he has used the orchestra creatively. The gem of the score is "The Broken Pianolita," where he has contrasted and intertwined a moony, sentimental tune sung by an old man and the brazen, angular and strident beat of an old piano-player that runs as fitfully as a jalopy.

And yet the music does not carry the show. The truth is that the music seldom will in the theatre. No matter how good the music there must be a story of some credibility or imagination to make it go. You may scoff at some of the librettos in the perennially popular operas, but nearly all have something in the way of action or character to redeem them.

Composers like Mozart and Verdi knew better than anyone else how vital to the success of an operatic project was a good libretto. Read the letters and biographies of Verdi and see how he fought year in and year out for stories about real people. It is no accident that his best operas are "Otello" and "Falstaff," for in Arrigo Boito he found at last a poet who understood the needs of the dramatic stage. Mozart, too, turned out his best-rounded operas in "Marriage of Figaro" and "Don Giovanni" when he found an able librettist in Lorenzo da Ponte.

In "Magdalena" Villa-Lobos had no such collaboration. What the composer might have achieved if he had had a play about people living in a credible world is something that can only be guessed at.

For Villa-Lobos who has something like 1,500 works to his credit, another try is not too much to expect. Some day he will hitch his music to a story of character, and the theatre will have something.

480

480 Howard Taubman (1907-1995), music critic of *The New York Times,* reviewed the work from a musical point of view (*The New York Times,* 26 September 1948).

the preparation of the work.

Magdalena had a mixed reception when it was produced in New York.

Villa-Lobos's most successful opera *Yerma* was a commission he received in 1955 from his old friend Hugh Ross and from John Blankenship, director of the drama department at Sarah Lawrence College, Bronxville, NY. Villa-Lobos finished the work in 1956. It was written partly in Paris, partly in New York. The work was acclaimed by the American press when it was posthumously premièred on 12 July 1977 at the Santa Fe Opera, Santa Fe, New Mexico. Basil Langton, the producer, who had previously commissioned Villa-Lobos to write music for the ballet based on Eugene O'Neill's play *The Emperor Jones,* tells the story of how *Yerma* came about in the programme of the première.

AT THE THEATRE

Heitor Villa-Lobos, Brazilian Composer, Has Written the Musical Score for 'Magdalena'

By BROOKS ATKINSON

Heitor Villa-Lobos, the Brazilian composer, has written the score for "Magdalena," which was put on at the Ziegfeld last evening. Although he has been certified as authentic by qualified musicologists, it is impossible to have much of an idea about the score for a very unfortunate reason. "Magdalena" is one of the most overpoweringly dull musical dramas of all time. Watching the slow process of the plot and production is like being hit over the head with a sledge hammer repeatedly all evening. It hurts.

Even bad musical plays do not need to be so profoundly dull as this one. Rummaging around among the old hats in the garret, the entrepreneurs of "Magdalena" have set the art of music drama back several generations, as though nothing had been accomplished since "The Prince of Pilsen." Since they are serious about this romantic "musical adventure," it is plain that their taste is definitely in favor of the old stencils of operetta and that they are uninterested in the modern achievements of "Brigadoon," "Finian's Rainbow," the Kurt Weill "Street Scene," to say nothing of "Oklahoma!"

    ✦   ✦   ✦

As a matter of fact, there is no intelligent reason why a serious composer need be introduced as though musical drama were written exclusively for humorless audiences that have disliked everything since "The Student Prince." Villa-Lobos has written a South American score with motives presumably taken from the native music of Magdalena River people. It includes a fine meditative poem about a jungle river and several ruefully beautiful religious songs, written for several voices and chorus. It also includes a pleasant Spanish waltz and an amusingly orchestrated burlesque of a broken-down mechanical piano. Disentangled from the appalling li-

bretto and lyrics of "Magdalena," the score might be stimulating, especially since the orchestrations are unhackneyed and an accomplished singing actress, like Irra Petina, can give her numbers brilliance and eloquence.

    ✳   ✳   ✳

But the men of letters and ideas who acknowledge authorship of "Magdalena" have insisted on hitching a contemporary Brazilian score to a threadbare show-shop formula with some egregious Continental flourishes. Not only is the form of the libretto with stock characters archaic, but the story is unintelligible. The production is elaborately old-fashioned and the direction is ponderous.

"Magdalena" is a production of the Los Angeles Civic Opera Association. It is reported to have been successful on the West Coast during the summer. If it honestly represents the taste of West Coast audiences, there is apparently a time-lag between East and West much more epochal than had been supposed. "Magdalena" is probably the sort of academic chore that put the Manaos opera house out of business.

The Cast

MAGDALENA, a musical adventure" in two acts and nine scenes, by Frederick Hazlitt Brennan and Homer Curran. Music by Heitor Villa-Lobos. Pattern and lyrics by Robert Wright and George Forrest. Presented by Mr. Curran and produced by Edwin Lester; staged by Jules Dassin; settings and lightings by Howard Bay; costumes by Irene Sharaff; choreography by Jack Cole; musical direction by Arthur Kay; choral direction by Robert Zeller. At the Ziegfeld Theatre.

Padre Josef	Gerhard Pechner
Manuel	Peter Fields
Solis	Melva Niles
Ramon	Henry Reese
Maria	Dorothy Sarnoff
Pedro	John Raitt
Major Blanco	Ferdinand Hilt
Doctor Lopez	Carl Milletaire
General Carabana	Hugo Haas
Chanteuse	Betty Huff
Cigarette Girl	Christine Matsios
Zoggie	John Schickling
Danseuse	Lorraine Miller
Teresa	Irra Petina
The Old One	Gene Curtsinger
Chico	Patrick Kirk
Juan	Leonard Morganthaler
Conchita	Betty Brusher
Major Domo	Roy Raymond
Balladora	Marie Groscup
Ballador	Matt Mattox

481

ABOUT YERMA

By BASIL LANGTON

In the early '50's, John Blankenship conceived the idea of having Lorca's play YERMA made into an opera, and he thought of Villa-Lobos. He asked his friend Dr. Hugh Ross to convey the idea to the composer.

Dr. Ross knew Villa-Lobos from Paris in 1930, when he was given the score of "Choros X" for the Schola Cantorum in New York. The Schola followed with premieres of his "Bachianas Brasilieras," Nonetto, his Mass, "Manducarara," and "Descobrimento do Brasil."

When *Yerma* was commissioned, Blankenship also asked Ross and the poet Alastair Reid to make an English translation. However, instead of waiting for this, or writing it in his native Brazilian tongue of Portuguese, Villa-Lobos bought a copy of the play in Spanish and went quickly to work. The libretto for the opera is identical with Lorca's great dramatic poem.

Dr. Ross tells an interesting story of visiting Villa-Lobos in his New York hotel and the composer exclaiming, "There is the finished score!" Ross picked up a large tome of music paper with nothing in it but bar lines. Like Wagner, Villa-Lobos had all the music of *Yerma* in his head before writing down a single note of it.

I first met Villa-Lobos myself in 1955, when as a producer for the Empire State Music Festival I commissioned him to write a dance work for José Limón, *The Emperor Jones*, based on the play by Eugene O'Neill. The composer conducted the premiere, and Limón has since performed the work with great success throughout the world.

After the premiere of *The Emperor Jones*, in 1956, which the composer conducted, I suggested to Villa-Lobos that he next write an opera for the Festival. I proposed that he use as his theme *Macbeth* and set it in Brazil. The composer smiled enigmatically and made no comment. I assumed, knowing that he was a good businessman, that he was waiting to be "commissioned."

After Villa-Lobos died in 1959, I learned by chance from Dr. Ross that he and Blankenship had indeed commissioned the composer to write an opera, and he showed me the score of *Yerma*. It was dated 1955, the same year that I had commissioned *The Emperor Jones!* The opera had never been published or performed, and Dr. Ross had one of the few existing copies of the score. I quickly resolved to promote, with all my heart, a first-class production of *Yerma* — the composer's only opera.

Promoting *Yerma* has been difficult, not only because of legal complications between the Lorca and Villa-Lobos estates, but above all because of my own conviction that the opera should be performed in Spanish. Both Covent Garden and Sadlers Wells expressed great interest when I showed them the score, but they wanted the work performed in English — in Europe it was wanted in German. I was resolved that the first performance should be in the language the composer had chosen for his text — Lorca's Spanish.

The story Dr. Ross tells of being shown a "finished" score with little more than bar lines and metric measures, convinces me that had the composer written the opera to an English text, the metric design of *Yerma* would have been entirely different.

It was this determination of mine to stage the work in Spanish that has, as much as anything else, delayed the first performance of *Yerma*.

We may have waited many years, but we could not now ask for a more appropriate setting for this first performance of *Yerma*.

Shortly before he died the composer wrote:

Consider minha obra como esto que escrevi à Posteridade, sem esperar resposta.

H. Villa-Lobos

"*I consider my works as letters that I write to posterity, without waiting for a reply.*"

The opera *Yerma* is dedicated: "*A'Dona Hermenegilda Neves D'Almeida, Rio 1955*" — to the mother of Arminda Villa-Lobos.

A DIRECTOR'S NOTE:

All life seeks to reproduce itself, and there exists in nature a blind instinct to procreate.

Man has always celebrated this force in life with fertility rites, spring festivals, and elaborate religious ceremonies. He gives praise to the eternal spirit of rebirth and resurrection. The seed that is fertile is blessed; the seed that is barren is cursed.

It is because this force in life is so powerful that society has always sought to confine it within strict rules of morality.

Perhaps today, the prospect of world famine has created a new morality. A permissive society encourages sex for pleasure and not for breeding. Fertility, not fornication, has beome the new sin.

However, the irony of modern times is that, though man is convinced that he can use his *reason* to control his destiny, his acts are still more often motivated by his *feelings* — feelings that are deeply rooted in his body's sexual instinct to procreate. We may rationalize our patterns of behavior and put our trust in our ability to obey the laws of the computer, but our bodies, being unreasonable, continue to respond blindly to biological instincts. Thus birth-control is more easily preached than practiced. The most enlightened of men, who support world legislation to control the population explosion, are invariably the first to have children of their own.

Yerma is not a particular woman, living in a particular place at a particular time, but like Electra and Medea she is the archtype of an idea. She is the tragic symbol of the life force in conflict with the moral laws of a society. Both Yerma and Juan are trapped in a vow of marriage that they cannot break, for they are both willing victims of a code of honor that has been decreed by the elders of their society. Their moral pride has condemned them to live, together without love, barren unto death: killing Juan, Yerma kills herself.

21

482

483 Brooks Atkinson returns to the subject once more in the Sunday Edition of *The New York Times* on 26 September 1948. Here is a quote from an article entitled 'On Musical Stages'.

484 Unedited transcript of an interview on *Yerma* between Arminda Villa-Lobos, Hugh Ross and Richard Gaddes on 31 March 1971, kindly provided by the Santa Fe Opera.

Brazilian Music

On the authority of Olin Downes, who works in the adjoining glass cage, Villa-Lobos is a rare creative composer whose "art is profoundly based upon his native folklore of melody and legend." And amid the stupor with which the show is drenched, it is possible to recognize what Mr. Downes is writing about. A good deal of the music is sicklied over with the pale cast of opera ideology, but much of it is rich, warm and original. Although Mr. Villa-Lobos writes songs, he does not confine his music to songs, but writes for many voices and uses choruses as integral parts of the music structure. It would be interesting to hear parts of this music in a concert hall.

For then it could be freed from the aggressively boring operetta that now encumbers it, bearing down on all sides with moribund ideas. "Magdalena" is the sort of light opera Gilbert and Sullivan were satirizing sixty and seventy years ago. It is the epitome of hack work. In the past six or seven years there has been a revolution in musical dramas—the healthiest thing that has taken place in the theatre for a long time. But give theatre handymen the job of introducing a serious composer to theatre audiences and they immediately retreat into the museums, and before you know it you are being afflicted again with the piquant dissipations of Paris and expected to swoon before the quaint innocence of hot-tempered lovers in the jungle.

Hollywood Influence

No one who lives in a glass cage should throw stones at Hollywood. But in assaying the values of "Magdalena" it is impossible to ignore the facts that Robert Wright and George Forrest, who did "the pattern" and lyrics, wrote the lyrics and musical adaptations for most of the Jeanette MacDonald and Nelson Eddy pictures; and that Frederick Hazlitt Brennan, who worked on the book, has written a lot of routine pictures, too.

Mr. Brennan has been enjoying a fine reputation in this neighborhood. He must have written his share of "Magdalena" out of a filing cabinet. For "Magdalena" is an elaborate, ponderous, murky formula-job that would have seemed old-fashioned before the first World War. It represents bankruptcy in taste. Mr. Villa-Lobos has been unfortunate in his collaborators. They are still carrying passports from Graustark, which, after the Anchluss, became a dependency of Ruritania, and has now disappeared from the cultural atlas and need never be explored again.

483

FROM: Margaret Carson Sherrod
SANTA FE OPERA
P. O. Box 2408
Santa Fe, New Mexico 87501
505) 982-3851

The following is an unedited transcript of an interview between Madame Arminda Villa-Lobos, widow of the composer, Dr. Hugh Ross, director of the Schola Cantorum, and Richard Gaddes, Artistic Administrator of the Santa Fe Opera Company. (March 31, 1971)

RG: It's a great honor for us, Madame Villa-Lobos, to be able to have the premiere in Santa Fe this year. By the way, I was reading some notes on Villa-Lobos and was interested to see that he was playing cello at the cinema when he met Artur Rubenstein.

Madame Villa-Lobos: He was performing with an orchestra that played at the cinema (Rio de Janeiro, 1919). They played several pieces in the lobby before the program. Rubenstein listened to some pieces that interested him, and he asked Villa-Lobos about it. Villa-Lobos was not happy at the time. Nobody accepted him. Nobody understood him. That's why he was not happy.

HR: But at times he was very gay. When I saw him in Paris first in 1929...

Madame Villa-Lobos: At that time he was very happy. At that time.

HR: There he gave me the Choros X which we played in New York the next year, and I thought he was like Sancho Panza, always joking.

Madame Villa-Lobos: Because at that time he was very happy. It was in the beginning, in Brazil, when he was unhappy, and sometimes he had to change his name in order for musicians to play his music.

RG: Was he a concert pianist at one time?

Madame Villa-Lobos: No. Violin-cello, but he played viola, too, and clarinet, but originally guitar, classical guitar. At that time, in Brazil, the guitar was nothing more than a rhythm instrument and his mother didn't want him to play guitar because he had to mix with popular musicians, and the popular musicians thought he was only playing with them to amuse

Unedited transcript
Page 2

himself. But it was not for that. Many times he told me he was there to catch the atmosphere, the popular Brazilian atmosphere. He thought it wise to be influenced by these because he wanted to create Brazilian music.

RG: But don't you think he was influenced to some extent by Dubussy?

Madame Villa-Lobos: Yes, but especially Puccini, because, you know, Debussy is already influenced by Puccini. He loved Puccini. He loved Wagner.

HR: And Bach.

Madame Villa-Lobos: Bach, for him, was the god. He was the God of Music for him. Especially when he discovered in the North of Brazil the people never listened to Bach. It was not like today because today it's easier. You have radio--many ways of communication--but at that time we do not have anything Bach! That's why he created the Bachianas Brasilieras. In the Bachianas Brasilieras you can find Brazil and Bach at the same time.

HR: Also, he took Bach Preludes and he made them for the Brazilian school children so that they could sing...

Madame Villa-Lobos: Choirs.

HR: He had children's singing many of the forty-eight Bach fugues. I've got copies of these things, where he arranged them for a children's choir to sing. The things that the Swingle Singers do today he was doing in Brazil with the children.

RG: He loved children, very much, didn't he?

Madame Villa-Lobos: Children, he loved them. He didn't like precocious children. He was afraid about precocious children. He loved children to joke, to play, but not to do serious music. I have a niece, and he understood that she had a talent and from the beginning she played at our house and that was all right, wonderful, but if she played in a recital he would say, "I won't go." Sometimes he did go because he loved her very much, and when she was fifteen he said "Now I can attend the concert because now I feel she is serious, not precocious He was afraid about precocious children because they begin wonderful but after they forget.

HR: He had a children's chorus in Rio.

Madame Villa-Lobos: Yes, he conducted 42,000. In a stadium. Once Nelson Rockefeller was in Brazil and he was invited to

484

232

attend a performance of the students. Our Minister asked Villa-Lobos to do a salutation to Nelson Rockefeller and the children sang "sale-sale-Rockefeller" and afterwards they waved flags, and Nelson Rockefeller said he would never forget that. Himself said it was the big emotion of his life and I can believe it because the children were spectacular. Villa-Lobos' idea was to gather the pupils of each town, especially students from the more aristocratic places, and from the poorest, and put them together in music.

RG: As a composer, he reached an almost unheard-of output.

Madame Villa-Lobos: More or less one thousand, but many are lost. He wrote a great deal of music that he never made copies of. It's very funny because one time Villa-Lobos sent a friend to a priest to ask for copies of a piece he had given him, and the priest said "No, Villa-Lobos made this for me." He would not give it back. But now I know he is dead, and I am going to pray because...

RG: It's not published then?

Madame Villa-Lobos: No. We have no copies.

RG: Do you remember the time when he was composing Yerma?

Madame Villa-Lobos: Yes. He finished in Paris.

RG: Can you tell us how that all came about?

Madame Villa-Lobos: Hugh Ross saw Villa-Lobos and said I have a friend, John Blankenship (Head of the Drama Department, Sarah Lawrence College), who wants to commission an opera based on Garcia Lorca's Yerma. At that time he intended to have a Negro cast. They organized the thing, and Villa-Lobos wrote very quickly. He finished in Paris, and when he finished the opera Dr. Ross wanted to record several excerpts because he wanted to show Villa-Lobos several voices for us to choose from. I remember when you brought us Adele Addison.

HR: And Betty Allen. You see, Blankenship wanted all black singers so I found Negro singers who were with us in Tanglewood. Adele Addison at that time was quite a star. Betty Allen wasn't yet, but she was obviously very good.

Madame Villa-Lobos: And the baritone, he was excellent, marvelous.

HR: Yes, I've forgotten his name at the moment because he hasn't gone any further.

Madame Villa-Lobos: I have it in my home.

HR: You have the record, yes.

Madame Villa-Lobos: The name, everything. When Adele Addison was in the hotel, you played the piano with her and Villa-Lobos himself cried. He was so moved when she sang. It was very funny because for that occasion it was translated into English because they had to sing in English, but I am very happy that it is going to be sung in Spanish because that is the original. But on that occasion they had to sing in English.

HR: You see, it was Dora Vas Consedos who got the whole thing together for Villa-Lobos. Dora Vas Consedos at that time was Consul General of Brazil in New York and it's rather rare that you have a lady to be that, but she was very artistic and indeed she was a great friend of Villa-Lobos and when wanted to help Blankenship and all of us to get something of the opera known. So I got all these singers together, I got some of my chorus from Tanglewood, who sang the chorus in the final scene, and also those two leads and the baritone to sing the parts. And of course Villa-Lobos was still here while we were doing it.

RG: But he actually completed the opera before he had the translation from you?

HR: Yes, he went out and bought a copy of the play in Spanish, and he started setting it in Spanish without waiting for us to do anything in English.

Madame Villa-Lobos: No, no, it was just in Spanish, exactly as Lorca wrote it. Villa-Lobos did not know any words in English, only "vanilla ice cream" because it was the best ice cream he ate in his life, and everyone knew that Villa-Lobos liked vanilla ice cream...vanilla ice cream and strong, strong coffee.

RG: And he chain smoked?

Madame Villa-Lobos: He smoked cigars. The only thing he learned to ask the American people was "vanilla ice cream" and "very, very strong coffee". But Villa-Lobos wrote quickly.

RG: How long did it take him to write the work?

Madame Villa-Lobos: Less than one year, less, he began in fifty-five and finished in fifty-six.

HR: Blankenship gave him the commission and the point was Alastair Reid (British poet) and I were supposed to translate it and give him the English but he didn't wait for that at all. He went and got the play and then he took it away

to Paris so that by the time we ever saw anything, it was already done in Spanish.

Madame Villa-Lobos: Everything. It was all in Spanish. He said to me that everything he wrote was as Lorca wanted to do. That was the ideal. He said "I think I am succeeding in achieving what Lorca wanted."

RG: Are you very happy that it's being performed in Santa Fe? You know it's an old Spanish city founded by the Conquistadores in 1610.

Madame Villa-Lobos: Yes, I'm very happy. Excited. And the singer is Spanish, no?

RG: Yes, Mirna Lacambra. Was Villa-Lobos very enthusiastic about conducting?

Madame Villa-Lobos: He didn't like conducting, he said he preferred to listen, but the only way he could listen to his music was to conduct it. Sometimes he put another composer on the program to mix, but he conducted his music everywhere and he recorded many of this things...he won the grand prix de disc.

RG: It's said that he could compose in the middle of tremendous noise and distraction.

Madame Villa-Lobos: In our home we didn't listen to good music. Just when he went out. He listened to everything, theatre, popular music, he knew everything. In the hospital once he wrote an "Ave Maria;" in 1950, the second time he went to the hospital here he wrote the Quartet #12. Many times he said his music was his biological problem.

RG: Was his approach mathematical? Did he really mark out the measures of music on manuscript paper?

Madame Villa-Lobos: Just a few notes. I have one famous phrase Villa-Lobos wrote for a program: "I consider my works as letters that I wrote to posterity without expecting reply."

RG: Did he compose at all times of the day and night?

Madame Villa-Lobos: All the time.

RG: He had no regular pattern of work?

Madame Villa-Lobos: Any time, and especially at night, and very late. He slept very little. He has another phrase that was put in a medal. I have the medal. It said "It is

in nature that Villa-Lobos finds his greatest inspiration."

RG: But he wrote eight or nine other operas.

Madame Villa-Lobos: He wrote several. For instance, he wrote one opera that we always thought would be wonderful for television, "The Children on Clouds." It was a history for children but after his death they performed it in Brazil but I didn't like the way they did it. Villa-Lobos told me it should have a lot of movement, and television is wonderful for that but I saw the singer stop, there was no action. Villa-Lobos thought, this is what he said, "The prima donna must be the orchestra and the orchestra sing more than the artists. The artists more respective but the orchestra sing more." He didn't love opera, not too much, but when he wrote it, he loved it.

RG: Do you think he considered Yerma as his greatest work?

Madame Villa-Lobos: He considered it a great work for him. He was very happy about it. Many times when he wrote, he showed me and said this must find this effect, and many times after he played, after he conducted a work, I would ask him did you mean this when you wrote it and he would say "exactly" because he felt exactly what he wanted. He was completely musical. He never studied piano, but when he played piano you would think he was a great pianist.

RG: But he composed at the piano.

Madame Villa-Lobos: No. Sometimes when he had written, he asked someone who played the piano here, play here for me, but it was already written, it was like a letter.

RG: Did he not play long passages at the piano himself?

Madame Villa-Lobos: It was like a letter at his table. I wrote a nice letter he said.

HR: You see, he thought it all out in his head. He had it in his head first, then he put it on paper, then, as she said, he got other people to play it.

Madame Villa-Lobos: Other people.

RG: Well, I understood from Jose Limon that he would sit down at the piano and play a passage and say, "Do you like this, or this, or will this do for your dance?"

HR: He was trying out technical ideas.

Madame Villa-Lobos: That was different.

485　Cast of *Yerma* at the première.

486　The Santa Fe Opera, looking south from the Opera Club Bar.

487　A scene from *Yerma* with (*left to right*) Mirna Lacambra in the title role and Frederica von Stade (*b.* 1945) as Maria. Mirna Lacambra was a Spanish singer who studied in Barcelona, sang in all the major Spanish opera houses and made guest appearances in Brussels, Berlin and Munich. She made her debut at Santa Fe Opera in 1969, followed by performances in New Orleans and the Milwaukee Opera.

Unedited transcript
Page 7

RG: He was choreographing.

Madame Villa-Lobos: Completely different, but the first time Jose Limon listened to the work, he was very moved about Emperor Jones. Did you hear?

RG: No.

Madame Villa-Lobos: Was wonderful...I know his life much better than my life. That's true. I have forgotten many things about myself, my family, but about him, even when I was not with him, I know because we spoke about it, we would meet and I would know everything.

RG: Were you with him in New York, on some occasions?

Madame Villa-Lobos: He conducted several concerts, since 1944, each year he conducted. Maybe I know the United States better than you. I know New York, Philadelphia, California, Miami, Seattle, Texas, Atlanta, Pittsburgh, Brooklyn, Boston, Chicago.

RG: Did he like New York, did he like big cities?

Madame Villa-Lobos: Yes. He liked it here in New York because it was like a home to him. He had an apartment and many people came to see him from all over the United States. He was very happy in the United States, especially he was very happy with the musicians. That's very important, the musicians that played with him. I remember one great emotion for him. He conducted the Philadelphia Orchestra for two concerts, one here, one in Washington, one in Baltimore, just his own works. When I came into the theatre during rehearsals I saw one musician receiving a gift from the other musicians. I didn't know what it was, but at intermission during the concert this musician said to Villa-Lobos, this is my last concert with the Philadelphia Orchestra, I am going to retire but I don't want to retire without playing with you. And he played. That made Villa-Lobos very happy. It was three concerts. For two concerts he was there. The third concert he was not. And Villa-Lobos said, did you see the orchestra wasn't so good today. And I said but the orchestra was so good. Yes, Villa-Lobos said, but I miss him very much...The next day he has a concert in New York. The musicians arrive and one man said to him, yesterday I was a little sick but I told the doctor I must get up because tomorrow I must play with Villa-Lobos. It was a big emotional thing for Villa-Lobos. The concerts he gave here, many, many times, musicians from other orchestras came to attend the concerts. He was very, very happy here. He loved the United States.

* * *

484

YERMA

An Opera in Three Acts
Music by Heitor Villa-Lobos
Libretto by Federico García-Lorca
by arrangement with Music Now, Inc.

Conductor
CHRISTOPHER KEENE

Production by
BASIL LANGTON

Choreographer
JOSE LIMON

Designer
ALLEN CHARLES KLEIN

Original Paintings by
GIORGIO DE CHIRICO

Lighting
GEORG SCHRFIBER

Dates of Performance: August 12 (*World Premiere*), and 18, 1971

This production is supported by the National Endowment for the Arts, a Federal Agency, and many generous private donors who have helped make this grant possible.

The Santa Fe Opera wishes to express its appreciation to Dr. Hugh Ross for his invaluable assistance and advice concerning the opera *Yerma*.

CAST

The Voice of a child	Jack Stanton
Yerma	Mirna Lacambra
Juan, *her husband*	John Wakefield
Victor, *a shepherd*	Theodor Uppman
Maria	Frederica von Stade
An old woman	Elaine Bonazzi
Women and Laundresses:	Barrie Smith, Ellen Vincent, Karen A. Barlar, Ellen Phillips, Barbara Sacks, Bonnie R. Bradley
A young girl	Roslyn Jhunever
Another girl, *daughter of Dolores*	Linda Rasmussen
Yerma's Sisters-in-Law:	Susan Treacy, Martha Ann Thigpen
Dolores	Judith Farris
Female singer	Barrie Smith
Male singer	C. Allen Barker

Male Mask, Female Mask, Chorus of villagers and boys
The scene is set in Southern Spain — near Granada

Act I.	Scene 1	Yerma's house
	Scene 2	A road to the fields
Act II.	Scene 1	A mountain stream
	Scene 2	Yerma's house
Act III.	Scene 1	Dolores' house
	Scene 2	Outside a mountain hermitage

485

486

487

Opera: 'Yerma,' by Villa-Lobos, Bows

By ROBERT SHERMAN
Special to The New York Times

SANTA FE, N. M., Aug. 13 —The Santa Fe Opera, consistently the most ambitious and adventuresome of companies, highlighted its 15th season with the world premiere of a major score written 15 years ago: "Yerma," by Heitor Villa-Lobos.

By no means an unflawed masterpiece, "Yerma" is nonetheless a strong, serviceable, compelling piece of operatic theater, sparked by many moments of striking beauty and others of high dramatic tension. With the Spanish soprano Mirna Lacambra in the title role and a fine production by Basil Langston, it received an admirable baptism here last night.

Interestingly, "Yerma" was originally commissioned as an English opera for an an all-black cast, but Villa-Lobos became so excited by the Federico Garcia Lorca play that he did not wait for the translation to arrive, and set his music directly to the Spanish text. Hugh Ross conducted excerpts from the score at Tanglewood shortly thereafter in English and with an all-black cast including Betty Allen and Adele Addison, but there the performances ended. The composer died in 1959, the rights were tied up in litigation for years, and the few opera companies that considered giving the premiere were put off by the proviso that the first production be in Spanish.

•

The plot of the opera is concise, almost simplistic. The word "yerma" in Spanish means barren, and the heroine, who lives only to fulfill her role as a mother, is childless. Tensions inevitably grow between Yerma and Juan, her sterile husband, yet honor prevents her from seeking the solution suggested subtly by one of the villagers and directly by another. Eventually, her torment too much to bear, she strangles Juan, knowing that

The New York Times
Christopher Keene
Conductor

Heitor Villa-Lobos
Composer

in killing him she kills herself as well.

This is, then, a play of ideas rather than action, and Villa-Lobos has countered the built-in static quality of the opera with music of fascinating complexity and changeability. Without disturbing the over-all forward thrust of the score, pages of angular power bump up against lush, semi-folklore sections, and clear-cut, almost Puccini-like vocal lines frequently soar above a harsh, thick-textured instrumental fabric.

"The prima donna must be the orchestra," the composer said, "and the orchestra sings more than the artists." Certainly much more was happening than could be grasped at first hearing, and while there were stretches that seemed musically arid, this listener was left eager for a second opportunity.

Creating the cruelly difficult role of Yerma, Mirna Lacambra richly deserved the ovation that brought tears to her eyes. On stage for all but a few moments of the opera, she combined a sure vocal command with intense dramatic projection, never overstating the emotional case, yet keeping her portrayal

vivid all the way through.

John Wakefield began rather stiffly, then contributed a well-etched portrait of the uncomprehending husband. Elaine Bonazzi and Judith Farris were excellent in smaller but significant roles. Frederica Von Stade was particularly impressive as Maria, a young friend of Yerma's; Theodor Uppman was sturdy, if unexceptional, as Victor, the other man in Yerma's life; and the other cameo roles were well taken by members of Santa Fe's Apprentice Program.

Skillfully shaping the whole performance, and pacing it with confident expertise, was the young conductor Christopher Keene, who once again revealed his ability to take charge of the most complicated scores with complete assurance.

"Yerma" is due for only one repeat here, on Tuesday, but let us hope that other companies will take it up. Particularly in English, with a listener able to follow more completely the psychological nuances, it should be an important and viable addition to the contemporary repertory.

488

Vivas for Villa-Lobos 'Yerma'

By Lynne Waugh
Santa Fe, N.M.

As the ovations at the dress rehearsal faded, a small group of brown-bereted barrio youth stood in the Santa Fe summer night and shouted, "Viva!"

On opening night two days later, the jewel-bedecked and formally gowned of society and the arts came to the oldest state capital in the nation to the world premiere of the opera "Yerma,"*to analyze minutely its form and style. They were moved to bravos by the exquisite music of the Brazilian composer, Heitor Villa-Lobos, by the magnificent performance of Spanish soprano Mirna Lacambra, and by the tragic simplicity of Yerma's story by Federico García Lorca.

Those who shouted "Viva" were responding to its Spanishness. The performance, sung in Spanish, is a word-by-word translation of Lorca's poem. It was a natural for Santa Fe and New Mexico, a state whose population is two-thirds Spanish and Indian. It is the fourth world premiere staged in the history of the Santa Fe Opera Company, and in the career of its founder-director, John Crosby. It is the 16th time in its 15 summers that an opera has made its American debut in the sleek, sculptured, contoured confines of the Santa Fe Opera pavilion.

Youth

Yerma's premiere here expresses a cultural commitment to Spanish-speaking people everywhere. In the 400-year-old plaza in the heart of Santa Fe on the weekend before Thursday's premiere, actors from La Juventude de barrio del Cristo Rey — a young neighborhood youth group in consort with the Museum of New Mexico — presented a dramatic narration of the play.

However, there is a serious question as to whether in the United States the theme of a barren woman is as worth considering in the decade of woman's lib and the population explosion as it was in 1934 when Lorca wrote the play.

As the wife, frustrated by her husband's lack of desire and inability to give her a child, Miss Lacambra presents a tour de force. But whether her childlessness is worth 2½ hours of on-stage agonizing is a question some first-nighters considered more than once.

Yerma's husband, Juan, is a doomed and tragic figure in Lorca's play. In the opera John Wakefield's performance in the role is more frustration and blindness than tragedy. The supporting roles, played by Theodor Uppman, Frederica von Stade, and Elaine Bonazzi are impeccable. Mr. Uppman and Miss Bonazzi already have established reputations in the opera world, and Miss von Stade marks herself as a major newcomer to opera.

Static music

Although students of Lorca and those who know him deny any symbolism or hidden meaning to the play, the opera seems to embody much symbolism. Juan's spinster sisters appear with bread and water. Mr. Uppman's idealistic Victor appears to be portrayed as a near-spiritual figure — a shepherd with a lantern. And Juan, who has denied his wife life, finds death.

The chorus is magnificent and represents the morality conflict over which the heroine agonizes.

The music itself, which was written by Villa-Lobos before his death in 1959, and has only now surfaced after the settlement of his estate, is a significant contribution to the whole body of opera.

The 25-year-old conductor, Christopher Keene, does an admirable job with an orchestra recruited from the New Orleans Symphony and other orchestras throughout the country. The opera's stage direction, by English director Basil Langton, may be revised as the opera makes its way to other opera houses throughout the world. José Limon is the choreographer. And the scenery is a perfect adaptation of a Spanish village with its whitewashed walls and protruding vigas.

The Santa Fe opera season runs through Aug. 28 and includes, besides the "Yerma" world premiere, performances of "The Magic Flute," "The Marriage of Figaro," (a specialty in its repertoire), "The Flying Dutchman," and . Offenbach's "Grand Duchesse der Gerolstein."

489

490

491

Stage works   237

492

492 Richard Gaddes (*b.* 1942), studied at Trinity College of Music in London, graduated in 1964. Artistic administrator of the Santa Fe Opera Company (1969-1978) at the time when *Yerma* was first performed. Assistant manager of Artists' International Management. Since 1976 general director of Opera Theatre of Saint Louis. Under his guidance the first TV film of an opera (Benjamin Britten's (1913-1976) *Albert Herring*) was made in the United States with collaboration from the BBC, London. Board member of the William Matheus Sullivan Foundation, New York City and frequent judge at auditions at the Metropolitan Opera, New York City (Photo by Ken Howard, courtesy Opera Theatre, St Louis).

493 Programme for the première of A *Menina das Nuvens* (The Girl on Clouds). It was performed twelve months after the composer died, on 29 November 1960, at the Teatro Municipal in Rio de Janeiro.

1 do Rio de Janeiro

Terça-feira, 29 de Novembro de 1960, às 21 horas
Domingo, 4 de Dezembro de 1960, às 10 horas

A Menina das Nuvens

em primeira audição mundial

Fantasia musical de
VILLA-LOBOS

baseada na peça de
LUCIA BENEDETTI
Três atos

Menina das Nuvens	— Aracy Bellas Campos
Corisco	— Assis Pacheco
Tempo	— Edison de Castilho
Variável	— Paulo Fortes
Marchinha	— Bailarina
Anita	— Lysia Demôro
Mãe	— Maria Henriques
Rainha	— Glória Queiroz
Príncipe	— Izauro Carrino
Soldado	— Guilherme Damiano
Lua	— Maria Helena Muccelli

Regência de Edoardo De Guarnieri
Regia de Gianni Ratto
Assistência de Assis Pacheco
Cenários de Gianni Ratto
Figurinos de Belá Paes Leme

DANÇAS

Coreografia de EUGENIA FEODOROVA

WANDA GARCIA e
as alunas da Escola de Danças Clássicas :
Wilma da Rocha Lima — Roseana da Silva Pires — Nora de Garcia Esteves — Maria Cristina Nunes — Norma Lobo Restier Gonçalves — Carmem Maria Fonseca Cavaliére — Lourdja Peixoto de Mesquita — Deborah de Oliveira Bastos.
Inspetor Técnico do Corpo de baile:
Sebastião de Araujo
Preparadores ao Piano :
Geraldo Rocha Barbosa
Jorge Vinicius Salles
Avisador: SEBASTIÃO FLORENÇO

493

Villa-Lobos wrote one more stage work, though it was not commissioned. It is nevertheless mentioned here as Arminda Villa-Lobos also alludes to it in the published interview referred to above. The composition, *A Menina das Nuvens,* written in 1957-58, shortly before Villa-Lobos's death, was performed posthumously.

Travels and concerts

After Villa-Lobos's return to Brazil following the enthusiastic reception of his works in the United States and with the end of World War II in sight, his lifestyle underwent fundamental changes. His dream had finally come true: he was given an opportunity to present his music in many places in the United States, in Europe and in some Latin American countries.

Notwithstanding the onset of his grave illness in early 1948 which necessitated two serious operations, one in 1948 and another in 1950, Villa-Lobos enthusiastically and with his customary joie de vivre savoured the sudden increase in requests for him to give concert appearances and to present his own compositions. This is not the place for a comprehensive account but it is

494 The Instituto Nacional de Bellas Artes in Mexico City where concerts and opera performances are held.

495 The Teatro Municipal in beautiful Santiago de Chile. It is used for opera and concert performances and is set against a background of the Cordilleras.

494

495

FESTIVAL VILLA-LOBOS

**Conjunto da
Sociedade Brasileira de Musica de Camara**

TEATRO MUNICIPAL
Quinta-feira, 11 de Abril
de 1946
—— ás 21 horas ——

PROGRAMA
DE OBRAS DE VILLA-LOBOS

I — QUARTETO No. 7 (1942)
(Dedicado ao Quarteto Borgerth)

Allegro
Andante
Scherzo
Allegro justo

Pelo Quarteto Borgerth
(Oscar Borgerth, Alda Grosso Borgerth, Francisco Corujo e
Iberê Gomes Grosso)

••

II — TRIO para Violino, Viola e Violoncelo (1945)
(Dedicado à Fundação Coolidge)

Allegro
Andante
Scherzo
Allegro preciso e agitado

Oscar Borgerth, Francisco Corujo e Iberê Gomes Grosso

••

III — CHÔRO No. 7 — SETTIMINO (1924)

Violino .... Oscar Borgerth
Violoncelo .... Iberê Gomes Grosso
Flauta .... Moacyr Liserra
Oboe .... João Breitinger
Clarinete .... Jayoleno dos Santos
Saxofone .... Francisco Miranda Pinto
Fagote .... José Lages da Rocha
Regencia de LEO PERACCHI

496

496   At a concert on 11 April 1946, arranged by the Cultura Artistica in Rio de Janeiro, an evening devoted exclusively to the work of Villa-Lobos.

possible to give an indication of Villa-Lobos's growing popularity on the concert circuit. For a composer-conductor from Brazil this was in itself quite an achievement; it was an honour both for him and his country. No other Brazilian composer prior to Villa-Lobos had ever participated in international concert programmes to the same extent. This focused the spotlight both on his music and on Brazil. The ovations, his success and the interest shown in him were, at the same time, a tribute to Brazil. He enjoyed both, no doubt, and the admiration accorded him outside Brazil also had its repercussions within his native country: he was suddenly acclaimed and cherished there as the great composer. Villa-Lobos's travels included Chile, Mexico, Israel, but principally the United States and Europe.

COMUNE DI ROMA
ACCADEMIA DI SANTA CECILIA
ISTITUZIONE DEI CONCERTI

STAGIONE ESTIVA 1947

ALLA BASILICA DI MASSENZIO
XII
(2948 dalla fondazione dei Concerti)

MERCOLEDI 6 AGOSTO 1947 - ORE 21.15

CONCERTO ORCHESTRALE
DI COMPOSIZIONI DI

ETTORE VILLA LOBOS

DIRETTE DALL'AUTORE

Rovine della Basilica di Massenzio (da una vecchia stampa)

La Basilica di Costantino, detta di Massenzio, fu iniziata tra il 306 e il 310 dopo C. dall'imperatore Massenzio sul luogo di un tempio della Pace che andò bruciato al tempo dell'imperatore Commodo (180-192 d. C.), e completata dal suo successore Costantino che lo vinse in battaglia.

Costruzione notevole come una delle ultime testimonianze del genio architettonico romano. Servi come corte di giustizia e anche come grande museo sotto l'impero.

Di una colossale statua di Costantino, già nella Basilica, si conservano i frammenti nel Museo Capitolino. Piastre di bronzo furono asportate dalle pareti nel VII sec. per la Chiesa di S. Pietro.

PROGRAMMA

1. *Bachianas Brasileiras* (prima esecuzione)
   Preludio
   Aria ' (Modinha)
   Tocata (Catira Batida)
   Fuga
2. *Choros n. 6* (prima esecuzione in Europa)
3. *Rude poema* (prima esecuzione in Enropa)

497 Programme for a Villa-Lobos concert at the Accademia di Santa Cecilia, Rome, 6 August 1947.

497

SATURDAY
5.0 p.m. to Close Down

Third Programme
514.6 m. (583 kc/s)   203.5 m. (1,474 kc/s)

8.0   MIRROR OF THE MONTH
A Magazine for the Microphone—March
The Channel Tunnel Story by Alex McCrindle
Battle of the Blues by Bernard Braden
Jump Sunday at Aintree with Frisby Dyke
Madrid Calling! from Jenny Nicholson
Public Voices with Wynford Vaughan Thomas
Salutes and Satires with George Benson, Cecile Chevreau, Deryck Guyler, Ronald Barton
Special contributions by Gordon Glover and Allan M. Laing
Music composed by Marr Mackie played by the Shoestrings
Conductor, Clifton Helliwell
Associate Editor, John Bridges
Edited and produced by Michael Barsley

8.45   TAKE YOUR PARTNERS
The Sydney Thompson Old-Tyme Dance Orchestra
Master of Ceremonies, Sydney Thompson

9.30   BBC CLOSE-UP
An 'O.B.' in the Making
Wynford Vaughan Thomas tells the story behind an Outside Broadcast and tests some would-be commentators

6.0 p.m. A HISTORY IN SOUND OF EUROPEAN MUSIC
General editor, Gerald Abraham
4—Early English Music to Dunstable
Introduced by Alec Robertson
(BBC recordings)
A weekly series of programmes, the first twelve of which are a résumé of those broadcast last year
Next programme: April 2
followed by an interlude at 6.40

6.45   'LAPSUS CALAMI'
A selection of the verse of J. K. Stephen (1859-92)
Arranged by Patric Dickinson
Reader, Carleton Hobbs
Produced by James McFarlan
(BBC recording)

7.10   SONG RECITAL
Settings of poems by Goethe
Elisabeth Schwarzkopf (soprano)
Bruce Boyce (baritone)
Frederick Stone (piano)
Mit einem gemalten Band...Beethoven
Wonne der Wehmuth........Beethoven
Wonne der Wehmuth.........Schubert
Geheimes..................Schubert
An Schwager Kronos........Schubert
Kennst du das Land?.........Liszt
Wer nie sein Brod mit Thränen ass......Liszt
Die Liebende schreibt....Mendelssohn
Liebeslied...................Schumann
Die wandelnde Glocke.....Schumann
Als ich auf dem Euphrat schiffte.Wolf
Die Spröde.................Wolf

9.5   THE PRINCE CONSORT
Alan Pryce Jones reviews a new life of the Prince Consort by Roger Fulford

9.25   ORCHESTRAL CONCERT
Part 2
(conducted by Heitor Villa-Lobos)
Symphony No. 7............Villa-Lobos
(first performance)
followed by an interlude at 10.5

10.10 THE ARAB REFUGEES
by Mabel C. Warburton, who has spent nearly thirty years in educational and missionary work in the Middle East
She recently visited the Arab refugee camps in Transjordan and reported on them to the organisations that have now taken over the administration of relief work in Palestine and the surrounding Arab countries
(BBC recording)

10.30 ITALIAN MUSIC
Antonio Saffi (harpsichord)
Suite in B minor......Domenico Zipoli
Two Sonatas: F, G minor...Cimarosa
Concerto in G..............Vivaldi—Bach

11.0   SYDNEY SMITH THE POLITICIAN
Last of four readings from the works of Sydney Smith
Read by Raf de la Torre

498

SALLE GAVEAU   SAMEDI 3 MARS 1951

HECTOR
VILLA-LOBOS

499

498   England and Italy broadcast Villa-Lobos's music. The BBC, London premièred Villa-Lobos's Symphony No. 7 on the Third Programme on 26 March 1949. Radio Italiana gave a Villa-Lobos concert on 16 April 1949.

499   Villa-Lobos conducting at the Salle Gaveau, Paris, 3 March 1951.

Sous les auspices de l'
ASSOCIATION FRANÇAISE D'ACTION ARTISTIQUE

CONCERT consacré aux Œuvres de VILLA-LOBOS

avec l'

ORCHESTRE DE LA SOCIÉTÉ DES CONCERTS DU CONSERVATOIRE

sous la direction de

Hector VILLA-LOBOS

Compositeur et Chef d'Orchestre

PROGRAMME

I. — BACHIANAS BRASILEIRAS N° 1

pour 8 violoncelles

a) PRÉLUDE (Embolada)
b) ARIA (Modinha)
c) FUGUE (Conversa)

(Bachianes brésiliennes) écrit en 1930 - pour 8 cellos

C'est le titre d'un groupe de compositions musicales écrites de 1930 à 1945, comportant neuf suites et appartenant à une série d'œuvres de Villa-Lobos, inspirées de l'ambiance musicale de J.-S. Bach, que l'auteur considère comme une ressource folklorique universelle, riche et profonde comme les musiques populaires de tous les pays, expression directe des peuples, tandis que Bach est un intermédiaire entre toutes les races.

Pour Villa-Lobos, la musique de Bach vient de l'infinité astrale pour s'infiltrer dans la terre comme musique folklorique et ce phénomène cosmique se reproduit sur toutes les superficies, se subdivisant dans les différentes parties du globe terrestre, avec une tendance à s'universaliser.

Bachianas Brasileiras N° 1 pour orchestre de cellos se subdivise en trois parties: Prélude (Embolada), d'une ambiance typiquement brésilienne; Aria (Modinha), construit en forme d'« aria bachiana » avec une longue mélodie; et une Fugue (Conversa), écrite à la façon de Satiro Bilhar, ancien compositeur de sérénades populaires de Rio-de-Janeiro. Dans le dernier mouvement, l'auteur a voulu rendre l'impression d'une causerie de quatre compositeurs de sérénades populaires brésiliens avec leurs instruments.

II. — 6ᵉᵐᵉ SYMPHONIE

a) Allegro non troppo
b) Lento
c) Allegro quasi animato
d) Allegretto

(Sur les Montagnes du Brésil - écrite en 1944)

Cette Symphonie est basée sur une ligne mélodique inspirée du contour des montagnes du Brésil, selon le principe adopté par Villa-Lobos.

Le but de l'échelle au millimètre est d'obtenir le dessin mélodique de la photographie d'une montagne, d'un paysage ou d'une colline, dont le profil est reproduit sur une feuille quadrillée, au moyen d'un pantographe placé dans l'échelle 1 × 1.000.

499

Villa-Lobos .. .. **CONCERTO**

Allegro
Allegro poco scherzando
Andante (Cadenza)
Allegro non troppo

Soliste • ELLEN BALLON • Soloist

90   Auditorium du Plateau,
Montreal, Canada. 31.I.
1951. Conductor: Ernest   **ERMISSION**
Ansermet.

INWAY PIANO

500

ORQUESTRA SINFÔNICA BRASILEIRA

Presidente: Dr. EUVALDO LODI

DIRETOR ARTÍSTICO E REGENTE TITULAR:
Maestro ELEAZAR DE CARVALHO

1952 — DÉCIMA SEGUNDA TEMPORADA — 1952

DÉCIMO SEGUNDO CONCÊRTO PARA O QUADRO SOCIAL
Sábado, 30 de agosto de 1952, às 16,30 horas - Série Vesperal

TEATRO MUNICIPAL

PROGRAMA

Festival Villa-Lobos

1a. Parte

I — BACHIANAS BRASILEIRAS N.º 8   (1944)

a) Prelúdio
b) Aria (Modinha)
c) Tocata (Catira Batida)
d) Fuga

II — EROSÃO — Sorimâo u Ipirungàua   (1950)

(A origem do Rio Amazonas) Lenda Amerindia N. 1
(Primeira audição no Brasil)

III — "Ouverture de l'home tel"   (1929)

(Primeira audição no Brasil)

2a. Parte

IV — SINFONIA N.º 2 — Ascenção   (1917)

a) Allegro non troppo
b) Allegretto Scherzando
c) Andante Moderato
d) Allegro Final

Regente: VILLA-LOBOS

501

TEATRO

MUNICIPAL

CARACAS
VENEZUELA

PROGRAMA

Jueves 22 de Enero de 1953, a las 9.15 p. m.

Director: HEITOR VILLA-LOBOS

I

Preludio y Fuga No. 6 (para órgano)	J. S. Bach
(adaptación para orquesta de H. Villa-Lobos)	
La Tumba de Chateaubriand	L. Aubert
Imbapara	O. Lorenzo Fernández

II

Descubrimiento del Brasil (la. Suite)	H. Villa-Lobos
a) Introducción	
b) Alegría	
Lloros No. 6	H. Villa-Lobos

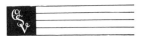

sociedad
RQUESTA SINFONICA VENEZUELA

502

PROGRAMA

FESTIVAL DE MUSICA SUDAMERICANA

I

LA VOZ DE LAS CALLES (1.ª audición) ALLENDE

OBERTURA CRIOLLA, Op. 20 (estreno) DRANGOSCH

IMBAPARA (estreno) ... ... FERNÁNDEZ

II

MOMOPRECOCE, Fantasía para piano y
orquesta (estreno)... ... ... VILLA-LOBOS

Solista: Ramón CASTILLO

III

EL RIO DE LAS SIETE ESTRELLAS
(estreno) ... ... CASTELLANOS

CHOROS NUM. 6 (estreno) ... ... VILLA-LOBOS

Maestro Director :

HECTOR VILLA-LOBOS

503

500   Ellen Ballon played
Villa-Lobos's *Piano Concerto
No. 1* under Ernest Ansermet
at the Auditorium du Plateau
in Montreal on 30 and 31
January 1951.

501   Villa-Lobos Festival in
Rio de Janeiro, 30 August
1952.

502   Villa-Lobos conducted
in Caracas, Venezuela on 16
and 22 January 1953.

503   Villa-Lobos conducted
in Barcelona on 8 March
1953, at the Gran Teatro del
Liceo.

SENDERGRUPPE

ROT-WEISS-ROT

WIEN – SALZBURG – LINZ

GROSSER KONZERTHAUSSAAL

Samstag, 14. März 1953 · Beginn 15 Uhr

Rot-Weiß-Rot-Konzert

der

Wiener Philharmoniker

Dirigent:

HEITOR VILLA-LOBOS (Brasilien)

EVENCIO CASTELLANOS: *El rio de las siete estrellas*

HEITOR VILLA-LOBOS: *Sinfonia Nr. 6*

Choros Nr. 6

504

PROGRAM—TUESDAY, JULY 28, 1953, at 8:30 P.M.

ALL NATIONS NIGHT

symphonies under the stars

(Co-sponsored by the Southern California Symphony Association)

LOS ANGELES PHILHARMONIC ORCHESTRA

HEITOR VILLA-LOBOS, Guest Composer-Conductor

BERNARDO SEGALL, Pianist

If necessary to leave before end of program, please do so during interval between numbers

VILLA-LOBOS PROGRAM

Bachianas Brasileiras No. 8

I. Preludio

II. Aria (modinha)

III. Toccata (Catira Batida)

IV. Fuga (Conversa)

Concerto No. 4 for Piano and Orchestra

I. Allegro non troppo

II. Andante con moto

III. Allegro vivace

IV. Allegro moderato

Mr. Segall

INTERMISSION

Symphonic Episode and Ballet, "O Papagaio do Moleque"
(The Youngster's Kite)

DANSAS AFRICANAS

I. Farrapos (Youth)

II. Kankikis (Infancy)

III. Kankukus (Old Age)

Mr. Segall uses the Steinway exclusively

The Steinway is the Official Hollywood Bowl Piano, Courtesy Penny-Owsley Music Co.
The official Organ is the Baldwin Electronic, Courtesy of Baldwin Piano Co.
Carillonic Bells Installation—Schulmerich Electronics, Inc., J. G. Corcoran, Carilloneur

505

504 Villa-Lobos led the Vienna Philharmonic on 14 March 1953.

505 An exclusively Villa-Lobos programme with the Los Angeles Philharmonic Orchestra on 28 July 1953.

506 Eleazar de Carvalho performed Villa-Lobos's *Madona* with the Vienna Philharmonic on 9 January 1954.

SENDERGRUPPE

ROT-WEISS-ROT

WIEN – SALZBURG – LINZ

GROSSER MUSIKVEREINSSAAL

Samstag, 9. Jänner 1954 · Beginn 15 Uhr

Rot-Weiß-Rot-Konzert

der

Wiener Philharmoniker

Dirigent: ELEAZAR DE CARVALHO
(Rio de Janeiro)

CAMARGO M. GUARNIERI: *Symphonie Nr. 2*

HEITOR VILLA-LOBOS: *„Madona", Poema sinfonico*

MANUEL DE FALLA: *El Amor Brujo*

506

San Antonio Symphony Orchestra

Founded by Max Reiter in 1939

VICTOR ALESSANDRO, Musical Director

Fifteenth Season—1953-54

enth Program

ary 30, at 8:30

ductor, HEITOR VILLA-LOBOS

THOVEN Overture to "King Stephen," Op. 117

FLEM "Magicienne de la Mer"
L'Appel de Dahut
Ys engloutie renait dans le reve

VEL Bolero

INTERMISSION

LA-LOBOS Bachianas Brasileiras No. 8
Preludio
Aria (Modinha)
Toccata (Catira Batida)
Fuga (Conversa)

LA-LOBOS Choros No. 6

San Antonio Symphony—STEINWAY PIANO—Dr. Alessandro—BALDWIN PIANO

507

GROSSER MUSIKVEREINS-SAAL
Mittwoch, 25. Mai 1955, 19.30 Uhr

4. Außerordentliches Konzert

DIE WIENER SYMPHONIKER

Dirigent:

HEITOR VILLA-LOBOS
(Brasilien)

Solisten:

FELICJA BLUMENTAL
(Klavier)

LEO CERMAK
Fagott)

P R O G R A M M :

Heitor Villa-Lobos

1.) Sinfonietta Nr. 1 über ein Thema von Mozart (1916)
Allegro justo — Andante non troppo — Andantino — Allegro

2.) Klavierkonzert Nr. 5 (1954)
Allegro non troppo — Adagio — Allegretto scherzando — Allegro
Solistin: **Felicja Blumental**

3.) Ciranda das 7 Notas für Fagott und Streichorchester (1933)
Allegro non troppo — Più mosso
Quasi Andante — Meno Allegro Solist: **Leo Cermak**

4.) Bachianas Brasileiras Nr. 2 (1930)
Preludio (O Canto do Capadócio)
Aria (O Canto da nossa terra)
Danca (Lembrança do sertao)
Toccata (O Trenzinho do Caipira)

Programmpreis: 90 Groschen

Kamar, Wien IV

508

507 Villa-Lobos conducting his music in San Antonio, Texas on 30 January 1954.

508 A Villa-Lobos concert with the Vienna Symphony on 25 May 1955.

New Orleans Philharmonic-Symphony Orchestra

TENTH SUBSCRIPTION CONCERT
TUESDAY, JANUARY 17, 1956

ALEXANDER HILSBERG, *Conductor and Musical Director*

HEITOR VILLA-LOBOS, Conducting

M. J. EUPHEMIE BLANC, Soloist

VILLA-LOBOS PROGRAM

SINFONIETTA NO. 1
(Played in memory of the 200th anniversary of the birth of Mozart)
Allegro Justo Andante Non Troppo Andantino

DANSES AFRICAINES (Danses des Indiens Métis)
Farrapós Kankukús Kankikís
(First performance in New Orleans)

Intermission (Continued on Page 5)

509

509 Villa-Lobos conducted his music in New Orleans, USA, on 17 January 1956.

THE ATLANTA SYMPHONY GUILD, INCORPORATED

presents

The atlanta symphony orchestra

in the

FIFTH SUBSCRIPTION CONCERT OF THE 1956-1957 SEASON

heitor villa-lobos, guest conductor

and

felicja blumenthal, pianist

Tuesday, December 4, 1956

Atlanta Municipal Auditorium

PROGRAM

Fantasia and Fugue No. 6 . . . . **Bach**
(Transcribed by H. Villa-Lobos)

Overture: *King Stephan* . . . . **Beethoven**

Prelude a la Conte de Fees . . . . . **A. LeGuillard**
(First performance in the United States)

Prelude to *Die Meistersinger* . . . . . . **Wagner**

INTERMISSION — Fifteen Minutes

Concerto for Piano and Orchestra No. 5 . **Villa-Lobos**
I. Allegro non troppo—Allegro Vivace
II. Poco adagio—Adagio piu mosso
III. Allegretto Scherzando—Cadenza
IV. Allegro
Mme. Blumental

Choros No. 6 . . . . **Villa-Lobos**

All concerts will begin promptly at 8:30 P.M. Trumpet fanfares will be sounded in the outer lobby at 8:25 and again five minutes before the end of the intermission. Late-comers will be admitted only at intervals between numbers. If necessary to leave early, please do so between numbers.

510

510 Villa-Lobos as guest conductor in Atlanta, USA, on 4 December 1956.

511 Villa-Lobos appeared as guest conductor in Miami, 17 and 18 November 1957.

Thirty-first Year

THE UNIVERSITY OF MIAMI
SYMPHONY ORCHESTRA

JOHN BITTER, *Conductor*

403RD *and* 404TH CONCERTS

Sunday Evening, November 17th *Monday Evening, November 18th*

HEITOR VILLA-LOBOS, *Guest Conductor*

FRANCES YEEND, *Soprano*

PROGRAM

I. *Prelude and Fugue No. 6 — *Johann Sebastian Bach*

II. Overture "Meistersinger" — *Richard Wagner*

III. 4 Danzas Sinfonicas — *Julian Orbon*
Obertura
Gregoriana
Declamatoria
Criolla
(first world premiere)

INTERMISSION

IV. Chant et Orchestra — *Heitor Villa-Lobos*
Eu te amo (Poem of Dora Vasconcellos)
(first performance in United States)
"Elsa's Dream" from Lohengrin — *Richard Wagner*
"Dich Theure Halle" from Tannhäuser — *Richard Wagner*

V. Dansas Africaines — *Heitor Villa-Lobos*
(Danses des Indiens Metis)
Farrapos
Kankukus
Kankikis

*Symphonic transcription by Heitor Villa-Lobos

Steinway Piano courtesy Morgan Piano Company

Patrons will not be seated during the playing of a composition, and are requested not to leave while the orchestra is playing.

Concerts start promptly at 8:30 o'clock

511

TEATRO COMUNALE GIUSEPPE VERDI
ENTE AUTONOMO

STAGIONE SINFONICA
PRIMAVERA 1959‒

Giovedì 23 Aprile alle ore 21

CONCERTO SINFONICO
della
ORCHESTRA FILARMONICA TRIESTINA
diretto dal Maestro
HEITOR VILLA-LOBOS

PROGRAMMA:

*) BACH - VILLA-LOBOS - Preludio e fuga N. 6

BEETHOVEN - «Re Stefano» - Ouverture

*) VILLA-LOBOS - Preludio, giga e fuga
da «Bachianas brasileiras n. 7»

───────

*) CHALLAN - Sinfonia N. 2 in Fa magg.
Allegro energico giocoso
Adagietto doloroso
Scherzo
Vivace

*) VILLA-LOBOS - Choros N. 6

*) Prima esecuzione a Trieste

512

512   Villa-Lobos gave a
concert in Trieste, Italy on
23 April 1959, seven months
before his death.

Villa-Lobos in Israel and Paris

Villa-Lobos's visit to Israel in 1952 had special
significance: he appeared as composer-conductor,
lectured about his educational system and was inspired
to write a composition dedicated to that country.
Bathya Bayer (*b.* 1928), once head of the Music
Department and National Sound Archives of the
Jewish National and University Library in Jerusalem,
wrote to the author on 28 December 1972 that,
according to information gathered from several
musicians, Villa-Lobos stayed in Israel for only three

513

513   Villa-Lobos
conducting the Israel
Philharmonic Orchestra on
18 June 1952.

514   Michael Taube (1890-
1972), Israeli conductor of
Polish origin who had lived
in what is now Israel since
1934. He had conducted in
Germany (Frankfurt and
Berlin) where he performed
rarely-performed works by
relatively unknown pre-
classical composers. Modern
composers often wrote
especially for him.

514

הקונצרט הסימפוני הראשון

ביום ראשון, 30 במאי, בשעה 9.00 בערב, באולם "ארמון"

התזמורת הפילהרמונית הישראלית

המנצחים: מיכאל טאובה, היינץ פרוידנטל

סולנים:	זדל סקולובסקי — פסנתר ; פרנק פלג — פסנתר.	

1. הייטור וילא־לובוס (ברזיל)
2. דאריוס מיהו

האודיסיה של גזע
קונצרטו מס' 4 לפסנתר

אנימה, מאריפה, סימפוניה

הפסקה

3. אדוח צ'י (איטליה)
4. אלכסי הייאף
5. אנדרה דזלוברט (צרפת)

שני אינטוננציות
קונצרטו־לפסנתר
סימפוניה

היטור וילא־לובוס הגה את רעיון יצירתו הסימפונית, המוקדשת לתחיית העם היהודי,
שעת ביקורו הראשון בישראל, בשנת 1952. הפואמה הסימפונית "אודיסיה של גזע"
חוברה בריאו דה־ז'ניירו, בספטמבר 1953. לא
זו בלבד שהמחבר הקדישה ליצירה, אלא שהוסיף ותרם את כל ההכנסות, שתובאנה, פרודוציה,
לקרנותיהם של אומני ישראל, שתחולקנה, לפי הוראת שר החינוך והתרבות.
ביצועה של הפואימה במסגרת הפסטיבל היא לה כידיעות־בכורה עולמי.

Heitor Villa-Lobos conceived the idea of a symphonic work dedicated
to the renaissance of the Jewish people when he visited Israel for the first time
in 1952. The Symphonic Poem "ODISSEIA DE UMA RAÇA" was composed in
Rio de Janeiro in September 1953 and the composer not only dedicated his work
to Israel but also donated all his royalties to artists' funds designated by the
Israel Minister of Education and Culture.
The composer's dedication reads :
"Na formação do Universo, Deus criou uma raça heroica que viveu
e sofreu, mas venceu em Israel".
The work is being given its world premiere on the occasion of the Festival.

Sunday, May 30th, at 9.00 p.m., "Armon"-Theatre

FIRST SYMPHONY CONCERT

Conductors: MICHAEL TAUBE, HEINZ FREUDENTHAL

Soloists:
Zadel Skolovsky, piano — Frank Pelleg, piano

1. Heitor Villa-Lobos (Brazil)
    L'Odyssée d'une Race
    Poème Symphonique
2. Darius Milhaud (France)
    Piano Concerto No. 4
    Animé — Très lent — Joyeux

INTERMISSION

Interval

1. Adone Zecchi (Italy)
    Due Intenzioni
2. Alexei Haieff
    Piano Concerto
3. André Jolivet
    Symphonie

first part of the concert.

על דאריוס מיהו ויצירתו — ראה עמודים 18, 19, 20.
על אלכסיי האייף — עמוד 52.

About Darius Milhaud and his works — see p. 18, 19, 20.
About Alexei Haieff — p. 52.

515
515

---

1 STUDY SCORES OF ORCHESTRAL WORKS AND CHAMBER MUSIC

15

HEITOR VILLA-LOBOS   הייטור וילה-לובוס

L'ODYSSÉE D'UNE RACE

נ ד ו ד י א ו מ ה

Poème Symphonique   שירה סימפונית

"Na formação do Universo, Deus criou uma
raça heroica que viveu e sofreu, mas venceu
em Israel"

Rio de Janeiro, September 1953

PRINTED AS FASCIMILE   נדפס בכתב יד הקומפוזיטור

ISRAELI MUSIC PUBLICATIONS

U. S. A.:	LONDON:	MILANO	AMSTERDAM:
LEEDS MUSIC CORPORATION	J. & W. CHESTER LTD	CARISCH S. A.	W. IKMANS & VAN POPPEL
322 WEST 48th STREET	11, GT. MARLBOROUGH St. W.1	VIA G. BROGGI 19	12. VAN BAERLESTRAAT
NEW YORK 36, N. Y.			
Sole representative for the	PARIS:	ZORICH	SCANDINAVIA:
Western Hemisphere	HEUGEL & Cie.	HUG & Co	WILHELM HANSEN Musik Fa.
	2 bis, RUE VIVIENNE, II e	LIMMATQUAI 24-28	COPENHAGEN, Gothersgade

TEL-AVIV, ISRAEL, P. O. BOX 6011 תל־אביב, ישראל, ת. ד.

516

---

515   Concert programme
which included the première
of *Odisséia de uma Raça*.

516   Title page of *Odisséia
de uma Raça* (Copyright by
Israeli Music Publications
Ltd., by kind permission of
the publishers.)

Villa-Lobos in Israel and Paris   251

Beginn von Villa Lobos' Sinfonischer Dichtung „Odisseia de uma Raça" (1953) in der Handschrift des Komponisten. (Mit Erlaubnis des Originalverlegers Israeli Music Publications Limited, Tel Aviv).

517 Facsimile of the first page of the score of *Odisséia de uma Raça* (Copyright by Israeli Music Publications Ltd., by kind permission of the publishers.)

days from 17 to 19 June. *The New York Times,* on the other hand, on 14 September 1952 reported that 'Villa-Lobos stayed in Israel six days'. On June 18 he conducted the Israel Philharmonic Orchestra including two of his own compositions: *Chôros No. 6* and the *Piano Concerto No. 2* with Maxim Shapiro as soloist.

At the invitation of his old friend Leo Kestenberg (1882-1962), whom he had first met at – and who had been responsible for his invitation to – the 1936 Prague International Congress for Musical Education, the Brazilian composer gave a guest lecture at Tel Aviv's Music Teachers' Training College of which Kestenberg was director.

Israel and her people inspired Villa-Lobos to write the symphonic poem *Odisséia de uma Raça,* composed the following year in September 1953. It was premièred during the 28th Festival (30 May – 8 June 1954) of the International Society of Contemporary Music (ISCM) in Haifa on 30 May 1954, with Michael Taube conducting.

Paris

518

Paris was Villa-Lobos's headquarters from 1952 until his death in 1959. He loved Paris and the Parisian life. Here he felt completely at home. He did not move into an apartment as he had done during the 1920s, but preferred to live in a hotel; because of his constant travelling he felt this to be more convenient. The author is not aware whether it was Villa-Lobos's idea or someone else's to reside at the Hotel Bedford, 17 Rue de l'Arcade. The Hotel Bedford was where the last Emperor of Brazil, Dom Pedro II, had lived out his remaining years after his dethronement when the Republic was proclaimed in Brazil in 1889. A memorial plate is affixed to the Hotel's façade in memory of the last Emperor of Brazil. On the eighty-fourth anniversary of the composer's birth (twelve years after Villa-Lobos's death) on the initiative of Consul-General and Minister Helio Scarabótolo and at the suggestion of the Brazilian Ambassador, General Aurélio de Lyra Tavares, a memorial tablet was placed above that of Dom Pedro II upon which was engraved (in French): The Brazilian composer, Heitor Villa-Lobos, great interpreter of the spirit of his country, stayed at this hotel from 1952 to 1959.

Opposite the Hotel Bedford was the restaurant L'Acropole. Villa-Lobos usually took his meals there in the company of friends and visitors.

Occasionally Villa-Lobos lunched somewhere else. On his birthday, on 5 March 1948, Brazilian friends fêted him in La Maison de l'Amérique Latine. His

518   A photograph of the memorial tablet at the Hotel Bedford.

519   Comments by Luiz Heitor Corrêa de Azevedo on Villa-Lobos and the restaurant L'Acropole (*Presença de Villa-Lobos*, Vol. 10, MEC/DAC/MVL, Rio de Janeiro 1977).

Muitas de suas obras do último período foram, se não inteiramente escritas, concebidas ou acabadas no Hotel Bedford, onde em seu quarto havia sempre um piano, posto à disposição do compositor, todos os anos, pela fábrica Gaveau.

Num restaurante situado do outro lado da rua, bem defronte do hotel, chamado l'Acropole e cujo proprietário era um grego de nome Papainac, vulgo Papa, ele fazia suas refeições e convidava amiude os amigos. Eram os seus momentos de folga, de pausa, pelo menos aparente, da atividade criadora. No cardápio do restaurante se achava inscrito um certo Café Villa-Lobos, mais caro que o ordinário, ultra-forte, destinado a satisfazer o gosto exigente do compositor, para o qual os outros eram mijo de gato e que, onde quer que fosse, ensinava os maîtres d'hôtel a preparar uma ìnfusão à brasileira, digna do nome de café.

519

---

520 To honour Florent Schmitt, who had recognised the talent of Villa-Lobos in reviews during the 1920s at the time when the composer was trying to secure a foothold in Paris, Villa-Lobos tried to persuade the French composer and critic to come to Brazil. The following year, in September 1949, Florent Schmitt visited Rio de Janeiro at the invitation of the Brazilian Academy of Music and the Conservatório de Canto Orfeônico. A reception was held and concerts were organised with Florent Schmitt, now almost eighty years old, conducting some of his works.

255

great admirer, Florent Schmitt, was invited to join the party.

To my knowledge there is just one letter presently available which testifies to the great friendship between Villa-Lobos and Florent Schmitt, written from Rio de Janeiro on 25 September 1951 and signed by Arminda Villa-Lobos and the composer.

The only place in Paris about which Villa-Lobos had some reservations was UNESCO, even though it had done much to honour him. In 1949 he was one of several composers commissioned to write a work for a gala concert commemorating the centenary of Chopin's death. Villa-Lobos responded with *Hommage à Chopin* for piano about which he and Irving Schwerké corresponded. On 3 November 1958, UNESCO premièred Villa-Lobos's *Bendita Sabedoria* on the occasion of the opening of the new UNESCO building in Paris at Place de Fontenoy. Even so, Villa-Lobos did not warm to this cultural organisation, though he did pay a visit to UNESCO on 15 June 1956 which is recorded in several photographs.

Villa-Lobos in pictures

521, 522, 523, 524, 525 These portraits depict the composer in similar poses. Only the photographs 524 and 525 (*overleaf*) show him markedly different, rather worn out and tired. They were taken in 1950 after he had undergone his second operation for cancer.

Portraits

The majority of the photographs of the composer which are still available date from the last fifteen years of his life, after he had emerged as a composer-conductor on the international concert circuit. In these pictures he is seen at work and at leisure. The likenesses include portraits, shots of the composer at work, playing instruments, conducting, with friends and in his leisure moments.

521

522

523

524

Villa-Lobos at work

526, 527, 528, 529   The
photographs show the
composer correcting proofs
and composing. In photo
526 Villa-Lobos is working
in the Hotel Bedford in
Paris; in photo 527 he is at
his desk in New York in
1956 and in photos 528 and
529 at his desk at the Hotel
Alrae in New York in 1957.

525

526

527

529

Villa-Lobos playing instruments

530, 531, 532   Villa-Lobos seen here playing the piano, the guitar, and (*overleaf*) the popular Brazilian percussion instrument reco-reco.

530

531

532

Villa-Lobos conducting

533   After a rehearsal with
the Symphony Orchestra of
Radio Italiana, 1953.

534   Villa-Lobos
conducting the Philharmonic
Orchestra in Havana.

533

534

Orquesta Filarmónica de la Habana

CONCIERTOS 629 y 630

TEMPORADA 1953-54

VIERNES 11 DE DICIEMBRE ● DOMINGO 13 DE DICIEMBRE

Teatro Auditorium

Director invitado: *Heitor Villa-Lobos*

Solista: *Iris Burguet*
Soprano:

PROGRAMA

I—BACHIANAS BRASILEIRAS No. 8 (1944)

    a) Preludio
    b) Aria (modinha)
    c) Tocata (catira batida)
    d) Fuga

II—SINFONIA No. 6 (1944)

    a) Allegro non tropo
    b) Lento
    c) Allegro quasi animato
    d) Allegretto

INTERMEDIO

III—SERESTAS (1926)

    a) Modinha
    b) Otoño
    c) Abril
    d) Cancao de Carreiro.

SOLISTA: **IRIS BURGUET**

IV—CHOROS No. 6.

PIANOS STENWAY

—9—

535

535 The programme which Villa-Lobos conducted in Havana on 11 December 1953.

536 Villa-Lobos conducting a concert at La Scala, Milan.

536

537 Title page of the
programme which he
conducted on 22-23 June
1953.

537

Villa-Lobos with friends

538 With Georges Auric
(1899-1983), French
composer and music critic
and a member of Les Six.

538

539 With Jenny Tourel (1910-1973) (*left*), Canadian mezzo-soprano of Russian origin who made her debut at the Metropolitan, New York in 1944. She was an outstanding interpreter of Villa-Lobos's music.

539

540

540 With Marguerite Long (1874-1966), French pianist and a teacher at the Paris Conservatoire (1906-1940), who founded her own school in 1920. Gave concert performances in Europe and the United States and known particularly as an interpreter of French music.

541 Cristina Maristany (*b.* 1918) and Villa-Lobos discussing some interesting points in the composer's work.

541

542 At a reception in honour of Villa-Lobos at the residence of Dora Alencar Vasconcellos (1910-1973) in New York in 1957, with his old friend Edgard Varèse.

543 With Phyllis Curtin (b. 1922), American soprano who made her debut in 1953 at the New York City Opera, and participated in 1959 at the Vienna State Opera and the Metropolitan in 1961. She is known as an interpreter of contemporary music. Here she is seen with Villa-Lobos in New York, December 1958.

544 With Queen Elisabeth of Belgium (1876-1965), who was married in 1900 to King Albert I (1875-1934) of Belgium, who ascended to the throne after the death of his father Leopold II (1835-1909) in 1909. She was renowned for her creative activities and cultural interests. She founded an annual international music competition in Brussels. Queen Elisabeth is seen here complimenting the Brazilian composer after his concert on 22 September 1958 with the Grand Orchestra Symphonique de la Radiodiffusion Nationale Belge. On the composer's left is Arminda Villa-Lobos.

542

543

544

Concert Symphonique

consacré à la musique brésilienne
sous la direction de

HEITOR VILLA-LOBOS

LUNDI, 22 SEPTEMBRE 1958

Grand Orchestre Symphonique
de la Radiodiffusion Nationale Belge

• • •

Programme

I. Prélude (N. I. de la « Bachianas
   Brasileiras N° 4 » . . . . . H. VILLA-LOBOS.

II. « O Café » (Suite de Ballet) . . C. SANTORO.
   Abertura - Passeio - Queimada
   (Ouverture - Promenade - Queimada)

III. Symphonie N° 12 . . . . H. VILLA-LOBOS.
   Allegro non troppo - Adagio
   Lento - Allegro poco moderato

• • •

IV. Abertura Concertante . . . C. GUARNIERI.

V. Abertura das 3 Mascaras Perdidas F. MIGNONE.
   (Ouverture des 3 Masques Perdus)

VI. Choros N° 6 . . . . H. VILLA-LOBOS.
   (Episode Symphonique)

545

545 Programme which Villa-Lobos conducted in Belgium.

546 Villa-Lobos with the Brazilian singer Bidú Sayão in 1959 during a rehearsal with the Symphony Orchestra of the Air for a recording of *Floresta do Amazonas*. Bidu Sayão (*b.* 1902) is a Brazilian concert and opera singer of international reputation. Made her debut in Rio de Janeiro in 1926, sang at the Colón Theatre in Buenos Aires and was a member of the Metropolitan Opera in New York (1932). She retired at the peak of her career.

546

547 Bidú Sayão (*right*) with Arminda Villa-Lobos (*left*) at the residence of the Brazilian Ambassador to the United States, Jaime de Barros, on 7 April 1959.

547

Villa-Lobos at leisure

548 During Walt Disney's visit to Villa-Lobos's office at SEMA in 1947, Disney took this photograph.

548

549 Villa-Lobos selects a book from the small library in his apartment.

550 Villa-Lobos tuning in to the radio in his apartment.

551 Villa-Lobos in 1956 selecting one of the many cigars he smoked incessantly every day.

549

550

551

Caricatures, aphorisms and decorations

Villa-Lobos was very rarely a subject for illustrators. To our knowledge there are only three such drawings:

During the latter years of his life, Villa-Lobos indulged in the business of jotting down his thoughts on himself and his views on life. He saw to it that these were widely distributed and indeed repeated on many occasions. His best known are to be found on p.269.

Villa-Lobos received many decorations and commemorative plates during his lifetime. Some of them are reproduced here, together with his baton.

552

553

552   A posthumous caricature from 1974, by Mário Mendez.

553   The earliest known sketch, drawn in Los Angeles by Sotomayor during the composer's visit to the United States.

554 A rather pensive
composer.

554

555 He considers his works
are like letters written to
posterity without expecting
an answer.

556 One of the composer's
aphorisms.

Consider minhas obras como cartas
que escrevi à Posteridade, sem esperar
resposta.

H. Villa-Lobos

555

Em todo caso, há sempre uma vantagem
nos meus adversários, eles obrigam-me
a ser cuidadoso nas minhas creações musicaes.

H. Villa-Lobos

556

557

558

557   Commemorative
plates.

558   Baton and
decorations.

559   Villa-Lobos's guitar
and some of his music.

559

Sculptures

560   Mário Cravo (*b.* 1923), at work when sculpting Villa-Lobos's bust in New York. Brazilian sculptor who studied in Brazil and the United States and exhibited in Brazil and other countries. Taught at the University of Bahia (1963-64) and was director of the Museum of Modern Art and Folk Art at Salvador, Bahia.

Several sculptors made a bust of Villa-Lobos. The first was by an Argentine, Luiz Perlotti, whose bronze bust has been in the Teatro Municipal in Rio de Janeiro since 1936. A copy, in white faience, made in 1938, was donated to the Museu Villa-Lobos by Arminda Villa-Lobos. Another copy was donated by Perlotti to the Museu Villa-Lobos on 19 November 1963 on the occasion of the fourth anniversary of Villa-Lobos's death. In 1948 Mário Cravo made a bust of Villa-Lobos in New York City.

Armando Sócrates Schnoor also made sculptures of Villa-Lobos.

There exist two more busts: one was made by Adriana Janacópulos (*b.* 1897); the other by Marta Elsa Winitzky in 1950 (1ft 8 in.).

560

561

562

561 Armando Socrátes Schnoor (*b.* 1913), Brazilian sculptor who studied at the Escola Nacional de Bellas Artes, and later taught at the same school. Member of the National Council of Culture. He made Villa-Lobos's death mask and a granite head which is at the Ministry of Education and Culture in Brasília. Schnoor is seen here with his bust of Villa-Lobos in the sculptor's apartment in the Rua Almirante Tamandaré 20, Flamengo, in Rio de Janeiro. The original is in the author's apartment. A bronze copy, made in 1974 (height: 1ft 8in.), is in the Brazilian Embassy in Paris.

562 The work was commissioned by the Brazilian Ministry of External Relations (*Itamaraty*). A bronze copy was offered to the Argentine in 1968, another copy to Uruguay and a third to the University of Maracai, Venezuela.

563

563 Leão Veloso (1899-1966) donated this life-size statue which he made in 1960 to the Museu Villa-Lobos. It is a maquette for a monument which the Brazilian newspaper, *Diário de Notícias,* had planned.

564

564 The original is in the Museu Villa-Lobos. A copy is in front of the Ministry of Education and Culture. The head is 3ft 4in. high. It was unveiled in Brasília on 14 January 1961 by Clóvis Salgado da Gama (*b.* 1906), then Minister for Education and Culture.

Seventieth-birthday celebrations

565

Villa-Lobos celebrated his seventieth birthday during the administration of Brazil's President Juscelino Kubitscheck de Oliveira.

The Brazilian composer happened to be in New York on his birthday. *The New York Times* honoured him with an editorial, the day before he turned seventy, and the following day John Briggs of *The New York Times* recorded the celebrations accorded to the Brazilian composer at New York's City Hall where he was cited 'for his achievements both as a composer and as a music educator'. A scroll, signed by Mayor Robert F. Wagner Jr, was presented by Abe Stark, President of the City Council.

Some time later, though the exact date is not known to the author, Villa-Lobos was fêted in Paris where a concert in honour of his seventieth birthday was given at the Théâtre de la Maison Internationale in the presence of the composer.

Brazil also celebrated her native son. He was made

565   Juscelino Kubitscheck de Oliveira (1902-1976), Brazilian politician who was President of Brazil from 1956 to 1961. He died in a car accident.

566   Editorial in *The New York Times*, 4 March 1957.

MUSICIAN AT 70

Heitor Villa-Lobos, Brazil's most famous composer and one of the truly distinguished men of music of our time, will be 70 tomorrow. His energy and enthusiasm are undiminished, and his creative powers remain at flood tide. He would be a remarkable figure in any age; in his own place and time he has been an enormously influential personality, leading his own people to a broadening of its culture and a rediscovery of its musical roots.

Senhor Villa-Lobos is a prolific composer. It is said that he himself cannot give an exact count of how many compositions he has written; he only knows that it is in the hundreds. Largely self-taught, he has instinctively expressed the spirit of his people and his native earth. He has not sought to be a self-conscious nationalist or patriot. He has immersed himself in the ways of his countrymen; he has soaked himself in the variety and immensity of Brazil. Without a deliberate effort to adopt a folk idiom, he has written music that sums up the quality of his land and its people.

More than a quarter of a century ago he persuaded the Brazilian authorities to let him prove what an original approach to musical education could accomplish. He organized a chorus of 12,000 voices, drawn from all classes, and in four months taught it to sing four-part a cappella music. He went on to devote ten years to reorganizing the Brazilian system of musical education. He inspired young Brazilian composers to do as he had done—to ignore the pedants and to translate in music the truth of their own and their people's intuitions.

On March 28 and 29 New York will have an opportunity to pay homage to this composer of fierce individuality when he will be guest conductor of the Philharmonic. Grateful as he may be for this observance, he will not need it to reinforce his pride in his convictions. For he is still the man who went to Paris in 1922, relatively unknown, to show the musical élite of Europe what he had done, not to beg for a chance to be heard. What he had done won wide respect, which has grown with the years.

566

567

567   New York City Hall.

568   Villa-Lobos takes a
bow after conducting at
Carnegie Hall on 28 March
1957 in honour of his
seventieth birthday,
celebrated on 5 March 1957.

569   Robert F. Wagner Jr
(1910-1991), American
politician who held several
public offices, including
Mayor of New York and
Ambassador to Spain (1968-
69).

568

569

Proper Way to Play the Reco-Reco

Heitor Villa-Lobos of Brazil playing a native instrument

Villa-Lobos, 70, Hailed by City; Composer Thumps in Brazilian

By JOHN BRIGGS

The Brazilian composer Heitor Villa-Lobos, 70 years old today, was honored yesterday at City Hall. He later demonstrated native Brazilian instruments. The instruments form part of the percussion section for Senhor Villa-Lobos' "Cantata Profana: Mandu-Carara." It will have its first New York performances by the Philharmonic-Symphony on March 28 and 29.

Senhor Villa-Lobos will conduct both concerts. They also will feature part of his "Bachianas Brasileiras No. 1" and first performances of works by Florent Schmitt and Camargo Guarnieri.

The Brazilian was cited at City Hall for his achievements both as a composer and as a music educator. A scroll signed by Mayor Wagner was presented, by Abe Stark, president of the City Council. It said Senhor Villa-Lobos had rendered "distinguished and exceptional service" in promoting cultural relations between the peoples of the Americas.

All the percussion instruments demonstrated are indigenous to Brazil, Senhor Villa-Lobos said, with no trace of European influence.

Drum Made of Goatskin

The camizaõ is a drum made of goatskin stretched over a square frame. It is used by musicians in the Negro and Indian voodoo processions of Rio de Janeiro.

The cabaça is a gourd filled with pumpkin seeds. On the outside are strung necklaces of seeds.

The reco-reco is a short bamboo tube with a goatskin over one end and notches filed down the side. The player sounds it by thumping it on the floor or by running a stick across the notches.

The caracaxa and xucalho are essentially the same as the maraccas used by conga and samba bands, except that Senhor Villa-Lobos insists the Brazilian instruments have "more masculine" tones.

With existing systems of musical notation, there is no way of writing down the variety of subtle effects that can be achieved with the Villa-Lobos percussion instruments. The composer solves this difficulty by himself demonstrating their use to orchestras that play his works. He communicates verbally in Portuguese and French.

ORCHESTRA LED BY VILLA LOBOS

Brazilian Conducts Three of His Own Compositions in Philharmonic Concert

By ROSS PARMENTER

Heitor Villa-Lobos brought the flavor of his native Brazil to Carnegie Hall last night when he led the New York Philharmonic-Symphony in a program that featured three of his own works.

This is the second time the Philharmonic has honored the Brazilian composer in a conspicuous way. In 1945, when his works were just becoming known in this country, it helped his fame by having him conduct several of them in a pair of February concerts. This time he was engaged to lead the orchestra in honor of his seventieth birthday, which was on the fifth of this month.

In many respects, the concert was like a crescendo. When Senhor Villa-Lobos first came on the stage there were only twelve 'cellists assembled in a semicircle and he led them in the first two movements of his Bachianas Brasileiras No. 1 for eight violoncelli. By the end of the concert the stage was thronged with instrumentalists, including many playing odd Brazilian percussion instruments, while on the left were ranged a girls' chorus from the High School of Music and Art and on the left an adult chorus from the Schola Cantorum.

'Cantata Profana' Heard

The work that employed all these forces—and it was much the best piece of the evening—was his "Mandú-Çarará," a composition he calls a "cantata profana," which was done with two-piano accompaniment in 1947 by the Schola Cantorum.

The program notes gave the story of the Brazilian version of "Hansel and Gretel" which suggested the work. But the actual piece does not follow the story in any detail. Nor do the choristers narrate it. Instead, they chant in a Brazilian Indian dialect, and the whole thing suggests a jungle ritual, with many natural jungle noises, as well as the drumming and chanting of the natives. It reaches an exciting climax and ends on a triumphant shout like an "Olé" at a bullring.

One of Senhor Villa-Lobos' chief gifts is for writing sustained, soulful melodies that sound very well when played by deep-toned string instruments. This aspect of his art was heard to particular advantage in the "Modinha" of his first Bachianas. That term, incidentally, is his own invention for Bach-like creations in Brazilian style.

Lavish Orchestra

The Latin Americans have a favorite phrase to the effect that there is more time than money. It tended to recur to the listener sitting through "Chôros No. 6," a thirty-five-minute piece that sounds like a pastiche of many different elements, including tangos, operetta melodies, folk songs and tunes out of minstrel shows. All of this employed the most lavish orchestral resources. To this listener it was disjointed and over-inflated, with only occasional touches of wit to save it from sounding like movie music.

One of the works the Brazilian composer led actually was movie music. It was the second suite that the French composer Florent Schmitt drew from "Salammbo," the score he wrote for a silent movie in 1926. It too was heavily orchestrated, but basically thin in its invention.

The remaining work of the program was Abertura Concertante by Senhor Villa-Lobos' fellow-countryman, Camargo Guarieri. It was agreeable and colorful, though there were times when it, too, seemed to be running on a little long, particularly in the slow middle section. The audience, which greeted Senhor Villa-Lobos like an old friend, was as cordial to the Guarieri piece as to everything else.

571 Ross Parmenter reviews the birthday concert in *The New York Times*, 29 March 1957.

572 Villa-Lobos accepting the distinction of an honorary citizen of São Paulo.

an honorary citizen of São Paulo where, from 23 to 28 September, a Festival – a 'Villa-Lobos Week' – took place. The Ministry of Education and Culture declared 1957 the 'Year of Villa-Lobos'.

Programme

I

1. SINFONIETTA N° 1 *(1916)*

(Sur 2 thèmes de Mozart)

a) ALLEGRO JUSTO
b) ANDANTE NON TROPPO
c) ANDANTINO

2. CIRANDA DAS 7 NOTAS *(1933)*

(Fantaisie pour Basson et Orchestre)

Soliste : Gérard FAISANDIER

3. BACHIANAS BRASILEIRAS N° 5
(1938 - 1945)

a) ARIA *(CANTILENA) Poème de R. V. CORREIA*
b) DANSA *(MARTELO) Poème de Manuel BANDEIRA*

Soliste : Eda PIERRE

II

1. SUITE POUR ORCHESTRE *(1933)*   *(1913)*

1 - au Brésil

2 - à l'Italie

Soliste : Homero de MAGALHAES

2. SAUDADE DA JUVENTUDE *(1940)*

Suite pour l'Orchestre N° 1

Direction : PIERRE CHAILLÉ

Sous la présidence de
Monsieur A. MARCHAUD, Recteur de la Cité Universitaire
et de Son Excellence
Monsieur CARLOS ALVES DE SOUSA, Ambassadeur du Brésil
en présence de
Monsieur H. VILLA-LOBOS

573

573 Programme for the concert at the Théâtre de la Maison Internationale in Paris in honour of Villa-Lobos's seventieth birthday.

UNIVERSITÉ DE PARIS

LE CENTRE CULTUREL INTERNATIONAL
DE LA CITÉ UNIVERSITAIRE DE PARIS
présente

CONCERT EN HOMMAGE A
VILLA-LOBOS
à l'occasion de son 70ᵉᵐᵉ anniversaire
- THÉÂTRE DE LA MAISON INTERNATIONALE -
11, BOUL. JOURDAN, XIV

573

São Paulo, 26 de setembro de 1957 — às 21 horas

PREFEITURA DO MUNICIPIO DE SÃO PAULO

SECRETARIA DE EDUCAÇÃO E CULTURA

CONCERTO SINFÔNICO

ORQUESTRA SINFÔNICA MUNICIPAL

Regente

Maestro HEITOR VILLA-LOBOS

PROGRAMA

VILLA LOBOS

1.a Parte

PACHIANAS BRAS!LEIRAS N.o 7
(Suite para orquestra)
a — Prelúdio (Ponteio)
b — Giga (Quadrilha caipira)
c — Tocata (Desafio)
d — Fuga (Conversa)

POEMA DE ITABIRA (Ópera de concerto)
(Canto e orquestra)
Poesia de Carlos Drummond de Andrade

Solista: MAGDALENA LÉBEIS

2.a Parte

11.a SINFONIA (1.a audição no Barsil)
a — Allegro moderato
b — Largo
c — Scherzo
d — Molto

574

574 Programme of the concert which Villa-Lobos conducted on 26 September 1957, during 'Villa-Lobos Week' in honour of his seventieth birthday.

Final honours

575

575 Guillermo Espinosa (*b.* 1905), Colombian conductor in Europe and the Americas, consultant on contemporary Latin American music and lecturer. Chief of the Music Division of the Organisation of American States (1952-1975). Founder and director of the Inter-American Music Festival, Washington, DC (1958-1974). Conductor at the Colón, Bogotá (1943-1944), founder and music director of the National Symphony Orchestra, Bogotá (1936-1958), winner of several prizes and recipient of many awards. He conducted the American première of Villa-Lobos's *Harmonica Concerto,* with John Sebastian as soloist and the National Symphony Orchestra of Washington. This took place on 24 April 1961 at the Cramton Auditorium of the Howard University during the Second Inter-American Music Festival (22-30 April) at a 'Brazilian Night' dedicated to Villa-Lobos.

With honours from the United States, Europe and Brazil, Villa-Lobos was a name to reckon with in the musical world. He relished the situation to the full. The memories of the long struggle at the beginning of his career were fading more and more into the background. He thoroughly and quite rightly enjoyed being in demand on the concert circuit, at festivals, and being honoured with distinctions and decorations. Amidst all this success Villa-Lobos remained the same delightful, jocular, cheerful person, the warm, lovable human being he had always been. His many friends in all countries cherished his spirit and felt drawn towards him now just as before.

In the year following his seventieth-birthday celebrations two further events took place in the United States to honour Villa-Lobos. The first came in April 1958 when he was invited to participate in the First Inter-American Music Festival, presented between 18 and 20 April in Washington by the Pan American Union whose chief of the Music Section since 1953 had been Guillermo Espinosa.

Villa-Lobos's music was included in three concerts, for two of which he offered compositions performed as world premières: the *String Quartet No. 15,* composed

576

576 The Pan American Union Building.

577 Title page of the programme for the First Inter-American Music Festival.

578 Coolidge Auditorium, Library of Congress.

The Pan American Union

p r e s e n t s

THE FIRST INTER-AMERICAN MUSIC FESTIVAL

April 18 - 19 - 20, 1958
in Washington, D. C.

organized by the Inter-American Music Center in collaboration with International House of New Orleans, the National Institute of Fine Arts of Mexico, the Elizabeth Sprague Coolidge Foundation of the Library of Congress, the Music Performance Trust Funds of the Recording Industries, and the Washington Board of Trade.

577

578

in 1954, and the *Symphony No. 12* which he had finished on his seventieth birthday. The *String Quartet No. 15* was performed at the Coolidge Auditorium of the Library of Congress by the Juilliard String Quartet on 19 April 1958.

Elizabeth Sprague Coolidge Foundation

was established in the Library of Congress by the late Mrs. Coolidge in 1925. It was a direct outgrowth of the chamber music festivals which she had been sponsoring in the Berkshires, near Lenox, Massachusetts since 1918. Generously endowing the Foundation in Washington, Mrs. Coolidge also gave to the Library of Congress an excellent concert auditorium, seating about 500 persons, which now bears her name. These gifts have made possible the adoption of a continuing program of importance to creative music and to the appreciation of chamber music.

The Coolidge Foundation began its career with a three-day festival of chamber music in the Coolidge Auditorium in 1925, and up to the present, twelve such festivals have been presented there. These have been internationally significant, both for content of programs and for standard of performance. The Foundation has extended commissions to many eminent composers for modern chamber works. Most of the commissioned works have received their world premieres at Coolidge Foundation festivals or at other concerts in the Library of Congress sponsored by the Foundation. Besides the concerts presented in Coolidge Auditorium, the Foundation also sponsors concerts in other places, usually at universities across the country. The two chamber music concerts were kindly offered to the Inter-American Music Festival by the Elizabeth Sprague Coolidge Foundation.

The Quartet No. 2 of Alberto Ginastera, which receives its world premiere at this time, was a recent commission of the Coolidge Foundation.

579

Saturday morning, April 19, 1958
11 a.m.
COOLIDGE AUDITORIUM
OF THE LIBRARY OF CONGRESS

THE JUILLIARD STRING QUARTET

Robert Mann, *first violin*
Isadore Cohen, *second violin*
Raphael Hillyer, *viola*
Claus Adam, *cello*

PROGRAM

* String Quartet No. 1, Op. 46 (1956)   JUAN ORREGO SALAS
  Adagio-Allegro
  Grazioso, quasi allegretto
  Assai lento e espressivo
  Presto energico
  (Commissioned by International House of New Orleans)

* String Quartet No. 15 (1954)   HEITOR VILLA-LOBOS
  Allegro non troppo
  Moderato
  Scherzo (Vivo)
  Allegro
  (Kindly offered by the composer)

INTERMISSION

* String Quartet No. 2 (1958)   ALBERTO EVARISTO GINASTERA
  Allegro rustico—Abbastanza meno mosso
    e piacevole—Tempo I°
  Adagio angoscioso
  Presto magico
  Libero e rapsodico (Theme with variations)
  Furioso
  (Commissioned by the Elizabeth Sprague Coolidge Foundation)

* World première   * World première

580

The Juilliard String Quartet was founded in 1946 by William Schumann, President of the Juilliard School of Music in New York, as the conservatoire's quartet-in-residence. All the members are principal teachers of chamber music at the Juilliard. The Juilliard String Quartet gives concert performances annually in the United States and Canada, and spends July and August each year on the faculty of the Aspen Music School, Colorado, performing at the Festival there. Numerous recordings by the Quartet include the quartets of Béla Bartók (1884-1945), Arnold Schönberg (1874-1951), and Alban Berg (1885-1935). The repertoire embraces four centuries of music, and includes more than 125 major works.

The second concert in which Villa-Lobos's music

581 The Juilliard String Quartet as it was in 1958. *From left to right:*

Robert Mann, first violin, born in Portland, Oregon, where he studied with Edouard Hurlimann. At the Juilliard he studied with Edouard Dethier, and won the Naumburg Award in 1941. After his debut he toured as a soloist, and became a member of the Juilliard faculty on his discharge from military service.

Isador Cohen, second violin, born in New York City. His musical education was acquired at the High School of Music and Art, Brooklyn College, and the Juilliard, where he was a pupil of Ivan Galamian. He has been a soloist with various orchestras and a member of chamber music organisations.

Raphael Hillyer, viola, born in Ithaca, New York. His musical education was acquired in private study with Serge Korgueff and at the Curtis Institute of Music in Philadelphia. Besides music, he has studied mathematics at Dartmouth College, and completed premedical studies at Harvard, Tufts, and the Massachusetts Institute of Technology. He has played in the Boston Symphony, the NBC Orchestra under Arturo Toscanini, and the Stradivarius (1644-1737) and NBC Quartets.

Claus Adam, cello, born in Sumatra, Indonesia. After attending schools in Holland, Germany, and Austria, he came to the United States with his family. Private instruction in cello and composition led to scholarships with Joseph Emouts and Emanuel Feuermann (1902-1942).

581

582

Sunday noon, April 20, 1958
12 noon
HALL OF THE AMERICAS
Pan American Union

THE CLAREMONT STRING QUARTET

Marc Gottlieb, *first violin*
Vladimir Heisman, *second violin*
William Shoen, *viola*
Irving Klein, *cello*

Assisted by Arthur Balsam, *pianist*

THE HOWARD UNIVERSITY CHOIR
WARNER LAWSON, Conductor

PROGRAM

* String Quartet — AURELIO DE LA VEGA
Allegro
Adagio
Scherzo
Rondo-Finale (Allegro)
(Kindly offered by the composer)

* Trio for Piano, Violin and Violoncello — VIOLET ARCHER
Allegro
Largo tranquillo
Allegro con brio, energico
Mr. Balsam, Mr. Gottlieb and Mr. Klein
(Commissioned by International House of New Orleans)

INTERMISSION

* World première

* Motet: Praise to the Lord, the Almighty, the King of Creation — NORMAND LOCKWOOD

** Two Songs — HEITOR VILLA-LOBOS
1. Invocação em Defensa da Patria
2. Cantos de Cairé

** Three Epitaphs — RODOLFO HALFFTER
(Text by Miguel de Cervantes)
1. Para la sepultura de Don Quijote
2. Para la sepultura de Dulcinea
3. Para la sepultura de Sancho Panza

* Improperium — RUSSELL WOOLLEN

* Two Madrigals
1. Velvet Shoes
2. Beauty

* World première
** First performance in the United States

583

Sunday evening, April 20, 1958
8:30 p.m.
LISNER AUDITORIUM

THE NATIONAL SYMPHONY ORCHESTRA OF WASHINGTON, D.C.
HOWARD MITCHELL, Conductor
Harold Wright, Clarinetist

PROGRAM

*** Second Symphony for String — HECTOR TOSAR
Allegro deciso
Andante sostenuto
Allegro con fuoco

** First Symphony — GUSTAVO BECERRA
Allegro, tenso e misterioso
Lento
Allegro scherzoso
Andante

INTERMISSION

* Chôro for Clarinet and Orchestra — MOZART CAMARGO GUARNIERI
Lento e nostalgico-Moderato-Lento-Allegro
(Commissioned by International House of New Orleans)

* World première
** First performance in the United States
*** First performance in Washington, D. C.

* Symphony No. 12 — HEITOR VILLA-LOBOS
Allegro non troppo
Adagio
Scherzo
Molto allegro
(Kindly offered by the composer)

Steinway Piano

* World première

584

He has played with the National Orchestral Association, at the Minneapolis Symphony, and was cellist of the New Music Quartet for seven years.

582 Lisner Auditorium.

583 Programme for the concert which included two songs by Villa-Lobos.

584 Programme for the concert which included Villa-Lobos's *Symphony No. 12.*

Heitor Villa-Lobos' name is the only one to appear more than once in the current Festival. He will be heard in three different media during the three days of concerts. Yesterday we heard his latest string quartet, his 15th, a work written in 1954. It has vivid rhythmic patterns at the opening of each of its four movements, and then, with the logic that infuses much of this great man's best formal works, it moves on in soundly conceived structures, conventional in harmonic devices but never uninteresting.

There is a "vivo" scherzo that must be one of the shortest on record, running about one minute in length.

585

586

585   Review of the première of Villa-Lobos's *String Quartet No. 15* in *The Washington Post and Times Herald*.

586   Howard Michell (*b.* 1911), American conductor who studied at the Peabody Institute and Curtis Institute of Music. In 1933 principal cellist of the National Symphony Orchestra. Received several awards and honorary doctorates. As director of the National Symphony Orchestra, Washington DC he toured Sweden and the Soviet Union in 1967, and thereafter became guest conductor.

was performed took place in the Hall of the Americas at midday on 20 April 1958.

On the evening of the same day, on 20 April 1958, Villa-Lobos's *Symphony No. 12* was first performed, in the Lisner Auditorium. Howard Michell conducted the National Symphony Orchestra.

The second outstanding event in Villa-Lobos's life during 1958 came at the end of the year, on 3 December, when an honorary doctorate was conferred upon him by New York University.

The National Symphony Orchestra of Washington, D.C.

was founded in 1931 by the late cellist and conductor, Hans Kindler, who remained its conductor until his retirement in 1949. In 1935 the orchestra inaugurated a summer series at the Watergate, playing from a barge to an audience gathered on the stone steps below the Lincoln Memorial. The annual series, which was discontinued in 1950 because of highway and air traffic noises, was one of the most popular summer music activities in the history of Washington. Under Hans Kindler the size of the orchestra was gradually increased until it numbered at one time 100 pieces, the season lengthened, and Washington had a resident symphony orchestra for the first time in the history of the Federal City.

Howard Mitchell, who succeeded Kindler as conductor, came to the orchestra as principal of the cello section in 1933. After appearances as a soloist, he made his debut as conductor at a "Pops Concert" in 1941, and later that year was named Assistant Conductor; in 1958 he became Associate Conductor, and was appointed permanent conductor on Kindler's retirement in 1949.

Under the leadership of Howard Mitchell, the orchestra now stands stabilized as an organization of 96 players, with a season of from 24 to 32 weeks, an extended touring season, and an increase in concerts to 184 per season. The annual turnover of the orchestra personnel is less than 5 per cent. Periodically, Mitchell has won awards for his services to American music, and the orchestra has become widely known for its services to the American composer.

587

588

Music: Inter-American Festival Ends

National Symphony Plays Last Concert

Three-Day Event in Washington Is a Hit

By HOWARD TAUBMAN
Special to The New York Times.

WASHINGTON, April 21—The First Inter-American Music Festival, which ended last night at Lisner Auditorium with a concert by the National Symphony Orchestra of Washington, was a success. A number of substantial works were introduced. The performances were on a high level. And a group of Latin-American composers was able to mingle and exchange views with North Americans.

•

Like other festivals presented in the past in Washington, this one was too concentrated. Five concerts devoted to largely unfamiliar pieces were crowded into two and a half days. Though such an arrangement is convenient for people who can spare only a week-end, it offered too much in too short a time. It tends to make an event of this kind a chore instead of an adventure to be savored at leisure.

Many individuals and institutions joined in providing the funds to make the festival possible. But official Washington, apart from John G. Dreier, United States Ambassador to the Organization of American States, did very little to give the visiting musicians anything like the warm, personal reception that was arranged in Venezuela when it held a Latin-American Festival last spring.

These observations are set down less in criticism than in

Heitor Villa-Lobos

a hope that the next Inter-American Festival—and there should be others in Washington in the years to come — will overcome this year's shortcomings.

The final program, led with precision and comprehension by Howard Mitchell, the National Orchestra's intelligent and imaginative conductor, embraced works by Hector Tosar, Uruguayan; Gustavo Becerra, Chilean, and Mozart Camargo Guarnieri and Heitor Villa-Lobos, Brazilians.

Señor Tosar's Symphony for Strings, which this listener heard in Caracas, improved on reacquaintance. At its best, in the intense, moving slow movement, it is a

score of profound feeling. Here is a work of strong individuality and genuine musical instincts. Señor Tosar manages to say something of his own in a relatively old-fashioned style.

Señor Becerra's Symphony No. 1 takes no more than ten minutes to traverse its four movements. It is an odd combination of Shostakovich and Webern influences. It leaves one with the feeling that this 33-year-old composer is still groping for a personal approach.

Señhor Camargo Guarnieri's Choro for Clarinet and Orchestra, which was commissioned by International House of New Orleans, is agreeable in a lightweight way. It reminds one a little of Gershwin and North American jazz. It wins an easy success. For all its slickness, one wonders whether this knowledgeable composer does not settle for less than his best capacities. Harold Wright was the skillful clarinet soloist.

•

Finally, there was the première of an exuberant Symphony No. 12 by the prodigally gifted Señhor Villa-Lobos. There was no indication of when this piece was written. But like everything else the composer does it overflows with ideas—good, bad and indifferent. Traces of romanticism, impressionism, orientalism and Slavism can be detected in the score. But it has an exhilarating fullness. It is expansive, oracular, full-blooded. Señhor Villas-Lobos, in short, revels in composition, and it is bracing fun to listen to him.

590

589

587   The history of the National Symphony Orchestra, Washington, DC, reproduced from the programme of the First Inter-American Music Festival, 18-20 April 1958, Washington, DC.

588   Villa-Lobos, delighted at receiving an honorary degree from New York University, being presented with the scroll. On this occasion unaccompanied choral pieces, settings of words from the Bible, assembled under the title *Bendita Sabedoria*, were performed at the suggestion of the American musicologist and librarian Carleton Sprague Smith, at that time chief of the Music Division of the New York Public Library, and a friend of Villa-Lobos since Smith's visit to Brazil during World War II. The music was sung by the Washington Square College Chorus under Maurice Peress.[27]

27) Maurice Peress (*b*.1930), American conductor and trumpeter. Attended New York University and Mannes College of Music, 1961, assistant director to Leonard Bernstein (1918-1990) at the New York Philharmonic Symphony Orchestra, 1962 music director at Corpus Christi Symphony Orchestra, 1970

Austin Symphony Orchestra and San Francisco Opera, 1974 music director of Kansas City Philharmonic Orchestra. Guest-conducted other American orchestras and also in Mexico and Vienna.

589   Carleton Sprague Smith (1905-1994), American musicologist and librarian. Chief of the Music Division of the New York Public Library (1931-1959).

590   Howard Taubman reviewed the Festival in *The New York Times*, 22 April 1958.

Last events in life of Villa-Lobos

The United States, which catapulted Villa-Lobos to international fame following his American debut in 1944, was also the country where the Brazilian composer was destined to make his final public appearance as a composer-conductor. This happened in the summer of 1959 at a concert which took place three years to the day after the world première of his music for *The Emperor Jones;* it was likewise presented at the Empire State Musical Festival.

On Sunday 12 July 1959, 'An Evening with Villa-Lobos' was presented which included the world première of *The Songs of the Tropical Forest* which *The New York Times* reviewed at length.

On the following day, 13 July, Villa-Lobos flew home to be present in Rio de Janeiro, on 14 July, at the golden jubilee of the Teatro Municipal and to receive yet another honour: the Carlos Gomes Medal.

In former years, on 7 September, Brazil's Independence Day, Villa-Lobos had conducted his

591   John Briggs reviews Villa-Lobos's final concert in *The New York Times,* 13 July 1959.

Villa-Lobos Leads Symphony of Air in His Own Works

Special to The New York Times.

BEAR MOUNTAIN, N. Y., July 12.— The first weekend of the Empire State Music Festival ended tonight with a concert of works by the Brazilian Heitor Villa-Lobos. The program was played by the Symphony of the Air, under the composer's direction, in the festival's temporary quarters at the Anthony Wayne Recreation Area in Harriman State Park.

The principal event of tonight's concert was the world première of Mr. Villa-Lobos' "Songs of the Tropical Forest." It is a big work for soprano and orchestra, based on W. H. Hudson's "Green Mansions," with lyrics by Dora Vasconcellos.

•The work is in four sections entitled "Song of the Sails," "Song of Love," "Twilight Song" and "Sentimental Melody." Only the first three sections were heard tonight, Mr. Villa-Lobos having decided to omit the final portion. The parts heard made a very favorable impression. They showed Mr. Villa-Lobos' skill in vocal writing, his inexhaustible imagination for rhythmic effects, the varied color of his orchestral texture and the deftness with which he utilizes the rich folk-music material of his native Brazil.

Elinor Ross, the soloist, displayed a pleasant-textured voice, which found especially congenial the broad sweeping cantilena of "Song of Love" and the odd, unexpected melodic contours of "Twilight Song." Mr. Villa-Lobos showed his gratitude by kissing the soprano's hand; the audience showed its pleasure by applauding until "Twilight Song" was repeated.

It is always interesting to hear music under the composer's direction, especially when the composer has Mr. Villa-Lobos' background as conductor and orchestral musician, and the music is a tricky work like "Choros No. 6," which ended the program. Mr. Villa-Lobos and the orchestra handled its rhythmic complexities with facility and brought the evening of music to a spirited conclusion.

Also heard were "Uirapuru" ("The Enchanted Bird"), in which Mr. Villa-Lobos uses the orchestra's resources to depict with skill and imagination the bird calls and other sounds of the Brazilian forest; "O Papagaio do Moleque" ("The Kite of the Street Urchin") and the Suite No. 1, "Discovery of Brazil."

JOHN BRIGGS.

591

Sterling Forest Research Center

presents

The Empire State
Music Festival

in cooperation with

The Palisades Interstate Park Commission

1959 Season

Sunday, July 12 at 7:15 PM

An Evening with Villa-Lobos

Heitor Villa-Lobos
Conductor

I.   Discovery of Brasil (First Suite) . . . . Heitor Villa-Lobos
        a) Introduction
        b) Alegria (Joy)

II. The Songs of the Tropical Forest (Music inspired on the
        classical history "Green Mansions" by Hudson) —
        Lyrics by Dora Vasconcellos . . . . Heitor Villa-Lobos
                a) Song of the Sails
                b) Song of Love
                c) Twilight Song
                d) Sentimental Melody
        Soloist: Elinor Ross, *Soprano*

   WORLD PREMIERE

III. O Papagaio do Moleque (The Kite of the Street Urchin) . . . . . Heitor Villa-Lobos

   INTERMISSION

IV. Uirapurú (The Enchanted Bird) . . . . Heitor Villa-Lobos

V.   Choros N. 6 . . . . Heitor Villa-Lobos

592   Programme of Villa-
Lobos's last concert.

592

593

595

594

593 Edoardo di Guarnieri
(1891-1968).

594 Pius XII (Eugenio
Pacelli) (1876-1958), who
was Pope from 1939 to
1958.

595 Villa-Lobos, visibly
tired and in poor health, seen
with Arminda Villa-Lobos at
the Teatro Municipal in Rio
de Janeiro on 14 July 1959.

596 Paul VI (Giovanni
Battista Montini) (1897-
1978), who was Pope from
1963 to 1978.

596

597 Facsimile of the
manuscript of the first page
of Villa-Lobos's final quartet,
String Quartet No. 17;
composed in 1957, and first
performed on 16 October
1959 by the Budapest String
Quartet in Washington.

597

UNITED NATIONS DAY

24 OCTOBER 1959

JOURNEE DES NATIONS UNIES

24 OCTOBRE 1959

PROGRAMME

New York Philharmonic

The Schola Cantorum (Musical Director: Hugh Ross)

Conducted by
Eleazar de Carvalho

Robert Casadesus

Mr. Dag Hammarskjold
Secretary-General of the United Nations

SINFONÍA INDIA . . . . Chávez

SYMPHONIC VARIATIONS . . . . Franck
Robert Casadesus

DESCOBRIMENTO DO BRASIL . . . . Villa-Lobos
Fiesta in the Forest
The Sailor's Vision
First Mass in Brazil

The Schola Cantorum

INTERMISSION

FINALE, SYMPHONY NO. 9 IN D MINOR, OP. 125: "ODE TO JOY". . . . Beethoven
Elisabeth Schwarzkopf, *soprano*
Maureen Forrester, *contralto*
Jan Peerce, *tenor*
Kim Borg, *bass*
The Schola Cantorum

598 Title page and
programme for the concert
given on United Nations
Day, 24 October 1959.

598

599

massed choir of some 40,000 schoolchildren in honour of the day's celebrations. Now, on 7 September 1959, though a very sick man, he was still able to attend the performance of his *Magnificat Aleluia*, conducted by Edoardo di Guarnieri at the Teatro Municipal, where, at the end of the concert, Villa-Lobos received an unforgettable ovation, a last farewell to a dying master.

Magnificat Aleluia, a setting for soloist, mixed choir and orchestra, of passages from the Bible, was commissioned by Pope Pius XII, transmitted by the Archbishop of Milan, subsequently Pope Paul VI, and composed in 1958.

Villa-Lobos's health began to deteriorate and he had to enter the Hospital dos Estrangeiros. There he received the news that his *String Quartet No. 17*, his last quartet, composed in 1957, would be premièred by the Budapest Quartet in Washington on 16 October 1959. He also heard that, on 24 October, United Nations Day, a concert was planned at which parts of his suite *Descobrimento do Brasil* would be performed.

Villa-Lobos was also visited by the Argentine composer Alberto Ginastera who was on his homeward-bound voyage from Europe. When Ginastera parted from Villa-Lobos it was with the feeling that he was seeing him for the last time.

The doctors could do no more for Villa-Lobos. The operation eleven years earlier had led to a massive congestion of the kidneys and uraemia had developed. The composer was allowed home so he could spend his last days there.

599   Alberto Evaristo Ginastera (1916-1983), Argentine composer who from 1970 lived in Switzerland. Twice recipient of Guggenheim Fellowships (1946 and 1969). He wrote operas including *Don Rodrigo* (1964), *Bomarzo* (1967) and *Beatrix Cenci* (1971).

600   Villa-Lobos leaves the Hospital dos Estrangeiros in good spirits as usual.

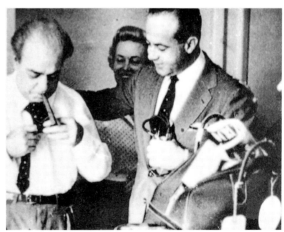

600

Last events in life of Villa-Lobos   291

Death

On 17 November 1959 Villa-Lobos died at home in the Rua Araújo Pôrto Alegre 56, Apt. 54. The news quickly spread throughout the world. Villa-Lobos was mourned in the United States, Europe and Brazil as the most significant Brazilian composer of his time and as a lovable, warm individual. *The New York Times* published several articles as a tribute. Villa-Lobos's old friend, the pianist Arthur Rubinstein, included in his New York recital at Carnegie Hall on 27 November 1959 – ten days after the composer's death – three small pieces by Villa-Lobos whom he had once helped to start his career.

Villa-Lobos's work continued to live on after his death. He was honoured in exhibitions, concerts and

VILLA-LOBOS DIES; COMPOSER WAS 72

Brazilian Noted for 'Choros,' Bachianas Brasileiras' and Many Other Compositions

MERGED MUSICAL IDIOMS

Folklorist Was Influenced by Impressionists, Moderns —Led Orchestras Here

Special to The New York Times.

RIO DE JANEIRO, Nov. 17—Heitor Villa-Lobos, world-famed Brazilian composer and conductor, died this afternoon of uremia at his home here. He had been ill since his return from a concert tour of Europe and the United States earlier this year. His age was 72.

Senhor Villa-Lobos' body was placed in the State Ministry of Education Building for burial here tomorrow.

He is survived by his widow, Arminda.

Leader in South America

By the time of his first arrival in the United States in 1944, Senhor Villa-Lobos had a reputation as South America's foremost composer. He quickly engaged to conduct his own works with such famous organizations as the Werner Janssen Symphony in Los Angeles, the Boston Symphony and the New York Philharmonic, and a special program of his works was given by the League of Composers.

Among his compositions those best known here are a series of "Choros" (the word is the composer's own) and a series of "Bachianas Brasileiras" and "Rudepoema," the last dedicated to Artur Rubinstein, the pianist.

Senhor Vila-Lobos' strong personality and bouncing energy made a great impression on those who met him. It was a matter of marvel that this man who had more than 1,000 compositions to his credit had time to become the director of his native Brazil's Department of Musical Education, a post he assumed in 1931; to invent new systems of musical notation, one of which consisted of hand signals to train musical illiterates; to establish choruses throughout his country, and to conduct them annually in massed performances, sometimes with as many as 20,000 school-children participating.

Primarily a Folklorist

Though Senhor Villa-Lobos had several styles, he was primarily a folklorist. He also was a musical sophisticate whose orchestral scoring could be ferocious and colorful, who could use a good deal of dissonance and who, disconcertingly, also wrote in an idiom very close to that of the French impressionists.

Some critics, as a result, denied him any style and called him a complete eclectic. Others pointed to his idiomatic use of Brazilian rhythmic and melodic elements—elements that, they said, he successfully fused into a very individual style.

An idea of his prolific qualities as a composer was evidenced in 1957 at the home of the Brazilian deputy consul in New York. Senhor Villa-Lobos was served a feojoda, Brazil's national dish, and he was so pleased with it that on the spot he wrote a musical composition celebrating that delicacy. He called it "A Fugue Without End," and wrote it in four parts: "Farina," "Meat," "Rice" and "Black Beans." Those are the essential components of the dish.

Senhor Vila-Lobos was born on March 5 in a year that he quoted variously as 1890, 1888, 1887 and 1886. Rio de Janeiro kept no birth records at that time. His father taught him the rudiments of the 'cello and it was said that the son's formal education went little further than that.

He is believed to have worked in restaurant and theatre orchestras at an early age, establishing his firm contact with his country's popular music. He is known to have made several trips through the northeastern part of Brazil, absorbing elements of Portuguese, African and Indian cultures that, appeared in his music in complex pagan rhythms and uncommon coloristic and percussive effects.

Worked in Paris

Limited Brazilian recognition had come to him by 1919, when he was "discovered" by Mr. Rubinstein. The new connection resulted in Senhor Villa-Lobos going to Paris, where he made it clear that "I didn't come to study with you; I came to show you what I've done."

Although Senhor Villa-Lobos already was well grounded as a composer, musicians noted in his music the effect of his contact with French impressionistic and neoclassic styles in the next seven years. Nevertheless, his music continued to show its distinctive Brazilian traits.

In his constant search for thematic material, the composer devised a system of graphs upon which he superimposed the profiles of Brazil's famous mountains. The resulting curves he translated into melodies, which he then harmonized. One of these works, composed about 1940, was based on the skyline of New York. When he visited this city later, he remarked that the score needed no alterations.

Senhor Villa-Lobos made many visits to the United States after his first one in 1944. His most recent appearance in the New York area was last July, when he conducted the Symphony of the Air at the Empire State Music Festival in a program of his works. Among his recent works was the music for the film, "Green Mansions."

601 *The New York Times,* 18 November 1959, pays tribute to Villa-Lobos.

601

VILLA-LOBOS IS BURIED

President of Brazil Leads Mourners for Composer

RIO DE JANEIRO, Nov. 18 (AP)—Heitor Villa-Lobos was buried today to the measured strains of two of his compositions. President Juscelino Kubitschek led Brazil and the world in paying tribute to the composer and conductor, who died yesterday at the age of 72.

An hour before the funeral procession, a choral group sang the composer's "Mass of São Sebastiao" from the steps of the Municipal Theatre, a block from his apartment. At the graveside in São Joao Batista Cemetery, a children's choral group sang his "Silence."

The principal religious ceremony in Senhor Villa-Lobos' memory will be a mass a week from now.

602

In the death of Heitor Villa-Lobos South America has lost an outstanding musical spokesman. Brazil its greatest musical figure, and the world its most prolific — by any standards a remarkable composer. Villa-Lobos died on November 17, 1959, aged 72, after a cerebral haemorrhage.

He was born at Rio de Janeiro on March 5, 1887. He grew up amid Brazilian traditional music, and was encouraged by his father to learn musical instruments. Eventually he made the cello his special study, and spent several years travelling through Brazil, using his cello as a principal source of livelihood, but primarily discovering and absorbing the music of Brazil which permeated his own work.

Bach was his idol, early and late, and the inspiration of his *Bachianas brasileiras* (which numbered nine at the last count), a curious blend of Bach's style, as Villa-Lobos saw it, with the spirit of Brazilian music: Villa-Lobos once declared that he regarded Bach as a monumental folk-source valid for all countries and periods. Some of these morganatic musical children suggested neither Bach nor Brazil: but the fifth of them, written for a soprano and an orchestra of cellos, evoked an individual atmosphere and has become, perhaps, the best known of Villa-Lobos's works.

The *chôros*, Brazil's famous musical music of the streets, inspired 15 works entitled *Chôros* from Villa-Lobos, scored (like the *Bachianas brasileiras*) for a variety of voices and or instruments; thus the first *Chôros* is written for guitar, the third for a mixture of wind, brass, and male voices, the fourteenth for choir, military band, and orchestra.

A series of highly attractive and often individual piano pieces were set off by the friendship which the composer struck up in 1918 with young Artur Rubinstein. The *Prole do bébé*, which date from this year, have become familiar through Rubinstein's recitals, as have, particularly, the *Rudepoema* and *Ciclo brasileiro*: England has also become acquainted with these, and with some of Villa-Lobos's five piano concertos, through the advocacy of Felicja Blumenthal and Ellen Ballon, who also dedicated themselves to the propagation of Villa-Lobos's music.

Often, one feels, it is not distinguished in its invention, often disparate in its resources, as might be expected of a composer whose natural genius and enthusiasm were never seriously disciplined by apprenticeship.

Besides Bach, Villa-Lobos was much influenced by his love of Wagner and Puccini, and later by Debussy. He underwent numerous ardent enthusiasms, mostly in the course of a lifelong zeal for musical education: choirs, and military and brass bands were among them. These influenced the direction that his own music took; all too often his compositions have appeared to be faulted by madcap infatuation of some temporary ideal. Yet in every one of his compositions that comes to performance (and there are so many that catalogues hesitate to list them all), an idealism and a strange individuality glow through the manifest miscalculations.

He was a pioneer, and even in his lifetime an interesting historical figure. Posterity must hesitate to judge whether he is the Bach or the Telemann of twentieth-century Brazil.

November 18, 1959.

603

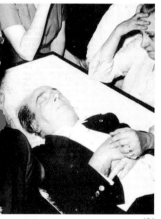

604

O amor que Villa-Lobos tinha pelo Brasil lhe era retribuído. Durante quase meio século, em seu país, ele fora discutido, mas poucos resistiam à sedução da sua personalidade. Havia sido um objeto de escândalo, de polêmicas, mas também de admiração e de orgulho para os brasileiros. Vivo, ainda, já o seu busto em bronze se encontrava no vestíbulo do Teatro Municipal do Rio de Janeiro. Morto, o Presidente da República veio inclinar-se diante do caixão florido em que se achava exposto o corpo, no edifício do Ministério da Educação. E um carro do Corpo de Bombeiros, cuja banda de música tinha sólidas tradições e havia, tantas vezes, prestado sua colaboração a Villa-Lobos, devia transportá-lo, procedido, em grande estilo, por batedores do Serviço de Trânsito, em suas motocicletas, e seguido, a pé, pelo Ministro da Educação e Cultura, o Prefeito de então Distrito Federal, o Reitor da Universidade do Brasil e a multidão de amigos do compositor, a que se juntavam os que não o haviam conhecido mas sua música havia conquistado. Diante do Teatro Municipal o cortejo parou e a orquestra do Teatro, colocada nas escadarias, executou a Marcha Fúnebre da Terceira Sinfonia de Beethovem. Era a apoteose. O tributo da Pátria estremecida ao seu filho bem-amado.

605

602 *The New York Times,* 19 November 1959, reports on the last farewell accorded to Villa-Lobos in Rio de Janeiro.

603 *The New York Times* obituary columns pay homage to Villa-Lobos on 18 November 1959.

604 Villa-Lobos in his coffin with a grief-stricken Arminda Villa-Lobos. (*O Cruzeiro,* Rio de Janeiro.)

605 Account of Villa-Lobos's funeral by Luiz Heitor Corrêa de Azevedo in 'Evocação de Villa-Lobos', *Presença de Villa Lobos* Vol.

10, 1977, p. 132, MEC/DAC/MVL, Rio de Janeiro.

HEITOR VILLA-LOBOS

HEITOR VILLA - LOBOS, the Brazilian composer, who died on Nov. 17, was an original. He had vast energy and imaginative powers. As a composer he was largely a self-made man. The quality of his work varied widely, but he wrote so abundantly that he could afford his share of inconsequential things.

At his best Villa - Lobos brought freshness and vitality to music. Steeped in the folk-lore of his country, he could quote literally from the sources he had explored in his safaris into the wild interior and he could invent ideas that had the directness and simplicity of folk music. He worked in all the forms, and his total output can only be conjectured. One does not envy the task of his executors in preparing a full account of all that he wrote.

Though the quality of his music fluctuated not only from piece to piece but also within a score, the finest Villa - Lobos will remain memorable. He was a remarkable melodist. His flair for rhythms reflected the music of his country. He had a highly personal sense of color. Having started as a 'cellist, he wrote with special affection and ingenuity for this instrument.

Nor was his creative achievement all that will carve his name in musical history. As a teacher and organizer, he did more than any other man to spread the gospel of good music in Brazil. He made Brazilians proud of their heritage, and he taught them to look beyond their borders. He was a protean musician.

606

606 *The New York Times,*
29 November 1959, again
reflects on Villa-Lobos's
career.

607 *The New York Times,*
28 November 1959, recalls
Arthur Rubinstein's
relationship with Villa-Lobos
when reviewing the virtuoso
pianist's Carnegie Hall recital.
Rubinstein had added three
little pieces by Villa-Lobos in
homage to his old friend.

Music: Artur Rubinstein

Pianist Pays Tribute to Villa-Lobos

By HOWARD TAUBMAN

ARTUR RUBINSTEIN played three brief pieces by Heitor Villa-Lobos at his Carnegie Hall recital last night. They were gay, charming, atmospheric and were played with the utmost grace. This was the pianist's tribute to the Brazilian composer, who died last week, and he had every reason to remember Villa-Lobos with an affectionate smile.

A long time ago, when both men were young, Mr. Rubinstein made a tour of Brazil. He was already a famous virtuoso. Villa-Lobos' fame, such as it was, was strictly local. He was writing music, getting very little of it performed and earning a meagre living playing the 'cello with a small ensemble in a café.

The pianist happened to hear the Villa-Lobos combo, as it would be described today. As one recollects the Rubinstein account of the occasion, it could have happened at a supper party after a recital. The pianist liked what Villa-Lobos played, complimented him and invited him to come to the hotel some time and show him more of his music.

Early the next morning—and it was especially early for a pianist who had given a recital and been out on the town—there was an unholy pounding on Mr. Rubinstein's hotel door. He got out of bed, cursing a hotel management that could let such things happen, and opened the door. There stood Villa-Lobos, carrying his 'cello, and behind him were the other members of his ensemble.

The bleary-eyed Rubinstein let the musicians take possession of his room, and he listened to them play music by Villa-Lobos. He could not help but admire the vigor and imagination in the pieces he heard. Later he made it a point to do what he could for the composer. Villa-Lobos got Government support to travel abroad, and the endorsement Rubinstein had given him was certainly helpful.

If the performance of the Villa-Lobos pieces were a sentimental touch at the first of Mr. Rubinstein's three Carnegie Hall recitals this season, it was only one of many. For a Rubinstein evening is a sentimental procession. The seats are sold long

Artur Rubinstein

The Program

Artur Rubinstein, pianist, Carnegie Hall.
Sonata in F minor.............Brahms
Sonata in F minor, Op. 5.....Brahms
Sonata in E flat, Op. 31, No. 3
.............................Beethoven
O Prole do Bebe (Mulatinha, Probre-Twelve Visions fugitives, Op. 22. March, from Love for Three Oranges
.............................Prokofieff
Berceuse; Polonaise in A flat minor
.............................Chopin

in advance, and an overflow crowd fills the stage beyond the piano. No matter what the pianist plays, he is sure to please those who have come eager to be pleased.

•

And they have every reason for pleasure. He brings ripe musicianship to every work he undertakes. On this occasion he chose largely to avoid bravura in the first half. How many times has one been oppressed by pianists who could not get under the skin of Brahms' long, romantic F minor Sonata? Mr. Rubinstein played with sustained poetry. One has space only to refer to the magic web of refined tone he wove in the Andante, which is like a whispered, ardent declaration of love.

Beethoven's E flat major Sonata had an airy, joyous reading as suited its modest frame. Prokofieff's "Visions Fugitives" were like vagrant improvisations, delicate in color and incisive in rhythm. As for the march from "The Love of Three Oranges," this is a Rubinstein specialty. So is Chopin, and this reporter can only lament having to leave before the pianist got to his favorite composer.

607

VILLA-LOBOS (*)

Luiz Heitor Correa de Azevedo

V ioleta escreveu a Você ontem. Eu, não tive tempo; mas ꞁei um telegrama. Todo o dia estive ocupado atendendo a ꞁidos de informação sobre o nosso queridíssimo amigo, vindos ꞁmuitas partes, e que procurei satisfazer na medida do possível.

ꞁn elementos que forneci o Jornal da Televisão pôde passar, ꞁem à noite, uma montagem filmada, em que se viam retratos de ꞁʰa em várias épocas, até aquele, no quarto do hotel, sob o ꞁdro do Imperador, autógrafos seus, a partitura de canto e piano ꞁ«Yerma», programas de concertos, etc. Não tenho muito mate-
e não sei como me desdobrar para emprestar fotografias de lado e de outro.

Eu não tinha ainda aberto o jornal de ontem, quando o nosso ꞁgo Pierre Vidal me telefonou, com uma voz em que logo ꞁcobri que uma desgraça muito grande havia acontecido. Efeti-ꞁⱡente, desde às 7 horas da manhã que a Rádio havia já ꞁꞁnciado a triste notícia. No dia 9 de dezembro o Pierre Vidal ꞁꞁnizará, no seu «Club des Trois Centres», onde vocês estiveram ꞁꞁas vezes, uma sessão consagrada à memória do Villa. Ele ꞁꞁvidará todos os seus velhos amigos, Mme. Long, Louis Aubert, ꞁꞁ Le Flem, Beaufils, e cada um contará à mocidade lembranças ꞁꞁsuas relações longínquas ou recentes com o grande músico ꞁꞁparecido. Em discos serão ouvidos, em seguida, o 6º Quarteto, ꞁꞁoneto e Erosão.

Sempre pensei, com horror, Arminda, no dia em que o per-ꞁꞁamos. Sei que esse pensamento também estava sempre presente

(*) Carta escrita em Paris — 19-11-1959.

ao seu espírito, e com uma acuidade infinitamente maior. Mas creia que sempre tive medo do que havia de sofrer, no dia em que uma tal notícia me fosse anunciada. Passei momentos amargos, em agosto, chegando ao Brasil. Tive um grande choque, ontem. Maria Cecília, que está trabalhando na Casa do Brasil, na Cidade Universitária, só de tarde, e no seu trabalho, teve notícia do que ocorrera, e desatou num pranto. Nós o queríamos tanto, Arminda, sem falar nesse buraco incomensurável que fica no Brasil, depois que ele cessou de existir. Para mim é como se tivéssemos passado de uma época histórica para outra, da Idade média para os Tempos Modernos.

Como compreender o Brasil sem Villa-Lobos? Tem-se a impressão que tudo acabou, e que é uma coisa nova e estranha que vai estar diante de nós, agora. Ontem à noite, no escuro da minha sala, e com os olhos cheios de lágrimas ouvi o 6º Quarteto, o 6º Choros e a 3ª Bachiana. Como ele está presente nessa música cheia de tanta ternura e de tanta vivacidade. Nunca mais hei de esquecer aquela tarde do dia 7 de outubro em que o deixei, pela última vez no apartamento da Araújo Porto Alegre, com seu copo de uísque ao lado, parecendo feliz e pronto para enfrentar as suas atividades habituais.

E Você, Arminda, de quanta coragem vai precisar. Saiba que estamos a seu lado como irmãos e conte com a nossa total dedica-ção. Tenho vertigem de pensar no abismo que essa perda representa, para Você. Mas seja corajosa, como sempre foi, porque muita coisa, ainda, precisa ser feita por ele, que só Você poderá fazer.

608

608 A moving letter by Luiz Heitor Corrêa de Azevedo written from Paris to Arminda Villa-Lobos on 19 November 1959 and published in *Presença de Villa-Lobos,* Vol. 8, 1973, p. 104, MEC/DAC/MVL, Rio de Janeiro.

festivals, and eventually a Museum was founded to perpetuate his name.

The New York Public Library was the first institution to pay respects to Villa-Lobos, early the following year. In its Fifth Avenue Branch, scores, books, photographs and drawings were displayed from early February to 23 April 1960.

On 29 April 1960 Brazil transferred her capital inland from Rio de Janeiro to the landlocked high plateau of Goiás. Here, the new capital, Brasília, was inaugurated five months after the composer's death and with it a new epoch began for Brazil: for the first time the country's capital which had remained for about 200 years in the city of São Salvador in the state of Bahia (1549-1763) and in the city of São Sebastião do Rio de Janeiro (1763-1960) was moved to the centre of the country.

In the autumn of that same year, in 1960, during the month in which the first anniversary of Villa-Lobos's death occurred, Rio de Janeiro honoured its great master with a Villa-Lobos Festival. The composer's works were performed in a series of presentations, which included some premières.

The following year, a Villa-Lobos Memorial Concert

609

Villa-Lobos Display Open
Heitor Villa-Lobos, the late Brazilian composer, is the subject of an exhibition of scores, books, photographs and drawings currently on display in Room 84 of the Fifth Avenue branch of the New York Public Library. The display is open on Mondays and Thursdays from 9 A.M. to 10 P.M., Sundays from 1 to 6 P.M., and other days from 9 A.M. to 6 P.M. It will be open until April 23.

610

609   Death mask by Armando Socrátes Schnoor, the Brazilian sculptor who was also to produce posthumous busts of the master.

610   *The New York Times,* 9 February 1960, announces a Villa-Lobos exhibition at the New York Public Library.

611   First page of Villa-Lobos's last will and testament, made on 11 August 1959, in the Hospital dos Estrangeiros, Rua General Góes Monteiro, Botafogo, Rio de Janeiro. (Published by kind permission of José Cândido de Andrade Muricy, Honorary President of the Brazilian Academy of Music and since 1939 music critic of the *Jornal do Commércio,* Rio de Janeiro.)

611

612

612   Brasília's Cathedral.

613   Programme of the Villa-Lobos Festival held in Rio de Janeiro on 21 November 1960.

21 de Novembro de 1960
Dia 21, segunda-feira — às 21 hs.

CONCÊRTO PELA O.S.B. SOB O PATROCÍNIO DO MINISTÉRIO DA EDUCAÇÃO E CULTURA, PROMOVIDO PELA RÁDIO MINISTÉRIO DA EDUCAÇÃO E CULTURA, EM COOPERAÇÃO COM A CAC

1a. Parte

Suite n. 1, para Orquestra de Câmara
(1a audição mundial)

Allegro
Pitoresco (poco andantino quase andante)
Fuga para brincar (allegro)
Pastoral
Danças

Suite n. 2, para Osquestra de Câmara
(1a. audição mundial)

Lamento (Andante cantabile)
Scherzo (vivace)
Passeio (andante quase allegreto)
Canção lírica (poco moderato)
Macumba

2a. Parte

MAGNIFICAT ALLELUIA

Côro Misto da Associação de Canto Coral
Côro dos Canarinhos de Petrópolis
Orquestra Sinfônica Brasileira

Regência — João de Souza Lima

613

614

614   Sculpture by Bruno Giorgi *Candangos* (to the workers who built Brasília).

615   Eugene Ormandy (1899-1985), American conductor of Hungarian birth who came to the United States in 1921, leading the Philadelphia Orchestra in performances of Villa-Lobos's *Symphony No. 9* in South America.

615

Music Institute To Be Assisted By Concert Here

UNISOMI Sponsoring Villa-Lobos Memorial Program on March 5

The Universal Symphony Orchestra and Music Institute, the aim of which is to "promote peace and to bring peoples and nations to warmer understanding and friendship through music, the universal language,"

is sponsoring the Villa-Lobos Memorial Concert at Carnegie Hall on March 5.

The concert, which will honor the birth of the Brazilian composer, will be held under the patronage of the government of his country. Jaime de Barros, Minister Plenipotentiary and Deputy Permanent Representative to the United Nations, and Senhora de Barros head the list of honorary patrons.

The concert also is being given to further friendship between the peoples of Brazil and the United States and the other American countries of the Western Hemisphere. Proceeds will aid UNISOMI and will provide funds for the establishment of

the Pablo Casals World Composers Music Scholarship.

An address of welcome will be given by Adolf A. Berle Jr., recently chosen by President Kennedy to coordinate United States policies on Latin America. Ninety members of the New York Philharmonic will participate in the concert, with Eleazar De Carvalho conducting. Soloists will be Anne Ayer, soprano, and Aldo Parisot, 'cellist

Permanent representatives to the United Nations from twenty-six countries are members of the honorary committee, and Mayor and Mrs. Wagner head the Villa-Lobos Memorial Committee. Senhora Jocy Oliveira De Carvalho, Bidu Sayao and

Senhora Arminda Villa-Lobos, widow of the composer, are honorary vice chairmen.

Among those serving as co-chairmen of the committee are Mrs. John Barry Ryan, Mrs. Frederick Ayer, Mrs. Samuel L. M. Barlow, Miss Marie R. Hall and Mrs. Horace Brock.

Vice chairmen include Mrs. Nicholas Goulandris, Mrs. Berle, Mrs. John Shubert, Mrs. Ellen Lewis Parisot, Mrs. Donald S. Stralem, Mrs. Goulandris, Mrs. Nathaniel Singer and Emma Alden Rothblatt, Deputy Commissioner of the Department of Commerce and Public Events.

Tickets may be obtained from the headquarters of UNISOMI at Suite 1020, 521 Fifth Avenue.

616

PAN AMERICAN WEEK 1963

The UNITED STATES AIR FORCE SYMPHONY ORCHESTRA

Colonel George S. Howard, Conductor
Captain Harry H. Meuser,
Associate Conductor
Guillermo Espinosa, Guest Conductor

Soloists: John Sebastian,
Harmonica virtuoso, and
Valerie Goodal, Soprano

Tuesday, April 16, 1963, 8:30 P.M.
HALL OF THE AMERICAS
Pan American Union, Washington, D.C.

PROGRAM

Eight Miniatures for Small Orchestra — Roque Cordero (Panama)
1. Marcha grotesca   5. Nocturno
2. Meditación   6. Mejorana
3. Pasillo   7. Plegaria
4. Danzonete   8. Allegro final

*Concerto for Harmonica and
Chamber Orchestra — Heitor Villa–Lobos (Brasil)
Allegro moderato
Andante
Allegro

Concertino for Harmonica and
Chamber Orchestra — Norman Dello Joio (U. S. A.)
With energy – Slowly – With spirit
GUILLERMO ESPINOSA, Guest Conductor
JOHN SEBASTIAN, Soloist

INTERMISSION

Overture for Woodwinds — Jerry H. Bilik (U. S. A.)

Sonata for Brass
Allegro non troppo
Andante cantabile
Rondo

Cantata I: Melora's Song, for Soprano
and Woodwinds — Duane A. Davidson (U. S. A.)

Nocturne for Winds and Percussion — Mark Bucci (U. S. A.)
Capt. HARRY H. MEUSER, Conductor
VALERIE GOODALL, Soloist

617

618

616   *The New York Times*, 12 February 1961, announces the Memorial Concert to be held in honour of Villa-Lobos's birthday, on 5 March 1961.

617   Programme for the Pan American Week 1963 held in Washington, DC.

618   The Ministry of External Relations (*Itamaraty*).

took place at Carnegie Hall on 5 March 1961 in honour of Villa-Lobos's birthday.

Two years later, on 16 April 1963, the United States Air Force Symphony Orchestra paid tribute to Villa-Lobos during Pan American week and included in a concert the *Harmonica Concerto* with a chamber orchestra and John Sebastian as soloist under the direction of Guillermo Espinosa.

Eugene Ormandy and the Philadelphia Orchestra also paid their tribute to Villa-Lobos during their South American tour in 1966 and performed his *Symphony No. 9* (composed in 1952) at Caracas, Venezuela on 16 May with subsequent performances in Rio de Janeiro on 18 May, São Paulo on 20 May and Pôrto Alegre on 23 May.

Among the soloists who continued to perform Villa-Lobos's music was Turíbio Soares Santos.

619   Turíbio Soares Santos (*b.* 1944), Brazilian guitarist who studied in Paris, obtained many prizes and recorded Villa-Lobos's *Preludes* and *Twelve Etudes.* After his return to Brazil in 1972, he toured the Soviet Union, the United States and Europe.

619

The Museu Villa-Lobos

620

621

620   Clóvis Salgado da Gama, Brazilian Minister of Education and Culture in 1960.

621   *Palácio da Cultura.* Until 1986, the Museu Villa-Lobos was on the ninth floor.

622   View of the Museum.

The most significant tribute paid to Villa-Lobos's memory was the creation of the Museu Villa-Lobos in Rio de Janeiro, seventeen months after the composer's death. The Museu had already been projected during the composer's lifetime, when in 1956, Amarylio de Albuquerque (*b.* 1902), then Director of the Secretariat of the Chamber of Deputies, had launched plans to preserve the composer's works and personal memorabilia in order to do him justice. Brazil probably experienced certain guilt feelings because of the indifference that had surrounded Villa-Lobos in his native land during his early career. But Villa-Lobos had emphatically rejected such a project being realised while he was still alive. The plans were therefore postponed. It was only after Villa-Lobos's death, on 22 June 1960, that Brazil's President, Juscelino Kubitscheck de Oliveira, signed the decree that established the Museu Villa-Lobos and Clóvis Salgado da Gama signed the enactment on 20 January 1961 which set up its administrative organisation.

The Museu was installed in the Palácio da Cultura, Rua de Imprensa 16, in the former building of the Ministry of Education and Culture before it moved to Brasília. There, on the ninth floor, the Museu had functioned until it moved in 1986 to its own premises (see illustration on p. 302). It was just a stone's throw away from the building where Villa-Lobos used to live.

622

623 Another view of the Museum.

624 Arminda Villa-Lobos (1912-1985), the composer's companion during the last twenty-three years of his life, and Director of the Museu Villa-Lobos until her death on 5 August 1985, is seen here on 2 October 1971, about ten years after the opening of the Museum.

623

624

The Museu Villa-Lobos is not a museum in the conventional sense. In addition to photographs, scores and memorabilia on display, it is splendidly equipped technically to provide copies of the composer's music and other material for scholars, students and performers. Once a year, lectures, concerts and contests are held during the week in which the anniversary of the composer's death falls. The Museu has published a catalogue of Villa-Lobos's works and recordings, an interesting series of books containing reprints of articles and specially written contributions under the title *Presença de Villa-Lobos,* and special studies on Villa-Lobos's music. It also has an attractively presented series of live recordings, with commentaries. A memorial Mass is held annually during the Villa-Lobos Festival Week in Rio de Janeiro's *Candelária* Church.

The Museu's high standards, international reputation, diverse activities and accomplishments in many realms, was due to the enterprising spirit and devotion of Arminda Villa-Lobos, the composer's companion throughout the last twenty-three years of his life. It is her organisational talent, administrative ability, aptitude as editor of books and recordings, and attention and assistance to scholars and students that have made the Museum possible. As Director, with the assistance of a small staff, she kept the flame aglow. The Museu Villa-Lobos is not therefore merely a shrine to the memory of the past but a place of lively activity.

625   Church of Our Lady of *Candelária*. Originally a hermitage for the fulfilment of vows in the seventeenth century, it was enlarged in 1634 and 1710, reconstructed in 1775 and opened to worship in 1811. As well as the great cupola of 1877, other outstanding features are the murals of the Candelária and the bronze portals. The church, located in the centre of Rio de Janeiro, is now surrounded by modern buildings.

626   The Museu Villa-Lobos at 200 Rua Sorocaba in the Botafogo quarter, 22.271 Rio de Janeiro. It moved to its own premises in 1986.

625

626

Appendix

Chronology
Brief survey of Brazil's history from its discovery until
    Villa-Lobos's death
Facts about Brazil
Glossary
Selected bibliography
Acknowledgments
Photo acknowledgments
Index of works mentioned
Index of names

Chronology

Only a selection of Villa-Lobos's major works is listed here under the dates they were composed.

1859	25 February: the composer's mother is born in Rio de Janeiro: Noêmia Umbelina Villa-Lobos, daughter of Antônio Santos Monteiro and Domitildes Costa Santos Monteiro.
1862	7 January: The composer's father is born: Raúl Villa-Lobos, son of Spanish parents: Francisco da Silveira Villa-Lobos and Maria Carolina Serzedelo Villa-Lobos.
1884	Marriage of the composer's parents.
1885	3 November: Birth of their first child, Bertha – nicknamed Lulucha – who dies in 1976 as Mrs Romeu Augusto Borman de Borges; she leaves three children: Clélia (*b.* 11 September 1908), Haygara (*b.* 10 May 1917) and Paulo Emygidio (*b.* 10 October 1922).
1887	5 March: Heitor Villa-Lobos is born.
1888	13 May: Princess Isabel, daughter of Emperor Dom Pedro II, signs – in her father's absence – the 'Golden Law' which abolishes slavery in Brazil. 10 October: the composer's sister, Carmen – nicknamed Bilita – is born. She dies on 20 April 1970 as Mrs Danton Condorcet da Silva Jardim; she leaves one daughter: Ahygara Iacyra (26 August 1933-1996).
1889	17 January: the composer and his sister, Carmen, are baptised at São José Church in Rio de Janeiro. 15 November: Proclamation of the Republic in Brazil. Villa-Lobos's father, Raúl, publishes the first of a series of scholarly books.
1890	16 October: Raúl Villa-Lobos finds work at the National Library in Rio de Janeiro. He gives up medical study for lack of funds; two years later, on 6 October 1892, he is promoted to librarian and, in 1896, entrusted to reorganise the Senate's Library.
1897	23 June: the composer's brother, Othon, is born who dies at age twenty-one in 1918; electrician married to Octavia.
1899	18 July: Raúl Villa-Lobos, at age thirty-seven, dies of malaria in Rio.
1899/1900	Heitor Villa-Lobos's first compositions: *Os Sedutores*, *Dime Perché* for voice and piano.
1901	3 April: Villa-Lobos enters Colégio Pedro II.
1904-07	Villa-Lobos composes short songs and piano pieces and sketches small chamber works; *Comédia Lírica*.
1905	Villa-Lobos moves in bohemian circles and mixes with popular composers and interpreters including Ernesto Júlio de Nazaré, Joaquim Francisco dos Santos (Quincas Laranjeiras), Eduardo das Neves, Anacleto Augusto de Medeiros, Irineu de Almeida, Francisca (Chiquinha) Hedwiges Gonzaga, Catulo da Paixão Cearense.

1906-07	Villa-Lobos sporadically attends courses at Rio de Janeiro's Instituto Nacional de Música (now: Escola de Música da Universidade Federal do Rio de Janeiro).
c. 1910	Villa-Lobos takes private harmony lessons with Agnello França and advice from composer Antônio Francisco Braga.
1911	*Piano Trio No. 1 op. 25*
c. 1911/12	Travels to Paranaguá, state of Paraná, where, for a short time, he works in a match factory, then to Belém, state of Pará, Bahia and Manaus.
1912	1 November: meets Lucília Guimarães (b. 26 May 1886 in Paraíba do Sul), a pianist, teacher and, later, interpreter of his music. *Suíte Infantil* No. 1 for piano.
1912/13	*Sonata Fantasia No. 1 (Désespérance)* for violin and piano. Villa-Lobos moves to Rua Souza Neves 15 in the Tijuca area. In the afternoons he plays the cello in a small ensemble to entertain guests at the Confeitaria Colombo in Rua Gonçalves Dias, and in the evenings in the Café Assírio in the Opera House's basement.
1913	September: The Ballets Russes, on its first visit to Rio de Janeiro, performs part of Borodin's *Prince Igor, Scheherezade, L'Après-midi d'un Faune*. Music of the Russians and French Impressionists influences Villa-Lobos who plays the cello in the Theatre's orchestra. 12 November: Villa-Lobos marries Lucília Guimarães; they move into the home of his wife and her brothers at Rua Fonseca Teles 7 in the São Cristóvão area.
1914-15	*Danças Características Africanas* for solo piano.
1915	29 January: A concert, given by the composer, Lucília and a friend in the nearby mountain village, Nova Friburgo, includes, for the first time, some of the composer's music. The concert takes place at Teatro D. Eugênia. March-June: *Cello Concerto No. 1 op. 50.* 31 July: For the first time, some of Villa-Lobos's music – *Suíte Característica for Strings* – appears in a concert programme in Rio de Janeiro, given by the Sociedade de Concêrtos Sinfônicos, conducted by Villa-Lobos's former teacher A.F. Braga. 13 November: Villa-Lobos organises in Rio de Janeiro the first concert consisting entirely of his own music.
1915/16	*String Quartet No. 12 op. 56.*
1916	February: *Cello Sonata No. 2 op. 66; String Quartet No. 3; Symphony No. 1 op. 112 (O Imprevisto).*
1917	Finishes *Miniaturas* for voice and piano. Villa-Lobos plays the cello in the Odeon cinema. He begins serious auto-didactical studies of theoretical treaties by Berlioz and Vincent d'Indy to school himself in instrumentation. 3 February: Villa-Lobos organises the second concert of his own music. July: Villa-Lobos's first acquaintance with the music of Stravinsky and Ravel performed by Diaghilev's visiting Ballets Russes in Rio. September: Alexander Smallens conducts *Tristan und Isolde.* Orchestral works: *Amazonas, Uirapurú, Naufrágio de Kleônikos.*

	17 November: Villa-Lobos organises the third concert of his own works.
1917/18	*Piano Trio No. 3.*
1918	Villa-Lobos, his wife and in-laws move to Rua de Paranaguá 11. He writes the fourth act of his opera *Izaht*. After meeting Arthur Rubinstein in Rio de Janeiro, he composes *A Prole do Bebé No. 1* for piano.
	15 August: Villa-Lobos organises, and partly conducts, the first concert of his orchestral works.
1919	May-June: He writes *Symphony No. 3 (A Guerra)*, as one of three composers who are each commissioned by the Director of the Instituto Nacional de Música to compose a symphony on the occasion of the Peace Treaty Commemoration.
	October: Villa-Lobos sketches *Symphony No. 4 (A Vitória)* and plans his *Symphony No. 5 (A Paz);* the latter is eventually finished in 1950.
	Villa-Lobos leaves the home of his in-laws and, together with his wife, moves to Rua Didimo 10 in the Tijuca area, the couple's home until May 1936.
	Beginning of public recognition: occasionally, conductors and soloists include his music in their concert programmes. To these interpreters the composer dedicates his subsequent compositions.
1919/20	*Carnaval das Crianças Brasileiras.*
1920, 1922	Felix Weingartner conducts music by Wagner in Rio de Janeiro and includes *Naufrágio de Kleónikos,* and *Dança Frenética* in one of his programmes.
1920, 1923	Richard Strauss conducts his compositions in Rio de Janeiro.
1921	*Boris Godunov* and other Russian music is performed in Rio de Janeiro. Vera Janacópulos sings three songs from *Miniaturas* in Paris, the first time that Villa-Lobos's music is heard there: *Quatuor, Epigramas Irônicos e Sentimentais, A Prole do Bebé No. 2.*
1922	During 'The Week of Modern Art' in São Paulo, Brazilian contemporary and avant-garde writers, poets, painters and composers organise lectures, recitals and exhibitions – including three recitals (13, 15 and 17 February) of Villa-Lobos's music – to promote Brazilian art and music.
	Villa-Lobos obtains a grant from the Brazilian government for a one-year stay in Paris.
1923	*Poème de l'enfant et de sa mère, Nonetto.*
	30 June: Villa-Lobos embarks for Europe on the S.S. *Croix.*
1924	In Paris, 15 February: Villa-Lobos conducts music by Latin American composers but none of his own.
	9 and 16 March: Villa-Lobos conducts Brazilian music, including his own, with the Orquestra Sinfônica Portuguêsa at the Teatro São Luiz in Lisbon.
	28 March: Villa-Lobos conducts Brazilian music in the Musée Galliéra, Paris.
	3 April: He gives a concert in Brussels.
	4 April and 11 April: During the Exposition d'Art Américain Latin in Paris, Villa-Lobos's music is played at the Musée Galliéra.
	9 April: The Sixth Jean Wiéner Concert includes a chamber

music piece by Villa-Lobos (*Trio for oboe, clarinet and bassoon,* composed in 1921).

30 May: Villa-Lobos conducts his works and premières his *Nonetto* in the Salle des Agriculteurs, Paris. This was his most important concert in Paris at that time.

In the summer Villa-Lobos returns to Rio de Janeiro. Here, the great breakthrough occurs: he creates his own musical style. *Chôros No. 2* and *No. 7.*

8 October: Villa-Lobos signs his first contract with the Paris publishing house Éditions Max Eschig. Previous works were mainly published by Arthur Napoleão in Rio de Janeiro.

1925   In January and February Villa-Lobos conducts Brazilian and French music in São Paulo and on 18 and 20 February a concert with his own works which met with success. *Chôros No. 3.*

On 1 and 17 June Villa-Lobos attends two chamber music concerts of his works in Buenos Aires. Upon his return to Rio de Janeiro he writes *Chôros No. 5* and *No. 8.*

On 30 November and 5 December he presents his new compositions in São Paulo.

1926   In Rio de Janeiro arranges a concert of his music. He regularly organises concerts to present his latest works as others are not inclined to include his music in their programmes. He gives three more concerts, 31 October, 15 and 19 November. The fertile period of composition continues throughout that year: *Chansons Typiques Brésiliennes, Três Poemas Indígenas, Serestas, Cirandas, Chôros No. 4* and *No. 10.*

December: He embarks for Paris with his wife, Lucília, sponsored financially by Arnaldo and Carlos Guinle, two Brazilian industrialists, to spend three-and-a half years in France.

1927   January: Villa-Lobos settles at 11 Place St Michel in Paris. Begins to arrange and edit the Guinle brothers' collection of folk- and children's songs. Publication, financed by the Guinle brothers, is foreseen. But no publisher is found. The collection is never returned to its owners, the Guinle brothers; the whereabouts of the collection has remained unknown ever since.

Villa-Lobos signs a further contract with Éditions Max Eschig. The composer meets internationally-renowned artists: Stokowski, Albert Wolff, Edgard Varèse, and Florent Schmitt, music critic of *Le Temps,* who becomes a great admirer of his music.

24 October and 5 December: Villa-Lobos presents his latest compositions with the Orchestre Colonne at the Maison Gaveau.

1928   *Quinteto em forma de Chôros, Twelve Études* and *Suite Populaire for guitar.*

23 and 24 November: Stokowski and the Philadelphia Orchestra perform Villa-Lobos's *Danças Características Africanas* in Philadelphia and, on 27 November, at Carnegie Hall in New York. This is presumably the first time that American audiences hear a work by the Brazilian composer.

1929   21 January: Villa-Lobos signs a further contract with Éditions Max Eschig.

	2/3 February: Albert Wolff and the Concerts Lamoureux perform *Chôros No. 8*. The composer writes *Deux Chôros* (*Bis*), *Suite Suggestive*. During the summer Villa-Lobos holidays in Brazil and conducts a series of concerts in Rio de Janeiro and São Paulo. *Mômoprecóce*. In early October Villa-Lobos embarks for Barcelona to conduct, on 18 October, Brazilian music including his own; then he travels to Paris.
1930	25 January and 21 March: Further contracts with Éditions Max Eschig.
	23 February: Villa-Lobos's *Mômoprecóce* is premièred in Salle Pleyel, Paris with the Brazilian soloist Magda Tagliaferro.
	1 April: Villa-Lobos attends a chamber music concert in Liège.
	3 April and 7 May: In Maison Gaveau, Paris Villa-Lobos presents his latest compositions. At the end of May, he and his wife, Lucília, leave Paris for Brazil. He is not to return to France until after World War II.
	During the second half of the year Villa-Lobos gives a series of concerts in São Paulo including his own works, interrupted only by Brazil's October Revolution with its forebodings of nationalistic tendencies. The composer begins his *Bachianas Brasileiras* series.
1931	Villa-Lobos with a group of musicians undertakes a musical pilgrimage into São Paulo's hinterland, organised in conjunction with the respective Municipalities, offering music in places otherwise deprived of cultural events.
	24 May: at the Campo São Bento in São Paulo, Villa-Lobos conducts his first massed choir with unexpected success. This marks the beginning of the composer's interest in choral singing and choral arrangements of folk- and children's songs. Villa-Lobos with his group of musicians visits São Paulo's hinterland twice more. On his return to the city of São Paulo, he conducts two more concerts on 6 and 21 October which include his newest choral arrangements. At the year's end he finally settles in Rio de Janeiro. *String Quartet No. 5*.
1932	18 April: SEMA (Superintendência de Educação Musical e Artística do Departamento de Educação da Prefeitura do (então) Distrito Federal) is decreed, to make choral singing in municipal schools mandatory. Villa-Lobos is nominated head of SEMA, a post specifically created for him. For the first time in his life, Villa-Lobos, aged forty-five, has a secure monthly income. He forms his music teachers' chorus, called Orfeão de Professores. *Caixinha de Boas Festas*.
1933	The composer creates the Villa-Lobos Orchestra, dismantled the following year for lack of funds, and conducts unorthodox programmes.
1934	On the occasion of the South American Theosophical Congress Villa-Lobos conducts two concerts on 18 and 20 June.
1935	In connection with his SEMA activities, Villa-Lobos organises a number of concerts between August and December.
1936	25 April: Villa-Lobos attends the First International Congress for Musical Education in Prague and returns via Berlin and Barcelona to Rio de Janeiro.
	28 May: Villa-Lobos decides to separate from his wife Lucília and leaves their home. *Ciclo Brasileiro*.

1937	*Descobrimento do Brasil, Missa São Sebastião.*
1938	Villa-Lobos composes the first movement of his *Bachianas Brasileiras No. 5* which was to become his most celebrated piece internationally. The second movement is composed seven years later.
1939	4-5 May: New York's World Fair; Villa-Lobos's music is heard during a Festival of Brazilian music. *As Três Marias.*
1940	16-20 October: At a further Festival of Brazilian music, held in New York's Museum of Modern Art, Villa-Lobos's music is performed. The composer gives concerts in Montevideo, Uruguay.
1942	July: First performance of *Chôros No. 6, No. 9* and *No. 11* in Rio de Janeiro. Villa-Lobos launches the Conservatório Nacional de Canto Orfeônico in Rio de Janeiro which is decreed on 26 November. *Bachianas Brasileiras No. 7.*
1944	26 November: Villa-Lobos's American debut in Los Angeles with the Werner Janssen Symphony Orchestra has little success. Five days previously he receives an honorary doctorate in law from Occidental College. *Bachianas Brasileiras No. 8, String Quartet No. 8.*
1945	*Fantasia for Cello and Orchestra, Bachianas Brasileiras No. 9, Piano Concerto No. 1, Symphony No. 7, Madona.* 28 January: The League of Composers offers a chamber music concert of Villa-Lobos's music at New York's Museum of Modern Art. 8 and 9 February: Villa-Lobos's first New York appearance with the Philharmonic Orchestra is followed by appearances in Boston and Chicago. 14 July: Villa-Lobos launches the Brazilian Academy of Music in Rio de Janeiro.
1946	13 March: Villa-Lobos's mother, Noêmia, dies.
1947	After a visit to Rome, Villa-Lobos travels to New York to receive from Edwin Lester, President of the Los Angeles Civic Light Opera Association, a commission to write the operetta *Magdalena.* From now on until the end of his life, the composer lives part of every year in the USA, Europe and Brazil, and guest conducts in other Latin American countries.
1948	9 July: Villa-Lobos enters New York's Memorial Hospital for a cancer operation on the bladder.
1950	*String Quartet No. 12.*
1951	*Guitar Concerto.*
1952	Villa-Lobos chooses the Hotel Bedford in Paris for his European headquarters. 17-19 June: Villa-Lobos conducts the Israel Philharmonic Orchestra. *Symphony No. 10, Piano Concerto No. 4.*
1953	*Odisséia de uma Raça, Fantasia Concertante, Harp Concerto, Alvorada na Floresta Tropical, String Quartet No. 14, Cello Concerto No. 2, Piano Concerto No. 5, String Quartet No. 15.*
1955	*Symphony No. 11, Harmonica Concerto.*
1955/56	Basil Langton commissions Villa-Lobos to compose music for

a ballet, based on Eugene O'Neill's *The Emperor Jones*, and John Blankenship commissions the composer to set Federico García Lorca's play *Yerma* to music.

1957	*Symphony No. 12, Quinteto Instrumental, String Quartet No. 17.* On the occasion of his seventieth birthday, Villa-Lobos is made an honorary citizen of São Paulo and in this city a festival takes place with his music during a 'Villa-Lobos Week' in September. The Brazilian government declares 1957 the 'Year of Villa-Lobos'.
1958	*A Menina das Nuvens:* MGM commission Villa-Lobos to write the music for the film *Green Mansions*, based on the novel by W.H. Hudson. *Bendita Sabedoria, Magnificat Aleluia.* 3 December: New York University confers an honorary doctorate on Villa-Lobos.
1959	12 July: In Bear Mountain, USA, Villa-Lobos conducts the last concert of his life. 14 July: In Rio de Janeiro, Villa-Lobos receives Carlos Gomes Medal. 11 August: Villa-Lobos, hospitalised for uraemia and kidney congestion, makes his will, in Rio de Janeiro. 7 September: Villa-Lobos attends the last concert of his life at the Municipal Theatre to hear *his Magnificat Aleluia.* 17 November: Villa-Lobos dies, at his home, in the Rua Araújo Pôrto Alegre 56, Apt. 54, in Rio de Janeiro.
1960	From February through April, the New York Public Library holds an exhibit in Villa-Lobos's memory with photographs, recordings, scores and books.
1961	20 January: The Museu Villa-Lobos in Rio de Janeiro – decreed on 22 June 1960 – opens its doors under the direction of Arminda Villa-Lobos, the composer's companion during his last twenty-three years. Since then, the Museum holds annual festivals and competitions and publishes books and recordings.
1966	25 May: Villa Lobos's wife, Lucília, dies.
1971	5 March: On the occasion of the eighty-fourth anniversary of Villa-Lobos's birth a memorial plate is affixed to the Hotel Bedford, Paris. 12 August: Première of *Yerma* at Santa Fe Opera, Santa Fe, New Mexico, USA.
1985	5 August: Arminda d'Almeida Villa-Lobos, the composer's companion, dies aged seventy-three in Rio de Janeiro (*b.* 26 July 1912).

Brief survey of Brazil's history from its discovery until Villa-Lobos's death

Discovery

7 June 1494	Treaty of Tordesillas divides the world between Spain and Portugal.
8 July 1497	First voyage to India by Vasco da Gama (1468 or 1469-1524)
22 April 1500	On his way to India, Pedro Álvares Cabral (1467-1520), a Portuguese navigator, discovers Brazil and disembarks the next day. The land is successively called Vera Cruz, Santa Cruz and Brazil. The word Brasil or Brazil means 'red wood' – derived from *brasa* (braze) – of which the land discovered by Cabral had an abundance. During the first thirty years after its discovery, Brazil is practically abandoned, and only the red Brazil wood is traded.
1501-1502	Amerigo Vespucci (1451 or 1454-1512), the Italian navigator, visits Brazil during his South American expeditions. On their exploration of the Brazilian coast, the fleet of Gaspar de Lemos and Amerigo Vespucci pass through the bay – on 1 January 1502 – and call it Rio de Janeiro.
1503	Expedition of Gonçalo Coelho establishes the first settlement in Rio de Janeiro at the mouth of the Carioca river.
1503	(Some sources give the date 1502 or 1506). King Dom Manuel I (1469-1521) of Portugal licenses Fernão de Noronha and other merchants to trade Brazil wood from the New World which yields more than five-hundred per cent profit.
1507	The name 'America' appears for the first time on a map of the German cosmograph Martin Waldseemüller (1470-1518?) in memory of the Italian navigator Amerigo Vespucci.
1519	Fernão (or Fernando) de Magalhães (*c.* 1480-1521) lands in Brazil on the first world circumnavigation.
1531	Expedition of Martim Afonso de Sousa (*c.* 1500-1571; some sources give the date 1500-1564, or 1530-1571) to colonise Brazil.
1532	First sugar cane introduced.

Captaincies (1534-1549)

1534	Brazil is divided into twelve donees or hereditary captaincies.
1538	First known shipment of slaves arrives from Africa.

Governors-General (1549-1714)

1549	The first governor of Portugal, Tomé de Sousa (1502 or 1503-1579) lands in Bahia de Todos os Santos and founds the city of São Salvador (1549-1763), which was to be the seat of government for about two centuries. Together with Tomé de Sousa come the first colonists with the first cattle and the Jesuits including Manuel da Nóbrega (*c.* 1519-1570) and, later, José de Anchieta (1534-1597) who play an

important part converting the heathens and in making the nation.

Creation of vast landed properties: sugar plantations in the northeastern coastal area and cattle ranches in the middle São Francisco area as far as Maranhão. This forms a society of two classes: aristocrats and slaves. With the Jesuits' opposition to the Indians' enslavement, the import of African Negroes is adopted as a solution, just as in the Mother country, Portugal, where low-class labour is performed by Negroes and Moors.

1551	First bishop in Brazil.
1554	Foundation of São Paulo by Padre Manuel da Nóbrega. Due to the absence of urban economy and a predominantly rural society, the colonists cling to the coast which, because of its enormous size, is rather defenceless. This is the reason for the success of the foreign invasion.
	10 November 1555 The French, under Admiral Nicolas Durand de Villega(i)gnon (1510-1575) land in Rio de Janeiro and establish a Huguenot colony.
1557	Hans Staden's book about Brazil *Zwei Reisen nach Brasilien* (*1548-1555*) appears in Marburg, Germany.
	1 March 1565 Estácio de Sá (1520-1567), nephew of Mem de Sá (1500-1572), founds the city of São Sebastião do Rio de Janeiro.
	20 January 1567 Mem de Sá expels the French and occupies Guanabara Bay.
1570	Population of Brazil is 35,000.
1580	Portugal is united with Spain.
1584-1616	Conquest of the coastal area: Foundation of Paraíba (1584), Natal and Rio Grande do Norte (1598), Ceará (1603), Maranhão (1615) and Belém (1616).
1600	Population of Brazil is 60,000.
1624-1654	Holland sends an expedition to Brazil.
1624	The Dutch capture Salvador da Bahia.
1630	The Dutch seize Recife and call it Mauritsstad.
1640	Portugal declares its independence from Spain.
1645	Revolt against the Dutch.
6 August 1661	Peace between Holland and Portugal.
1694	Gold is discovered in Minas Gerais.

Viceroys (1714-1808)

1714	Governors-General are henceforth called Viceroys.
1714 or 1721-22	Discovery of diamonds.
1727-32	Francisco de Melo Palhêta (1670?-?) introduces coffee to Brazil.
1737	Foundation of Rio Grande do Sul.
1748	Foundation of Goías and Mato Grosso.
	13 January 1750 The Treaty of Madrid abandons the Treaty of Tordesillas of

	1494 and establishes the boundaries between Spanish America and Portuguese America (Brazil), thus confirming the conquest by recognition of *uti possidetis*.
3 September 1759	Expulsion of the Jesuits.
1761	Treaty of El Pardo annuls the Treaty of Madrid.
1763	The capital is transferred from Salvador da Bahia to Rio de Janeiro where it remains for almost two centuries until 1960.
28 May 1774	First Brazilian bishop arrives in Rio de Janeiro.
1777	Treaty of Sto Idelfonso remakes the Portuguese-Spanish frontiers.
1789	The Inconfidência Mineira, a conspiracy to establish a Republic, is exposed.
21 April 1792	The Inconfidência's leader, Joaquim José da Silva Xavier (??), known as Tiradentes, is executed.
1807	After the invasion of Portugal by Napoleon, (1769-1821) the Portuguese court is transferred to Brazil and leaves on 27 November 1807.

State of Brazil in the Kingdom of Portugal and Algarves (1808-1815)

23 January 1808	Queen Maria I (1734-1816) of Portugal and Algarves, her son Dom João (1767-1826), acting head of the ruling House of Braganza, and the royal court arrive in Bahia.
7 March 1808	The royal family arrive in Rio de Janeiro. Henceforth, the ports open to world trade, restrictions on manufacturing is lifted, the Bank of Brazil is founded, cultural life is furthered and the first printing press is established. The Brazilian population is estimated at three-and-a half million, including almost two million slaves. Sugar, cotton, coffee and cacao are exported.
1810	Treaties with Great Britain give that nation commercial dominance over Brazil. *The History of Brazil* by Robert Southey, London, appears.

United Kingdom of Portugal, Brazil and Algarves (1815-1821)

1815	Brazil is raised to the status of Kingdom and Rio de Janeiro becomes the capital of the United Kingdom of Portugal, Brazil and Algarves. The seat of government is installed in the former Palace of the governors and of the viceroys.
1816	Upon the death of Queen Maria I, her son is crowned King as Dom João VI.
	5 November 1817 Leopoldina, Archduchess of Austria, and future Empress of Brazil, arrives in Rio de Janeiro.
1818	First non-Portuguese immigrants settle in Petropolis, Nova Friburgo and Southern Brazil.
4 October 1819	First steamship goes into operation from Bahia to Cachoeira.
26 April 1821	Dom João VI returns to Portugal, leaving his son, Dom Pedro, to govern as Regent.

1821-1822	*Kingdom of Brazil (1821-1822)* Dom Pedro, the Prince Royal, becomes regent of Brazil which is elevated to the status of Kingdom. Dom Pedro shares the desire for independence, advocated by José Bonifácio de Andrade e Silva (1763-1838).
	The First Empire (1822-1831)
7 September 1822	Dom Pedro, the Prince Regent, proclaims Brazil's independence and is crowned as Dom Pedro I, Emperor of Brazil.
1824	Dom Pedro promulgates the first constitution.
	Second Empire (1831-1889)
7 April 1831	Dom Pedro I abdicates and leaves for Europe. During the minority of his son, Dom Pedro II, Brazil is governed, for nine years, by regents. The period is filled with revolutions in Pará, Rio Grande do Sul and Maranhão.
1834	Additional Act to the 1824 constitution institutes federalism.
28 March 1835	First steamship sails from Rio de Janeiro across the bay to Niteroi.
22 July 1840	Dom Pedro II is declared of age and ascends the throne on 23 July 1840.
1843	First steamboat navigates the Amazon.
1850	Brazil has seven million inhabitants, two million of which are slaves. The Queiróz Law abolishes the slave trade. Capital previously invested in the slave trade is now applied to public utilities: railways, shipping companies, telegraph.
1851	First regular steamship line to Europe is inaugurated.
30 April 1854	First railway in Brazil.
1857	Publication of José Martiniano de Alencar's novel *O Guarani*.
1865-1870	War against Paraguay.
1867	The Amazon is opened to international trade.
1871	Law of the Free Womb frees all children born to slaves.
1873	Italian immigrants surpass those from Portugal.
1874	Transatlantic cable between Brazil and Europe goes into service.
1875	Brazil's population surpasses ten million.
1885	28 September 1885 The Saraiva-Cotegipe Law frees all slaves at age sixty.
1888	13 May 1888 The Golden Law, signed by Dom Pedro II's daughter, Princess Isabel, regent during her father's absence, abolishes slavery without compensation for slaveholders.
1889	*Republic (1889-* 15 November 1889 The fall of the monarchy is the consequence. The Emperor is dethroned by the army, led by Marshal Manuel Deodoro da Fonseca who becomes head of the provisional government (1889-1891). Proclamation of the Republic introduces an American-style Federation which replaces the British-style monarchy. Centralisation is replaced by autonomy of the states.

1890	Church and State separate.
1891	Death of Dom Pedro II in exile in Paris.
1891-1894	Marshal Floriano Vieira Peixoto becomes President.
1894-1898	Law and order is reestablished with President Prudente José de Morais Barros (1841-1902).
1898-1902	Finances stabilise under President Manuel Ferraz de Campos Salles (1841-1913).
1899	Alberto Santos Dumont (1873-1932) flies around the Eiffel Tower in Paris.
1902	Euclydes (Rodrigues Pimenta) da Cunha publishes *Os Sertões* and José Pereira da Graça Aranha *Canaan*.
1906	The Third Pan American Conference meets in Rio de Janeiro.
1907	At the Second Hague Conference, Brazil participates in her first worldwide conference.
20 July 1910	Indian Protection Service is established.
1917	Brazil declares war on Germany and joins Allied forces.
1922	'Week of Modern Art' in São Paulo initiates a new phase of national culture. First university is established to replace scattered faculties. Brazil's population surpasses thirty million.
1930	Brazil's population reaches more than thirty-four million. Revolution brings Getúlio Dornelles Vargas (1883-1954) to power, as head of the provisional government (1930- 1934), President (1934-1937) and Dictator (1937-1945).
1932	Revolution in São Paulo and civil war.
10 November 1937	'New State' is established.
22 August 1942	Brazil declares war on the Axis Forces.
1944	Brazil sends expeditionary corps to Europe.
1945	Vargas is deposed by the military.
18 September 1946	Promulgation of a new constitution.
1950	Brazil's population surpasses fifty million.
31 January 1951	Vargas assumes Presidency, constitutionally elected by free vote.
24 August 1954	Vargas commits suicide.
31 January 1956	Juscelino Kubitscheck de Oliveira assumes Presidency. During his administration Brasília is built.
21 April 1960	The capital of Brazil moves from Rio de Janeiro inland to Brasília. Brazilian population reaches seventy million.

Facts about Brazil

Brazil is the largest country in Latin America and the fifth largest in the world, exceeded only by the USSR, Canada, China and the United States. Brazil ranks seventh amongst the most populous countries in the world, with approximately 160 million inhabitants which represents about 50 per cent of South America's inhabitants. Its population has more than doubled since Villa-Lobos's death. The chief centres of population are in the southeast (about 40 per cent of the total), northeast (around 30 per cent) and south (about 21 per cent). The urbanisation process is striking. By 1970 the urban population was equivalent to more than half (60 per cent) of the total. At that time, sixty Brazilian cities had more than 100,000 inhabitants.

Brazil is a Federal Republic with twenty-three states, three Federal territories and one Federal District where its capital, Brasília, is located. Inaugurated on 21 April 1960, it is on a central plateau, 3,350 ft (1,100 metres) above sea level and 560 miles (900 km) from the coast. Rio de Janeiro, the former capital, remains the country's leading cultural centre. Its metropolitan area with 8.3 million inhabitants, is exceeded only by São Paulo, with ten million people (1975), which is Brazil's largest industrial complex and ranks first in Latin America.

Elected for a five-year term, the President of the Republic wields the Executive Power. The National Congress wields the Legislative Power and comprises two Houses: The Federal Senate and the House of Representatives. The Federal Supreme Court is the chief institution of the Judiciary Power.

Discovered in 1500 by the Portuguese navigator Pedro Álvares Cabral and colonised by Portugal, Brazil declared her independence and became an Empire on 7 September 1822 which lasted until the proclamation of the Republic on 15 November 1889.

Glossary

Information is derived from the following sources:

Cascudo, Luís da Câmara (1898-1986), *Dicionário do Folklore Brasileiro*, 4th ed. S. Paulo, 1979.

Encyclopedia of Latin America, New York, 1974.

Pequeno Dicionário Brasileiro da Língua Portuguêsa, 9th ed. Rio de Janeiro, 1951.

Smith, T. Lynn, *Brazil, Portrait of Half a Continent*, New York 1951.

Smith, T. Lynn, *Brazil, People and Institutions*, Baton Rouge, 1963.

Aldeia	Village
Agogô	Double-bell instrument of African origin
Amarelo	Yellow
Angóias	(see *chocalho*)
Apito	Whistle
Atabaques	Conical drums; in Bahia known as lê, rumpi and rum
Aviararé	Five-tube panpipe
Bairo	District or section of a city
Batuque	Generic designation of Negro dances accompanied by percussion instruments. It has no specific choreography
Berimbau	Musical bow, also with *caxixi* (small basket rattle) used to accompany the stick strokes
Bicho	Animal or beast
Branco	White
Buzina	Horn
Cabaça	Gourd filled with little stones which rattle when moved Similar to *chocalho* (cf.)
Caboclo	In colonial Brazil a term (literally: copper-coloured) used to refer to an uncultured Indian. Now it denotes a mixed-blood Brazilian of European and Indian ancestry. Currently, widely used to refer to any lower-class rural male
Cacique	Head of an Indian village or tribe, a local strong man
Caipira	Hillbilly; designation for lower-class rural Brazilian
Caixa	Drum
Calunga	Doll made of cloth, wood, bone or metal
Candomblé	A highly ritualistic cult of African origin. It was brought to Brazil by slaves from West Africa, with its centre in Bahia and uses the nagô language in Brazil. African deities are worshipped
Candongueiro	Drum
Canzá	A type of *reco-reco* (cf.)
Capadócio	A charlatan, quack, braggart, impostor
Capitania	Designation for the state or province during part of the colonial period
Caracaxá	A type of *reco-reco* (cf.)

Carioca	Designation for the inhabitants of the city of Rio de Janeiro or the cultural traits of the city. The name is derived from the carioca brook in Rio de Janeiro
Cascavel	Rattlesnake or rattle
Caleretê	In the south of Brazil a rural dance of African origin known since the colonial period in São Paulo, Minas Gerais and Rio de Janeiro
Catir a Batita	(cf. *Caleretê*)
Caxambu	A great drum. It is also the name of a dance which is performed to the sound of this instrument, yet the instrument is also played for other dances
Chocalho	Wooden or metal rattle
Chôro	This is a generic name. It signifies a group of instruments usually consisting of flute, clarinet, ophicleide, trombone, guitar, *cavaquinho* (*ukelele* type of instrument) – with one of them as soloist – and a few percussion instruments. It is also the term for a piece of music played by these instruments in the open air and perhaps comparable with a serenade. It is also known as *assustados* or *arrasta-pé*, a sort of popular ball. 'Chôro was something that had come to Brazil from the other side of the Atlantic...from the African coast where the Kaffir tribes practised a sort of vocal concert with dance, called *xôlo*.... The Brazilian Negroes called their balls which they staged on St John's Day or the other holidays on the big country estates where they were employed *xôlos* which through some confusion with a Portuguese paronym turned into *xôro*. When this *xôro* moved into urban regions it became *chôro*.' (Renato Almeida: *História da Música Brasileira,* 2nd edition, Rio de Janeiro, 1942)
Ciranda	Children's dance, a round-dance which came to Brazil from Portugal where it was an adult dance; also known as *Cirandinha*
Colégio	An educational institution at the secondary level
Cruzeiro	The Brazilian monetary unit which replaced the milreis on 1 November 1942
Cuíca or Puíta	A friction drum, a small cylindrical musical instrument much used by carnival groups in *candomblés* (cf.) and *macumba* (cf.). Almost indispensable at popular, *mestizo* and Negro balls. It came to Brazil with the Bantu Negroes from Angola where it was called *puíta*. In Portugal it is known as ronca, in Spain as *zambomba*
Currupira	A malignant little mythical being which, according to superstition, is a demon in the woods. His feet are turned backwards so that anyone seeing his tracks and trying to run away from him, will speed to destruction at his hands. He is said to be responsible for the mysterious disappearance of hunters, sudden anguish and forgetting the right track
Desafio	A contest in dialogue, usually in verse and as improvisation, between two singers, each in turn seeking to answer the opponent's question. It came from Portugal, is known all over Brazil but especially in the northeast, and there, more in the *Sertão* (wilderness), than on the coast. The accompanying instruments – in the north – are viola and the rabeca (a type of violin of lower timbre with four strings and a melancholy sound) and – in the south – the *sanfona* and the guitar
Embolada	Poetic musical form in the northeast of Brazil in binary, rapid rhythm, used by soloists, with choral refrain. May be

	improvised. As a dance it is called *coco de embolada*
Engenho	Old-fashioned sugar mill
Exu	One of the *orixas* (cf.) of the Afro-Brazilian religious cult. He is the incarnation of evil and generally associated with the devil. He accepts as offerings chickens and black goats and is the messenger between the gods and human beings. He is clad in red and black
Farrapos	A much used piece of cloth; rags
Favela	Slums on some hills surrounding Rio de Janeiro
Freguesia	Church parish
Fazendeiro	The owner of a plantation (*Fazenda*); a farmer, a rancher on a large scale
Filha do Santo	A female who after long ceremonial preparations has been consecrated as a devotee in an Afro-Brazilian fetish cult.
Ganzá	Cf. *Canzá*
Gaúcho	A native of Rio Grande do Sul
Ginásio	An educational institution at the secondary level
Iara	A fantastic being, a sort of water-nymph of the rivers and lakes. Also known in Brazil as *Mae d'Agua,* blond, half fish, it sings to attract lovers who then die by drowning
Interior	All of the state or province lying outside the capital city
Jurupari	A demon or bad spirit of the *Tupi* Indians
Liceu	An educational institution at the secondary level
Lundú	Of Bantu origin, it is a dance accompanied by songs of comic character. It was popular in Portugal in the sixteenth century and came to Brazil in the eighteenth century. In the nineteenth century the dance was replaced by a song of cheerful character. In Portugal it was accompanied by guitar, *bandolim* or viola, in Brazil by viola and guitar
Macumba	A fetish ceremony of African origin with Christian influence accompanied by dances and songs to the sound of drums
Mae d'Agua	Cf. *Iara*
Mameluca	The offspring of European and Indian parents
Maracá	A wooden or clay hollow gourd, filled with dried seeds or little stones which make a noise when rattled. It serves to keep the demons away. The Indians used this instrument in songdances. It was the first Indian instrument in Brazil. Various sizes exist, in simple or double form, sometimes ornamented, or painted, or covered with straw, feathers or animal fur, according to the tribes' tradition
Maracatú	A carnival group which, in the north of Brazil, dances and sings accompanied by percussion instruments. It is of Negro origin and the most luxurious carnival ensemble of the people with a king, queen, princes, dames and the like
Marimba	An African instrument, very popular in Brazil until the beginning of the twentieth century but little used at present
Martelo	Poetic music used for the verses sung by the soloist in the *Desafios* (cf.)
Matraca	Wooden rattle
Maxixe	An urban Brazilian dance which appeared around 1870
Mestiço	A person of mixed parentage. If the person has mixed European-Indian lineage, he is a *caboclo* (cf.), if he has European African parents, he is a *mulato* (cf.)
Milreis	Brazilian monetary unit which prevailed until 1942. One milreis, written 1$000, was replaced by the *cruzeiro* (cf.)
Miundinho	Formerly a dance known in less aristocratic salons. Very successful, its geography consists of short delicate steps. At the

	time of the Regency it was a dance of society and much in fashion
Modinha	Brazilian sentimental art song, cultivated in the nineteenth and twentieth centuries by Portuguese and Brazilian composers. During the Second Empire in Brazil it acquired the character of the Italian opera aria and eventually became a folklore type of strongly lyrical character. Opinions concerning its origin vary, but most agree that the romantic song came from Portugal to Brazil under the name of *Modinha*, a designation derived from *Mote* (Motto) or *Moda* (Fashion). The *modinha* is a drawing-room romance, a sentimental and whining aria about motives for love…with strong influences of Italian cantabile. It is usually in binary form (Renato Almeida: *História da Música Brasiliera*, 2nd edition, Rio de Janeiro, 1942)
Moleque	Small Negro; also designation of any boy who is bad or unruly
Mulato	A person of mixed European and Negro parentage
Orixas	The *orixas* are divinities between the supreme God and human beings. The most important, *Oxalá*, is considered the father. Friday is his consecrated day. Clad in white, he is the divinity of the creation and his instruments are the shepherd's staff, the crown, the hearts and bracelets. His offerings include white chicken, pigeons and goats
Oxum	Clad in yellow, this is the divinity of vanity. His instruments are the crown, two fishes, spade, harpoon on the back and bracelets. His consecrated day is Saturday when chickens, goats and duck are offered
Padre	Priest
Pagé	An Indian medicine man, counsellor of the tribe, sorcerer
Pai-do-Mato	In traditional Alagoas folklore the *Pai-do-Mato* is a very great beast with enormous hair and thirty-foot-long nails
Palma	Palm
Paulista	Native of São Paulo
Pé	Foot
Pica-Pau	Woodpecker. More than seventy different species are known in Brazil. There are several legends concerning this bird. One legend has it that he who finds a woodpecker's feather and keeps it, will lack nothing because luck is with him
Pifes	Flutes
Pio	Bird-call whistle used by hunters to attract birds; it is made of wood, bone or clay
Plantar	To plant
Praça	Public square
Puíta	Friction drum. The same as *cuíca* (cf.). This designation is mostly used in the north of Brazil
Quínjengue	Drum
Reco-reco	Wooden scraper, also called *canzá* (cf.) or ganzá (cf.)
Rudá	It is the aborigines' god of love, entrusted to promote reproduction in human beings by creating love in their hearts and thus making them yearn to return to their tribe from their long and repeated peregrinations
Saci-Pereré	A fantastic, ill-spirited mischievous being, common in Brazil's south. A little Negro with only one leg, red hood, agile, astute and pipe-smoking, he announces himself by persistent and mysterious whistling. He amuses himself by creating domestic difficulties, frightening cattle and burning food. The colonists never mention him. It seems that he first appeared in the

	nineteenth century
Sanfona	Of European origin, it is also known as *acordeona, concertina, fole, limpa banco* and sometimes *gaita de fole*
Saudade	An untranslatable expression which means roughly that pleasant memories, homesickness and deep yearnings are involved
Selvas	Rain forest
Seringueiro	Worker who taps rubber trees and coagulates raw latex
Sertanejo and Sertanista	A hillbilly who lives in the *Sertão* (wilderness)
Sertão (plural: Sertões)	Wilderness, a dry, arid, mainly uninhabited backland region in Brazil's northeast. The drought often lasts for three years, disrupts agriculture, kills crops and causes the death of cattle
Tambu	A drum, often used in the jongos, a sort of samba in São Paulo, Minas Gerais, Espírito Santo and the state of Rio de Janeiro. The choreography differs from one locale to the other. Sometimes the tambu is attached to the player's body by a string. It is then known as *Candongeiro*
Teiru	A typical flute of the Parecis Indians, also designating a melody from the same tribe
Tupinambá	Generic designation of various tribes that occupied Brazil's littoral in the sixteenth century. They spoke Tupi-Guarani language until the nineteenth century, which today is still known in the Amazon region under the name of *nheengatu*. Between 1560 and 1575 settlers of Rio de Janeiro launched a military campaign against the Indians which forced them to move to the interior. Survivors moved north to Pará and Maranhão where in the seventeenth century they were again harassed. The Tupinambá are a fierce, warlike people. They live on hunting and cultivation of manioc, sweet potatoes and beans. Their gods and supernatural beings still exist today with such names as *Jurupary* (cf.) *Currupira* (cf.) and others. The Tupinambás are the most studied tribes about which there exists the most extensive bibliography
Ualalocé	A typical flute of the Parecis Indians, often considered a holy instrument
Uirapurú	A Brazilian bird which sings beautifully. According to legend it brings luck to those who own it, dried or stuffed. When it sings, all other birds fall silent to listen to it
Vaqueiro	A cowboy. This term is used most frequently in the northeast
Xangô	One of the *orixas* (cf.), he is the god of lightning and thunder. Clad in red and white squares, and cockerels and lambs are offered in his honour on Wednesdays

Selected bibliography

Books

Barros, Carlos, Marinho de Paula: *O Romance de Villa-Lobos*, A Noite, Rio de Janeiro, 1951

Beaufils, Marcel: *Villa-Lobos, Musicien et poète du Brésil*, Livraria Agir Editóra, Rio de Janeiro, 1967; Museu Villa-Lobos, Rio de Janeiro, 2nd edition, 1982

Béhague, Gerard: *Heitor Villa-Lobos*. Austin, Texas, 1994

Druesdow, John: *The Chamber Works for Wind Instruments by Villa-Lobos*, Typescript, Latin American Music Centre, Indiana University, Indiana, 1963

Estrela, Arnaldo: *Os Quartetos de Cordas de Villa-Lobos*, Ministério da Educação e Cultura, Museu Villa-Lobos, Rio de Janeiro, 2nd edition, 1978

França, Eurico Nogueira: *Villa-Lobos, Síntese. Crítica e Biográfica*, Ministério da Educação e Cultura, Museu Villa-Lobos, Rio de Janeiro, 1978

França, Eurico Nogueira: *A Evolução de Villa-Lobos na Música de Câmera*, Museu Villa-Lobos, Rio de Janeiro, 1976

Giacomo, Arnaldo Magalhães de: *Villa-Lobos, Alma Sonora do Brasil*, Edições Melhoramentos, São Paulo, 5th edition, 1968

Guimarães, Luiz and collaborators: *Villa-Lobos, Visto da Platéia e na Intimidade, (1912-1935)*, Rio de Janeiro, 1972

Homenagem a Villa-Lobos, Ministério da Educação e Cultura, Rio de Janeiro, 1960

Horta, Luís Paulo: *Heitor Villa-Lobos*, Edições Alumbramento, Livroarte Editora, Rio de Janeiro, 1986

Johnson, Robert L.: *Villa-Lobos's Chôro No. 10*, Analysis and critical survey. Typescript, Latin American Music Center, Indiana University, Indiana, 1963

Kiefer, Bruno: *Villa-Lobos e o Modernismo na Música Brasileira*, Porto Alegre, Movimento, 1981

Lima, João de Souza: *Comentários sobre a Obra Pianística de Villa-Lobos*, Ministério da Educação e Cultura, Museu Villa-Lobos, 2nd edition, Rio de Janeiro, 1976

Mariz, Vasco: *Heitor Villa-Lobos*, Zahar, Rio de Janeiro, 1983

English edition: *Heitor Villa-Lobos, Life and Work*, Brazilian American Cultural Institute, Inc., Washington DC, 2nd edition, 1970

French edition: *Hector Villa-Lobos, L'homme et son œuvre*, Collection: Musiciens de tous les temps, No. 31, Editions Seghers, Paris, 1967

Muricy, José de Andrade: *Villa-Lobos, Uma Interpretação*, Ministério da Educação e Cultura, Rio de Janeiro, 1961

Neves, José Maria: *Villa-Lobos, O Chôro e os Chôros*, Ricordi, São Paulo, 1977

Nóbrega, Adhemar: *As Bachianas Brasileiras de Villa-Lobos*, Ministério da Educação e Cultura, Museu Villa-Lobos, Rio de Janeiro, 2nd edition, 1976

Nóbrega, Adhemar: *Os Chôros de Villa-Lobos*, Ministério da Educação e Cultura, Museu Villa-Lobos, Rio de Janeiro, 1975

Palma, Enos da Costa, and Edgard de Brito Chaves Júnior: *As Bachianas Brasileiras de Villa-Lobos*, Companhia Americana, Rio de Janeiro, 1971

Peppercorn, Lisa M.: *Heitor Villa-Lobos, Leben und Werk des brasilianischen Komponisten*, Atlantis, Zurich, 1972

Peppercorn, Lisa M.: *Villa-Lobos* in The Illustrated Lives of the Great Composers, Omnibus Press, London, 1989

Peppercorn, Lisa M.: *Villa-Lobos, The Music*, Kahn & Averill, London, 1991

Peppercorn, Lisa M.: *Villa-Lobos, Collected Studies*, Scolar Press, Aldershot, 1992

Peppercorn, Lisa M.: *The Villa-Lobos Letters*, translated, edited and annotated, Toccata Press, Kingston-on-Thames, England, 1994

Riedel, W. Rudolph Emmen: *Trois Grades ad Parnassum, Les Derniers Quatuors à Cordes*

(*Nos. 15, 16 et 17*) *de Heitor Villa-Lobos*, Den Haag, Musiekhandel Albersen & Co. b.v. 1977

Santos, Turíbio: *Heitor Villa-Lobos e o Violão*, Museu Villa-Lobos, Rio de Janeiro, 1975

Schic, Anna Stella: *Villa-Lobos, Souvenirs de l'indien blanc*, Actes Sud, Arles, 1987

Tarasti, Eero: *Heitor Villa-Lobos, The Life and Works 1887-1959*, McFarland & Co, Inc. Jefferson, North Carolina and London 1995

Wright, Simon: *Villa-Lobos*, Oxford Studies of Composers, Clarendon Press, Oxford, 1992

Selected studies, articles in newspapers and periodicals

Bush, Randall: *The Piano Works of Heitor Villa-Lobos*, Clavier, Northfield, Illinois, February 1985

Chase, Gilbert: *A Guide to the Music of Latin America*, Pan American Union, Washington DC, 1962

Enciclopédia da Música Brasileira: Erudita, Folclórica, Popular, São Paulo, 1977

Fernandez, Oscar Lorenzo: 'A Contribuição Harmónica de Villa-Lobos para a Música Brasileira', *Boletín Latino-Americano de Musica*, VI, April 1946

Gustafson, Ralf: 'Villa-Lobos and the Man-eating Flower: A Memoir', *The Musical Quarterly*, Spring 1991, Vol. 75, No. 1, pp. 1-11

Marx, Walter Burle: 'Brazilian Portrait', *Modern Music*, New York, Oct/Nov. 1939

Musik in Geschichte und Gegenwart, Vol. 13, Kassel, 1966

New Grove Dictionary of Music and Musicians, pp. 763-67, vol. 19, London, 1980

Orrego-Salas, Juan A.: 'Heitor Villa-Lobos, Man, Work, Style', *Inter-American Music Bulletin*, No. 52, Pan American Union, Washington DC, March 1966

Peppercorn, Lisa M.: 'A Villa-Lobos Opera', *The New York Times*, 28 April 1940

Peppercorn, Lisa M.: 'Uma Opera de Villa Lobos', *Musica Viva*, Rio de Janeiro, Ano I, No. 3, July 1940

Peppercorn, Lisa M.: 'Musical Education in Brazil', *Bulletin of the Pan American Union*, Washington, DC, Vol. 74, No. 10, Oct. 1940

Peppercorn, Lisa M.: 'Violin Concerto', *The New York Times*, 8 June 1941

Peppercorn, Lisa M.: 'New Villa-Lobos Works', *The New York Times*, 11 Oct 1942

Peppercorn, Lisa M.: 'Some Aspects of Villa-Lobos's Principles of Composition', *The Music Review*, Cambridge, Vol. 4, No. 1, 1943

Peppercorn, Lisa M.: 'The History of Villa-Lobos's Birth Date', *The Monthly Musical Record*, London, Vol. 78, No. 898, July/August 1948

Peppercorn, Lisa M.: 'Villa-Lobos's Brazilian Excursions', *The Musical Times*, London, Vol. 113, No. 1549, March 1972

Peppercorn, Lisa M.: 'Villa-Lobos: Father and Son', *Américas*, Washington, DC, Vol. 24, No. 4, April 1972 (English, Spanish, Portuguese)

Peppercorn, Lisa M.: 'The Villa-Lobos Museum', *Américas*, Washington, DC, Vol. 25, Nos. 11/12, Nov./Dec. 1973 (English and Spanish)

Peppercorn, Lisa M.: 'Heitor Villa-Lobos, Festanlässe zum Todestag des brasilianischen Komponisten', *Neue Zürcher Zeitung*, Zurich, No. 489, 19 November 1974

Peppercorn, Lisa M.: '*Villa-Lobos*, entry in *The International Cyclopedia of Music and Musicians*, 10th Edition, New York, 1975, 11th edition, 1985

Peppercorn, Lisa M.: 'Le Influenze del Folklore Braziliano nella Musica di Villa-Lobos', *Nuova Revista Musicale Italiana*, Rome, Anno X, No. 2, April/June 1967

Peppercorn, Lisa M.: 'Foreign Influences in Villa-Lobos's Music', *Ibero-Amerikanishes Archiv*, West Berlin, N.F, Jg. 3, Heft 1, 1977

Peppercorn, Lisa M.: 'The Fifteen-Year-Periods in Villa-Lobos's Life', *Ibero-Amerikanisches Archiv*, West Berlin, N.F., Jg. 5 Heft 2, 1979

Peppercorn, Lisa M.: 'Villa-Lobos's Last Years', *The Music Review*, Cambridge, Vol. 40, No. 4, Nov. 1979

Peppercorn, Lisa M.: 'Villa-Lobos: Il Burlone', *Nuova Revista Musicale Italiana*,

Rome, Anno XIV, No. 3, July/Sept. 1980

Peppercorn, Lisa M.: 'Correspondence between H. Villa-Lobos and his wife Lucília', *Music and Letters*, Oxford, Vol. 61, Nos. 3/4, July/Oct. 1980

Peppercorn, Lisa M.: 'Heitor Villa-Lobos en zijn Familie', *Mens en Melodie*, Utrecht, Vol. XXXV, Sept. 1980

Peppercorn, Lisa M.: 'A Villa-Lobos Autograph Letter at the Bibliothèque Nationale (Paris)', *Latin American Music Review*, Austin, Texas, Vol. 1, No. 2, Oct. 1980

Peppercorn, Lisa M.: 'A Letter of Villa-Lobos to Arnaldo Guinle', *Studi Musicale*, Rome, Vol. X, No. 1, 1981

Peppercorn, Lisa M.: 'The Paris Bibliothèque Nationale's Autograph Letter of Villa-Lobos to his Sponsor', *The Journal of Musicological Research*, New York/London/Paris, Vol. 3, Nos 3/4, 1981

Peppercorn, Lisa M.: 'Villa-Lobos's Stage Works', *Revue Belge de Musiologie*, Brussels, Vol. XXXVI-XXXVIII, 1982-1984

Peppercorn, Lisa M.: 'Menschen, Masken, Mythen: Heitor Villa-Lobos und die brasilianische Musik', *Neue Zeitschrift für Musik*, Mainz, Sept. 1984

Peppercorn, Lisa M.: 'Hoe Villa-Lobos de vader werd van de brasiliaanse Muziek', *Mens en Melodie*, Buren, Oct. 1984

Peppercorn, Lisa M.: 'Villa-Lobos's Commissioned Compositions', *Tempo*, London, No. 151, December 1984

Peppercorn, Lisa M.: 'Profilo del Compositore Brasiliano', *Nuova Rivista Musicale Italiana*, Rome, Vol. XIX, No. 2, April/June 1985

Peppercorn, Lisa M.: 'Heitor Villa-Lobos in Paris', *Latin American Music Review*, Austin, Texas, Vol. 6, No. 2, 1985

Peppercorn, Lisa M.: 'The Villa-Lobos Family', *The Music Review*, Cambridge, England, Vol. 49, No. 2, May 1988

Peppercorn, Lisa M.: 'Villa-Lobos in Israel', *Tempo*, London, No. 169, June 1989

Peppercorn, Lisa M.: 'Villa-Lobos 'ben trovato'', *Tempo*, London, No. 177, June 1991

Presença de Villa-Lobos, Vol 1-12, Ministério da Educação e Cultura, Museu Villa-Lobos, Rio de Janeiro, 1965-1981

Round, Michael: 'Bachianas Brasileiras in Performance', *Tempo*, London, No. 169, June 1989

Smith, Carleton Sprague, and Marcos Romero: 'Heitor Villa-Lobos', *Inter-American Music Bulletin*, No. 15, January 1960, Pan American Union, Washington, DC

Wright, Simon: 'Villa-Lobos: The Formation of his Style', *Soundings*, Cardiff, Wales, 1979

Wright, Simon: 'Villa-Lobos and the Cinema, A Note', *Luso-Brazilian Review*, Vol. 119, No. 2, 1982, Madison, WI

Wright, Simon: 'Villa-Lobos: Modernism in the Tropics', *Musical Times*, March 1987, Vol. 128, No. 1729

Unpublished studies

Boff, Ruy Celso: *Les Chóros de Heitor Villa-Lobos*, Dissertation, Université Catholique de Louvain, n.d.

Elkins, Laurine Annette: *An Examination of Compositional Technique in Selected Piano Works of Heitor Villa-Lobos*, M.A. Thesis in Music, University of Texas at Austin, Texas, August 1972

Farmer, Virginia: *An Analytical Study of the Seventeen String Quartets of Heitor Villa-Lobos*, Ph.D. Thesis in Musical Arts, University of Illinois, Urbana-Champaign, Urbana, Illinois, 1973

Rubinsky, Sonia: *Villa-Lobos's Rudepoêma, An Analysis*,Thesis for the Doctor of Musical Arts, The Juilliard School, New York, April 1986

Wright, Simon: *Heitor Villa-Lobos: His Life, Works and Aesthetic Principles, 1915-1930*, M.A. Thesis, University of Wales, Cardiff, 1978

Wright, Simon: *Villa-Lobos and his position in Brazilian Music after 1930*, Ph.D. Dissertation, University College, Cardiff (University of Wales), 1986

Iconography

Catálogo Iconográfico, Museu Villa-Lobos, Rio de Janeiro, 2nd edition, n.d.

Recordings

Discography (in categories): Selection of foreign-made recordings published in Vasco Mariz: *Hector Villa-Lobos, L'Homme et son œuvre,* Collection: Musiciens de tous le temps, No. 31, Edition Seghers, Paris, 1967

Discography (alphabetical) compiled by the Museu Villa-Lobos, Rio de Janeiro, in Eurico Nogueira França: *Villa-Lobos, Síntese Crítica e Biográfica,* Ministério da Educação e Cultura, Museu Villa-Lobos, Rio de Janeiro, 1970

Discography (Brazilian and Foreign) in categories, published in: *Villa-Lobos, Sua Obra,* Ministério da Educação e Cultura, Museu Villa-Lobos, Second Edition, Rio de Janeiro, 1972

Discography in *Enciclopédia de Música Brasileira, Erudita, Folclórica, Popular,* São Paulo, 1977

Discography in: Appleby, David P. *Heitor Villa-Lobos, A Bio-bibliography,* Greenwood Press, Westport, CT, 1988

Catalogues of compositions

Composers of the Americas, Biographical Data and Catalog of Their Works, Vol. 3, Villa-Lobos, Pan American Union, Washington, DC, 1957 and 1960 (English and Spanish)

Muricy, José de Andrade: *Villa-Lobos, Uma Interpretação,* Ministério da Educação e Cultura, Rio de Janeiro, 1961 (Portuguese)

Villa-Lobos, Sua Obra, Ministério da Educação e Cultura, Museu Villa-Lobos, Rio de Janeiro, 1965, 1972, 1989

Villa-Lobos entry in *Enciclopédia de Música Brasileira, Erudita, Folklórica, Popular,* São Paulo, 1977

Villa-Lobos entry in *The New Grove Dictionary of Music and Musicians:* Macmillan, 1980

Appleby, David P.: *Heitor Villa-Lobos, A Bio-bibliography,* Greenwood Press, Westport, CT, 1988

Acknowledgments

Every effort has been made to secure permissions for copyright material. In the event of any material being used inadvertently, or in those cases where it proved impossible to trace the copyright owner, acknowledgment will be made in any reprint of this book.

I. Reprints of material from articles, books and programmes

1. The essays from *The Musical Quarterly*, New York City, are reproduced by permission of the Journal's Editor.

2. The article from *The Christian Science Monitor*, Boston, is reproduced by permission of the author and the Christian Science Publishing Society, copyright 1971. All rights reserved.

3. The articles from *The New York Times* are reproduced Copyright © 1940/41/42/44/45/48/55/56/57/58/59/60/61/71 by The New York Times Company, reprinted by permission.

4. Permission to reprint extracts from the article by Luiz Heitor Corrêa de Azevedo, published by the American Musicological Society, Inc., 1946, pp. 85-96, has been granted.

5. Some material and illustrations concerning Villa-Lobos's first stay in Paris appeared in the *Latin American Music Review*, Vol. 6, No. 2, Fall/Winter 1985 and are reprinted by permission of The University of Texas Press, Austin, Texas, and courtesy of the other copyright owners.

6. Some material concerning Villa-Lobos's 'Commissioned Compositions' first appeared in *Tempo*, No. 151, December 1984, Boosey & Hawkes, Music Publishers, Ltd, London and are reprinted by permission.

7. Some material and illustrations concerning Villa-Lobos's own studies first appeared in *Neue Zeitschrift für Musik*, Heft 9, September 1984, and are reprinted by permission of Verlag Schott's Söhne, Mainz.

8. Some material and illustrations from *História de Arte Brasileira* by P.M. Bardi are reprinted by permission from the author and Companhia Melhoramentos, São Paulo, 1975.

9. The engravings by Thomas Ender are reproduced by kind permission of the Akademie der Bildenden Künste, Kupferstichkabinett, Vienna.

10. BBC programmes of 1949 (courtesy BBC Written Archives Centre, Caversham Park, Reading).

II. Facsimile Letters

Brazil

Oldemar Guimarães, Rio de Janeiro

Letter from Villa-Lobos to his wife Lucília Guimarães Villa-Lobos

Canada

University Archives, Dalhousie University Library, Ellen Ballon Papers, Halifax, Nova Scotia

A letter to Ellen Ballon

United States of America

1. The Library of Congress, Music Division, Washington, DC with the consent of Arminda Villa-Lobos, Rio de Janeiro, Brazil.

A letter to Irving Schwerké

2. Janet Collins, Seattle, Washington

Letter to the author

III. Musical Quotes

No. 158   Manuscript page of first four bars of *Sexteto Místico*

No. 444   First page of score for *Cello Concerto No. 2* (Editions Max Eschig)

No. 517   First page of score for *Odisséia de uma Raça*, courtesy Israeli Music Publications Ltd., Tel Aviv, Israel

No. 597   First manuscript page of score for *String Quartet No. 17* (Editions Max Eschig)

Nos. 444 and 597 are reproduced by authorisation of Editions Max Eschig, Paris, proprietors of the works.

Photo acknowledgments

Every effort has been made to locate and credit copyright holders, and the publishers apologise for any omissions.

American Wind Symphony Orchestra, Pittsburgh 456, 458

Américas, Organisation of American States, Washington DC, Vol. 9, No. 6, June 1974: 273, 274; Vol. 26, No. 8, August 1974: 339; Vol. 27, No. 1, June 1975: 331

Alcey Maynard Araújo, *Folklore Nacional*, Vol. II, São Paulo 1964 (copyright: Cecilia Macedo de Araújo, São Paulo, 1974) 263, 264, 265, 266, 268, 270

Arquivo Geral da Cidade do Rio de Janeiro 327

Associação Brasileira de Imprensa, Rio de Janeiro 153

Atlas Cultural do Brasil, Rio de Janeiro 1972 609

Luiz Heitor Corrêa de Azevedo, Paris 520

P.M. Bardi, *Historia da Arte Brasileira*, Co. Melhoramentos de S. Paulo 1975 112

Gustavo Dodt Barroso, *Mythes, Contes et Légendes des Indiens*, Paris 1930 134, 207, 208, 209, 210, 211, 212, 213

Henry Walter Bates, *The Naturalist on the River Amazon*, London 1863 421

Bedford Hotel, Paris 518

Biblioteca Nacional, Rio de Janeiro 13, 14, 15, 16, 52, 59, 60, 65, 73, 76, 124, 125, 129, 130, 132, 140, 141, 142, 154, 156, 175, 176, 177, 178, 179, 252, 254, 260, 303, 327, 345, 375

B. Brandt, *Kulturgeschichte von Brasilien*, Stuttgart 1922 111

Raquel Braune, London 215, 287, 341, 464, 465, 554, 557, 558

Brazilian Chamber of Deputies, Brasília 188, 189, 190, 191

Brazilian Ministry of Education and Culture, Brasília 38, 39, 43, 49, 50, 90, 95, 96, 97, 99, 116, 117, 120, 121, 135, 136, 147, 148, 149, 151, 167, 168, 170, 174, 180, 181, 184, 185, 201, 250, 251, 258, 259, 261, 266, 284, 285, 300, 304, 318, 337, 371, 412, 531, 591

Brazilian Ministry of External Relations, Brasília 40, 41, 45, 88, 89, 90, 91, 92, 93, 94, 107, 108, 109, 110, 146, 255, 256, 277, 279, 319, 320 337, 338, 379, 380, 381, 382, 384, 416, 455, 565, 566, 612, 614, 618

Oscar Canstatt, *Brasilien, Land und Leute*, Berlin 1877 20, 103

Làzinha Luiz Carlos, *A Colombo na Vida do Rio*, Rio de Janeiro 1970 69, 70, 71

Chicago Symphony Orchestra 439

The City of New York 567

Colbert Artists Management, New York 581, 585

College of Philosophy, São Paulo 332

Companhia Melhoramentos de São Paulo 51, 53, 54, 57, 72, 206, 254, 330, 332

Concerts Pasdeloup, Paris 300, 376

Convento Santo Antônio, Rio de Janeiro 357

Ruth Valladares Corrêa, Rio de Janeiro 372

Courier-Journal and Louisville Times, Louisville, Ky 454

O *Cruzeiro*, Rio de Janeiro 144, 323, 429, 568, 604
Jean Baptiste Debret, *Voyage pittoresque et historique au Brésil, depuis 1816 jusqu'en 1831 inclusivement*, Paris 1834-39 3, 4, 5, 102, 234, 236, 237, 238, 239, 262, 269
M. Ferdinand Denis, *L'Univers Brésil*, Paris 1846, 276
Éditions Max Eschig, Paris 194, 195, 196, 197, 198
L. E. Elliott, *Brazil Today and Tomorrow*, New York 1917, 115, 118
Enciclopédia Universal Ilustrada Europeo-Americana, Bilbao 1927 199, 200
O velho Rio de Janeiro através das gravúras de Thomas Ender, Melhoramentos, São Paulo 1957 (Original: Akademie der Bildenden Künste, Wien) 8, 24, 243
Escola de Música da Universidade Federal do Rio de Janeiro 78, 79, 375
Alexandre Rodriques Ferreira, *Viagem filosófica pelas Capitanias do Grã Pará, Rio Negro, Mato Groso e Cuiabá, 1783-1792* 95, 250, 261, 264, 267, 271, 276
Gilberto Ferrez, *A Praça 15 de Novembro*, Rio de Janeiro 1978 11, 151
Gilberto Ferrez, *O que ensinam os antigos mapas e estampas do Rio de Janeiro*, Instituto Histórico e Geográfico Brasileiro, Vol. 278, Jan/March 1968, pp. 87-104, Rio de Janeiro 1, 9, 10, 18, 19, 82
Gilberto Ferrez-Weston J. Naef, *Pioneer Photographers of Brazil 1840-1920*, The Center for Inter-American Relations (Americas Society), New York 1976 36, 41, 44, 81, 125, 243
Fon-Fon, Rio de Janeiro, 18 August 1917 124, 140
Fotografie Lateinamerika von 1860 bis heute, Zürich 1981 17, 23, 80
Geralda França, Rio de Janeiro 74, 75
Concert Program, Geneva 138
Hermann M. Goergen, *Brasilien*, Essen 1967 105, 106
Peter Gradenwitz, Tel Aviv 517
Peter Gradenwitz, *Die Musikgeschichte Israels*, Kassel 1961 344
Grande Encyclopédia Delta-Larousse, Rio de Janeiro 1974, 72, 98, 101, 102, 125, 127, 128, 172, 204, 272, 285, 286, 293, 296, 349, 356, 359, 360, 361, 363, 364, 366, 368, 369, 370, 402
Joaquim Cândido Guillobal, Coll. Paulo Geyer, Rio de Janeiro 260
Oldemar Guimarães, Rio de Janeiro 28, 29, 30, 31, 32, 113, 114, 150, 306, 308, 316, 317, 321, 322, 353
Hebrew University, Jerusalem 514
Instituto Brasileiro de Geografia e Estatística, IBGE, Rio de Janeiro 86, 87, 165, 278, 279, 280, 281, 282, 283, 330
Instituto Hans Staden, São Paulo 217, 218, 219, 220
Instituto Histórico e Geográfico Brasileiro, Rio de Janeiro 36, 46, 47, 48, 122, 123, 319, 565
Jornal do Brasil, Rio de Janeiro 275, 366, 427, 563, 622, 623, 624
C.von Kosteritz, *Bilder aus Brasilien*, Leipzig and Berlin 1885 21, 22, 37
Olga Koussevitsky, New York 401, 405
Basil Langton, Los Angeles 461
Jean de Léry, *Histoire d'un voyage faict en la terre du*

Nicolas Slonimsky, Los Angeles 374
Société Philharmonique de Bruxelles et Société des
  Concerts Populaires 155, 432
Société Philharmonique de Bruxelles, R. Kayaert,
  Brussels 432
Hans Staden, *Wahrhaftige Historia und Beschreibung
  einer Landschaft der wilden, nackten, grimmigen
  Menschenfresser in der neuen Welt Amerika gelegen*,
  Marburg 1557 133, 218, 219, 220
Suiza-America Latina, Basel 1973 100, 380
Suhrkamp Verlag, Frankfurt/Main 490
Carolina Penteado da Silva Telles, São Paulo 159,
  161, 162
Théâtre des Champs-Elysées, Paris © Richard de Grab
  438
University Archives, Dalhousie:
  University Library, Ellen Ballon Papers, Halifax,
  Canada 423, 424, 425
Ary Vasconcellos, Rio de Janeiro 145, 186, 187, 205,
  292
Ary Vasconcellos, *Panorama da Música Popular
  Brasileira*, São Paulo 1964 62, 64
Vatican, Rome 594, 596
La Ville de Rio de Janeiro et environs, Rio de Janeiro
  1909 84, 85, 152
Robert Wagner Jr. 569
Prince Maximilian Wied-Neuwied, *Reise nach
  Brasilien in den Jahren 1815-1817*, Frankfurt/Main
  1820 225
Herbert Wilhelmy, *Südamerika im Spiegel seiner
  Städte*, Hamburg 1952 35, 335, 336, 340, 413,
  414, 415
Robert Wright and George Forrest, New York 473,
  477

Index of works mentioned

Illustration numbers are given in italic

Index of names

Illustration numbers are given in italic

Fortes, Paulo *223*
França, Agnello *42*, 42, *43*, 44
França, Geralda *42*, *43*, 305
Frederico, Orlando 65, *85*
Freire, Maria Emma *83*
Fried, Oscar *139*
Frontin, André Gustavo Paulo de 60

Gaddes, Richard *233*, *238*
Galamian, Ivan *282*
Gama, Clóvis Salgado da *272*, *300*, 300,
Gama, Vasco da 311
Gangl, Celia Flores 11
Gassmann, Remi 187
Gilman, Lawrence 141
Giorgi, Bruno *297*
Ginastera, Alberto Evaristo *237*, *291*, 291
Glória, Maria da 23
Gomes, Alfredo *65*, 65, *184*
Gomes, Antônio Carlos, 88, 286, 310
Gonçalves, João Octaviano 71,
Gonzaga, Francisca (Chiquinha) Hedwiges 36, *37*, 304
Gradenwitz, Peter *156*
Grosso, Iberê Gomes *170*, *184*, 186
Guanabarino, Oscar 71, *73*
Guarnieri, Edoardo di 222, *223*, *288*, 291
Guimarães, Alvaro de Oliveira *59*, 144
Guimarães Filho, Luís *47*, *66*
Guimarães, Luiz 10, *59*, 144, 306
Guimarães, Lucília *see* Villa-Lobos, Lucília
Guimarães, Oldemar 10, *59*, 144, 306
Guinle, Arnaldo *70*, 76, 130, *136*, 143, 144, 145, 160, 307
Guinle, Carlos *70*, 76, 130, *134*, *136*, 143, 144, 145, 160, 307
Guinle, Eduardo 39, *70*
Guinle, Guilherme *70*
Guinle, Otávio *70*

Hartley, Walter E. 175,

Haydn, Joseph 21,
Heifetz, Jacha *178*
Heinz (Mrs) Clifford S. *217*
Hendl, Walter *204*
Henriques, Maria *222*
Hillyer, Raphael *282*
Houston, Elsie *133*
Howard, Ken *238*
Hudson, W.H. 310
Hurlimann, Edouard *282*

Indy, Vicent d' 305
Isabel, Princess 28, *29*, *30*, 304, 314

Janacópulos, Adriana 271,
Janacópulos-Staal, Vera *74*, 76, 90, 306
Janssen, Werner 176, *176*, 309
Jardim, Danton Condorcet da Silva 24, 304
Jardim, Ahygara Iacyra 24, 304,
João VI, Dom *19*, *28*, *118*, 313
Joseph I, King Maximilian *105*
Judson, Arthur 214,

Keene, Christopher *236*, *237*
Kestenberg, Leo *156*, 253
Korgueff, Serge *282*
Koussevitzky, Natalie 186, *186*
Koussevitzky, Olga 186
Koussevitzky, Serge 181, 183, *184*, 185, *186*, *186*

Lacambra, Mirna *234*
La Fontaine, Jean de *64*
Lamas, Dulce Martins 10, 19
Lamber, Juliette, 139
Lamoureux, Charles 170
Landsdorff, Georg Henrich 113
Langton, Basil *219*, 220, 229, *231*
Laranjeiras, Quincas *see* Santos, Joaquim Francisco dos
Lau, Percy *126*, *127*
Lawrence, Sarah *204*, 229
Lebrão, Manuel José 40
Lebreton, Joachim

(Joaquim), *109*
Leiser, Henri *178*
Lemos, Gaspar de 311
Leopold II, King of the Belgians *264*
Leopoldina (Maria Leopoldina Josefa Carolina of Habsburg) *23*, 28, *28*, *105*, 313
Léry, Jean de *99*, 100, 101, *103*, 103, 104, *104*, *123*, *168*
Lester, Edwin 222, *223*, *228*, 309
Levy, Alexandre 88,
Lifar, Serge *99*, 100
Lima, João de Souza *145*, *148*, *199*, *201*
Limón, José Arcadio *219*, 220
Lindbergh, Charles 130
List, Eugene 208, *210*, *211*
Lobo, Laurinda Santos 76
Long, Marguerite *263*
Lorca, Federico García *219*, *237*, 309
Louis XVI 41, *62*
Luboshutz, Pierre *144*

Machado, José Gomes Pinheiro 92,
Machado, Pery *85*
Machado, Vieira *42*, 42
Magalhães, Fernão (Fernando) 311
Magalhães, Jr., Raimundo *237*
Malfatti, Anita *85*
Malta, Augusto César *73*
Mandel, Leon 187
Mann, Robert *282*
Manuel I, King of Portugal 164, *167*, *168*, 311
Maria I, Queen of Portugal 313
Marietti, Jean *91*, 92
Marietti, Philippe *91*, 92
Maristany, Cristina *213*
Martinon, Jean *200*, *201*
Martius, Carl Friedrich Philipp von *16*, 104, *105*, *109*
Marx, Walter Burle *156*, *157*, 159, *202*
Massé, João *124*
Massenet, Jules *43*
Matte, Ch. *109*